Literary Theory from Plato to Barthes

GW00994010

By the same author

Theoretical and academic titles
SUPERSTRUCTURALISM
BEYOND SUPERSTRUCTURALISM

Science fiction, fantasy, horror
THE VICAR OF MORBING VYLE
THE DARK EDGE
TAKEN BY FORCE

Literary Theory from Plato to Barthes

An Introductory History

Richard Harland

Published by
PALGRAVE
Houndmills, Basingstoke, Hampshire RG21 6XS and
175 Fifth Avenue, New York, N.Y. 10010
Companies and representatives throughout the world

PALGRAVE is the new global academic imprint of
St. Martin's Press LLC Scholarly and Reference Division and
Palgrave Publishers Ltd (formerly Macmillan Press Ltd).

ISBN-13: 978-0-333-71421-8 hardcover
ISBN-10: 0-333-71421-0 hardcover
ISBN-13: 978-0-333-71422-5 paperback
ISBN-10: 0-333-71422-9 paperback

This book is printed on paper suitable for recycling and
made from fully managed and sustained forest sources.
Logging, pulping and manufacturing processes are
expected to conform to the environmental regulations
of the country of origin.

A catalogue record for this book is available
from the British Library.

Printed and bound in Great Britain by
CPI Antony Rowe, Chippenham and Eastbourne

For Anne, Gerry, Graham, Kate, Paul
and all colleagues in the English Program at Wollongong

Contents

Preface   xi
Acknowledgements   xiii

1 **Literary Theory in Classical Times**   1
  • Rhetorical Criticism   3
    (*the Sophists, Aristotle, Demetrius, Cicero, Dionysius of Halicarnassus,*
    Quintilian)
  • Plato   6
    (*also the Neo-Platonists*)
  • Aristotle   10
  • Horace   15
  • Longinus   18

2 **Literary Theory in the Middle Ages**   22
  • Allegorical Exegesis   24
    (*Porphyry, Proclus, Macrobius, St Paul, St Augustine, Fulgentius, Dante,*
    Boccaccio)

3 **The Rise and Fall of Neoclassicism**   29
  • The Question of Language   31
    (*Dante, du Bellay*)
  • The Idealising Strain   33
    (*Giraldi, Sidney*)
  • The Italian Aristotelians   36
    (*Minturno, Scaliger, Castelvetro*)
  • Neoclassicism and the Purification of Language   39
    (*Montaigne, Malherbe*)
  • French Neoclassical Theory   41
    (*Boileau, Bouhours, Rapin, [Pope, Johnson]*)
  • The British Version of Neoclassicism   45
    (*Jonson, Dryden, Johnson, Addison*)

- British Theory in the Age of Sensibility   49
  (*Johnson, Young, Joseph Warton, Thomas Wharton, Hurd,*
  Edmund Burke)
- Vico, Diderot, Lessing   55

4 **Romantic Literary Theory**   60
  - Herder and the Spirit of the Time   62
    (*also Schiller, Friedrich Schlegel, Hegel*)
  - The Influence of Kant   65
    (*also Schelling, Coleridge, Goethe, Schiller, Schopenhauer*)
  - The Organic Principle   69
    (*A. W. Schlegel, Coleridge, Schelling, Goethe*)
  - The Role of the Critic   72
    (*Herder, Friedrich Schlegel, Schleiermacher*)
  - Some British Themes   74
    (*Wordsworth, Coleridge, Keats, Shelley*)
  - Sainte-Beuve, Emerson, Poe   77

5 **Social Theories of the 19th Century**   81
  - Belinsky and the Three Radicals   83
    (*Belinsky, Chernyshevsky, Dobrolyubov, Pisarev*)
  - Matthew Arnold   87
  - The Beginnings of Sociological Criticism: Taine and Marx   90

6 **Naturalism, Symbolism and Modernism**   96
  - French Naturalists   98
    (*Flaubert, Zola, the Goncourt brothers*)
  - French Symbolists   103
    (*Gautier, Baudelaire, Mallarmé, Valéry*)
  - British Aestheticism and Henry James   109
    (*also Pater, Wilde*)
  - Modernism and the Avant-Garde   113
  - Hulme and Pound   116
  - T. S. Eliot   120

7 **New Developments in Theory**   125
  - Nietzsche   125
  - Freud   130

- Saussure   135
- Marxism and Literary Theory   137
  (*Engels, Lukács, Benjamin, Brecht, Adorno*)

8 **20th-Century Russian Theory**   **146**
   - Russian Formalism   146
     (*Shklovsky, Eikhenbaum, Tomashevsky, Tynyanov, Jakobson*)
   - Propp   153
   - Czech Structuralism   155
     (*Mukarovsky*)
   - Bakhtin and his Circle   157
     (*also Voloshinov, Medvedev*)

9 **Anglo-American Criticism, 1900–60**   **166**
   - Richards and Empson   168
   - Leavis and the Leavisites   176
   - The New Criticism: Southern Phase   182
     (*Ransom, Tate*)
   - Kenneth Burke   184
   - The New Criticism: Hegemonic Phase   187
     (*Brooks, Penn Warren, Wimsatt, Wellek*)
   - Myth Criticism and Northrop Frye   194

10 **Phenomenological Criticism in France and Germany**   **200**
    - Poulet and the Geneva School   201
    - From Ingarden to Iser   204
    - From Gadamer to Jauss   208
    - De Beauvoir and Two Predecessors   213
      (*also de Staël, Woolf*)

11 **French Structuralism**   **219**
    - Paradigmatic Structural Relations   221
      (*Jakobson, Lévi-Strauss*)
    - Structuralist Narratology   225
      (*Greimas, Bremond, Todorov, Barthes*)
    - Structuralism as a Poetics   231
      (*Todorov, Barthes*)
    - Barthes   234

Epilogue: Into the Postmodernist Period　　　　　　　　**238**

Time Charts　　　　　　　　　　　　　　　　　244
Glossary　　　　　　　　　　　　　　　　　　247
Notes　　　　　　　　　　　　　　　　　　　264
Further Reading　　　　　　　　　　　　　　287
Index　　　　　　　　　　　　　　　　　　　293

Preface

In 'telling the story' of literary theory, this book incorporates several recognitions which have become standard in recent years. In the first place, the recognition that there is no non-theoretical literary criticism. Theoretical assumptions and implications lurk behind even the most 'practical' forms of criticism, even the most text-oriented interpretations or evaluations. In referring to critical writings about literature, I shall speak sometimes of 'literary theory' and sometimes of 'literary criticism', depending upon the explicit focus presented in the writing; but my concern will be always with the theoretical underpinnings, whether explicit or implicit.

In the second place, it is nowadays generally recognised that critical discussions of literature do not constitute one single kind of activity. We are not looking at a body of knowledge gradually accumulated in relation to some single stable object according to some single consistent methodology. For a start, the nature of the object itself changes, as Eagleton, amongst others, has demonstrated: the net of 'literature' pulls in quite different kinds of fish in different periods. (I shall continue to speak of 'literature', with embarrassment, only because there is no adequate alternative: some of the major historical changes will be indicated as they occur.) What's more, discussions of 'literature' have been produced from many disparate sites for many disparate purposes. The story I shall be telling does not have a unified plot converging towards some ideal goal of 'true' literary theory or criticism. That old New Critical dream is dead. I shall take it for granted that there is no 'true' form of literary theory or criticism, only a congeries of discourses which appear and disappear according to different needs, in different periods and different institutional contexts. The periods and contexts are a necessary part of the story, and will be described as fully as space allows.

A third recognition is the recognition that literary theory is international. To look only at British or Anglo-American discussions of literature is to perceive mere fragments of a larger body. Structuralism in America depends upon French Structuralism, which depends upon Russian Formalism; British criticism of the Restoration/Augustan period depends upon French Neoclassicism, which depends upon Italian Aristotelianism; and so on and so forth. This book proposes to tell the *whole* story, because it is only as a whole that the story makes sense.

Of course, the whole story cannot be told without simplification. I have aimed to present the largest and most fundamental theoretical trends; and I have typically stated those trends point-blank, without mentioning the possibility of further complications and higher-level qualifications. For example: on p. 41 I describe the period of French Neoclassicism as a period of 'unusual theoretical unanimity'. And so it was – when compared with the literary theories of the Renaissance or the nineteenth century. But it may not appear so unanimous when compared with the degree of unanimity proposed by earlier commentators; and it is relative to this tacit standard that several recent critics have in fact emphasised the *non*-homogeneity of French Neoclassicism. It should be borne in mind that further complications and higher-level qualifications of this kind are always possible. For the sake of economy, let me then issue a single blanket proviso: no statement in this book should ever be taken as the *final* word upon anything. The book will have achieved its aim if it has managed to utter a good first word.

At the same time, my understanding of theoretical trends can hardly have escaped the influence of my own theoretical position. That position is on record in *Beyond Superstructuralism: The Syntagmatic Side of Language*. No doubt my understanding is also affected by my 'other' career as a writer of SF/fantasy fiction. But if the deeper kinds of personal bias are unavoidable, I have nonetheless tried to avoid making personal judgements on the trends presented (with the exception of a few obvious and deliberate indulgences). Above all, I have tried to 'step into the shoes' of earlier theoretical perspectives without prematurely condemning their inadequacies from the more sophisticated vantage-point of contemporary theory. It has been my general aim to show how such perspectives can make perfect sense in their own terms, no matter how odd or unappealing they may appear nowadays.

Acknowledgements

My gratitude goes out to several excellent research assistants who helped in the gathering of material for this book: especially to Saeed Ur-Rehmann, and also to Matthew Tubridy, Richard Lever, Colleen McGloin and Jon Knowles.

I would also like to re-express my deep respect and appreciation for Professor Jonathan Culler, whose generosity of spirit launched my career as a writer of theoretical texts many years ago.

Another kind of debt I owe to the students I have taught at the University of Wollongong. If this book manages to be clear and comprehensible on difficult subjects, then they have trained me well!

My thanks also to the Australian Research Council and the CRITACS program (University of Wollongong) for contributing financial support towards the project.

Finally, I would like to thank Penguin Books for permission to draw a particularly large number of quotations from *Classical Literary Criticism* (trans. T. S. Dorsch, 1965).

1 Literary Theory in Classical Times

Fictions, narratives, dramatisations, special poetic modes of language – these have been produced in all societies from the very earliest times. But it is one matter to produce them, another to think and theorise about them. As in so many other areas, it was the Greeks who first recognised that there were questions to be asked and answered about these forms of verbal composition.

Not that the Greek forms were equivalent to 'literature' in our modern understanding of the term. In the first place, they were tied in very tightly to specific social occasions. Thus, plays were performed only during certain festivals; there were special occasions for the recitation of Homeric epics; and epinician or victory odes were composed during the actual ceremonies of celebration. Such forms belonged within larger rituals, quite unlike the free-floating books of modern literature. It is no wonder that concepts of genre sprang up almost automatically in Greek 'literary' theory. The different genres did not have to be discovered by a sampling of contents; they were defined in advance by different categories of social occasion.

At the same time, the element of ritual was modified by the element of *agon* or contest. In the Athenian drama festivals, for example, the plays of different dramatists were presented competitively, for judging and the awarding of prizes; and a similar competitiveness applied to many other occasions of poetic performance. This suggests an evaluative stance on the part of the audience going beyond pure communal involvement in ritual. An evaluative stance naturally leads on to a critical stance, to asking questions about what makes one work better than another.

It is important to note that Greek plays, epics and odes were all performed to an audience. The modern poet may be able to think of the production of the text as a transaction between her/himself and the words on the page. But for the Greek poet, the role of the audience was inescapable. Even when written language eventually supplanted spoken language as a means of presentation, still the act of composition was directed towards a very specific audience. It should come as no surprise that 'literary' theory was almost always *affective*.

As for the textual object of Greek 'literary' theory, I have used the Greek term *poiesis*, which translates into our modern term 'poetry'. But the focus of the two terms is very different. When we think of poetry nowadays, we think primarily of lyric poetry. But in Greek culture, lyric poetry played a much smaller part than epic and drama. When Plato and Aristotle theorise about *poiesis*, their conceptual framework derives from epic and drama, and is not well suited to the lyric form at all. In fact, Plato and Aristotle theorise mainly with a view to the most strikingly successful forms of their own particular period: the Athenian tragedy of Aeschylus, Sophocles and Euripides, the Athenian comedy of Aristophanes and Menander.

The textual object of Greek 'literary' theory differs not only in itself from the object of present day theory, but also in its relations with neighbouring areas of verbal composition. In particular, Greek thinking makes no clear separation between the language of *poiesis* and the language of legal debate, or political debate, or public speaking. The boundary lines are differently drawn. In Theophrastus' famous formulation: 'poetry and rhetoric are concerned with the orientation towards the hearers. . . . The philosopher on the other hand is primarily concerned with the orientation of discourse towards the facts.'[1] *Poiesis* opens out onto oratory; and oratory covers the vast majority of practical utterance. The modern ideal of objectivity (as espoused by scientists and journalists, for example) does not feature strongly in Greek culture. For the Greeks, most discourse has designs upon its audience, seeking to persuade and convince.

It is interesting that recent critical theory has swung around to a somewhat similar view. Now that the ideal of objectivity (in science, in journalism) has become suspect, there is increasing interest in the role of persuasion in *all* language. With the growth of Cultural Studies, the boundary between literature and other forms of discourse once again dissolves. And as the category of literature has been called into question, so the concept of rhetoric has tended to come back into fashion.

Rhetorical criticism
(the Sophists, Aristotle, Demetrius, Cicero, Dionysius of Halicarnassus, Quintilian)

In Classical times, the study of rhetoric was far more widespread than the study of *poiesis*. However, such study was not undertaken in the spirit of contemporary Cultural Studies. On the contrary, the skill of speaking persuasively in legal and political arenas was an advantageous career asset for educated Greeks; and the Schools of rhetoric which taught this skill revealed the tricks of the trade not for purposes of critique but for purposes of replication. A how-to-do manner pervades the thinking of the rhetorical critics. At bottom, even their most critical writings are guides or handbooks offering useful strategies for would-be practitioners. The ends of persuasion are as if taken for granted; it is the practical means that matter.

Nonetheless, the study of rhetoric required an understanding of what we would nowadays consider literary techniques, even if not directed towards what we would nowadays consider literary goals. In Classical times, it was the rhetorical critics who discussed rhythm, diction, and figurative language of all kinds. Moreover, the teaching of rhetoric involved many fictional exercises, including the retelling of a narrative or anecdote, the invention of a speech to be spoken by some mythological or historical character, the description of a scene or object. And in all teaching by example, the works of famous poets were mined for sample passages no less than the works of famous orators.

The very highest claims for persuasive language were made by the very first rhetorical critics, the Sophists of the fifth and fourth centuries BC. For the Sophists, the power of language was overwhelming and irresistible. 'Speech the persuader forces the persuaded mind to agree with what is said and what is done,' says Gorgias; and 'the alliance of speech and persuasion shapes the mind as it wishes'.[2] According to Gorgias, the effect is almost physical: 'The effect of speech bears the same relation to the constitution of the mind as the prescribing of drugs does to the nature of the body.'[3] And if so much power can be claimed for persuasion, then the claims of truth must be correspondingly reduced. Thus Protagoras apparently believed 'that things are to me as they appear to me, and that they are to you as they appear to you.'[4] The Sophists took a relativistic, tactical view of the world, where the local pragmatics of language could always undermine any single overarching version of reality. There are obvious similarities here to the contemporary views of such thinkers as Foucault and Lyotard. It is a pity that so little direct evidence about the Sophists has survived.

After the Sophists, the study of rhetoric became more technical and less philosophical. Aristotle's *Rhetoric* was doubtless influential in directing rhetorical critics into more modest channels. Through Hellenistic and Roman times, the study of rhetoric continued to flourish, increasingly systematic in its classifications and terminology. But there were no further challenges to the ideal of truth. Instead, truth and morality were reintroduced by the back door, as it were, with the assertion that the orator *ought* to be an honest and upright man. Roman writers, in particular, were eager to reconcile morality and persuasion by tacking on separate standards in this way. The underlying theoretical clash of interests was passed over.

After Aristotle, the next major surviving works of rhetorical criticism belong to the first century BC, by which time two important systems of classification had become established. On the one hand, there was a division of stylistic registers into the high (or grand), the middle (or moderate), and the low (or plain). Naturally enough, the grand style calls for strong emotion and elevated language, while the plain style calls for quiet simplicity and relatively unadorned language. Less obviously, the middle style also has its own characteristics: a quiet but not simple style, it calls for sweetness, smoothness, flowingness. Each style is considered appropriate for specific audiences and specific forms of persuasion. As explained by Cicero and Quintilian, the grand style serves to sway an audience to resolution and decision, the middle style serves to win an audience by charming conciliation, and the plain style serves to convince by argument. From the rhetorical point of view, no one style is superior to any other: they are different tools for different jobs.

Equally important but much more complicated was the system of tropes and figures. In standard rhetorical terminology, a trope is a deviation from the normal use of an individual word, while a figure is a deviation from the normal arrangement of words or the normal sequence of thought. The tropes include metaphor (commonly defined as the use of a term that belongs to something separate but comparable, e.g. the sea *bristles*), synecdoche (commonly defined as the use of the part for the whole, e.g. houses referred to as *roofs*), and metonymy (commonly defined as the use of a term that belongs to something co-occurring, e.g. Africa the continent substituted for its inhabitants in 'Horrid Africa shakes with terrible tumult').[5] Altogether the system runs into many dozens of labelled categories, although the recurrence of labels from writer to writer does not always indicate an identical definition.

Figures and tropes are here viewed as ornaments or clothing for an already existing material, and the same may be said of all other stylistic devices discussed by rhetorical critics. This perspective follows inevitably from the context in which the teaching of rhetoric took place. What the would-be practitioner wanted to learn was a persuasive manner of expression for future use: that is, a manner to be acquired in the present for a material to be acquired in the future. The traditional separation of form and content is above all a tradition of rhetorical criticism. Even when rhetorical critics advise that the form should match or mirror the content, a primary separation of form and content is still presupposed.

Another feature of the rhetorical tradition is the emphasis upon details at the expense of larger wholes. Large-scale unity is not a major concern for the rhetorical critics. Again, the practicalities of the teaching situation must be borne in mind: it would be difficult to expound a general technique of *unifying* without determining the particular potentialities of a particular material. Large-scale principles of structural organisation are another matter; but when rhetorical critics expound principles of effective structural organisation, they do not turn to the poets for examples. After all, the structures of narrative epic and drama, or even non-narrative lyric, have very little relevance to the structures required for oratory. Rhetorical criticism converges with literary criticism mainly on the local level of linguistic expression.

Overall, rhetorical criticism was a very conservative discipline. The names of even its most notable proponents – Demetrius, Cicero, Dionysius of Halicarnassus, Quintilian – are ultimately of less importance than the tradition itself. Compared with the broad accumulating stock of pedagogical know-how, the contributions of individual writers seem relatively small. The history of rhetorical criticism contains no drastic challenges or revolutions of the kind associated with later literary criticism. For literary criticism has typically been affected by the changeability of its object, literature; whereas oratory, a craft rather than an art, remained largely beyond the currents of taste and fashion. Even when public speaking lost much of its pragmatic usefulness during the more autocratic period of the Roman Empire, the practice of declamation still continued along established channels. Nor did the upheavals of the Middle Ages and the Renaissance have any marked impact; as will be seen, rhetorical criticism preserved its heritage for twelve hundred years after the Fall of the Roman Empire.

Plato
(*also the Neo-Platonists*)

Plato spoke from a very different site. The Schools of philosophy in classical Athens were training grounds, as were the Schools of rhetoric, but oriented towards theoretical rather than practical skills. At the same time, their interests were not specialised in the manner of philosophy nowadays; the Greek philosophers were all-round thinkers who applied themselves to every kind of topic. For Plato, *poiesis* was just one of many areas to be examined in the light of his larger metaphysical and socio-political concerns. And *poiesis* comes out of the examination very badly – especially in Books II, III and X of the *Republic*.

Plato defines *poiesis* as imitation or *mimesis*. '[Poetical] imitation imitates men performing actions either forced or voluntary, and believing that they are either successful or not in these actions, and feeling pain or pleasure as a result of it all.'[6] The emphasis here is not only upon the reproduction of something not literally present, but upon the dramatised quality of the reproduction – in the sense that a play or an epic (or arguably even a lyric) re-creates a full experience, puts the audience in the scene, encourages us to live through a situation as if we were there. Even nowadays, this quality of dramatisation is one of the three most plausible criteria for defining 'literature'. Of the other two criteria, Plato was unlikely to invoke the quality of fictionality, since Greek poets drew their stories from history (albeit mythical history); nor was he likely to invoke a special figurative quality of language, since that quality extended beyond *poiesis* to all persuasive discourse.

Plato also uses the term *mimesis* in a more restricted, though still related, sense. That is, he distinguishes between *mimesis* as the speech of a character directly reproduced, and *diegesis* as a narration of doings and sayings where 'the poet speaks in his own person, and does not try to turn our attention in another direction by pretending that someone else is speaking'.[7] In this restricted sense, drama is entirely mimetic, while epic is mimetic when it reproduces dialogue directly, diegetic when the poet tells the story. Plato disapproves of both imitation in general and dramatised dialogue in particular.

His disapproval is at bottom a disapproval of any form of copying. Drawing upon ethical notions of honesty, his philosophy aspires towards *the true*, where *the true* is equated with the original, the authentic, the source. In an incidental argument since made famous by Jacques Derrida, he suggests that writing is dangerous and dishonest because it copies (phonetically) from speech and because it can be distanced from its author, separated from its origin.[8] Plato believes in seeing through to the most real reality, and is deeply suspicious of all secondary realities.

As regards dramatised dialogue, Plato objects to the way in which such dramatisation encourages people to live many lives other than their own. This applies in the first place to actors and reciters, who step into someone else's shoes as they impersonate someone else's words. It also applies to members of an audience, who impersonate a dramatic character through identification and sympathetic experience. Such impersonations, in Plato's view, rub off very readily onto the impersonator, becoming lasting dispositions of personality. 'Haven't you observed that imitations, if persisted in from childhood, settle into habits and fixed characteristics of body, voice, or mind?'[9] In modern phraseology, Plato is warning against the moral danger of unsuitable role models; and, like many a modern moraliser, he especially emphasises the effect of role models upon the impressionable young. Plato disapproves of copies precisely because he sees them as so powerful, so easily capable of taking over and becoming primary.

Plato's disapproval is intensified by the kinds of characters and incidents which poets typically choose to dramatise. For Plato values the philosophical state of mind, as that which sees through to the most real reality, and denigrates less rational states where the mind is swayed and blinded by emotion. But as he points out, the philosophical state of mind is not exactly suited for dramatic representation:

> the quiet and sensible personality, always very much on the same level, is difficult to imitate – and difficult to detect if someone does try to imitate it . . . the imitative poet is obviously not made for this element in the mind . . . but for the indignant and variable personality.[10]

While admitting that 'indignant' and 'variable' characters are more interesting, Plato does not want audiences to impersonate or identify with them. As for incidents, the poet will naturally choose emotion-provoking incidents for imitation, as in tragic drama. But Plato distrusts the grief stirred up by scenes of suffering: 'the consequences of others' experience invade one's own, because it is difficult to restrain pity in one's own misfortunes when it has grown strong on others' [misfortunes]'.[11] Again, the assumption is that a temporary excess of feeling will infect the audience with a long-term habit of uncontrollable emotionality.

Plato's case against *mimesis* in the unrestricted sense focuses upon the fact that drama and epic (and lyric) imitate the world of perceptual appearances. Compared with philosophy or science or any such form of abstract understanding, *poiesis* has always a sensory concrete element. For Plato, this means that *poiesis* can have no claim upon the truth. He is particularly concerned to refute the commonly-held belief of Greek times that poets can teach and impart wisdom. To grasp the logic of his case, it will be necessary to take a detour through his larger metaphysical theory.

Plato sees the world of perceptual appearances as secondary and derivative. His most real reality is a reality of underlying abstractions. In this, he is not unlike the scientist who trusts to mathematical equations to capture the real workings of mechanics or gravity or electromagnetic force. For the scientist too sees the world of perceptual appearances as secondary and derivative: the actual movement of a rolling ball as secondary to the pure theoretical movement of a body under inertia, the actual look of a hot glowing object as secondary to the pure theoretical behaviour (impossible to visualise in concrete terms) of quanta levels within the atom. Not that Plato is a scientist: his most real reality is more of an Otherworld, and the abstractions he puts there include many strange and non-mathematical entities. Still, he does recognise the mysterious objectivity which abstractions may possess – that objectivity which prevents us from changing the laws of geometry as easily and capriciously as we may change our more subjective mental imaginings. Plato, it might be said, has taken one of the two founding steps of modern science. (The other step, the practice of empirical observation, had to wait for nearly another two millennia.)

According to Plato, the world of perceptual appearances is nothing more than an (imperfect) imitation of the reality of abstractions. So when poets imitate perceptual appearances, they are in fact imitating what is already an imitation. Instead of moving closer to *the true*, they are moving yet further away from it. Their works 'are "third" removes from the reality and are easy to make even if you don't know the truth. They are images, not realities.'[12] Moreover, in imitating individual people and particular events, they are also moving further away from the universality of the abstract. The unnecessary multiplication of sensory representations only distracts from the important business of trying to see through to the most real reality.

Whatever one thinks of Plato's case, it must be conceded that he lays down a fundamental challenge of extraordinary scope. Even the more modest attack upon dramatised dialogue is remarkable, given that the forms of *poiesis* were an established, institutionalised part of Greek life. Whereas the rhetorical critics never look up from their own small groove of practical study, Plato refuses to take anything for granted. He reveals himself, in all the books of the *Republic*, as perhaps the very first thinker to question society on the basis of a theoretical perspective.

Mention of a theoretical perspective may suggest analogies to more recent thinking; and in fact there is a close analogy to one trend in current literary theory – the challenge to Naturalistic realism. The notion of *mimesis* as a mere copying of perceptual appearances is peculiarly appropriate to Naturalistic realism, even though no such realism existed in Greek times. And Plato's argument that mere copying blocks our way to an understanding of *the true* parallels the current argument that Naturalistic realism, by reproducing the perceived face of reality as a natural state of affairs, fails to see through to the ulterior political motivations by which the perceived face of reality is *socially constructed*. On the current argument, the realists fail to consider the ideological forces shaping their own assumptions about what is to count as reality. Although the politics of current theorists are about as far removed from Plato's politics as possible, the same essential logic can be nonetheless observed in both cases.

There is a small tailpiece to add to this account of Platonic theory. In the third, fourth and fifth Centuries AD, the Neo-Platonists reinterpreted Plato's 'Otherworld' abstractions in a more mystical light as the Thoughts of God. Unlike Plato's original abstractions, these new abstractions were not limited to a philosophical, logical or mathematical understanding, but seemed more within the purview of the artistic mind. So the Neo-Platonists began to suggest that perhaps the artist might bypass the world of sensory appearances and achieve direct access to *the true*. The arts, said Plotinus, 'give no bare reproduction of the thing seen, but go back to the Reason-Principles from which Nature itself derives'.[13] And according to Proclus, the highest kinds of poetry '[set] the soul amid the principles that are the causes of existing things' or 'afford means of recalling to mind the periods of the soul and the eternal principles and various powers contained in these'.[14] The Neo-Platonists did not theorise much about *poiesis* as such; but the new twist they gave to Platonic theory foreshadows later claims for the poet as visionary, the poet's truth as a visionary truth.

Aristotle

Aristotle was Plato's pupil, and later set up his own School of philosophy in Athens. Compared with Plato, he appears as a less *absolute* theorist, more interested in describing and classifying things as they are, with less regard to ultimate principles. In the *Poetics*, his main surviving work of literary theory, he follows Plato in defining poetry as mimesis, specifically the imitation of an action. But whereas Plato condemns mere copying, Aristotle views the impulse to mimicry as a natural healthy human impulse:

> The instinct for imitation is inherent in man from his earliest days; he differs from other animals in that he is the most imitative of creatures, and he learns his earliest lessons by imitation. Also inborn in all of us is the instinct to enjoy works of imitation.[15]

Implicitly if not explicitly, the *Poetics* can be seen as a refutation of Plato's attitude to poetry.

The difference between Aristotle and Plato arises not merely from a difference of temperament but from a difference of general conceptual framework. Aristotle's way of thinking about the world is dominated by the model of the biological organism. The ideal for Aristotle lies not in some Otherworld reality of pure abstractions, but in the potential which each living being strives to realise in itself. Thus the acorn and sapling strive to realise the ideal of the fully-grown oak tree. This is the concept of *entelechy*: the assumed purposiveness whereby biological organisms 'want' to achieve their own particular fulfilment.

In our post-Darwinian age, such a concept has lost much of its scientific appeal; but as applied to poetry, it can be related to the often reported experience of writers who find that characters and stories seem to grow by their own principles, quite away from the writer's original plans. 'Art imitates Nature' is Aristotle's general principle, in the sense that the arts, like Nature, work to unfold the potentials hidden within things.[16] Indeed, since a great many accidental factors intervene to prevent things from growing as they 'want' in the real world, Aristotle even suggests that the arts may 'on the basis of Nature, carry things further than Nature can'.[17]

Clearly, the Aristotelian version of mimesis is no mere matter of passive copying. Aristotle's position must not be confused with later notions of realism and the realistic. Although Aristotle asserts that 'the characters [in tragedy] should be lifelike', he also asserts that 'comedy aims at representing men as worse than they are nowadays, tragedy as better'.[18] Elsewhere he talks of the poet representing things 'either as they were or are, or as they are said to be or seem to be, or as they ought to be'.[19] The second clause here makes room for mythological subjects and traditions of the marvellous; while the third clause points once again to the presence of the purposive ideal in Aristotle's theory. On this version of *mimesis*, detailed factual accuracy is of secondary importance.

Aristotle claims for poetry a higher kind of truth: not the reporting of factual details but the understanding of underlying generalities. Again, this is a rebuttal of Plato and his view that poetry is cut off from the universal because it is cut off from the reality of pure abstractions. Aristotle envisages another kind of generality: the generality of the species. For the ideal form of the fully-grown oak is the same for all acorns, even though intervening factors cause actual oaks to differ. On this ground, Aristotle makes a very clear separation between poetry and the type of narrative chronicle history written by Greek historians. 'Poetry is something more philosophical and more worthy of serious attention than history; for while poetry is concerned with universal truths, history treats of particular facts.'[20] Dealing with potential rather than real-life people and events, the poet must understand the principles by which potentialities operate.

It is this concept that underlies Aristotle's claims that 'probable impossibilities are to be preferred to improbable possibilities' and 'a convincing impossibility is preferable to an unconvincing possibility'.[21] Our sense of the probable comes from general principles of behaviour which poet and audience understand; other behaviours may be possible as a result of intervening accidental factors, but will not seem convincing if we do not understand the principles behind them. Aristotle is here pointing to an undeniable fact of experience, and doubtless our sense of probability must be explained along some such lines. But the topic is enormously complicated, as Aristotle himself recognises in his off-the-cuff remark that 'it is probable enough that things should happen contrary to probability'.[22] Unfortunately, this level of complication gets left behind in practice, and Aristotle's examples often appear to modern eyes as not only excessively simple but also theoretically naive. 'For example, a character may possess manly qualities, but it is not appropriate that a female character should be given manliness or cleverness.'[23] Aristotle's purposive ideal for women is not a matter of real potential but of socially constructed stereotype. Similarly, the human ideal for a fully-grown oak tree might be an ideal imposed by human beings and not what the acorn itself 'wants' at all. Who decides what things 'want' to be? This kind of difficulty haunts many arguments in Aristotle's theory.

The 'species' way of thinking also emerges in Aristotle's theory of genres. Each genre, like each species of plant, has its own distinctive principles of growth and fulfilment. An epic poem does not have to live up to the same goals as a tragedy, nor a tragedy to the same goals as a comedy. What's more, each genre evolves in itself and comes to fruition over time. 'Little by little tragedy advanced, each new element being developed as it came into use, until after many changes it attained its natural form and came to a standstill.'[24] Indeed, it would be difficult not to apply evolutionary thinking to the step-by-step development of Greek tragedy in the two centuries before Aristotle – though the supposed 'standstill' is more questionable.

The advantage of a genre theory is that on the one hand it avoids judging all works by the same set of goals, whilst on the other hand it avoids attributing to each individual work such uniquely individual goals that they can be discovered only by perusing the private mind of the author. But in practice Aristotle does not really escape the first of these two traps. He considers the genre of tragedy superior to the genre of epic, and when, in the *Poetics*, he finally comes around to a very brief discussion of epic, he reinvokes essentially the same set of goals which he has earlier proposed for tragedy. Even within tragedy, his thinking is shaped by a special partiality for Sophocles' *Oedipus*

Tyrannus. As so often, there are evaluative preferences lurking behind the philosophical theorising.

The main goal that Aristotle proposes for both tragedy and epic is the goal of unity – a natural enough goal when works of art are conceived on the biological model. Since he has defined poetry as the imitation of an action, he envisages this unity as primarily a unity of action, where incident leads on to incident in necessary sequence. Just as the limbs and organs of an animal work together in dissimilar but complementary roles, so too with the parts of an action. Aristotle's criterion for unity of action is that the 'various incidents must be so arranged that if any one of them is differently placed or taken away the effect of wholeness will be seriously disrupted'.[25]

Other goals proposed by Aristotle have to do with audience-effect. The work of art must take account of the capacities and limitations of the audience at which it is aimed. So questions of size are referred to the size of the audience's memory:

> Now in just the same way as living creatures and organisms compounded of many parts must be of a reasonable size, so that they can be easily taken in by the eye, so too plots must be of a reasonable length, so that they may be easily held in the memory.[26]

This is an audience-oriented requirement on top of the more text-oriented goal of unity; and it is this additional requirement which enables Aristotle to proclaim tragedy, with its relatively compacted kind of unity, superior to epic, with its relatively spread-out kind of unity.

For tragedy, Aristotle also defines a specific tragic effect, a distinctive emotional response which the genre seeks to arouse in the audience. Tragedy, he says, 'should represent actions capable of awakening pity and fear'.[27] (In the lost second part of the *Poetics*, he would doubtless have spelled out the distinctive emotional response to be aroused by the genre of comedy.) In this formula, pity and fear should be seen as influencing one another. What is to be aroused is a fear-charged kind of pity rather than pity as sentimental pathos; and what is to be aroused is a pity-charged kind of fear rather than fear as self-centred terror. A pity-charged kind of fear would presumably involve awe and a sense of 'the terrible'.

In focusing upon emotional effect, Aristotle is promoting that very aspect of poetry to which Plato most objected. But then Aristotle does not regard the emotions as intrinsically harmful but as a natural part of human life. What matters is to keep them healthy and balanced. As for fictionally-created emotions, the fact that such emotions are superfluous to real life does not prevent them from being beneficial. Specifically, Aristotle claims that the emotional experience of a tragedy brings about a catharsis (*katharsis*) of pity and fear in the audience.[28] The exact meaning of Aristotle's term is still under debate; but it is now widely agreed that *katharsis* refers to some sort of improving or refining – whether through an intellectual clarification of emotional capacities, or through a stronger emotional control, or through an enhanced sense of emotional proportion. By 'working through' emotions in a particularly intense form, we become more capable of coping with emotion-provoking situations in real life. Aristotle challenges Plato's assumption that people who 'indulge' in fictionally-created emotions will become prone to excessive emotionality in their lives generally.

Having defined the appropriate effect of tragedy, Aristotle goes on to consider the type of hero required to produce this effect. According to Aristotle, the fall of a wholly good man does not generate pity and fear (in fact, sentimental pathos would be the most likely effect). Nor can pity and fear be generated by the fall of an evil man who fully deserves his punishment. The appropriate type of hero is a man remarkable for neither virtue nor vice, for neither justice nor depravity, but a man whose fall is due to some error or weakness, some *hamartia*.[29] Three important features of Aristotelian theory are visible in this argument. First, it reveals the subordinate status of character, which must fit in with action (the 'fall') in such a way as to produce the required emotional effect. Secondly, it shows how *mimesis* diverges from realism, when the ultimate goal of generating pity and fear renders large areas of reality unsuitable for imitation. Thirdly – and most generally – it illustrates Aristotle's teleological procedure, working backwards from end to means.

Aristotle's teleological procedure leads to a teacherly mode of discourse: once the goals are established, he imparts instruction on how to achieve them. 'I must go on to say what is to be aimed at and what guarded against in the construction of plots'[30] – such is the recurring tone of much of the *Poetics*. In similar spirit, he introduces examples from existing plays typically as models which should or should not be followed. His discourse is authoritative, but not in the modern manner of 'objective' scientific description. There is no reason to suppose that his instruction was directed towards the dramatists of his time, no reason to suppose that he was trying to influence the kind of plays being written. But the typical how-to-do framework of the Classical literary theory also pervades his way of thinking. As has been noted, the concept of *mimesis* strongly distinguishes the object of Aristotle's literary theory from the object of rhetorical criticism. However, his tone and tactics are not dissimilar.

Horace

While Greek culture spread far beyond the original city-states, Greek political power soon vanished beneath the advancing hegemony of the Roman Empire. However, it was the Romans who sought to imitate and emulate the superior culture of their Greek subjects. In Horace's famous line: 'Greece, now captive, took captive its wild conqueror, and introduced the arts to [Rome].'[31] Throughout the period of the Roman Empire, Greek was the obligatory second language of all educated Romans, but very few Greeks ever bothered to learn Latin.

Roman poets thus looked to Greek models before creating their own poetry. There were debates as to just how much deviation and novelty might be permissible; but there was never any doubt that the primary inspiration must come from the great Greek texts of the past. From the very beginning, Roman forms of *poesis* (the Latin spelling of the Greek *poiesis*) existed in a state of willing secondarity. And the same is naturally true of Roman literary theory.

Horace, writing in the Augustan period, is the most important figure here. His literary theory appears especially in *Epistles* 2.1 and 2.2, and above all in the epistle that has come to be known as the *Ars Poetica*. Horace writes as a poet, but he is not the kind of poet, familiar to later ages, who sets out a programme justifying his own special brand of poetry. Horace's stance is that of the experienced practitioner, passing on valuable advice. In the *Ars Poetica*, this advice is addressed to two would-be poets, the sons of Piso.

The elements of Horace's theory are drawn almost entirely from Aristotle. But Horace's reformulation has a much more peremptory tone:

> I will teach the poet his duties and obligations; I will tell him where to

find his resources, what will nourish and mould his poetic gift, what he may, and may not, do with propriety, where the right course will take him, and where the wrong.[32]

Whereas Aristotle expounds principles, Horace lays down rules:

> If you want your play to be called for and given a second performance, it should not be either shorter or longer than five acts. A *deus ex machina* should not be introduced unless some entanglement develops which requires such a person to unravel it. And there should not be more than three speaking characters on the stage at the same time.[33]

One might compare the difference between Aristotle and Horace to the difference between the Chomskyan linguist, who claims to describe an existing intuitive sense of grammar, and the schoolroom grammarian, who aims to *inculcate* a sense of grammar. The Chomskyan linguist idealises the evidence, but the schoolroom grammarian is not even dealing with evidence. Like the schoolroom grammarian, Horace speaks the language of right and wrong, the language of social duty.

Horace's concept of genre is thus prescriptive in a way that Aristotle's was not. Talking of the themes of lyric poetry and the metre of tragedy and comedy, Horace says: 'If I have not the ability and skill to adhere to these well-defined functions and styles of poetic forms, why should I be hailed as a poet?'[34] Horace recognises a larger number of genres than Aristotle, including his own favourite genre of satire. But his approach is actually more limiting: less an examination of genres which happen to exist, more a designation of genres which may be allowed to exist.

A similar shift occurs in the case of Horace's key concept of *decorum*. Decorum refers to the criterion of 'fittingness' which comes into play whenever elements must be appropriate in the service of some ultimate goal. In the service of character plausibility, for example, there must be an appropriate match between age and behaviour: 'you must note the behaviour of people of different ages, and give the right kind of manners to characters of varying dispositions and years'.[35] And Horace goes on to prescribe the attributes appropriate for the child, for the beardless youth, for the grown man, for the old man. But although such rules of thumb may be useful in their way, there is always the danger of following the rules without remembering the rationale behind them. Aristotle too was always concerned to discover what elements are appropriate in the service of some ultimate goal. But in Horace's way of thinking, the ultimate goal is more easily lost sight of.

Of course, rules of thumb are what a *craftsman* needs, and Horace consistently views *poesis* as a craft. Training is necessary, though not in itself sufficient: 'I myself cannot see the value of application without a strong natural aptitude, or, on the other hand, of native genius unless it is cultivated.'[36] In Horace's thinking, 'native genius' is indeed akin to 'aptitude': a matter of inventiveness rather than inspiration. Too much originality is undesirable, and the 'mad poet' is held up for derision. Addressing his two would-be poets, Horace insists 'you must have nothing to do with any poem that has not been trimmed into shape by many a day's toil and much rubbing out, and corrected down to the smallest detail'.[37] He further suggests that they submit any completed writings to the critical judgement of others.[38] In all of this one can see the modest stance of Roman literature, conditioned from the outset by its acceptance of an essential secondarity vis-à-vis the great Greek texts of the past.

This secondarity vis-à-vis the great Greek texts of the past also gives a new angle to Horace's concept of *mimesis*. He continues to speak of imitating from reality: 'the experienced poet, as an imitative artist, should look to human life and character for his models, and from them derive a language that is true to life'.[39] But he also speaks of 'imitating another writer', and claims that 'a theme that is familiar can be made your own property as long as you do not waste your time on a hackneyed treatment'.[40] From a modern point of view, the imitation of literary models looks like the very opposite of imitating from real life. But the modern point of view is coloured by modern notions of realism. From Horace's point of view, the great Greek texts contain the same general principles of human behaviour as are present in real life; and the poet may draw equally from either source.

Another shift appears in Horace's new emphasis upon moral value in poetry. This shift can be plausibly related to the more sternly moral, more duty-oriented atmosphere of Roman society, at least in the time of the Republic and early Empire. (By contrast, Greek writers in the same period had been throwing the emphasis increasingly upon 'beguilement'.) Aristotle had argued that *poiesis* can have an improving effect, emotionally through the refining of catharsis and intellectually through the learning of general truths about human nature. These are intrinsic virtues of *poeisis*, in the sense that the learning and refining are automatically involved in the particular kind of pleasure which mimetic art offers. Horace however institutes a bifurcation of virtues. '[The poet] who has managed to blend profit with delight wins everyone's approbation, for he gives his reader pleasure at the same time as he instructs him.'[41] Aesthetic value and ethical value are not two aspects of the same thing, but two separate things; and their coexistence in a single work is fortunate rather than inevitable. From this it becomes natural to think of moral teaching as an ingredient which needs to be added separately. The notion of poetry as a nasty-tasting pill of instruction wrapped up in a sweet coating of delight can be traced back to Horace.

In general, Horace's importance to the history of literary theory lies not in any profoundly original ideas, but in the new twist that he gave to the ideas of Aristotle. When the concepts of Classical criticism were taken up again in the Renaissance and Neoclassical periods, it was through Horace that the *Poetics* was viewed; and Horace's reinterpretation of Aristotle then came to be carried even further in the same direction.

Longinus

While Roman culture looked back to the great Greek texts of the past, Greek culture developed a backward-looking orientation of its own. This had begun even in the Hellenistic period of Alexander the Great and his successors. The Hellenistic period was a Golden Age of textual editing, philology and historical commentary, thanks to the growth of such central royally-funded institutions as the vast library of the Ptolemies in Alexandria. Already Alexandrian scholars took it upon themselves to draw up a *kanon* (or canon), a list of those works deemed most worthy of preservation and study. Later, when the entire Greek-speaking world was incorporated into the Roman Empire, the same backward-looking orientation encouraged a fashion for 'Atticism', requiring writers to imitate the supposedly pure vocabulary and syntax of Greek oratory from the fourth century BC. Such is the context into which the strangely original figure of Longinus intrudes.

Longinus lived probably a hundred years after Horace, although his dates are still uncertain and may be much later. His real name is unknown: the name of 'Longinus' was attributed to him only by confusion with another writer. His sole surviving work is the treatise *Peri Hupsous*, commonly translated as *On the Sublime*, in which he deals with elevated or grand language, and tries to explain the causes of *ekstasis*, or transport and rapture.

At first glance, Longinus belongs squarely in the tradition of rhetorical criticism. In manner and methodology, *Peri Hupsous* is a how-to-do guide for orators, laced with positive and negative examples. In his Preface, Longinus speaks of 'the practical help that it should be the writer's main object to supply'.[42] Like all rhetorical critics, he concentrates upon local linguistic effect rather than the overall structure of a work; like all (later) rhetorical critics, he deals in a technical jargon of hyperbaton, polyptoton, asyndeton, metaphor, periphrasis, hyperbole, etc. But there is a special quality about Longinus that far exceeds these resemblances.

In the first place, Longinus *preaches* the sublime. Certainly, the sublime has features in common with the high or grand style, as traditionally discussed. But for Longinus, the sublime is not just one option out of a range of options. It is the essence of all great poetry and oratory. Pinning supreme value to a special use of language, he has no time for concepts of genre. Nor is he interested in the usual rhetorical goal of persuasion: 'the effect of elevated language is, not to persuade the hearers, but to entrance them . . . what transports us with wonder is more telling than what merely persuades or gratifies us'. As for the traditional figures of hyperbaton *et al.*: 'Sublimity and the expression of strong feeling are, therefore, a wonderfully helpful antidote against the suspicion that attends the use of figures. The cunning artifice remains out of sight. . . .'[43] Longinus makes the successful deployment of figures dependent upon a larger emotional force which sweeps through the poet's language Without such force, the figures remain painfully visible as mere technical devices.

The element of preaching in Longinus is reminiscent of more recent manifestos in which poets or novelists have proclaimed their own new way of writing as the only true way. But Longinus stands in outright opposition to the literary tendencies of his time. Greek poets of the first century AD were still following Callimachus' ideal of the small but perfectly polished masterpiece. 'A big book is a big evil,' according to Callimachus.[44] Longinus takes the very opposite view: 'we admire, not, surely, the small streams, beautifully clear though they may be, and useful too, but the Nile, the Danube, the Rhine, and even more than these the Ocean'. And he considers 'grandeur accompanied by a few flaws' clearly superior to 'mediocre correctness'.[45] Indeed, a lack of final polish is almost regarded as a virtue, a testament to raw power. It is the raw power of the early Greeks that Longinus most admires: Homer, Pindar, Demosthenes, Sophocles. Like the Atticists, he seeks a return to Greek roots: but his conception of those roots is less constrained by contemporary interests, his empathy more profound.

For Longinus, the sublime is a matter of reader response. It is true that he also invokes the author and the need for grand ideas impregnated with a noble inspiration. 'Sublimity is the echo of a noble mind,' he writes.[46] But his theory is essentially affective, not self-expressive. Tacitly appealing to the sympathetic introspection of his readers, he starts from the feelings actually aroused – transport or tedium, rapture or ridicule – which he then tries to explain by the language of the text. And indeed, the line which divides transport from tedium, rapture from ridicule, appears as a very fine one. Unlike the rhetorical critics who offer reliably efficacious techniques, Longinus is interested in an extremity of effect that is always in danger of toppling over into absurdity.

The paradox is that the sublime as defined by Longinus is virtually beyond language, or at least ordinary literal language. He is concerned with what a text communicates rather than the writer's uncommunicated soul; but the communication that he studies works through suggestion rather than through ordinary processes of meaning. Thus, the greatest of works 'leave more food for reflection in [the reader's] mind than the mere words convey'.[47] Naturally this points towards a degree of creative activity on the part of the reader. We feel, says Longinus, 'as though we had ourselves produced what we had heard'.[48] This is a most unusual emphasis in classical literary theory, and runs completely counter to the standard rhetorical view of the audience as a mere passive material to be moulded.

Not surprisingly, Longinus finds his examples of the sublime where words and syntax are under strain and language itself is almost breaking down. A single illustration must suffice, a case of hyperbole taken from Herodotus' account of the battle of Thermopylae:

'Meanwhile though they defended themselves with swords (those who still had them), and with hands and mouths, the barbarians buried

them with their missiles.' What is meant by fighting armed men with mouths or being buried with missiles? Still, it is credible. . . . As I keep saying, acts and emotions which approach ecstasy provide a justification for, and an antidote to, any linguistic audacity.   [My italics][49]

Limited by the linguistic tools at his disposal, Longinus nonetheless gestures towards a poetic 'rightness' which somehow transcends the literal meanings involved. His topic is the almost indefinable, the almost incomprehensible – yet he struggles constantly to define and comprehend it.

To talk of words and syntax under strain may seem to suggest twentieth-century notions of poetic language. But Longinus is interested in a special grandeur of meaning, not a maximum wealth or multiplicity of meaning. He regards concision as generally inimical to the goals of transport, wonder and awe. 'Excessive conciseness in expression reduces sublimity, for grandeur is marred when it is too closely compressed.'[50] Instead he favours the appropriate use of *amplification* and *periphrasis*, two standard devices in the rhetorician's armoury.

Longinus appears to have had almost no influence upon the writers and thinkers of his own time. *Peri Hupsous* did not resurface until the Renaissance, and achieved importance only during the brief period of the eighteenth century. Unfortunately for Longinus, his arguments became tainted by association with the precious post-Miltonics of that period; and the Romantics discarded his theory even as they brought their own kind of raw power and grandeur back into poetry.

2   Literary Theory in the Middle Ages

On the last day of AD 406, a coalition of Teutonic tribes crossed the Rhine into Gaul: a convenient single date for the Fall of the Roman Empire. But the full political story is much more messy and protracted, and the cultural story even more so. Long before the end of the fourth century, the growth of Christianity had introduced new and incompatible forms of thinking into Greco-Roman culture; conversely, Greco-Roman culture persisted in many adaptations under many transient regimes for centuries after the Empire had ceased to exist politically in the West.

Christianity was both a force for preservation and a force for change. It absorbed many elements from Greco-Roman culture, and what it absorbed it preserved. But such elements were drastically transformed even in the process of absorption. The details might look similar, but the framework was different. For Christianity was not simply a new religion replacing the old Roman gods and goddesses: it redrew the whole map of human thinking. Even in preservational mode, it could not help but alter everything it touched.

From the point of view of literary production, it is the later Middle Ages which are important. The Age of Faith, from the eleventh to fifteenth centuries, produced remarkable new vernacular literatures in France, Germany, England and Italy. This is the period of *The Romance of the Rose*, *Parzifal*, *The Divine Comedy*, the *Decameron*, and *The Canterbury Tales*. But there was very little new thinking *about* literature to accompany the sudden surge in cultural energy. The later Middle Ages merely continued to deploy critical concepts which had been developed in the centuries immediately after – and even before – the Fall of the Roman Empire. From the point of view of literary theory, it is the early Middle Ages that are important: the period of declining Greco-Roman culture, the period during which Christian thinking came to terms with the Greco-Roman heritage. And whereas the culture of the later period spread out from France and the Paris region, the cultural centres for this earlier period are mainly in the more strongly Romanised areas around the Mediterranean. Many of the mainstream elements of Classical literary theory were impossible for Christian thinking to accept. The concept of *mimesis* had been developed by Plato and Aristotle especially in relation to drama. But drama was violently condemned by all the early Church Fathers, who viewed the emotional immediacy of dramatic enactment as too simply pleasurable, not sufficiently instructional. In consequence, drama disappeared from the scene until the very last phase of the Middle Ages, and the concept of *mimesis* accompanied it into oblivion.

The situation is more complicated as regards concepts of style and figurative language. The Middle Ages inherited a theoretical knowledge of Classical rhetoric, even though Greco-Roman forms of oratory were no longer practised. This knowledge was applied specifically to the art of poetic composition in a sudden flurry of handbooks appearing around 1200. Added on top of the already multitudinous categories of late Roman rhetoric, the medieval love of hair-splitting classification produced some truly mind-numbing results:

> Colours of words and thoughts [i.e. figures of speech] are repetitio, complexio, traductio, contentio, exclamatio, interrogatio, ratiocinatio, sententia, contrario, membrum, articulus, compar, similiter cadens, similiter desinens, annominatio (in 13 mutations), conduplicatio, subjectio, gradatio, diffinitio, transitio, correctio, occupatio, disjunctio, conjunctio, adjunctio, interpretatio, commutatio permissio, dubitatio, expeditio, dissolutio, precisio, nominatio, prenominatio, denominatio, circuico, transgressio, superlatio, intellectio, translatio, abusio, permutatio, conclusio.[1]

So wrote John of Garland. But there was very little new thinking in all of this. The application of Classical rhetoric to the art of poetic composition merely transferred to poetry the old rhetorical assumption that subject-matter comes first and persuasive presentation in language follows after. In the words of Geoffrey of Vinsauf: 'If a man has a house to build, his impetuous hand does not rush into action. . . . The mind's hand shapes the entire house before the body's hand builds it.'[2] Whatever the merits of this approach in relation to the pragmatics of oratory, it encourages a merely ornamental notion of style in relation to poetry.

It is the third criterion for literature that comes to the forefront in the Middle Ages: the criterion of fictionality. The recurring terms *fabula* and *figmentum* (roughly, 'unreal story' and 'something made up') mark the space of the problem. From a Christian perspective, the events described in Classical literature could only be seen as untrue – and what's more, dangerously untrue, invoking false gods and false miracles. (By contrast, the events described in the Bible were understood as literal historical fact.) Could such lies be reconciled with some ulterior form of truthful instruction? This was where the characteristic medieval strategy of allegorical exegesis entered the debate.

Allegorical exegesis
(*Porphyry, Proclus, Macrobius, St Paul, St Augustine, Fulgentius, Dante, Boccaccio*)

Allegory comes from a Greek term meaning 'other-speaking'. From Roman times onward, definitions of allegory typically focused upon the way in which something has to be understood other than what is literally said. The earliest known example goes back to the sixth century BC, when Theagenes of Rhegium propounded an allegorical interpretation of a passage in Homer. But the allegorical method rose to major prominence only as religious and mystical thinking rose to prominence in the later period of the Roman Empire. Neo-Platonists and Christians were the main practitioners.

In conjunction with the beliefs described at the end of the section on Plato above, Neo-Platonic philosophers viewed the particular appearances of the world as signs standing for ulterior truths. Only the philosophically initiated could see through to the meanings of such signs, which were hidden from vulgar minds. This world-view provided fertile ground for allegorical thinking. When they reversed Plato's judgement on poets, Neo-Platonic commentators typically discovered high metaphysical truths hidden behind 'mere' plot and characters. In the third century AD, Porphyry of Tyre justified the cave of the nymphs episode in *The Odyssey* by claiming that the nymphs represent souls descending to be born and the cave represents the *kosmos*, or, alternatively, that the cave represents the Intelligible essence as understood by Neo-Platonic philosophy. In similar fashion, Proclus (already mentioned at the end of the section on Plato) interpreted Homer's account of the marriage between Zeus and

Hera as signifying a union between Mind and the creativity of the Demiurge, or between Monad and Dyad. Also written in the fifth century AD was Macrobius' highly influential allegorical reading of a text by Cicero, the so-called *Dream of Scipio*. After Macrobius and Proclus, Neo-Platonic philosophy went into a decline and became submerged under the stronger influence of Christianity.

The Christian religion took a similar view of the world as signs. The world was a text, God's book, full of messages set out for Christians to read. Nor was this the only motivation to allegorical thinking. Christ's own method of teaching through parables clearly involved an understanding of something other than what was literally said. And there was a further special motivation for Christian interpreters of the Bible: the need to find ways of bringing the Jewish Old Testament into harmony with the very different ethos of the New Testament. The Bible was the text upon which Christian strategies of allegorical interpretation first developed and mostly flourished.

The earliest example appears in one of St Paul's letters, *Galatians* 4:21–31. Paul interprets the Old Testament episode in which God tells Abraham to cast out his slavewoman wife, Hagar, in favour of his freewoman wife, Sarah. According to Paul, 'Hagar' is the Arabic term for Mount Sinai and therefore represents the Old Law, the Old Covenant of Moses; whereas the freewoman wife is the symbolic mother of all New Covenant Christians who trust in the free gift of God's grace. In effect, Paul turns the Old Testament against itself. The cross-referencing by which an Old Testament episode is made to foreshadow something revealed in the New sets a pattern for all subsequent Biblical exegesis, as does the etymological tactic of calling up the supposed derivations of a name.

Strategies of allegorical interpretation were further developed by Alexandrian theologians, most notably Origen, and decisively confirmed in the writings of St Augustine (AD 354–430). Gradually a system was established for reading the Bible on three, then four, separate levels of meaning. But on any level above that of literal meaning, several different readings could be equally valid. The only criterion limiting possible interpretations was Augustine's 'principle of charity', according to which all interpretations had to be consistent with Christian teaching. A charitable principle indeed! But such wide allowance made perfect sense in terms of the natural Christian assumption that Holy Scripture had been written down under direct inspiration from the Holy Spirit. The intentions and knowledges of a particular human writer were irrelevant when that writer was merely the channel for a higher authority.

The allegorical strategies thus developed were used throughout the Middle Ages. Given the enormous proliferation of preaching, teaching and theological thinking focused upon the one sacred text, some such method for producing meaning was no less than an institutional necessity. But could the same strategies be applied to secular texts? St Augustine, St Isidore of Seville and St Thomas Aquinas thought not. After all, there was no Divine inspiration to justify higher levels of meaning in the *fabulae* and *figmenta* of poets. Nonetheless, allegorical readings of some secular texts were produced during the Middle Ages – especially readings of Virgil.

Clement and Origen of Alexandria were perhaps the first to notice that Virgil's Fourth Eclogue could be understood as a Messianic prophecy foretelling the coming of Christ. This encouraged the medieval view of Virgil as a proto-Christian and the greatest of all poets. In the sixth century AD, a full-scale allegorical interpretation of the *Aeneid* was put forward by Fulgentius, a North African Christian. According to Fulgentius' *Exposition of the Content of Virgil*, Virgil's epic begins with the shipwreck of Aeneas on the shore of Carthage because

> the shipwreck symbolizes the perils of birth in which the mother suffers birth-pangs, and the infant endures the danger of being born. . . . And to make this meaning very plain, the shipwreck is caused by Juno, the goddess of childbirth.[3]

Similarly, when Aeneas fixes the golden bough, which he has carried through the underworld, on the sacred doorposts at the entrance to Elysium, this shows that 'learning is fixed in the memory forever'.[4] And so on and so forth. Often etymology plays a role in these readings. The nymph Marica represents 'merica', that is, *counsel*;[5] while Aeneas gains in maturity when he buries the character Misenus, because 'misio' means *spite* and 'enos' means *praise*, thus demonstrating that 'unless you reject ostentatious and vain praise you will never reach the secrets of wisdom'.[6] In general, every tiny detail of Aeneas' adventures becomes part of an allegory about the progress of the human soul from innocence to wisdom.

Fulgentius' *Exposition* is in the form of a commentary, working through Virgil's poem from first line to last. The tradition of commentary had become established in Hellenistic Alexandria; and for both sacred and secular writings, commentaries were the most common form of critical discourse throughout the Middle Ages. A commentary might explain the meanings of difficult words, give background on historical or mythological allusions, point out figures of speech, and propound allegorical interpretations. But given the concentration upon successive local details, a commentary was always unlikely to characterise the text as a whole, let alone delve into larger questions of theoretical principle. Interestingly, medieval scribes often left a space or margin when hand-copying a text, allowing for the insertion of later commentary, also hand-written. In medieval thinking as in recent Poststructuralist thinking, the text was not finalised or bounded by an original conception, but remained open to further expansions and outworks of meaning.

Throughout the Middle Ages, commentaries and other critical forms (such as the handbooks of poetical composition) were invariably written in Latin, the language of thought. The barrier of language doubtless helps to explain why the arrival of the new vernacular literatures had so little impact. Cut off from the new cultural growing-points, Latin had its own inertia and its own affinities. There was remarkably little direct interaction between the the critical analysis of allegory and the allegorical practice of the new vernacular poets.

One poet who challenged this situation was Dante Alighieri. In the first chapter of Book II of the *Convivio* (*The Banquet*) and in the 'Epistle to Cangrande', Dante argues that the full four levels of meaning in Biblical exegesis can also be found in secular, vernacular poetry.[7] These four levels are the literal, the allegorical (in a more specific sense here), the moral, and the anagogical. To illustrate the allegorical level, Dante refers to Ovid's story of how Orpheus with his music tamed the wild animals and caused trees and stones to move closer to him: allegorically, this 'signifies that the wise man with the instrument of his voice makes cruel hearts gentle and humble, and makes those follow his will who have not the living force of knowledge and of art'.[8] To illustrate the moral level (elsewhere called the tropological level), he refers to Christ's selection of only three Apostles to accompany Him when He ascended the Mount: the moral instruction here is that 'in the most secret things we ought to have but little company'.[9] To illustrate the anagogical level (elsewhere called the spiritual level), he refers to the Old Testament passage telling how Judaea was made holy and free when the people of Israel departed out of Egypt: interpreted for its eternal theological meaning, this means that 'in the Soul's liberation from Sin (or in the exodus of the Soul from Sin) it is made holy and free in its powers'.[10] Admittedly, these last two examples are not in fact secular; but Dante's argument is more ambitious than his examples.

Boccaccio followed Dante in making high claims for poetry. His *Genealogy of the Gentile Gods* is a compendium of interpretations of Greek mythology on all four levels of meaning. 'These [Greek] myths contain more than a single meaning,' he states. 'They may indeed be called "polyseme" i.e., of multifold sense.'[11] Moreover, the last two books of *Genealogy of the Gentile Gods* are a *defence* of poetry, in which Boccaccio tries to raise poetry up from its relatively humble position in the medieval scheme of things. More specifically, he represents the new Humanism in opposition to the logical- or abstract-minded Scholasticism of the later Middle Ages. His four-level exegesis may be a quintessentially medieval technique (and hardly very relevant to his own *Decameron*), but, in so far as he uses it to exalt the status of poetry, he points ahead to the forthcoming Renaissance. The *defence* is a new form of critical discourse – especially as written by a practising poet.

In general, the distinctive achievement of the Middle Ages was to set up an enormously powerful interpretive strategy which was, at least sometimes, applied to secular texts. But the medieval mind felt no need to ground this strategy in a critical theory. It was enough that the strategy yielded the desired results, the appropriate kinds of moral and religious message. The complete conceptual framework was already supplied by Christian theology.

3   The Rise and Fall of Neoclassicism

The Humanism of Boccaccio and Petrarch in the fourteenth century gathered pace through the fifteenth century, to become the dominant mode of Renaissance thinking. For Humanists, the recovery and re-reading of Classical texts was above all an attempt to reinhabit the cultural and intellectual perspective of Ancient Greece and Rome. Medieval thinkers, for all their enormous humility towards Classical authority, had never stepped for a moment outside of their own medieval Christian perspective. But Renaissance thinkers sought to re-establish vital connection with what they admired. Soon the Middle Ages began to appear as 'the Dark Ages', a long interruption to the true line of Western cultural and intellectual development. For literature, this 'rebirth' of the Classical spirit meant that literary texts were to be judged by literary rather than religious values.

But these literary values were still social values. In particular, they tied in with the interests of the newly emerging Renaissance élite, the court aristocracy. The fifteenth century saw an increase in the power of central rulers at the expense of the old local dukes and barons of the feudal system. Court circles expanded accordingly, as did capital cities. And although court circles were still composed of people of birth and title, yet birth and title no longer simply determined ranking within court circles. Indeed, many titles had been only recently acquired. The court aristocracy was internally competitive, with the general competitiveness of Renaissance individualism. And the grounds of competition were no longer military prowess and military virtues. Instead, 'advancement' depended upon education, manners and literacy. The new élite based its superiority upon values of the kind spelled out in Castiglione's *The Courtier* (1528).

Literature featured as a key element in the new constellation of values. Association with literature, whether by writing or by patronage of writers, became a marker of social prestige and a significant means of advancement. Many poets ceased their literary efforts as soon as some sought-after appointment was achieved. At the same time, criticism of literature flourished in a new institutional setting, especially in Italy, where self-constituted 'academies' of gentleman amateurs discussed matters of poetic theory and practice.

By this special relationship to an élite social class, literature enhanced its prestige but also became more specialised. In medieval times, an audience for poetry typically included people of all social levels, and a poem such as *The Canterbury Tales* offered many different kinds of appeal. But literature in the new conception defined itself by appealing exclusively to the more discerning élite; while the élite defined itself by its more discerning taste for literature. It is now that literature separates off from general entertainment and lays claim to a superior, high-art status. The implications of quality in the modern term 'literature' first become relevant in relation to Renaissance literature.

A further factor in this change of status was that the new literature was accessible only to those who could read and write. In medieval times, texts had been written down mainly for purposes of storage, and oral performance continued as the normal mode of transmission. But in the Renaissance, it was the written text itself which passed from hand to hand. (Not yet the *printed* text, in spite of the new technology: for printed copies were considered vulgar and lowering amongst the court aristocracy, and poets preferred to enhance their social prestige by circulating scriveners' handwritten copies.) The implications of 'letters' and 'literate' in the modern term 'literature' first become relevant also in relation to Renaissance literature.

The role of 'letters' is even more explicit in the common Renaissance term for the new literature: 'belles-lettres'. The concept of 'belles-lettres', or 'gentleman's reading' as one might call it, continued to dominate throughout the seventeenth and eighteenth centuries (and has perhaps never entirely disappeared). However, the boundaries of 'belles-lettres' ran somewhat differently from the modern boundaries of 'literature'. Essays and histories were clearly included; contemporary prose narratives of popular appeal (such as Nashe's picaresque tale *The Unfortunate Traveller*) were clearly excluded; while contemporary plays might go either way. But there was no argument about any work which could claim strong derivation from the Greek and Roman classics. Needless to say, Homeric epic and Classical drama were now accorded the status of 'gentleman's reading', even though performed to non-exclusive audiences in their own time.

The question of language
(*Dante, du Bellay*)

One early battle in the Renaissance was fought between those who believed that the new literature should be written in Latin and those who believed that it should be written in the national vernacular. On the one hand, the Humanist enterprise led to the recovery of a 'pure' Roman Latin, as distinct from the degraded Church Latin of the Middle Ages. What better way to re-establish a vital connection with the Classics than by writing in the same language? On the other hand, the growth of the court aristocracy corresponded to the growing power of the centralised ruler; and the growing power of the centralised ruler corresponded to a growth of national consciousness. The Renaissance saw the rise of the new nation-states: England, Spain, France, Portugal. And the defining ground for national consciousness was a common national language. This curious contradiction between cultural forces and socio-political forces was resolved in favour of the socio-political forces. In the last analysis, the poets depended upon the courts; there was no new *institutional* base for the new Latin comparable to the old international Church of the Middle Ages.

The battle was fought out first in Italy – always far ahead of the rest of Europe throughout this period. The earliest reasoned argument for a vernacular literature appeared in the early fourteenth century, with Dante's unfinished *De Vulgari Eloquentia*. (It is a significant comment on Latin's medieval status as the language of thought that even a treatise on behalf of a non-Latin literature was itself written in Latin.) Inevitably, the argument also became a debate between different forms of the vernacular: courtly or everyday? past or present? Dante envisaged a high form of the vernacular which should be 'illustrious, cardinal, courtly, and curial', but was forced to conclude that no existing dialect measured up to his requirements.[1] However, the continuation of the debate into the early Renaissance eventually resulted in a victory for the School of Pietro Bembo, and the establishment of the Tuscan dialect as the medium for literature – the Tuscan dialect as it had been written two centuries ago by Petrarch, Boccaccio and Dante himself. The vernacular thus triumphed over Latin, but a Classical form of the vernacular triumphed over the contemporary language of the streets.

In France, the key event was the appearance in 1549 of du Bellay's *Defence and Illustration of the French Language*, a defence of poetry and a manifesto for the Pléiade group of poets. In this text, du Bellay speaks up for the French language and claims that France can produce literary works to equal those of Greece and Rome. The note of patriotism is particularly strong. At the same time, du Bellay presents an aristocratic conception of the poet's role, and insists that French poets should be fully familiar with the Classics in order to compete with them. He also wants to improve the French language by naturalising new words from Greek, Latin or Italian sources. The poet, he says, 'should not fear to invent, adopt, or compose in imitation of the Greeks some French words'.[2] French critical theory has always been very conscious of the role of language, and the language-oriented insights of French Structuralism and Poststructuralism tie in with a tradition going back all the way to du Bellay.

A side-skirmish in the battle between Latin and the vernacular was waged between quantitative and accentual metre. Whereas Classical quantitative verse had been patterned in terms of long and short vowels, medieval poets had shifted to a patterning in terms of strong and weak stresses. An accompanying shift had introduced rhyme as a further form of patterning. But many voices in the Renaissance were raised in favour of a return to unrhymed quantitative verse. One such voice in Elizabethan England was that of Thomas Campion; another poet, Samuel Daniel, wrote a *Defence of Rhyme* (c.1603) rejecting Campion's claims for the superior subtleties of Greek and Roman forms. Indeed, Daniel even vaunted the virtues of medieval culture generally.

In hindsight, the triumph of the vernacular and rhymed accentual verse seems inevitable. But it was not a simple triumph. The victorious discourse was not the discourse of medieval poetry, but a 'higher' discourse which had taken on Classical words, Classical manners, Classical assumptions. When Renaissance poets sought to compete against the classics of Antiquity, they felt obliged to judge and prove themselves against the same Classical standards. In many ways, the situation may be compared to the emulation phase of postcolonial culture, with the 'mother culture' here distanced in time rather than space.

The idealising strain
(*Giraldi, Sidney*)

But the Renaissance period was still creative in its relation to Antiquity. In literature as in architecture, it had not yet arrived at the directly imitative attitude of the Neoclassical period. For one thing, its knowledge of Antiquity was less accurate and less overwhelming. One particular inaccuracy occurred in the Renaissance reading of Plato. The Florentine Academy of Marsilio Ficino launched Platonism as the main philosophical influence at the start of the Renaissance. But Ficino and his followers failed to recognise the irony in Plato's statements about the *furor poeticus*. Notions of poetic frenzy and divine inspiration had been common in early Greek culture; Plato invoked such notions in the *Ion* and *Phaedrus* mainly in order to lower the status of the irrational poet. But the idea of the poet as inspired creator passed into Renaissance orthodoxy, and served to explain the more imaginative productions of the period.

For literary theory, the most important imaginative production of the period was Ariosto's *Orlando Furioso* (1516), the first best-seller in Western publishing history. Like Spenser in the *Faerie Queene*, Ariosto filled his romance with fantastic beings and events; and audience reaction clearly showed that such novel inventions had a special appeal of their own. The justification of marvels and the marvellous became one significant strand of Renaissance theory. So Giovambattista Giraldi (also known as Cinthio) found it necessary to claim in 1554 that the romance was an entirely new genre outside of Aristotle's scheme, a genre which called for entirely different criteria of judgement. 'Hence romances should not be subjected to classical laws and rules, but left within the limits set by those among us who have given authority and reputation to this species of poetry.'[3] As relevant criteria, he proposed maximum variety, multiplicity of action, digression and discontinuity – all plainly at odds with Aristotle's criteria for tragedy and epic. Similar but more philosophical theories were developed by two of the period's most interesting critics: Jacopo Mazzoni, in his defence of the dream-reality of Dante's *Divine Comedy*; and Francesco Patrizi, in his full-scale assault upon the Aristotelian concept of *mimesis*.

Moreover, the Renaissance was still a Christian age. For all the fascination of the pagan Classics, there were certain Christian attitudes that could not be left behind. Above all, literature had to be justified as morally useful. From the start of the Renaissance, theorists adopted Horace's formula of the *utile dulci,* profit combined with delight. But Horace's formula, which was already more moralistic than anything in Aristotle, now underwent a further tilt towards the side of instruction. So Tasso, the Italian poet, wrote that the goal of epic and indeed all poetry is 'to profit by delighting, that is, delight is the cause why no one fails to obtain benefit, because delight induces him to read the more gladly'.[4] Here teaching becomes the ultimate end, to which delight is merely the means.

To justify poetry on moral grounds was the main purpose of Sir Philip Sidney's *An Apology for Poetry* (written between 1579 and 1583, and sometimes referred to by its other title, *The Defence of Poesy*). Sidney – poet, courtier, scholar, and all-round Renaissance gentleman – was probably responding to a violent attack on poetry by Stephen Gosson. Like Boccaccio, he wrote to defend poetry against religious condemnation: specifically, the kind of condemnation increasingly voiced by English Puritans in the latter half of the sixteenth century. But unlike Boccaccio, he did not resort to the old medieval strategy, the old claim of an allegorical level of theologically-sound truth. Sidney's strategy has a distinctive Renaissance flavour.

Drawing upon Renaissance notions of 'divine' inspiration and marvellous invention, Sidney effectively outmanoeuvres the whole issue of truth. The poet's utterances never claim to apply as true or false: 'for the poet, he nothing affirmeth, and therefore never lieth'.[5] Instead, the poet seeks to create an alternative world (as Sidney himself had done, in his pastoral romance, *Arcadia*). What matters is the power of the creative imagination:

> the poet . . . lifted up by the vigour of his own invention, doth grow, in effect, into another nature, in making things either better than nature bringeth forth, or quite anew, forms such as never were in nature, as the heroes, demi-gods, cyclops, chimeras, furies, and such like.[6]

The poet refuses to be tied down and subjected to mere factual reality.

Such alternative worlds not only delight but also teach, precisely in so far as the poet's 'golden' world is superior to the 'brazen' (= brass) world of nature. Poets 'borrow nothing of what is, hath been or shall be; but range . . . into the divine consideration of what may be and should be'.[7] It is their task to set up role models, patterns of desirable behaviour. 'What philosopher's counsel can so readily direct a prince, as the feigned Cyrus in Xenophon?' Sidney demands. 'Or a virtuous man in all fortunes, as Aeneas in Virgil?'[8] The moral philosopher or theologian can teach virtue only in the abstract, but the poet paints images of ideal characters, and makes virtue appear attractive by example. Virtue can appear even more attractive when rewarded, especially if punishments are simultaneously meted out to vice. In this respect, the poet's feignings serve the purposes of moral instruction far better than the historian's facts:

> For, indeed, poetry ever setteth virtue so out in her best colours, making Fortune her well-waiting handmaid, that one must needs be enamoured of her. . . . And, of the contrary part, if evil men come to the stage, they ever go out . . . so manacled, as they little animate folks to follow them.[9]

This is the concept of *poetic justice*, which now appears in full force in Western critical thinking. As divinely inspired sub-creator, the poet must follow God, the supreme creator, in dispensing morally appropriate rewards and punishments. The Greeks and Romans, who had no such concept of an omnipotent omniscient God, also had no such concept of poetic justice.

Sidney sums up most emphatically the idealising strain in Renaissance literary thinking; but his views were not unusual. Many other writers also talked in terms of improving upon reality, setting up role-models, and teaching by example. Theoretically, this idealising strain can be related to Renaissance Platonism, with its dreams of a higher world and ideal forms. Of course, Renaissance Platonism conveniently inverted (where it did not simply misinterpret) Plato's opinions on the subject of poetry: allowing the poet access to the ideal and focusing upon the positive rather than the negative potential of role-models. The same idealising strain also showed itself strongly in the literature of the time. But the idealising strain was only one tendency in Renaissance critical theory – and, in the long run, not even the most important.

The Italian Aristotelians
(*Minturno, Scaliger, Castelvetro*)

The other strain was Aristotelian. Whereas Horace's *Ars Poetica* had been at least known throughout the Middle Ages, Aristotle's *Poetics* had almost completely disappeared from view. Rediscovered early in the Italian Renaissance, the *Poetics* began to have a major impact only when translated into Italian in 1549. Then followed an immediate flurry of commentaries and systems of theoretical poetics. Minturno's *De Poeta* (1559), Scaliger's *Poetices libri septem* (1561), and Castelvetro's *Poetica d'Aristotele vulgarizzata et sposta* (1570) were probably the three most influential texts. They were also particularly massive texts, all well over 500 pages long. In the second half of the sixteenth century, Italian writers produced works of literary theory on a scale and with a professionalism never seen before.

What Aristotle seemingly offered was a short-cut to the most admired qualities of the Classics. Despising the supposed formlessness of medieval writing, the writers of the Italian Renaissance aspired above all to the Greek and Roman sense of form. The rediscovered *Poetics* appeared to reveal the secrets of that sense of form, laid out in clear general principles. Aristotle in his own time had derived his general principles from the actual evidence of Greek tragedies and epics; but now the Renaissance Aristotelians turned them into *a priori* goals. The new literary theory was less concerned to describe an existing state of literature than to lay out the route to a desirable state of literature.

The Aristotelian strain in Renaissance theory cannot be separated from the Platonic strain by any simple division of critics. Sidney himself imported some Aristotelian notions of unity into his *Apology*, while the Italian Aristotelians typically believed in the moral function of literature and the creation of exemplary characters. (Even catharsis was reinterpreted as a kind of moral improvement.) Still, there is a significant difference in emphasis and commitment. The Aristotelians may refer to the *furor poeticus*, but their overwhelming interest is in the poet's conscious craft. And they may allow a role for 'invention' and 'the marvellous', yet nonetheless wish to exclude fantastic beings of the kind that Ariosto creates and Sidney promotes. Indeed, they prefer to focus upon a marvelling audience-response, produced by striking natural possibilities. Ideal golden worlds are unable to flourish under the Aristotelians' crucial principle of *verisimilitude*.

Verisimilitude means, literally, likeness to reality. The Italian Aristotelians derived the principle from Aristotle's concept of *mimesis*, or imitation, and his statements about achieving probability in representation. For Aristotle, though, imitation was not so much a criterion of value as a defining property of *poiesis*: he valued a work in proportion to its emotional effectiveness rather than in proportion to the believability of its imitation. With the principle of verisimilitude, the Italian Aristotelians gave more weight to believability, less to emotional effect. But verisimilitude is still far distant from modern notions of realism and the realistic.

In the first place, verisimilitude has nothing to do with everyday realism or the imitation of how a majority of people spend the majority of their lives. Literature is expected to focus upon specially important events in specially important lives – above all, the high-status lives of the noble and powerful. There is no role for the 'recognition factor' of everyday realism – the pleasure of being able to say 'That's exactly how I know it in my own life, that's exactly how it happens in my own environment'. And since the events imitated are far removed from personal experience, their likeness to reality can not be judged by a direct matching of item to item. Convincingness becomes a matter of general laws of probability. Poetry, according to Sperone Speroni, deals 'with what . . . is true according to reason because according to reason it should be like this'.[10]

This is still the way we tend to judge credibility in relation to public events. Given a newspaper report suggesting corrupt behaviour by a particular policeman, we say: 'I don't believe it, because the police are generally upright honourable people'; or, more recently: 'That would be true, because it's just the kind of corrupt behaviour you'd expect from the police'. However, we seem to work by different standards when judging the realism of a fictional imitation. What convinces us nowadays in fiction is the individual and unpredictable, the singularities which *don't* conform to stereotype. We believe in the awkward reality of what simply exists *in spite of* our understanding. In descriptions of scenes and objects, a proliferation of random details appears realistic to the modern mind. But random details and singularities have no place in sixteenth-century literary theory. According to the principle of verisimilitude, credibility depends upon probability, probability depends upon truth-to-type. And although the types envisaged by the Italian Aristotelians are not the same as ideal Platonic types, yet they are not *wholly* different either.

Of all the Italian Aristotelians, Castelvetro is the most interesting. He comes closer to the spirit of the *Poetics* than Scaliger or Minturno; at the same time, he does not elide his disagreements with Aristotle, but explicitly criticises and attempts improvements. Alone amongst his contemporaries, he is concerned with what appeals to a popular rather than an élite audience, and envisages a goal of pleasure rather than moral instruction. In many ways, his views are consciously cynical; certainly they are at the opposite pole to the idealising Platonic strain of Renaissance thinking.

Particularly extreme is his insistence upon verisimilitude. A popular audience has very little power of imagination, he claims, and will not become involved with events and characters unless it can believe in them as real. Visible divergences from known historical facts will jeopardise this kind of credibility, so Castelvetro insists upon a very literal adherence to known historical facts. Similarly with the known facts of nature: even the writer of comedies does not have 'license to make up for himself new cities that he has imagined, or rivers or mountains or kingdoms or customs or laws, or to change the course of things in nature, making it snow in summer and putting harvest in the winter'.[11] Similarly again with the known facts of human nature: it is 'necessary' that a mother (such as Medea) who resolves to kill her innocent children should do so only with great perturbation of soul.[12]

Considerations of verisimilitude also apply to presentation and performance. Castelvetro's focus is upon the theatre and the experience of drama as staged. He notes that drama involves the audience's physical senses as well as its understanding of words, and asserts that the physical senses cannot be deluded as to the real passage of time. This is surely correct so far as it goes: three sentences of narrative in a book can carry us across days or years or centuries, but it is impossible to think how this could happen with three sentences of continuous dialogue exchanged by characters on stage. Castelvetro applies this reasoning to entire plays:

> Nor is it possible to make [the audience] believe that several days and nights have passed when they know through their senses that only a few hours have passed, since no deception can take place in them which the senses recognise as such.[13]

What he is rejecting here, of course, is the possibility of letting time lapse in the discontinuities between scenes, between periods of continuous representation. His conclusion is that 'the time of the representation and that of the action represented must be exactly coincident'.[14] Or, allowing for a slight stretch, the events represented in a play must not exceed a time span of twelve hours. This is the unity of time, which had been already adumbrated by Scaliger and Minturno. The unity of place was entirely Castelvetro's own invention. 'The scene of the action must be constant,' he states, 'being not merely restricted to one city or house, but indeed to that one place alone which could be visible to one person.'[15] Again his argument is based upon claims about what the audience will be able to believe, again he rejects the possibility of letting space lapse in the discontinuities between areas of representation. The unity of place and the unity of time combine with the unity of action to constitute the notorious *three unities*. Only the unity of action has any real foundation in Aristotle: the requirement that representation be restricted to a single focused plot, a single nexus of convergent events. Ironically, the unity of action mattered least of the three to Castelvetro, and he endorsed it for fairly secondary reasons.

The interpretations of the Italian Aristotelians, still very much under debate in the second half of the sixteenth century, developed into the standardised rules of French Neoclassicism. This line of theoretical development curiously bypassed the intervening creative phase of the Baroque. For all the enormous achievements of Gongorism in Spain, Marinism in Italy and the Metaphysicals in England, the Baroque remained largely unthought and untheorised. Sforza Pallavicino (1644) and Emmanuele Tesauro (1654) in Italy, and Balthazar Gracián (1648) in Spain, praised the pleasures of deliberate artifice, and promoted a play of simile and metaphor for their own sake. But their suggestions scarcely amount to an overall theory of literature. Perhaps this lack of conceptual justification helps to explain why the Baroque, when it fell from creative fashion, disappeared so rapidly and remained for so long forgotten.

Neoclassicism and the purification of language
(*Montaigne, Malherbe*)

The fanatical religious wars in the first half of the seventeenth century brought on a reaction in the second half. The mood of Europe swung towards reason and reasonableness. The swing was strongly influenced by the growing success of the physical sciences, culminating in the great unifying system of Newton's *Principia* (1687). It seemed that the universe ran according to fixed unalterable laws, which could be understood by the rational, mathematical human mind. Culturally, France led the way. This was the age of the geometrical gardens of Versailles, the age of developing *haute cuisine*, the age of style and elegance in furniture, the age of Neoclassical literature. Naturally the literature partook of the general rational spirit. The poems of Dryden and Pope have a cerebral rather than an emotional appeal; the tragedies of Racine unfold with a clear, implacable logic. Much writing is satirical; some writing makes straightforward truth-statements about the world and humanity (e.g. the *Maximes* of La Rochefoucauld, or Pope's *Essay on Man*). At the same time, there was a simplifying standardisation of forms: the alexandrine and the heroic couplet became standard for all poetry in France and England respectively.

The impulse to simplifying standardisation also affected language. The Renaissance had been a time of spectacularly proliferating vocabulary and do-it-yourself linguistic innovation. But now came a movement to agree and regulate usage for society as a whole, so that everyone everywhere could understand one and the same meaning for one and the same word. What's more, there were to be fewer words. From the very start of the seventeenth century, the wholesale naturalisation of foreign terms advocated by du Bellay was reversed by François de Malherbe, who sought to restrict and stabilise language in the interests of clear communication. Arguing specifically against the poet Desportes, he condemned as wilful the quirkishness and difficulty – and even the *variety* – of Baroque usage. The regulation of the French language was institutionalised with the founding of the Académie Française in 1635.

Above all, the new focus was upon the content and reference of language. Michel de Montaigne, arguably the first writer of clear modern prose, foreshadowed the Neoclassical view as early as the 1580s: 'Away with that eloquence that enchants us with itself, and not with actual things!'[16] Flourishes of language indulged in for their own sake obscure the all-important subject-matter. Of course, a referent-oriented approach to language was well adapted to the needs of science. Conversely, the teaching of rhetoric, which had been revived as an appropriate element in a gentleman's education during the Renaissance, now vanished finally from the scene. During the

Neoclassical period, the accolades go to *perspicuity*, that is, the quality of 'see-through-able-ness' in language. Indeed, Neoclassical writers have a general predilection for analogies to sight and light and seeing: sight being the most objectifying sense, where the subject observes at a distance and the object appears as if untouched and unmediated.

French Neoclassical theory
(*Boileau, Bouhours, Rapin, [Pope, Johnson]*)

France became the centre of literary theory following the wholesale importation of Italian Aristotelianism by Jean Chapelain in the early seventeenth century. Key ideas were taken from Castelvetro, notably the three unities; however, the main influence overall was the less individualistic, more respectful Scaliger. The French theorists added little of their own; the most prominent figures – Bouhours, Rapin, and above all Boileau – were expounders and summarisers rather than original thinkers. Their role was to simplify and standardise the work of the Italians, shedding incompatible elements and producing a coherent, homogeneous system. The period of French Neoclassicism was a period of unusual theoretical unanimity. The Neoclassical mood spread across the Channel as a direct consequence of the 1660 Restoration, when Charles II and his court returned to England after exile in France.

One might suppose that the dramatic example of the new physical sciences would inspire a similar revolution in literary theory: a similar willingness to re-examine the actual evidence, to rethink fundamental principles. But in fact the critics of the period were deeply conservative, with their eyes fixed firmly upon the old Aristotelian principles reinterpreted into rules by Horace and the Italians. However, Neoclassical literary theory does relate to the new scientific spirit in other less obvious ways.

In the first place, there is the characteristic Neoclassical concern for generality, for the universal and the eternal. Renaissance theorists had emphasised generality, but their notion of teaching by example had been oriented towards moral improvement rather than towards general truths about the world and humanity. In the Neoclassical period, the universality expected of the writer seems almost on a par with the universality of the new scientific laws. The most famous

statement on the topic comes from a late Neoclassical critic of the
mid-eighteenth century, Samuel Johnson. In Johnson's *Rasselas*, the
character Imlac asserts:

> The business of the poet . . . is to examine, not the individual, but the
> species; to remark general properties and large appearances; he does
> not number the streaks of the tulip, or describe the different shades
> in the verdure of the forest . . . he must disregard present laws and
> opinions, and rise to general and transcendent truths, which will
> always be the same.[17]

The individual and particular have no larger relevance, no wider
application. Why would anyone be interested in a merely local case?
In similar vein, Johnson claims that 'great thoughts are always
general, and consist in positions not limited by exceptions';[18] and
praises Shakespeare for creating characters who are not merely individuals but every one 'a species'.[19]

For Johnson, the individual and the particular should know their
place and not get carried away by self-importance. The rational attitude is objective and looks out beyond what merely happens to be in
the immediate vicinity of the subject. This is also the scientific attitude – and in the seventeenth century, scientists had had to pull down
human pride in a very drastic way, displacing the Earth from the
centre of the universe. Ideally, the scientific attitude involves a kind of
modesty in the face of the world, a willingness to accept self-reducing,
self-controlling laws. And there is a further modesty on the part of the
individual scientist vis-à-vis the scientific community; other scientists
must confirm the individual's results, which will be absorbed or
rejected by the community of scientists as a whole. A similar modesty,
towards the world at least, can be seen in twentieth-century
Structuralist theory, which also proclaims scientific de-centring and
the unpalatable acceptance of self-reducing, self-controlling laws.

Neoclassical literary theorists embrace this kind of modesty almost
for its own sake. Critics must recognise their own limits, says
Alexander Pope in his *Essay on Criticism* (the most direct reflection of
French Neoclassical ideas in English):

> Be sure your self and your own Reach to know,
> How far your Genius, Taste, and Learning go,
> Launch not beyond your Depth [20]

But it is not by looking out to the observable factual evidence that Neoclassical critics transcend the subjective point of view. They bow to other forms of objective authority: the authority of the past and the authority of the social consensus. They adopt the scientific attitude without the science.

As regards the authority of the past, Neoclassical critics believe that the writer can be just as true to Nature by imitating the Greek and Roman classics as by imitating actual reality. This was originally Horace's notion – and in general, the Neoclassical spirit is closer to the Romans, who accepted their own secondarity, than to the Greeks. Pope proposes the example of Virgil, who as a young poet supposedly 'scorned to draw' from any other source than 'Nature's Fountains':

> But when t'examine ev'ry Part he came,
> Nature and Homer were, he found, the same.[21]

There is a sense of self-centred pride reduced to a proper humility.

The authority of the past was also accepted on the subject of genres. The medieval and early Renaissance genre of the romance was banished. Neoclassical theory allowed only a small number of genres, and no mixing between genres. (The idea that a mixing of, say, tragedy and comedy can be ruled out *a priori* seems very strange nowadays, although reviewers continue to blame the failure of a particular novel, play or film upon mixed purposes or incompatible emotional effects – *a posteriori*.) There was also a hierarchical arrangement of genres, which followed Aristotle in placing epic and tragedy at the top, but followed the majority of the Italian Aristotelians in placing epic above tragedy. The interesting thing here is that this hierarchy was accepted in spite of the fact that Neoclassical poets were quite incapable of producing .epics. The necessary mood for epic poetry had passed; and in England, the mood for dramatic tragedy had passed too. We are accustomed to literary theory which boosts the possibilities of the present writing scene, but Neoclassical theory tended to self-disempowerment.

As regards the authority of the social consensus, Boileau expresses the typical Neoclassical view: 'The bulk of mankind will not always be mistaken in their judgement of writers and writing.'[22] The operation of this form of authority shows clearly in the Neoclassical notion of Taste. Just as a taste for avocadoes may not manifest itself as an immediate liking but can be acquired, so too with a taste for works of literature. If a particular work has always been valued by the social consensus (of educated, cultivated people), then there must be something there to value; it is only your own loss if you can't learn to value it too. David Hume, far more conservative in his aesthetics than in his epistemology, draws an analogy between the appreciation of literature or art and simple sensory appreciation:

> Some particular forms or qualities . . . are calculated to please, and others to displease; and if they fail of their effect in any particular instance, it is from some apparent defect or imperfection in the [receiving] organ. A man in a fever would not insist on his palate as able to decide concerning flavours; nor would one, affected with the jaundice, pretend to give a verdict with regard to colours.[23]

A failure to appreciate is not an alternative point of view, but a lack in the subject, a missing capacity.

As for the reader, so too for the writer. According to Neoclassical critics, the poets of the Baroque had indulged in self-glorifying virtuosity in order to show off their own cleverness. Neoclassicism saw itself as a reaction against such egotistical excesses. Boileau, in his *L'Art Poétique,* roundly condemns poets who 'feel that they would demean themselves . . . if they were to think what somebody else was equally capable of thinking'.[24] There is a kind of manners, in poetry as in social life, which respects the intelligence of those addressed. Bouhours disapproves of 'authors who do not control their ideas or their words, and leave nothing to be thought or said on the subjects they treat'.[25] Sheer proliferating creativity for its own sake is to be condemned: in this period, what matters is not only what a poem says, but what it excludes, what it forbears to say. Neoclassical taste takes a gourmet delight in things that are done *de justesse* – just enough and no more.

This attitude helps to explain the Neoclassical concept of Nature. 'First follow NATURE', declares Pope[26] – but clearly he is not using the term in the sense later popularised by the Romantics. This is not a Nature of scenes and phenomena uncontaminated by human hand, but a Nature which includes and centres upon *human* nature. And not even human nature in primitive or spontaneous form, but human nature in social and cultivated form. We need to think of Nature as in the sense of 'speaking naturally', i.e. without forcing or straining for effect. The Neoclassical period considers itself natural specifically in contrast to the willed, false showiness which it attributes to the period of the Baroque.

Another recurring Neoclassical concept is decorum, described by Rapin as the 'most essential' rule, 'without which the other rules of poetry are false'.[27] Decorum means 'fittingness', as for Horace. But Neoclassical critics give the term a bewildering multiplicity of applications. Decorum is transgressed when style becomes inappropriate to its context; or when characters temporarily behave in ways inconsistent with their overall characterisation; or when particular emotional responses are out of keeping with the overall emotional tone of a work; or when onstage episodes of violence or vulgarity contravene the general social standards of the audience. What all these cases have in common is the prohibition upon developing local intensities without regard for larger context. The Baroque period was condemned for allowing the individual part to dominate over the whole – as in the flourishes of ornamentation which can seem to submerge the overall structures in Baroque architecture. By contrast, the Neoclassical age was determined to avoid indulging in what Pope called 'a Love to Parts'.[28]

The deliberate control of creativity requires the exercise of a separate mental faculty: the faculty of *judgement*. As arbiters of judgement, critics acquired unusual power in the Neoclassical period. Such power was naturally assisted by the impressive coherence and homogeneity of the Neoclassical critical system – which was in turn perfectly homogeneous with the larger social system. One defining moment in the establishment of French Neoclassicism was the trial of *Le Cid* in 1637, when Corneille was summoned to defend his play against the strictures of the Académie Française. But more often, of course, the power of critical theory was internalised by the writers themselves. Not until the Postmodern era – and then for very different reasons – does critical theory come into so close a conjunction with creativity, or claim so near an equality of status.

The British version of Neoclassicism
(*Jonson, Dryden, Johnson, Addison*)

Although systematicity was the source of its power, French Neoclassical theory habitually admitted one small escape clause. It was recognised that, on top of all the rules and requirements, an additional unpredictable element lifts literature to the very highest level. This is Boileau's 'je ne sais quoi', the indescribable 'I-don't-know-what' ingredient. Pope converts the concept into English as 'a Grace beyond the Reach of Art'.[29] Since this ingredient is by definition beyond theorisation, theory feels under no obligation to say anything further about it.

In the English version of Neoclassicism, there were typically many more escape clauses. Most of the important English critics were prac-tising poets and/or dramatists, and therefore less inclined to lay down absolute standards, more inclined to observe appropriate tactics in the contemporary writing scene. They did not aspire to challenge or out-think the general theory, but they did want to make a generous allowance for individual exceptions.

English Neoclassicism began early, and independently of French influence, with Ben Jonson. Jonson's ideas were taken from Italian sources, especially by way of the Dutch professor Daniel Heinsius. Himself an autodidact, Jonson placed great emphasis upon hard work and craftsmanship, and questioned Shakespeare's easy genius: 'he flowed with that facility that sometime it was necessary he should be stopped'.[30] His version of Neoclassicism was strongly oriented towards 'brevity' and 'vigour', in opposition to his contemporaries, the Metaphysicals.[31] It is an illuminating comment upon the use of gendered terminology that Jonson praised these Neoclassical virtues as 'manly', whereas later opponents of Neoclassicism condemned the 'effeminacy' of the Neoclassical style.

By the time of John Dryden, writing during the Restoration period, French influence had arrived in full strength. In many of his critical statements, Dryden shows himself wholly in agreement with the new trend. But he is also aware of a distinctively English literary tradition, with specific reference points in Shakespeare, Beaumont and Fletcher, Jonson, and Chaucer. He insists that different national audi-ences have their own temperaments and requirements: 'the climate, the age, the dispositions of the people to whom a poet writes, may be so different that what pleased the Greeks would not satisfy an English audience'.[32] The Neoclassical assumption of an essential human nature that is constant across cultures and history is here under chal-lenge. Dryden's most important piece of literary criticism, *An Essay of Dramatic Poesy,* is in large part a defence of English practice as against French theory.

In *An Essay of Dramatic Poesy,* drama is defined as 'a just and lively image of human nature'.[33] From the strict Neoclassical point of view, the important term is 'just', i.e., the image must be accurate according to the standards of verisimilitude. But Dryden's spokesman, Neander, throws the emphasis upon 'lively', and thus upon the value of local intensities.[34] The implications of 'lively' fly in the face of the Neoclassical rule of decorum. And Neander wants a richness, a multiplicity, a variety of such local intensities.

Variety is a recurring concept in Dryden's criticism. The exact criteria for applying the concept or assessing the degree of variety have never been spelled out, by Dryden or any other critic: throughout its long critical ancestry, the concept has remained *ad hoc* and intuitive. But it enables Dryden to justify 'the variety and copiousness of the English [plots]' as against 'the barrenness' or 'thinness' of the French.[35] And it enables him to justify a diversity of emotional responses, even including tragic and comic effects within the same play. 'Contraries when placed near, set off each other.'[36] Above all, it enables him to argue in favour of a large number of strongly individualised characters: 'the variety of [human] images being one great beauty of a play'.[37] Or, as he says a propos of Chaucer's character-gallery: 'here is God's plenty'.[38] The weighting of character above action had already been advanced by the Italian Aristotelians, but Dryden gives it a distinctively English twist.

Dryden is more important as a practical than as a theoretical critic. His appreciations and evaluations of particular authors, often working by a method of comparison and contrast, would loom much larger in a history of practical literary criticism. Similarly with Samuel Johnson, whose criticism is remarkable for judgements and insights into particular authors rather than for any development of a consistent theoretical position. Like Dryden, Johnson is essentially Neoclassical in his attitudes, but with certain very significant reservations.

Like Dryden, Johnson values variety: 'the great source of pleasure is variety. Uniformity must tire at last, though it be uniformity of excellence.'[39] He also places great emphasis upon imitating real life, and dismisses abruptly the imitation of past works of literature: 'No man was ever great by imitation.'[40] Nor will he allow an *a priori* absolute status to the Neoclassical rules: 'there is always an appeal open from criticism to nature'.[41] Thus he accepts the mixture of tragedy and comedy in Shakespeare's plays on the grounds that Shakespeare 'exhibit[s] the real state of sublunary nature, which partakes of good and evil, joy and sorrow, mingled with endless variety of proportion and innumerable modes of combination'.[42] On similar grounds, he suspects the artificial conventionality of the well-established classical genre of the pastoral. Too many writers of pastoral, he claims, 'have written with an utter disregard of both life and nature, and filled their productions with mythological allusions, with incredible fictions, and with sentiments which neither passion nor reason could have dictated'.[43] Not that truth to real life is his only criterion: he also insists upon the moral role of literature, and requires the writer to select from nature with a moral end in view. But in so far as truth to real life is one of his primary criteria, he believes in starting from actual observation, like the British Empiricist philosophers. Moving away from the apparatus of Neoclassical verisimilitude, he takes a step in the direction of modern notions of realism and the realistic.

Many of Johnson's critical opinions appeared as essays in *The Rambler*, a weekly periodical. The market for periodicals had sprung up earlier in the century, servicing a new middle-class reading public: *The Tatler* in 1709, *The Spectator* in 1711. Throughout the eighteenth century, the British middle classes were growing and expanding their political power, well ahead of any other European nation. And with growth and power came leisure, literacy and a desire for 'culture'. The periodicals fed this desire with non-specialist essays designed to extend the 'culture' of the élite to the would-be élite.

The most notable writer in the new critical form was Joseph Addison. Addison promoted such non-Neoclassical works as Milton's *Paradise Lost* and the old English ballad 'Chevy Chase', though his reasons for approval were notably less advanced than his tastes. He also placed overwhelming emphasis upon the value of vivid *visual* imagery – a distinctly English emphasis which was to resurface in the Anglo-American criticism of the twentieth century. But by and large, Addison remained very much within the Neoclassical tradition. The originality of his criticism was not so much a matter of content as of context – both material and intellectual.

The new intellectual context out of which Addison wrote was the new field of philosophical aesthetics. The first full-scale work of aesthetics was Shaftesbury's *Characteristics*, published in 1711; Addison's essays on 'The Pleasures of the Imagination' appeared in *The Spectator* in 1712; and many others, including Hume, followed after. Not since the time of Plato, Aristotle and Plotinus had literary theory been so directly generated from a fundamental philosophical framework. And whereas Aristotle had asked questions specifically about *poiesis*, the new aestheticians asked questions about *beauty* in general – whether in art, literature, music, or natural landscape. The answers were sought in terms of universal human response: but response now understood in terms of individual subjectivity rather than public or social affect. Addison was typical in invoking the new philosophical psychology of such thinkers as Hobbes and Locke. As yet, the answers did not differ significantly from the standard Neoclassical conclusions; but the new framework opened the way for future developments.

British theory in the Age of Sensibility
(*Johnson, Young, Joseph Warton, Thomas Warton, Hurd, Edmund Burke*)

Eventually, inevitably, the growth of the middle classes in Britain changed the nature of literature. The passive acceptance of tastes handed down from above gave way to a more active shaping role: the new reading public wanted its own kind of reading material. And this reading public was new not only in terms of class but also in terms of gender: a large proportion of readers were female. Although middle-class women were not taught Latin or Greek, they were nonetheless educated and literate, and now had leisure for reading. Circulating libraries sprang up to satisfy the new market, hiring out books as video shops nowadays hire out videos. And a new network of communication came into being, bypassing the traditional social centre of London, relying entirely upon the printed word as a means of transmission. At the same time, new Copyright Laws set up the modern royalties system, whereby writers received ongoing payments according to the number of books sold. Combined with the vast expansion of the reading public, this system made it possible for writers to live – as never before – upon the proceeds of book sales. Patronage, which had long been the most valuable source of funding for any writer above the 'hack' level, now became increasingly irrelevant. Writers were tied to the demands of the marketplace, but they were no longer tied to the demands of particular members of the political aristocracy.

Middle-class tastes brought on the Age of Sensibility or Age of Sentiment. In the latter half of the eighteenth century, cerebral wit and satire were displaced by feeling and emotional response. *Enthusiasm* became a common term of approval, along with *sympathy*. Sympathy was especially called for in relation to the newly developed form of the novel, which encouraged readers to a more intense and personal identification with the experience of the characters. The Richardsonian novel in Britain set the fashion for the whole of Europe. Novels as such were little discussed in literary theory, being as yet scarcely admitted to the status of serious reading. But literary theory was very much influenced by the Richardsonian mood.

Britain was at the centre of developments in literary theory as in literature. The decade of the 1750s was particularly rich in new ideas. Many theorists were moved by a new spirit of nationalism and a newly assertive pride in the achievements of English literature from before the Neoclassical period. Shakespeare had long been an example of what British genius could achieve unshackled by rules and laws; now Shakespeare was joined by Spenser and Milton. While changes in taste led the way and explicit theorisation followed haltingly behind, yet one by one the fundamental principles of the Neoclassical system were assaulted.

One such assault was launched by Samuel Johnson. Johnson has already featured as being in some respects an upholder of strict Neoclassicism, and in some respects a pragmatic modifier of Neoclassicism. But in one respect at least, he was an outright opponent of Neoclassicism – namely, in his rejection of the unities of time and place. Many had doubted these two unities, but it was Johnson who finally kicked out the theoretical props on which they rested. Ever since the time of Castelvetro, they had been justified by 'the supposed necessity of making the drama credible'.[44] But Johnson denied that any such credibility existed. 'The spectators', he said, 'are always in their senses, and know, from the first act to last, that the stage is only a stage, and that the players are only players.'[45] Plays, he insisted, are not credited with the credit due to real life, but only with the credit due to a drama.

Castelvetro's argument had turned upon the fact that the senses are fully engaged in watching a play (as not in reading a book); combined with the assumption that the evidence of the senses is primary and foundational; and leading to the conclusion that the senses must be deluded if the drama is to be believed. But Johnson saw that the evidence of the senses is not always primary and foundational, but can be overridden by the projective interpretations of the mind. The audience sees the stage, but *takes it* as being Alexandria or Rome. The things observed are not terminal realities, but signs for something further. And, to the extent that signifying is involved, a play is like a book and can direct its representations to different times and places. Even in his attacks upon the Neoclassical unities, Johnson still speaks with the objectifying reasonableness of Neoclassical discourse. By contrast, Edward Young speaks with a new kind of passion and a new subjectivist appeal. 'Thyself so reverence, as to prefer the native growth of thy own mind to the richest import from abroad.'[46] Such subjectivism relates to the subjectivist basis of Nonconformist Protestantism, the predominant religious background of the rising middle class. At one significant moment in his *Conjectures on Original Composition,* Young draws an analogy to the Protestant notion of individual conscience: 'Genius can set us right in composition, without the rules of the learned; as conscience sets us right in life, without the laws of the land.'[47]

Conjectures on Original Composition is a proclamation of originality as an absolute virtue. Young attacks the Neoclassical writers' acceptance of secondarity and subservience to authority. Foreshadowing the Romantics, he envisages creative power in organic terms:

> An original may be said to be of a vegetable nature; it rises sponta-
> neously from the vital root of genius; it grows, it is not made:
> [whereas] imitations are often a sort of manufacture wrought up by
> those mechanics, art and labour, out of preexistent materials not
> their own.[48]

He also foreshadows the Romantics in describing the creative power as 'the stranger within thee', which may be unknown to the consciousness of its possessor.[49]

The Neoclassical way of thinking emphasised the common nature of human beings, so that even a writer who managed to ignore all influence of past models or the social consensus would not 'naturally' produce anything very different from other writers. But Young's notion of originality ties in with an assumption of individual differences. The extent to which a writer differs from other writers becomes in itself a criterion of value. In relation to past models: 'All eminence and distinction, lies out of the beaten road; excursion, and deviation, are necessary to find it; and the more remote your path from the highway, the more reputable.'[50] And in relation to the social consensus: 'Genius often then deserves most to be praised, when it is most sure to be condemned.'[51] This is original genius as we still think of it today: recognisable by the very fact that society condemns it. As for the poetry produced by original genius, Young claimed that 'There is something in poetry beyond prose-reason.'[52] A similar view appears in Joseph Warton's *Essay on the Genius and Writings of Pope.* Warton distinguishes between different levels of poetry:

> In the first class I would place our only three sublime and pathetic poets: *Spenser, Shakespeare, Milton.* In the second class should be ranked such as possessed the true poetical genius in a more moderate degree, but who had noble talents for moral, ethical, and panegyrical poetry. . . . In the third class may be placed men of wit, of elegant taste, and lively fancy in describing familiar life, though not the higher scenes of poetry.[53]

It is on this lower third level that Pope belongs. One mark of the distinction between levels is that Pope's poetry can be successfully paraphrased, whereas it is impossible to 'lower and reduce' Homer or Milton or Virgil 'to the tameness of prose'.[54] Of course, Pope himself would not have disputed his own paraphraseability ('What oft was Thought, but ne'er so well Express'd'); and Warton does not suggest that Pope fell short of anything he tried to achieve. Only, there are different levels of achievement.

Joseph's younger brother, Thomas, was involved in another anti-Neoclassical development. The middle decades of the eighteenth century were a period of intense editorial activity, especially following Theobald's pathbreaking edition of Shakespeare (1733–4). Editorial activity encouraged historical scholarship – and the most notable historical scholar was Thomas Warton. Challenging the Neoclassical view of the Middle Ages as a period of mere barbarism, the younger Warton insisted that the code of chivalry had its own kind of validity, its own cultural logic. Such a code might even be seen as particularly fertile ground for the production of poetry. Thus, medieval romances 'contribute, in wonderful degree, to rouse and invigorate all the powers of imagination: to store the fancy with those sublime and alarming images which true poetry best delights to display'.[55] In general, according to Thomas Warton, a work from an earlier period must always be viewed in the light of the customs and beliefs then prevailing. So, when considering Spenser, he examines the critical writings of the time in order to discover the standards by which the Elizabethans themselves judged poetry. Such an approach clearly contradicts the Neoclassical postulation of a constant, transhistorical human nature, from which eternal standards of true taste may be derived.

Richard Hurd was less of a scholar than the younger Warton, but more wholeheartedly enthusiastic about medieval literature and about the *Faerie Queene*. Reversing the connotations of 'Gothic', a term which Neoclassical writers had used to condemn the Middle Ages, he proclaimed the superiority of 'Gothic' tradition to Classical tradition. Neoclassicism might have gained 'a great deal of good sense', but it had lost 'a world of fine fabling'.[56] As for the *Faerie Queene*, Hurd recognised that the separate adventures of the knights lacked Aristotelian unity of action, yet argued that the poem still possessed 'an unity of another sort . . . resulting from the respect which a number of related actions have to one common purpose'.[57] This 'unity of *design*' grew naturally out of Spenser's subject-matter and the whole chivalric way of thinking.

Meanwhile, another crucial new concept had been gradually making its presence felt: *the sublime*. The term has already appeared in quotes from Joseph and Thomas Warton. Longinus' *On the Sublime* had been translated by Boileau – of all people – at the height of the Neoclassical period. The general reverence for everything Classical meant that Longinus' views had to be given a place in Neoclassical thinking; for a long time, however, the sublime was restricted to a superficial quality of style. But Longinus, whose critical approach is fundamentally different from Aristotle's and even more fundamentally different from the Neoclassical version of Aristotelianism, was a time-bomb ticking away. Around the start of the eighteenth century, John Dennis began to draw a different message from *On the Sublime*. Conventionally Neoclassical in most of his opinions, Dennis nonetheless regarded passion as the essential feature of poetry, and gave highest praise to religious poetry (such as Milton's) because of its power to generate sublime feelings of admiration and awe. Again, the Bible-reading background of the rising middle classes is relevant here.

The most important theorist of the sublime was Edmund Burke, who published his *Philosophical Enquiry into the Origin of our Ideas of the Sublime and Beautiful* in 1757. Burke belongs to the line of philosophical aestheticians. All the arts are his field of discussion, and his method is a psychological analysis of human response. He distinguishes between two quite different forms of aesthetic response: our sense of the beautiful versus our sense of the sublime. Although both are valuable in their own ways, it is clear that a higher level of value is associated with the greater intensity of the sublime.

For Burke, the beautiful is pleasant, attractive, appealing. We find it, he claims, in smoothness, smallness, subtle variation, delicacy, and mild colours. This is very much a Neoclassical version of beauty – the version of beauty implicit in such favoured Neoclassical critical epithets as 'grace', 'charm', 'delicateness'. By contrast, our sense of the sublime is inspired by ruggedness, irregularity, vastness, power and obscurity. (It is no coincidence that in this very period European travellers first discovered a liking for spectacular mountain scenery.) Going beyond Longinus, Burke links the sublime with terror: 'Whatever is fitted in any sort to excite the ideas of pain, and danger . . . or operates in a manner analogous to terror, is a source of the *sublime*.'[58] And terror and fear are mind-numbing, reason-numbing emotions: 'No passion so effectually robs the mind of all its powers of acting and reasoning as fear.'[59] To seek out such emotion is a novel and paradoxical twist of human sensibility. But, as the Romantics more fully demonstrated, it is indeed possible to admire the non- or anti-human, to be fascinated with what overpowers us, and to enjoy dallying with the prospect of our own annihilation.

The role of obscurity calls for special comment. Longinus had already pointed out that the imagination is most stirred to activity when things are suggested rather than plainly stated. Burke relates this to the notion that plain statement, like plain vision, gives us a sense of control. 'When we know the full extent of any danger, when we can accustom our eyes to it, a great deal of the apprehension vanishes.'[60] Emotions such as terror, which involve a loss of control, are therefore heightened when we are denied clear knowledge: 'dark, confused, uncertain images have a greater power on the fancy to form the grander passions than those have which are more clear and determinate'.[61] Needless to say, Burke's argument is completely at odds with the Neoclassical virtue of perspicuity.

What is more, Burke challenges the whole Neoclassical analogy between the workings of language and the workings of visual perception. Appealing to intuitive introspection in the typical manner of the eighteenth century psychological philosopher, he denies that the meanings of language are simple visual images:

it is not only of those ideas which are commonly called abstract . . .
but even of particular real beings, that we converse without having
any idea of them excited in the imagination; as will certainly appear
on a diligent examination of our own minds.[62]

For Burke, language *acts* – and acts *subjectively*. Its meanings are not
static reflections of external objects, but effects directly wrought upon
the mind and feelings of the receiver. Writers, therefore, should not
attempt to convey pictures, but should use the peculiar energies of
their own medium:

> poetry and rhetoric do not succeed in exact description so well as
> painting does; their business is to affect rather by sympathy than
> imitation; to display rather the effect of things on the mind of the
> speaker, or others, than to present a clear idea of the things them-
> selves.[63]

Burke's argument suggests a natural affinity between language and
the sublime.

In the Age of Sensibility, British critics moved beyond admitting
particular exceptions to the Neoclassical system and began setting up
alternative kinds of poetry, alternative kinds of response. Also during
this period, many terms began to shift from their Neoclassical sense
towards their Romantic (and modern) sense: 'imagination' (which
had previously meant little more than the summoning up of visual
images); 'Nature' (which had centred upon human nature); 'genius'
(which had been scarcely distinguished from 'talent'); and 'inspiration' (which had been scarcely distinguished from 'invention'). But
none of the British critics – not even Burke – managed to develop a
general theoretical framework capable of replacing Neoclassicism as a
whole. In their writings, residual elements of Neoclassicism exist
strangely in suspension with proto-Romantic elements. The age was
transitional, in its criticism as in its poetry.

Vico, Diderot, Lessing

In the mid-eighteenth century, British literary theory becomes a
movement that is greater than any of its individual members. The
opposite applies to Continental literary theory, where it is now the

separate single figures who most impress. The first such figure is the most out-on-a-limb of all: the Neapolitan thinker Giambattista Vico. Almost single-handedly, Vico founded the scientific study of culture – or would have founded the scientific study of culture, but for the fact that his ideas were largely ignored for a century and only fully appreciated after two centuries.

In his *Scienza Nuova* (published 1725, heavily revised 1730, further revised 1744), Vico hypothesises about the earliest stage of human society. Without in any way sentimentalising primitive culture, he recognises that the earliest stage of human society must have possessed its own quite different way of thinking: namely, mythological or 'poetic' thinking. Mythological thinking, he claims, was determined by the early state of human language, which lacked abstract terms. Concrete particular terms were therefore required to take on conceptual and explanatory roles, as *imaginative universals*. Mythical gods and heroes are one type of imaginative universal: 'if . . . a nation is unable to name some abstract, or general, property, it must . . . name some particular man who possesses it'.[64] The early state of language is thus metaphorical, and myth is a metaphorical way of thinking. Such language and thinking call for powers of imagination rather than powers of reason. Nonetheless, this way of thinking has its own 'poetic' logic, and provides a means of rendering the world intelligible.

Although Vico was not greatly concerned with poetry in the usual narrower sense, his arguments evidently entail a complete rejection of the Neoclassical perspective. Viewed in relation to myth, poetry is no longer something merely added on top of ordinary rational thinking. Poetry is not entertainment or amusement but a mode of thinking – and even the necessary original mode of all thinking. Poetic thinking is the very base from which rational thinking has evolved. Nor are figures of speech merely added on top of ordinary prose sense. Whereas Neoclassical critics often warned poets against allowing metaphor to run off on its own and take over from clear thinking, Vico argues that metaphor *is* thinking. 'All the first tropes are corollaries of this poetic logic, and of these the most luminous, and hence the most necessary and frequent, is metaphor.'[65] What's more, modern literal language is actually founded upon dead metaphors, as in the case of such modern phrases as 'the mouth of a river', 'veins of minerals', 'murmuring waves', or 'weeping willow'.

If Vico's 'new science' points ahead to Romantic literary theory and twentieth-century anthropology, some of Denis Diderot's ideas seem to foreshadow late nineteenth-century Naturalism and Symbolism, and late twentieth-century Postmodernism. Even Diderot's paradox-loving manner foreshadows Postmodernism, with a play of extremes which refuses to be reduced to overall consistency. Diderot's writings are perfect models of Bakhtinian *dialogism*, not simply because they are commonly in the form of dialogues, but because their voices argue for themselves as if unchecked by any controlling author. Early in his career, Diderot was especially a proponent of sensibility and the virtues of natural emotion. But the natural was not such a simple matter for Diderot as for the British critics. In his 'A Letter on the Blind', he alludes to the case of a blind man who seems to use visual terminology effectively and yet lacks the basic experience upon which such terminology is supposedly founded.[66] Language already operates at a very great distance from the natural. In his 'A Letter on the Deaf and Dumb', Diderot further argues that sequential verbal utterance is already an artificial arrangement of simultaneous thought and perception. And the natural becomes even more inaccessible when literary 'imitation' is involved. In *The Paradox of Acting*, Diderot points out that an actor who is sincerely overcome by the emotion to be represented would lose control and fail to communicate anything successfully. The actor 'must have in himself an unmoved and disinterested onlooker'.[67] Similarly with poetry: the impression of spontaneous utterance in the heat of a real emotional moment is an illusion that has to be faked. 'One writes of one's falling tears, but they do not fall while one is hunting a strong epithet.'[68] Given the conditions of literary production, 'getting back to' the natural actually introduces a further level of artifice. Like many more recent French theorists, Diderot recognises that the natural and artificial do not lie simply at the opposite ends of a single spectrum, but constantly double back and forth over one another.

Such a recognition suggests two options for the writer: either a more determined pursuit of the truly natural, or, on the contrary, a conscious assertion of the artifice in art. By analogy to the nineteenth century, these might be called the 'Naturalist' and 'Symbolist' options respectively. Diderot embraces the 'Naturalist' option when he proposes a theatre where visual tableaux and bodily gestures would be offered to simultaneous sensory perception and articulate utterance would be minimised. Instead of the artifice of language, inarticulate cries, weeping and silence would express emotion naturally.[69] At the same time, the play would be acted as if the audience were not present, as if the front of the stage were merely the fourth wall of a real domestic interior.[70]

Elsewhere Diderot embraces the 'Symbolist' option. Speaking in this voice, he claims that there is a pleasure in being aware of art *as* art. The planned and composed order of a work of art moves away from Nature, improves upon Nature. 'What, then, is truth for stage purposes? It is the conforming of action, diction, face, voice, movement, and gesture, to an ideal type invented by the poet.'[71] Diderot comes uncannily close to Symbolism when he focuses upon 'relationships' as the secret order of art, and when he suggests that words in poetry are 'a tissue of hieroglyphs heaped upon each other'.[72] Admittedly, these are only passing hints, but it is tempting to see Diderot as the connecting link between French Neoclassicism and French Symbolism – two very different movements which share a common orientation towards deliberate literary artifice.

Gotthold Lessing is a more straightforward representative of the Age of Sensibility. Reacting against the French-style Neoclassicism imported into Germany by Gottsched, he attacked the unities and other mechanical rules. His praise of Shakespeare did much to propel a growing worship of Shakespeare in Germany. But his main work of criticism, *Laocoön* (1766), dealt with a topic of general aesthetics: the difference between the verbal arts and the visual or plastic arts. Like Burke, Lessing tended to favour language over visual perception, as being less tied down to the physical and offering greater possibilities for imagination.

It is the contrast of simultaneity versus sequentiality that he most dwells upon. In painting or sculpture, 'signs arranged together side by side can express only subjects which, or the various parts of which, exist thus side by side', whereas in language, 'signs which succeed each other can express only subjects which, or the various parts of which, succeed each other'.[73] This leads to the conclusion that 'succession in time is the sphere of the poet', and that 'actions form the proper subjects of poetry'.[74] Conversely, the poet is at a relative disadvantage when attempting to present static objects and spatial relations. (To take a modern example: how often we fail to grasp the exact layout of a room in a novel, no matter how precise or lengthy the description!) Lessing praises Homer for avoiding static description wherever possible: '[Homer] paints nothing but continuous actions, and all bodies, all single things, he paints only by their share in those actions, and in general only by one feature.'[75] In *Laocoön*, the old Neoclassical rules have fallen away, but the new limiting laws of the medium are starting to emerge.

Goethe in his autobiography testified to Lessing's enormous impact upon the young writers of the forthcoming 'Sturm und Drang' school. It is not difficult to see a general connection between Lessing's insistence upon action and the Romantic emphasis upon movement and energy. More specifically, the temporal dimension to which Lessing drew attention becomes increasingly important in the Romantic period. In such 'process-poems' as Coleridge's 'Frost at Midnight' or Keats' 'Ode to a Nightingale', the time of the language is made to correspond to the time of the experience, causing the poet's state of knowledge to shift as if during the course of writing the poem. And in the Gothic novel, with its newly prominent mystery interest, the time of language is made to correspond to the time of the characters, heightening the sequentiality of anticipation and revelation. In such cases, language is deployed *within* rather than *over* or *above* time.

4   Romantic Literary Theory

The cultural revolution of Romanticism began towards the end of the eighteenth century, spreading out initially from Germany. At the same time, a political revolution was taking place in France, and an industrial revolution in Britain. But the cultural revolution was not in obvious agreement with the two other revolutions. In Britain, for example, Romantic reverence for Nature clearly clashed with the effects of industrialisation. In France, the culture of the Revolutionary and Napoleonic periods held back the arrival of Romanticism. And in Germany, Romanticism kept company with a revival of Christian mysticism and reactionary political attitudes.

In terms of artistic production, the Romantic period was a great period of music and poetry. Not only were the literary energies of the period channelled into poetry rather than prose, but the poetry itself aspired to peaks of poetic intensity and exaltation. For the first time, the short lyric became the model and norm for all literature. Coleridge, for one, insisted that 'a poem of any length neither can be, nor ought to be, all poetry'.[1] The concept of 'poetry' is here turning into an inner essence, a quality of thought and vision, rather than a simple recognisable category of outward form.

Also intense and exalted was the role of the poet as genius. Byron stands as perhaps the most notable example of the new glamour surrounding the figure of the poet. And, as in the case of Byron, this glamour was reinforced by the poet's new anti-social, outsider status. The poet became the standard-bearer of Romantic individualism. Such a stance would have been impossible in the age of patronage, when the poet depended for survival upon the ruling class of an existing social structure. But now the poet could reject the existing social structure and envisage drastic alternatives. There is a world of difference between the pragmatic 'inner circle' politics of a Dryden and the ideal Utopian politics of a Shelley. Through the medium of print transmission, the poet no longer addresses a small, well-defined social group, but sends forth messages towards an unknown general audience. Correspondingly, the reading of poetry tends to become an increasingly private kind of activity.

Romantic literature in Britain grew almost in parallel with Romantic literature in Germany, but Germany was overwhelmingly the source of the most important developments in literary theory. German literary theory was produced by poets like Goethe and Schiller, by journal-critics like Friedrich and August Wilhelm Schlegel (especially in their journal, the *Athenaeum*), and by academic philosophers like Kant, Schelling, Schopenhauer and Hegel. The last group was especially significant, in that the advent of German Idealist philosophy impacted very directly upon Romantic literary theory. Indeed, the German intellectual scene exhibits an unusual degree of interaction between academics and creative writers throughout this period, often involving close circles of friendship and personal acquaintance.

The new literary theory in Germany moved beyond the emotional–sensory perspective of the Age of Sensibility, towards a more abstract–idealist perspective. Of course, many of the arguments against Neoclassicism continued as before: the dismantling of the rules, the acclamation of originality and inspiration, the emphasis upon the sublime, and so on. These themes have already been observed in the previous chapter, and will not be re-examined here. Amongst British critics, only Coleridge fully adopted the German perspective; and in the following four sections, only Coleridge will be discussed alongside the German theorists.

First, though, a note on the term 'Romantic'. German usage gives the term a very narrow application, in literature as in music; specifically, it refers to a group of writers who began writing around the turn of the century. In line with common English usage, I have opted for a much wider application, taking in the Sturm und Drang movement of the 1770s, and not necessarily excluding even the late eighteenth century forms of German 'classicism'. For the so-called 'classicism' of Goethe, Schiller and Hölderlin was in no sense a reversion to Neoclassicism, or even Renaissance classicism. It turned upon a very sharp distinction, initiated by Winckelmann, between the inspired original Greeks and the imitative secondary Romans. When German writers turned with admiration to Greek culture, they simul-

taneously turned away from Latin culture – and away from French
Neoclassicism.

Herder and the spirit of the time
(*also Schiller, Friedrich Schlegel, Hegel*)

Johann Gottfried Herder was the most important influence upon the
Sturm und Drang movement. His vision in many ways resembled that
of Vico. But whereas Vico saw himself as a new kind of scientist,
Herder was a proselytiser. In fact, much of his writing was in the
special form of the *fragment*, deliberately incomplete, with sudden
jumps of topic and moments of elevated poetic rhapsody. The fragment form was popular with many subsequent German theorists,
who similarly enacted their rejection of Neoclassical systematisation
in their own writings.

Herder's vision was a vision of what he called 'the collective individuality of a society'. Every culture and every age has its own unique
character, its own distinctive way of thinking and experiencing. And
crucial to this distinctive way of thinking and experiencing is a
distinctive language. 'The language [of a nation] is its collective treasure, the source of its social wisdom and communal self-respect.'[2] For
Herder, a language is a living organism with its own principles of
growth and change – a view which later inspired the early nineteenth
century triumphs of German philology. And just as a language is
inseparable from a particular culture, so too a literature is inseparable
from a particular language and particular culture. Herder sees literature as the self-expression, not of an individual, but of a whole society.
He is not interested in what a poem imitates or is about, but in where
it comes from. To explain a poem is to explain its role within its own
home culture.

The connection between a poem and its home culture is especially
visible in the case of folk-poetry. Herder was a central figure in
encouraging the great rediscovery of folk-poetry which took place in
Germany, as in Britain, during the latter half of the eighteenth
century. Folk-poetry fits in well with Herder's view of the poem as a
communicative act between people: not an autonomous created
object, but voices speaking. It also usefully exemplifies Herder's ideal
of a poetry that is produced by a whole community, rather than by
one exclusive segment or class. (Admittedly, Herder was often starry-

eyed about the degree of communal involvement, especially when he stretched the concept of folk-poetry so far as to include Dante!)

By contrast, the French Neoclassical age shows what happens when literature becomes divorced from its home culture. As Herder saw it, the writers of the French Neoclassical age had subjected themselves to principles taken from a totally different state of society. In Greek drama, the unities arose naturally out of the conditions of Greek life; but they were artificial when imposed upon French culture two thousand years later. '[French Neoclassical] drama is not the same, because it has nothing in common with Greek drama at its very heart: neither action, nor customs, nor language, nor purpose – nothing. So what is the point of all these externals . . . ?'[3]

Leaving aside such cases of artificiality, Herder delights in all genuine products of all cultures and periods. Different sorts of poetry appeal precisely because of their differentness, because of their individuality. 'Each age has its own tone, its own colour; and it gives a peculiar pleasure to characterise it correctly in contrast to other times.'[4] But by the same token, individual cultures and periods are essentially incommensurable. It is as great a mistake to judge Shakespearian drama by the criteria of Greek drama as to judge Greek drama by the criteria of Shakespearian drama. One can only say that 'out of the soil of the age there grew a different plant'.[5] Herder arrives at the kind of relativism that was implicit, but only implicit, in the historical approach of Hurd and Thomas Wharton.

Herder was not greatly concerned to define *the spirit of the time* for his own contemporary society and its literature. That definition was undertaken by the dramatist Friedrich Schiller, in a famous essay 'On Naive and Sentimental Poetry'. Schiller sets up a large-scale contrast between early 'naive' poetry and late 'sentimental' poetry – where 'sentimental' is given an unusual meaning, virtually equivalent to 'reflective' or 'self-conscious'. 'Naive' literature is especially exemplified by Homer and the Greeks; 'sentimental' literature potentially applies to the whole Christian period, but seems to relate most closely to Romanticism (and particularly German Romanticism).

Schiller's contrast is between integration and separation. 'Naive' poets are at one with Nature; 'sentimental' poets admire Nature precisely because they see it as something apart, something lost. 'Naive' poets present the object impersonally in concrete description; 'sentimental' poets present the object always through themselves, subjectively and self-consciously. 'The sentimental poet . . . *reflects* upon the impression that objects make upon him, and only in that reflection is the emotion grounded which he himself experiences and which he excites in us.'[6] Other separations include an alienation of the poet from the community, and a dissociation between the poet's sensuous and intellectual faculties. For the Greeks, 'sense and intellect did not as yet rule over strictly separate domains; for no dissension had as yet provoked them into hostile partition and mutual demarcation of their frontiers'.[7] By contrast, mind and spirit predominate in the 'sentimental' poets, who aspire towards the Idea, the unattainable ideal. So, whereas 'naive' poetry is harmonious and satisfied within the limits of the real world, 'sentimental' poetry is filled with unbalanced energy and a longing for the infinite.

While it might seem desirable to recover the integrated sensibility of the past, the German theorists found it difficult to believe in the possibility of such recovery. The new historical sense precluded it. Instead, various future forms of reconciliation were projected. Schiller hoped for a unification of 'naive' and 'sentimental' impulses; Friedrich Schlegel, A. W. Schlegel, and Schelling called for the creation of an original mythology. But there were no generally agreed solutions. The Romantic critics continued to hover between the irrecoverable ideal of the integrated past and the unattainable ideal of the spiritual present. And in this respect, they reflected the true condition of Romantic poetry, which had discovered the curious appeal of being in a state of unfulfilled desire.

The new historical sense opened up another possibility for criticism: the possibility of stepping back from contemporary struggles and surveying the large-scale phases of literature in grand historical sequence. The many-sided Friedrich Schlegel was busy here too, producing early examples of such surveys, and theorising about an organic version of history where one phase would be seen as necessarily unfolding out of another. This approach was confirmed by the later influence of G. W. F. Hegel, who, amongst all his other unfoldings, produced a dialectical historical sequence for art. The first phase in this sequence is the 'symbolic' phase, when 'the idea has not as yet found the formative principle within itself', and 'natural objects are thus in the first instance left just as they are, while, at the same time, the substantive idea is imposed upon them as their significance'.[8] (Hegel's sense of the 'symbolic' is actually closer to what other Romantic theorists were defining as 'allegory'.) Hegel locates the 'symbolic' phase in Oriental and Egyptian art generally; for literature, the animal fable illustrates the case of a conceptual idea which is merely imposed upon an embodied narrative. By contrast, the second, 'classical' phase achieves a perfect fusion of idea and sensuous embodiment, in what Hegel calls 'the concrete spiritual'.[9] Supremely exemplified by Homer and Sophocles, 'classical' art represents for Hegel, as for so many other German theorists of the period, a state of perfect balance. The third, 'romantic' phase is less satisfactory as art, but higher in spiritual level. The idea has now developed to a point where sensuous embodiment is no longer adequate to its needs: 'it is to complete fundamentally this higher perfection that [the idea] withdraws itself from the external element'.[10] 'Romantic' art has moved on into a new state of imbalance.

As can be seen, Hegel drew mainly upon the existing contrast between 'classical' and 'romantic', adding only the earlier 'symbolic' phase. Nor did art rate very significantly in the Hegelian scheme of things: 'romantic' art being subsumed into the higher dialectic of religion, which was in turn subsumed into the higher dialectic of philosophy. Nonetheless, the Hegelian method exercised enormous influence over all the large-scale histories of literature produced during the nineteenth century.

The influence of Kant
(also Schelling, Coleridge, Goethe, Schiller, Schopenhauer)

If Herder was one key source of Romantic literary theory, Immanuel Kant was the other. Kant's philosophy of aesthetics is contained in *The Critique of Judgement* (1790), which follows on from his earlier revolutionary *Critique of Pure Reason* (1781). The *Critique of Pure Reason* itself theorises about epistemology, not art or literature; nonetheless, it too impacted upon literary theory, as other thinkers pursued the implications of Kant's new perspective.

Kant's new perspective overthrows the essentially passive view of perception which had prevailed in philosophy ever since Descartes, Hobbes and Locke. In passive perception, stimuli are transmitted through the nerves and received as images or sense-data in the mind. But how can an image in the mind bear in itself the proof that it actually corresponds to an out-there object? Or how can a merely subjective association between co-occurring images ever justify the belief that the tilting of the table actually *causes* the cup to fall to the floor?

The most general features of experience such as objective existence or causality cannot be observed in the same way that patches and shapes of colour can be observed. Kant therefore concludes that such general features must pre-exist the particular evidence of the senses. And, since we don't *receive* impressions of objectivity and causality from the outside world, we must ourselves *impose* them upon what we do receive. All human minds, according to Kant, are constituted in such a way as to interpret sense-data in terms of objects (so far as possible) and to interpret successive events in terms of cause-and-effect (so far as possible). We create what we see – without ever being conscious of our own creativity.

Also involved in this unconscious creativity is the special kind of combining called *synthesis*. When we interpret numerous varying shapes of colour in terms of one and the same tree, we unify the sense-data in a manner which goes beyond any mere linkage or agglomeration. A tree as an object both incorporates and *transcends* all the countless images we may have of it. Such synthesising activity involves a fundamental leap of the imagination.

Of course, imagination in literature is something more special and unusual. But the proponents of imagination in literature could draw strength from Kant's basic conception. Thus A. W. Schlegel suggested that the 'imagination through which the world first originated for us and through which works of art are created, is the same power, only in diverse kinds of activity'.[11] And F. W. J. Schelling claimed that the imagination which *unconsciously* creates the real world, *consciously* creates the ideal world of art. Schelling also proposed a distinction between primary and secondary imagination, which reappeared in Coleridge's *Biographia Literaria* (1817). As Coleridge expressed it:

> The Primary IMAGINATION I hold to be the living Power and prime Agent of all human Perception. . . . The Secondary Imagination I consider as an echo of the former, co-existing with the conscious will, yet still as identical with the primary in the *kind* of its agency, and differing only in *degree*, and in the *mode* of its operation.[12]

Two levels of imagination: but the higher, secondary level grows out of the lower, primary level. Imagination in literature is no longer a mere sport or indulgence, but a more extended exercise of our most vital human faculty.

In the older, eighteenth-century sense of the term, 'imagination' in literature had been defined essentially by opposition to 'imitation'. On the one hand, invention and making things up; on the other, the verisimilar reproduction of objective reality. But Kant's new perspective had dissolved the objectivity of objective reality: the world we experience is *always* partly created by our own minds. This undermines not only the goal of imitation but the whole dichotomy of imitation versus imagination. Under the new approach, the secondary imagination in literature may refer to real experience no less than the primary imagination – only with a more strongly active degree of creativity. So, according to Coleridge, the imaginative faculty in Wordsworth works by 'modifying the objects observed', and by spreading 'the depth and height of the ideal world around forms, incidents, and situations, of which, for the common view, custom had bedimmed the lustre'.[13] What the poet presents is neither plain reality nor fantastic fiction, but *individual vision.*

This new version of imagination also supersedes the Age of Sensibility's notion of a purely emotional response to literature. Not that the Romantic theorists ever reject emotion: but passivity of feeling is now combined with activity of understanding. The new version of imagination may not be rational but it is nonetheless *cognitive.* Thus Coleridge thinks of the secondary imagination as operating not only in poetry but also in philosophy – and even in moments of creative scientific insight. A similar convergence is proclaimed by Schelling, whose own philosophy elevates artistic vision to the very highest position, above all other forms of human understanding.

Kant himself did not develop a theory of higher or poetic imagination; when he turned his attention to aesthetics, he focused upon the psychology of response rather than the psychology of creation. According to *The Critique of Judgement*, an aesthetic response involves a distinctive cast of mind imposed by the subject upon experience. Aesthetic pleasure is no mere passive reception of sensations; once again, what we see depends upon our own mental activity. It is in line with this approach that Kant draws his examples more from aesthetically appreciated works of nature – flowers, living creatures, crystal formations – than from works of art. In a modern context, Kant's view could be referred to the case of *art trouvé*, when the aesthetic framing of a familiar everyday object encourages us to look at that object in a whole new light.

The aesthetic cast of mind is distinctive, according to Kant, because it is *disinterested.* It sets aside considerations as to whether an object is useful or morally approvable or even exists. As Kant puts it: 'One must not be in the least prepossessed of the real existence of the thing, but must preserve complete indifference in this respect.'[14] This state of mind is free in the sense that it is detached from all our usual personal interests and purposes. We delight in the object simply for its own sake.

The concept of aesthetic disinterest undermines the long-held Horatian view, which even the Age of Sensibility had never really challenged, that the purpose of literature is to teach as well as delight. Goethe and Schiller immediately seized upon Kant's argument as a justification for downgrading the moral function in literature. Thus Goethe allows only that poetry 'should draw our attention to something worth learning: but it should be left to us to draw the lesson from it, just as we learn from life'.[15] And when describing the after-effects of a play, he seems to doubt whether any moral improvement is to be expected at all:

> The complication [of the plot] will confuse him [the spectator], the solution will enlighten him, but he will not go home a better person. Rather, he would be amazed at himself – if he were unusually observant – for coming back home just as frivolous or stubborn, as aggressive or meek, as kind or unkind as he was when he left.[16]

Schiller similarly argues that it is 'self-contradictory' to think of 'a fine art which teaches (didactic) or improves (moral); for nothing is more at variance with the concept of beauty than the notion of giving the psyche any definite bias'.[17]

Nor is it only Horace's additions to Aristotle that come under fire. Also incompatible with the free state of aesthetic disinterest is Aristotle's own orientation towards producing certain calculated emotional effects in an audience. Again Goethe and Schiller follow Kant's lead. Thus Schiller suggests that arts which affect the passions, such as tragedy, 'are the more perfect, the more they respect the freedom of the spirit even amid the most violent storms of passion'.[18] And Goethe regards the audience as a potential limitation upon all staged drama: '*We* struggle for the perfection of a work of art, in and by itself, *they* think of the effect outside, which does not concern the genuine artist at all'.[19] Clearly, the contempt for calculated emotional effects fits in with the Romantic promotion of the author as genius.

The most extreme version of the anti-effect view came later in the

Romantic period, in the writings of Arthur Schopenhauer. For Schopenhauer, everything in human existence is governed by blind will and desire, which consciousness merely rationalises after the event. Everything, that is, except art. The contemplative disinterest of the aesthetic response represents a momentary release from the insatiable urge of selfish desire. But such disinterest manifests itself rarely: 'Most men . . . seek [in objects] only some relation to their will, and with everything that has not such a relation there sounds within them, as it were like a ground-bass, the constant, inconsolable lament, "It is of no use to me".'[20] Schopenhauer specifically disapproves of wish-fulfilling fictions which gratify their readers' desires: 'the imaginary object is used to build castles in the air, congenial to selfishness, and to one's own whim'.[21] The very elevated role assigned to art goes hand in hand with a very pure and selective conception of art. It is not surprising that music is for Schopenhauer the supreme art-form.

The organic principle
(A. W. Schlegel, Coleridge, Schelling, Goethe)

The organic model appears everywhere in Romantic literary theory: organically developing culture, organically developing language, organically developing literature. Kant suggested an organic model for the aesthetic object itself when he pointed to an impression of *purposiveness* in the way that its parts combine into wholes. The application of the model to literary form was especially the work of August Wilhelm Schlegel, who formulated a crucial distinction between organic and mechanical form:

> Form is mechanical when, through external force, it is imparted to any material merely as an accidental addition without reference to its quality; as, for example, when we give a particular shape to a soft mass that it may retain the same after its induration. Organical form . . . is innate; it unfolds itself from within, and acquires its determination contemporaneously with the perfect development of the germ.[22]

In effect, mechanical form imposes itself regardless of the inherent tendencies of the content, like an elephant-shaped mould imprinted upon soft chocolate. By contrast, organic form is produced when the

essence of an idea is allowed to unfold according to its own nature –
like the growing of a real live elephant.

Aristotle himself had proposed an organic model, even if his principles had been mechanically applied during the Neoclassical period.
But for Aristotle it was the completed work, the drama and its action,
which resembled a living organism; whereas Romantic theory is more
interested in the growing process which takes place in the author's
mind. The quality of the organic is referred to the synthetic powers of
the creative imagination.

Inevitably, there are also differences as to what constitutes organic
unity of form. Although Romantic theorists talk no less frequently
than Aristotle about wholeness and unity, their emphasis is upon
inclusion rather than exclusion. A subjectively-grounded unity of
interest or mood can take in almost anything. A. W. Schlegel sees this
kind of unity as distinctively Romantic:

> the romantic delights in indissoluble mixtures; all contrarieties: nature
> and art, poetry and prose, seriousness and mirth, recollection and
> anticipation, spirituality and sensuality, terrestrial and celestial, life and
> death, are by it blended together in the most intimate combination.[23]

In fact, the term 'Romantic' was first coined by Friedrich Schlegel as a
derivation from the German *roman*, a potpourri kind of novel which
skips over and between all other genres.

The same way of thinking appears in Coleridge's definition of
poetry as 'proposing to itself such delight from the *whole*, as is
compatible with a distinct gratification from each component *part*'.[24]
Clearly, the value of the whole does not preclude a counterbalancing
emphasis upon the value of the individual parts. Coleridge also
suggests that 'the reader should be carried forward, not merely . . . by
a restless desire to arrive at the final solution; but by the pleasurable
activity of mind excited by the attractions of the journey itself'.[25]
Multiplicity and unity can be reconciled thanks to the (Secondary)
Imagination, 'modifying a series of thoughts by one predominant
thought or feeling', like a landscape behind which lies 'a single
energy, modifying *ab intra* in each component part'.[26] Such unity is
contrasted against mere connection by association, where 'each part
[is] separately conceived and then put together as the pictures on a
motley screen'.[27] This latter kind of connection Coleridge attributes to
the inferior faculty of the Fancy, which links through passive acciden-

tal analogies or continuities, in the manner favoured by the Empiricist and Associationist philosophers.

The organic model also helped justify the Romantics in their concentration upon the particular or individual as against the general or typical. The overthrow of Neoclassical attitudes can be seen in Goethe's statement: 'apprehension and representation of the individual is the very life of art'.[28] The Neoclassical view had resembled the scientific view: just as the scientist considers planets or pebbles as elements in a larger natural system, so too the Neoclassical theorists had considered even human beings as elements in a larger (social) system. But the Romantic theorists were less interested in the laws than in the achievements of Nature. They saw Nature as evolving its highest and most complex forms – organisms generally, supremely the human mind – in the direction of ever-increasing individuality. And as with Nature, so with art. 'In nature and art, essence first strives for the realisation or representation of itself in singleness,' says Schelling; and 'since much of the power of singleness, and therefore individuality as well, is manifested in living character, a negative conception of [singleness] necessarily results in an inadequate and erroneous view of the characteristic in art'.[29] Here appears the crucial Romantic concept of *the characteristic;* that is, the qualities which make the individual special and unique. On this approach, everything is to be considered as an end in itself – in the way that we normally think of individual human beings.

However, this concentration upon particulars is only a 'first' step, as indicated in the above quote from Schelling. Though hostile to the kind of typical generality inherent in the Neoclassical view, Romantic theorists, especially in Germany, were unwilling to surrender all claim to the universal. Instead they proposed a reconciliation of the individual and the universal in *the symbol.* The concept is initially suggested by Goethe, further elaborated by Schelling, and eventually transposed into English by Coleridge. The symbol, Romantically defined, identifies a particular image with a general idea – but not an idea in the form of a clear-cut abstract concept. In fact, the symbol is invariably defined in opposition to allegory. Thus Coleridge:

> an allegory is but a translation of abstract notions into a picture-language . . . On the other hand a symbol . . . is characterized by a translucence of the special [i.e. the species] in the individual, or of the general in the special, or of the universal in the general . . .[30]

Symbolism involves a kind of thinking in images not unlike that which Vico attributed to mythological thinking in pre-rational cultures.[31] That is, a particular image *has* to be used precisely because there exists no adequate abstract term in which the general idea might be otherwise conceived.

The role of the critic
(*Herder, Friedrich Schlegel, Schleiermacher*)

Romantic theory also revolutionised assumptions about the role of the critic. From Aristotle through to the eighteenth century, the critic had typically taken up a position with the audience, evaluating the success of the effects produced and generalising about the means for producing such effects. But under the new dispensation, the critic proposed to take up a position with the author, sympathetically identifying with the creative act. This revolution changed not merely the way that critics went about their business, but the kind of business that they were expected to go about.

The groundwork was laid in Herder's approach to individual cultures. Herder believed that, with a sufficient effort of the imagination, one could feel one's way into different mentalities, no matter how unfamiliar. The 'feeling into' process was captured in the German term 'Einfühlung'. (Vico had insisted upon a similar effort of the imagination even for the *scientific* understanding of other cultures.) Herder himself applied the process to individual authors when he declared that one should strive to 'live in the spirit of an author'.[32] Moreover, the critic should seek to become the 'servant of the author, his friend', seeking out values rather than finding faults.[33] Criticism here becomes *appreciation* in the 'praise of beauties' mode which was to persist throughout the nineteenth century.

Friedrich Schlegel argued specifically in favour of the theory of imaginative creation, which he called 'fantastics', as against the theory of audience reception, which he called 'pathetics'. He followed Herder in emphasising positive appreciation and the attempt to identify with the particular goals of the particular work. 'Criticism', he said, 'is not to judge works by a general ideal, but is to search out the *individual* ideal of every work.'[34] He especially promoted a genetic form of criticism, which begins by intuiting 'the author's secret intentions, which he pursues in silence and of which we can never assume too many in a genius',[35] and then proceeds to hypothesise the growth and unfolding of those intentions into the fully realised work. Like Herder – and like the entire historically-oriented nineteenth century – Friedrich Schlegel believed that 'origins show the nature of a thing'.[36] Friedrich Schlegel also advanced a common theme of Romantic theory when he asserted that 'the first condition of all understanding, and hence also of the understanding of a work of art, is an intuition of the whole'.[37] This top-down approach follows from the way in which parts relate to whole under the Kantian notion of synthesis. To take a simple perceptual example: no sheer accumulation of tree-images will ever bring us to the idea of an objectively-existing tree; the objectively-existing tree is beyond or behind the images, and we reach it by a kind of imaginative jump to a different level. Similarly with a work of literature. The work as a whole is something more than the sum of its parts, and can never be reached by a mere addition or assembling of part to part. The reader or critic must juggle between parts and whole on two different levels simultaneously.

The most subtle analysis of such juggling was developed in *hermeneutics* or the theory of interpretation, a distinctively German discipline growing out of the Lutheran Church's interest in Biblical interpretation. Friedrich Schleiermacher, the founder of modern hermeneutics, drew specific attention to what he called *the hermeneutic circle*. If the parts must be understood as shaped and modified in the light of the whole, nonetheless the whole has no existence other than in and through its parts. So where does understanding begin? Schleiermacher envisaged an act of 'divination' on the part of the interpreter, an intuition of the whole beyond the parts. 'The detail can be understood only by the whole, and any explanation of detail presupposes the understanding of the whole.'[38] Like Friedrich Schlegel, Schleiermacher opted for a strongly top-down theory of interpretation.

Schleiermacher also expounded a philosophical aesthetics in which he carried a general trend of Romantic thinking through to its logical conclusion. The work of art, he claims, exists most truly in the mind of its creator. 'The inner image is the work of art proper.'[39] However, this inner image is not something about which the creator can inform us; on the contrary, Schleiermacher claims to be able to understand authors better than they have understood themselves. 'We must seek to bring into consciousness much that could remain unconscious for him.'[40] This is not the unconsciousness of a special hidden domain of the mind, as in the Freudian model; but it is the unconsciousness of a special activity of creation, as typically conceived by the Romantics.

Some British themes
(*Wordsworth, Coleridge, Keats, Shelley*)

Always excepting Coleridge, British literary criticism was predictably less theoretical. Essay-critics writing for periodicals, such as Lamb and Hazlitt, tended to produce author-appreciations in the 'praise of beauties' mode. More important were the poet-critics, such as Wordsworth, Shelley and Keats, whose agendas were typically determined by their own particular poetic practices. The poet-critics developed many of the same themes as the Germans, albeit in their own way: poetry as self-expression, the action of the imagination upon the outside world, unconscious creation, criticism on the side of the author, etc. But some themes were peculiarly British: and one such theme was the debate over the language appropriate to poetry.

The debate was launched by the Preface to the *Lyrical Ballads* volume, written by Wordsworth in 1800 and expanded in 1802. According to Wordsworth, his poems in the volume would be found to contain 'little of what is usually called poetic diction', drawing instead upon 'a selection of the language really spoken by men'.[41] The selection would be special only to the extent that Wordsworth chose to imitate the language of 'low and rustic' men, 'because in that condition, the essential passions of the heart . . . are less under restraint, and speak a plainer and more emphatic language'.[42] But in general, Wordsworth envisaged no essential difference between the medium of poetry and the medium of prose.

Wordsworth's enemy was eighteenth-century poetic diction. The British poets of the Age of Sensibility had reformulated their goals but had remained hamstrung by the forms of Neoclassical diction. How could a poet convey sublimity or personal emotion when sunbeams automatically appeared as 'Phoebus' rays', or fish as 'the finny tribe'? The situation called for the overthrow of an entrenched artificial language – just as the entrenched artificial language of Victorian poetry had to be overthrown by the Modernists a century later. Indeed, the notion of a return to real or natural language has been a recurring motif in the history of British and American literature. Like British and American philosophers, British and American poets have always had a fear of language flying off on its own, losing contact with its roots. But did Wordsworth's poems in fact employ 'the language really spoken by men'? Coleridge thought not, and most critics since have agreed with him. Wordsworth's style – at least in his more successful poems – achieves a solemn grandeur far removed from ordinary prose. As Coleridge argues, the words themselves may be common, but not their placement or the constructions in which they participate. Only a poet would think of using the ordinary word 'busy' in the way that Wordsworth uses it in 'The thrush is *busy* in the wood.'[43] Coleridge concludes that Wordsworth is 'a poet, whose diction, next to that of Shakespeare and Milton, appears to me of all others the most *individualized* and characteristic'.[44] Such individualised language differs from both conventional poetic diction *and* the ordinariness of everyday language.

As for the distinction between poetry and prose, Coleridge turns Wordsworth's argument on its head. Looking beyond the aberration of eighteenth-century poetic diction, he claims that ordinary prose is typically corrupted 'by the vicious phraseology which meets us everywhere, from the sermon to the newspaper, from the harangue of the legislator to the speech . . . announcing a *toast* or sentiment'; whereas 'in poetry it *is* practicable to preserve the diction uncorrupted', precisely because the poet takes special pains over language.[45] Coleridge's view here harks forward to Symbolist and Modernist theory, which gives the poet special responsibility for guarding the health of the language.

Another theme of the British poet-critics concerns the moral effect of poetry. If German thinkers rejected the traditional requirement of teaching and instruction, the British poet-critics came up with a new moral effect which could operate in a more indirect manner. Thus Wordsworth talked of the poet as 'carrying every where with him relationship and love', and as 'widening the sphere of human sensibility'.[46] Behind these vague effusions may be discerned yet another application of the general Romantic virtue of sympathy or 'Einfühlung'. It is the poet's business not to inculcate any specific moral code, but to encourage in the reader a wide-minded openness and responsiveness to others. Wordsworth saw such openness and responsiveness as particularly called for in his own period of increasing urbanisation and economic rationalism.

Keats was even more firmly opposed to the inculcation of any specific moral code. 'We hate poetry that has a palpable design upon us,' he wrote in one letter.[47] Far from wishing to prescribe behaviour, the poet must be forever entering into other minds, taking on the colour of other perspectives. 'What shocks the virtuous philosopher, delights the chameleon Poet.'[48] Openness of sympathy here appears as an ultimate virtue, overleaping judgements of right or wrong, good or evil.

Shelley's 'Defence of Poetry' brings this line of thinking to a decisive formulation. Like Wordsworth, Shelley believed that human sensibility had become peculiarly dulled and deadened by 'an excess of the selfish and calculating principle' in his own period.[49] Poetry alone can restore sensibility because, unlike ethical science, it can compel us 'to feel that which we perceive, and to imagine that which we know'.[50] Above all, it can compel us to imagine ourselves empathetically in the place of others. In this respect, it does its work not upon morality but upon imagination as the cause of morality. The poet's 'own conceptions of right and wrong' are inevitably limited, 'usually those of his time and place'.[51] But the exercise of the imagination is a good which transcends historical relativity: 'poetry strengthens that faculty which is the organ of the moral nature of man, in the same manner as exercise strengthens a limb'.[52] As with any form of exercise, no immediate specific outcomes are to be expected.

The definition of the poet is another favourite theme of the British poet-critics. 'What is poetry? is so nearly the same question with, what is a poet?' says Coleridge;[53] and Wordsworth clearly judges the poem by the poet when he claims that 'Poems to which any value can be attached, were never produced on any variety of subjects but by a man who, being possessed of more than usual organic sensibility, had also thought long and deeply.'[54] In fact, Wordsworth throughout the Preface to the *Lyrical Ballads* is concerned to characterise a distinctive poetry-producing sensibility rather than any distinctive qualities of the text produced. Especially famous is his assertion that 'Poetry is the spontaneous overflow of powerful feelings: it takes its origin from emotion recollected in tranquillity'.[55] As so often with poet-critics, Wordsworth's definition – especially the second half of it – applies far more readily to his own writing than to anyone else's.

On such an approach, what matters for the text is the authenticity of its relation to the poet's feelings. In his 'Essays upon Epitaphs', Wordsworth introduces 'a criterion of sincerity, by which a Writer may be judged'.[56] For Wordsworth, epitaphs illustrate the general fact that 'our sensations and judgement depend upon our opinion or feeling of the Author's state of mind'.[57] In his examples, he discovers insincerity whenever facility in language and imagery predominates; sincerity whenever a sense of personal thought and feeling pushes its way through, often almost in spite of crude or inadequate verbalisation. Language here is becoming less of a channel of communication, more of a symptom for psychological hypothesis.

Shelley also describes poetry in terms of the poet. More radical than Wordsworth, he resembles Schleiermacher is his view that the highest poetry exists not on the page but in the poet's mind. 'When composition begins, inspiration is already on the decline, and the most glorious poetry that has ever been communicated to the world is probably a feeble shadow of the original conception of the poet.'[58] He further resembles Schleiermacher in his view that poetic creation is to a considerable extent unconscious: 'Poetry . . . is not subject to the control of the active powers of the mind, and . . . its birth and recurrence has no necessary connexion with consciousness or will.'[59] Most interesting here is the way in which the moral superiority of the poem becomes the moral superiority of the poet: 'A poet . . . ought personally to be the happiest, the best, the wisest, and the most illustrious of men.'[60] The notion that a writer should be more than ordinarily moral and upright had appeared often enough before, in the Renaissance and in the criticism of the Latin rhetoricians. But Shelley elevated the claim to an unsustainable pitch.

Sainte-Beuve, Emerson, Poe

As the Romantic fashion progressed from country to country in the opening decades of the nineteenth century, the ideas of the German literary theorists accompanied it. The same ideas continued to influence the discussion of *poetry* throughout the nineteenth century, even when new critical approaches were generated by the rise of the realistic novel. In this section, I shall look at just two significant developments of Romantic theory, in France and in the USA.

Romantic theory arrived late in France, but was soon taken up by a critic whose reputation eventually outshone all others: Charles-Augustin Sainte-Beuve. Sainte-Beuve derived his distinctive methodology from the Romantic idea of tracing poetry back to its origins in the poet. His favoured form was the 'portrait', in which he characterised the sensibility of an author with reference to both works and life. A famous quotation sums up his approach:

> Literature, literary production, as I see it, is not distinct or separable from the rest of mankind's character and activity. I may enjoy a work, but it is hard for me to judge it independently of my knowledge of the man who produced it, and I am inclined to say, *tel arbre, tel fruit* – the fruit is like the tree.[61]

Drawing upon letters, memoirs and biographical information, he seeks to enter into the individuality and taste the distinctive quality of different minds. 'Criticism is for me a metamorphosis. I try to disappear in the character I am reproducing.'[62]

However, Sainte-Beuve was less impressed by genius than were the German and British Romantics. Often he preferred to draw attention to interesting minor writers. Nor did he share Shelley's belief in the moral nobility of the poet. On the contrary, he took it for granted that every writer has a vice or weakness. He was especially attracted to cases where 'an author, when writing, throws himself into the excess or affectation directly opposed to his vice or secret penchant, so as to disguise it'.[63] The writing and the life are connected, but not necessarily similar.

The biographical approach affected Sainte-Beuve's judgement in the usual ways: that is, he tended to value sincerity, and he tended to think more highly of authors whose lives, as well as works, were admirable. For these and other reasons, the biographical approach was later condemned by Modernist writers and related schools of criticism, and Sainte-Beuve's reputation plummeted. Sainte-Beuve is simply not writing criticism as the twentieth century understands it – nor biography either. Instead, he should perhaps be viewed as a kind of creative writer – the creative writer he always wanted to be. His portraits of writers depict a gallery of individual character types, in some ways analogous to the character galleries of the great nineteenth-century novelists.

It is true that criticism in the Postmodernist age has again claimed the right to creativity and the right to range beyond the text. There is even a resemblance to Deconstruction in Sainte-Beuve's technique of reading unintended implications into key words: 'Every writer has his favourite word which occurs frequently in his speech and inadvertently betrays a secret wish or partiality.'[64] But Sainte-Beuve's psychology remains pre-Freudian, and the territory where he ranges remains unfashionable. Also unfashionable is his claimed ability to discard prejudices and beliefs as a precondition for entering into the individuality of someone else's mind. In fact, Sainte-Beuve's judgements were greatly influenced by his own political beliefs and personal antipathies, as has long been recognised.

Although Sainte-Beuve's criticism grew out of Romantic theory, his personal tastes swung increasingly away from Romantic literature. His concept of a 'classic' was wide, but inclined towards the classical French virtues of balance and moderation. By contrast, the dominant Puritan ethos in the USA. amplified certain tendencies of Romanticism, and Romantic theory was carried to new extremes by Emerson and Poe, albeit in different directions.

Tracing the ideas of Coleridge and Thomas Carlyle back to their sources in German Idealism, Emerson developed a Transcendentalism in which the physical appearances of Nature are envisaged as merely the outward manifestation of an immanent *Over-soul*: 'the world is mind precipitated'.[65] The poet represents the individual soul in its encounter with the Over-soul. The typical Romantic concentration upon the poet is carried even further by Emerson, who places comparatively little value upon the poem as a creation in language. He proposes a particularly strong version of organic theory in which the poet's experience entirely determines the content, and the content entirely determines the form. 'The sense dictates the rhythm. ... Ask the fact for the form.'[66] He even prophesies a time when literature as such will become unnecessary, when everyone will become a poet reading Nature for themselves.

Emerson's importance as a critic lies in his notion of how Nature may be read. His New England religious background magnifies the Romantic concept of the symbol. In Puritan *typology*, the world is God's book (as in medieval Christianity), and natural phenomena are signs to be interpreted for ulterior meanings. Substituting the Over-soul for God, Emerson claims that 'Nature offers all her creatures to [the poet] as a picture-language. Being used as a type, a second wonderful value appears in the object, far better than its old value.'[67] Nor does 'Nature' here exclude human constructs:

Readers of poetry see the factory-village and the railway, and fancy

that the poetry of the landscape is broken up by these; for these
works of art are not yet consecrated in their reading; but the poet sees
them fall within the great Order not less than the beehive or the
spider's geometrical web.[68]

At the same time, such readings do not produce determinate once-
and-for-all meanings. 'All symbols are fluxional,' says Emerson,
implicitly endorsing the Romantic disapproval of allegory.[69] But his
emphasis upon symbols is more widespread than anything in the
German theorists, or Coleridge, or Carlyle.

It was a different feature of the Puritan sensibility that acted upon
Poe, and in a negative rather than a positive way. The Puritan insistence that literature should be morally instructive inspired Poe to
violent opposition. Proclaiming 'the heresy of *The Didactic*', he
condemned all kinds of moral effect, and stated point-blank that 'the
obstinate oils and waters of Poetry and Truth' are irreconcilable.[70]
Poetry should concern itself only with 'Beauty', and Poe envisaged a
very pure form of Beauty far removed from the practicalities of everyday life.

Poe's anti-didacticism was an extreme version of a common
Romantic attitude; but in another respect, he advanced beyond
Romanticism. For Poe did not believe in inspiration and spontaneity,
and the authenticity of personal emotion; he believed in craft.
Challenging the myth of the poet as overwhelmed by 'a species of fine
frenzy – an ecstatic intuition', he pointed to the reality of 'cautious
selections and rejections' and 'the faculty of analysis'.[71] His account
of how he composed *The Raven* (in 'The Philosophy of Composition')
goes to extraordinary lengths to present creation as an impersonal,
calculated, almost mathematical process. Poe's view of the poem as a
carefully wrought object harks forward to Symbolism and Modernism, as does Emerson's extended theory of symbols.

5 Social Theories of the 19th Century

In most European countries, Romanticism began to give way to realism from about 1830 onwards. Unlike the dramatic revolution which had introduced Romanticism itself, the Age of Realism entered quietly and unobtrusively – as quietly and unobtrusively as the Baroque after the Renaissance, or Postmodernism after Modernism. There was no violent contestation between contrary positions; this was a revolution which was reflected upon largely after it had already happened. The inevitable momentum of the new trend appears only with the benefit of hindsight: the less realistic generation of Dickens, Gogol and Balzac leading on to the more realistic generation of Eliot, Tolstoy and Flaubert, in turn leading on to the hyper-realistic generation of the Naturalists. It was not until the advent of Naturalism that the claims of Realism were articulated in a theoretically confrontational manner.

At first sight, the gap between Romanticism and Realism looks much deeper than that between Renaissance and Baroque, or between Modernism and Postmodernism. But there is one significant continuity in the concept of *the characteristic*. Romantic theory had overthrown the old reverence for the general or typical in favour of an interest in the unique individuality of things. When Romantic displays of poetic subjectivity ceased to occupy the front of the stage, this interest remained. The realism of the nineteenth-century novel is fuelled by a fascination with the sheer *thusness* of life. Individual human characters, local regional settings, particular details of experience are all to be enjoyed for their own distinctive flavour. And as regards individual human characters, the psychological concerns of the nineteenth-century novel clearly benefit from the Romantic model of the human psyche: more personalised, more complicated and less rational than the Neoclassical model.

Another continuity may be traced in the concept of history.

Romantic theory had launched the idea that every historical period has its own distinctive outlook; and Sir Walter Scott in his historical novels had tried to 'feel into' the way of life in earlier cultures. The historical novel carried through into the Age of Realism, but often with a much more recent setting – as in the case of *War and Peace* or *Middlemarch*. It was only one small further step to the notion of actually chronicling contemporary society under a historical perspective. Thus Balzac, in the novels of his *Comédie Humaine*, saw himself as the historian of the present, recording the distinctive feel of French Restoration society even as the march of history left it behind. Looking back now, we are mainly conscious of a sharp contrast between Romantic imagination versus 'true-to-life' observation, between historical romance versus realistic novel. But we should not underestimate the extent to which a great realist like Tolstoy thought of himself as following in Scott's footsteps. The sharpness of the contrast is elided by a more gentle transition from historical romance to contemporary history.

However, the historical perspective inevitably brings with it a social perspective – and here a definite difference must be recognised. The typical mid-nineteenth-century novel unfolds a broad panorama across many sections of society and a multitude of character-types; and the character-types are (increasingly) depicted in terms of their social interactions and relationships. The pivotal shift between Romantics and first-generation Realists was above all a shift from subjectivity to social perspective. And the same shift made itself felt in literary theory.

Not that the shift in literature was necessarily the cause of the shift in theory. Social theories of literature were often responding to wider intellectual trends of the time: to the general growth of academic historicism, to the rising prestige of science, to the declining power of religion. Such various influences encouraged various new developments in literary theory. But there was no single predominant thrust of thinking of the kind that tends to occur – as during the Romantic period – around the promotion of a particular new way of writing.

Perhaps things would have been different if the novelists themselves had sought to defend their practices. But the mid-nineteenth-century produced no novelist-critics comparable to the Romantic poet-critics. If novelists took themselves seriously, it was as shapers of public opinion, not as artists. The novel had still not acquired the kind of status assigned to poetry. And on its own level, the novel needed no defending. A general middle-class readership consumed novels in voluminous quantities, and the royalties system ensured a comfortable living for a great many writers. There was no pressing need to compete intellectually or theoretically. The modern bifurcation between 'highbrow' literary novels and 'lowbrow' popular novels had not yet arrived.

The criticism of the Age of Realism was produced not by novelists but by journalist-critics and by academics. Periodicals for the non-specialist audience continued to flourish, as they had flourished ever since the eighteenth century; and there was an ongoing demand for reviews, informative essays, and the general dispensation of knowledge. More of a novelty was the role of universities, which for the first time began to set up chairs for the study of literature. Often such study was purely historical and scholarly, devoted to factual research and the editing of texts.

Belinsky and the three radicals
(*Belinsky, Chernyshevsky, Dobrolyubov, Pisarev*)

In the nineteenth century, Russian novelists took to realism as if to the manner born (in spite of the virtual absence of a true middle class – a fact which must surely qualify the automatic conjunction of 'bourgeois' with 'realism'!). At the same time, a distinctively Russian movement in literary criticism sprang up, different from anything that had gone before. The difference can be largely explained by the political situation in nineteenth-century Russia, where a feudal social structure was colliding with modern influences from Western Europe. In this crisis-ridden atmosphere, the critics, like the novelists, tended to develop a strong sense of social mission. Whether the solutions proposed were pro-Western or pro-Eastern, the issue of Russia's national destiny was always implicitly on the line.

This pressure-cooker intensity was increased by censorship of press and publishing. On the one hand, cultural life was growing and flourishing in numerous new periodicals; on the other hand, the Czarist regime could and did suppress all direct political criticism – and the writers of such criticism. However, articles on literature and book reviews were able to convey a political message less overtly, and were less likely to attract the censor's eye. Not only did the discussion of literature veer naturally towards political discussion, but political discussion could find an outlet through the medium of discussion of literature.

The most important Russian critic of the nineteenth century was Vissarion Belinsky (also Belinski or Belinskii: for all Russian writers, it needs to be remembered that different methods of transliteration from the Cyrillic alphabet yield different forms of the same name). Belinsky changed direction several times in the course of his career, but his overall trend was away from German Romantic theory and towards a distinctively Russian social theory. 'However rich and sumptuous may be a man's inner life . . . it is incomplete if it does not take upon itself the interests of the world external to itself, of society and humanity.'[1] Subjectivity must give way to wider, less egotistical concerns.

For Belinsky, such wider concerns were especially national concerns. In response to influences from Western Europe (which Belinsky generally favoured), it was imperative to develop a national literature that would give expression to the true spirit of Russia. But not the Russia of the past. Belinsky did not believe in going back to roots; traditional Russian folk-poetry he associated with the traditional evils of serfdom. The true spirit of Russia was still to be fully defined and realised, and Belinsky looked to the writers to define and realise it.

This perspective colours Belinsky's advocacy of realism. 'We demand not the ideal of life,' he asserts on the one hand, 'but life as it is. Be it good or bad, we do not wish to adorn it.'[2] But on the other hand he dismisses precise observation, and argues that a great novelist like Gogol 'has not made a copy of actuality. He has beheld it all in a prophetic vision.'[3] Writers of the new generation must actively mould society. 'What is the art of our times? A judgement, an analysis of society, consequently criticism. . . . For our time, a work of art is lifeless if it depicts life only to depict it.'[4] Realism for Belinsky is necessary to the extent of establishing a connection between literature and life. But that connection is then to be used causally, productively, for the sake of social impact. Belinsky is not interested in realism as an end in itself, or in measuring the value of a work by its relative accuracy as a *reflection* of life.

The connection to life is above all a connection to contemporary life. For Belinsky, a work of literature must be in tune with the historical moment of its writing; and the more in tune, the better the work. 'Every creation, in whatever genre, is good . . . if by its spirit and form it bears upon itself the stamp of its age and satisfies the demands of that age.'[5] It is the writer's special gift to be aware of current social trends and to bring to public consciousness developments which are only just starting to take shape. Belinsky's admiration for Pushkin was qualified by his belief that Pushkin had become outdated; by contrast, Turgenev 'is a son of our time, who bears in his breast all its sorrows and questions'.[6] Belinsky is particularly interested in the recognition of emerging social types, new classes and kinds of people – an interest continued in the writings of his followers (especially Dobrolyubov).

This is a revolution against the trans-temporal generalities beloved by Neoclassical critics and the universality of theme favoured by Romantic critics. Quantitatively outweighed by the vastness of all human existence, the brief moment of the present has nonetheless its own overwhelming importance as the pivot upon which the whole future turns. Belinsky's perspective was clearly influenced by the sense of crisis in nineteenth-century Russia, the sense that the nation's future direction had to be – and was about to be – decided once and for all. There is something very modern about the way in which Belinsky consistently invokes 'our age' and 'our time' as the ultimate reference point in his discourse. The notion of *catching the wave of the future* here makes its first appearance in literary theory; a notion now so familiar as to be taken for granted – and not only in the field of literary theory.

Not surprisingly, Belinsky had little time for questions of artistic form or style. 'Only content – not language or style – can save a writer from oblivion.'[7] His criticism is focused upon such characters and situations as can be directly referred to contemporary social reality. But if the artist's *socio-political* vision is what he values, nonetheless he values the *artist's* socio-political vision rather than that of the socio-political theorist. In this respect at least, literature is never subordinated to extra-literary requirements. Belinsky in fact maintained a remarkable record as an evaluative critic throughout his career. His increasing emphasis upon contemporary relevance in no way undermined his uncanny knack for discovering precisely those Russian writers whose reputations would prove long-lasting.

Belinsky's self-proclaimed followers in the next generation had far less respect for writers and literature. Often called 'the three radicals', Chernyshevsky, Dobrolyubov and Pisarev were radical in their demands that literature should serve a social purpose, and even more radical in their doubts as to whether literature could ever have enough of a social purpose to justify its continuing existence. Needless to say, these two attitudes did not always sit happily together, but they sprang from a common source: namely, a belief that the Russian society of the future ought to be shaped by a spirit of rationality oriented towards science and hard facts.

In the criticism of the three radicals, the overriding emphasis upon rationality allows no room for any distinctively aesthetic mode of knowing. The kind of socio-political *vision* valued by Belinsky is discarded. Nor is there room for any distinctively aesthetic pleasure or aesthetic emotion. The beauties of art and literature are borrowed from the beauties of real life – and, as borrowed, are automatically inferior. 'Art cannot stand comparison with living reality and completely lacks the virility which reality possesses,' says Chernyshevsky (gendering reality in a very revealing way!).[8] Even more extreme is Pisarev, who, in his deliberately provocative essay 'The Destruction of Aesthetics' (1865), argues that notions of beauty can be ultimately reduced to biological requirements. It follows that there can be no debate between different evaluative preferences, since preferences reduced to the biological level are simply a matter of individual biological constitution. As all rights to objectivity accrue on the side of factual scientific reason, a total relativism rules over responses to literature.

What remains for art is the strictly limited role of providing raw material for someone else's understanding. Such raw material must be accurately reproduced from contemporary reality, for only thus will it include the real social forces at work. The three radicals advocate realism for essentially negative reasons. 'The principal merit of the author-artist', according to Dobrolyubov, 'lies in the *truth* of the images he creates; if they were not true, false conclusions would be drawn from them.'[9] But the drawing of conclusions is what ultimately matters, and this is too important a business to be entrusted to the author. The rational understanding of real social forces and the directing of future social change require the separate input of the social or political theorist: in this case, specifically, the social or political theorist *as critic.*

Compared with the passive reality-reproducing writer, the critic thus takes on a very active role. Belinsky had already claimed that the critic expresses the same consciousness of reality as the writer, striving similarly to improve the state of society. The three radicals take the further step of attributing superior rational powers to the critic, who is capable of seeing more clearly than the writer into the nature of both real and fictional worlds. Dobrolyubov in particular develops the important principle that 'the important thing for us is not so much what the author *wanted* to say, as what he said, even unintentionally, simply in the process of truthfully reproducing the facts of life'.[10] According to Dobrolyubov, 'it is precisely the function of criticism to explain the hidden meaning of the images the artist creates'.[11]

Some parallels may be noted to the recent political phase of Postmodernist literary theory. In both cases, there is a refusal to accept the merely secondary status of commenting upon a writer's commentary upon life. Recent theorists are critics in the very largest sense: not so much critics of literature as critics of social reality, with literary texts serving as a particularly useful point of entry. However, recent theory seeks to attain a higher theoretical awareness, not rationalistic, scientific insights.

Matthew Arnold

It may seem strange to place Matthew Arnold alongside the Russian social critics in any respect other than that of chronology. Whereas their views are radical, his are conservative; whereas they look to the future, he looks to the past; whereas they demote the importance of the aesthetic, he raises it to new heights of supremacy. Nonetheless, the same overall frame defines his perspective, the same appeal to the larger social good. He too is a critic of his own contemporary society at least as much as a critic of literature. And he too gives to both criticism and literature the vital mission of redeeming that society from its failings.

That Arnold's particular conclusions are almost diametrically opposed to those of the Russians may be partly attributed to the difference between mid-nineteenth-century Russia and mid-nineteenth-century England. Victorian society in Arnold's time had no sense of being in a state of crisis; on the contrary, it was unusually smug and satisfied with its own successes. At least, it could observe the rest of the world struggling to follow in its economic, scientific and political footsteps. Arnold condemned such smugness as a surrender to self-interested materialism. 'Our august Constitution sometimes looks . . . a colossal machine for the manufacture of Philistines,' he declared.[12] Living human culture was being sacrificed to mere mechanism and technology: 'The idea of perfection as an *inward* condition of the mind and spirit is at variance with the mechanical and material civilisation in esteem with us.'[13] Arnold stands at an interesting historical moment of bifurcation between two forms of middle-class ideology, the genteel and the entrepreneurial.

It is in his attitude towards rational science that Arnold is most at odds with Chernyshevsky, Dobrolyubov and Pisarev. Science, he claims, can give us only knowledge in the form of endless separate facts. But human beings have a psychological need to unify separate facts into some larger picture: 'every one knows how we seek naturally to combine the pieces of our knowledge together . . . and how unsatisfactory and tiresome it would be to go on for ever learning lists of exceptions, or accumulating items of fact which must stand isolated'.[14] Arnold's version of the larger picture is moral and aesthetic: 'We experience . . . the need of relating what we have learnt and known to the sense which we have in us for conduct, to the sense which we have in us for beauty.'[15] Only thus can knowledge become 'touched with emotion'.[16]

Against materialism, mechanism and arid factual knowledge, Arnold pits – literature. For the great majority of mankind, literature 'will call out their being at more points, will make them live more'.[17] Or, elsewhere: 'poetry reconciles [man] with himself and the universe'.[18] Arnold is asking literature to take on the role previously filled by religion, of providing a sense of meaning in life. With the advances in nineteenth-century science, simple religious belief was becoming increasingly impossible for educated Victorians, who nonetheless lamented its loss. Arnold proposed to fill the space of that loss with literature.

Arnold is especially eager for literature to re-create the old religious sense that there is something greater than the egotistic concern of the self-centred individual. He cordially dislikes 'our strong individualism, our hatred of all limits to the unrestrained swing of the individual's personality, our maxim of "every man for himself"'.[19] For Arnold, the study of the very greatest literature is a practical lesson in humility and respect – not merely as an end in itself, but as a teaching tool in a larger programme of social improvement. To achieve a truly 'classical' taste is to overcome eccentric whims and personal prejudices. Arnold insists upon 'elementary, permanent feelings', and inveighs against the vice of 'provinciality'.[20] Any special favour towards that which is close to oneself in time or place is condemned as a fallacious 'personal estimate':

Our personal affinities, likings, and circumstances, have great power to sway our estimate of this or that poet's work, and to make us attach more importance to it than in itself it really possesses, because to us it is, or has been, of high importance.[21]

Arnold himself most admires the distant writers of classical Greece, and has almost no interest in the major novelists of his own time.

Arnold's version of literature is removed not only from the contemporary but also from the practical world. The appreciation of literature helps us to 'keep aloof from what is called "the practical view of things"'.[22] True criticism must 'refus[e] to lend itself to any of those ulterior, political, practical considerations about ideas, which plenty of people will be sure to attach to them'.[23] Such disinterestedness is important not simply for the sake of literature, but as a desirable social attitude generally:

It is said that a man with my theories . . . is full of antipathy against the rougher or coarser movements going on around him, that he will not lend a hand to the humble operation of uprooting evil. . . . But what if rough and coarse action, ill-calculated action, action with insufficient light, is, and has for a long time been, our bane? What if our urgent want now is, not to act at any price, but rather to lay in a stock of light for our difficulties?[24]

Arnold has great faith in the possibility of rising above one's own class political interests to a state of contemplative impartiality.

The paradox of Arnold's position is that literature serves the social purpose he prescribes not by becoming more socially purposive, but by remaining, above all, literary. Instead of preaching religion or teaching morality, literature must itself take on the status of a kind of religion, a kind of morality. Arnold insists upon morality as forcibly as he rejects didacticism: 'a poetry of revolt against moral ideas is a poetry of revolt against *life*; a poetry of indifference towards moral ideas is a poetry of indifference towards *life*'.[25] In fact, Arnold sees literature as promoting a general capacity for morality rather than directing any specific line of conduct. This is very much in the vein of Wordsworth and Shelley, as described above in the section on 'Some British Themes'. And, like Wordsworth in particular, Arnold tends to equate moral capacity with a certain kind of mood: a quasi-religious mood of deep solemnity.

He discovers this quasi-religious mood as much in the style as in the content of great literature. He especially values what he calls 'the grand style', which moves and elevates in an appropriately solemn manner. This orientation towards style is taken to an extreme in the famous – or notorious – theory of *infallible touchstones*. The theory is presented in 'The Study of Poetry', where Arnold quotes a selection of very short samples of poetic language, and claims that 'these few lines, if we have tact and can use them, are enough even of themselves to keep clear and sound our judgements about poetry'.[26] Milton's '. . . *which cost Ceres all that pain / To seek her through the world*' is one of his touchstones, as is Dante's '*In la sua volontade è nostra pace*'. Although such isolated fragments are almost meaningless in themselves, he believes that in their language we can feel the authentic accent of the very greatest poetry, against which all other poetry may be measured. Predictably, his samples are characterised by a tone of deep solemnity.

The stress upon feeling is significant. Arnold presents his concrete samples in order to avoid the elaboration of a general theory of poetic value. 'Critics give themselves great labour to draw out what in the abstract constitutes the characters of a high quality of poetry . . . characters [which] . . . are far better recognised by being felt in the verse of the master, than by being perused in the prose of the critic.'[27] Perhaps he suspects that conceptual analysis would undermine the impact of the quasi-religious mood. But a little more theoretical self-awareness might have helped Arnold to be more honest about his own responses. For what he feels when reading his touchstone fragments is surely very much determined by the larger assumptions that he brings to his reading: assumptions not only about the whole context of *Paradise Lost* and *The Divine Comedy*, but also about the special status of Milton and Dante in the Western literary pantheon.

The beginnings of sociological criticism: Taine and Marx

In their very different ways, Arnold and the Russian social critics were primarily concerned about the *effects* of literature – and the criticism of literature – upon society. For another kind of nineteenth-century critic, society entered the picture as the *cause* of literature. Herder and Hegel had already encouraged the habit of viewing individual works as arising out of a larger *Volksgeist* (the spirit of a people) or *Zeitgeist* (the spirit of a time); and many nineteenth-century literary historians followed in their footsteps. The mid- to late-nineteenth century was a Golden Age for large-scale narratives describing the evolution of a national literature or genre in relation to the history of a particular society. De Sanctis, Brunetière and Brandes are some of the more prominent names in the field – though all far less prominent now than in their heyday.

However, these literary historians still envisaged literature as the expression rather than as the product of a society. In this respect, they merely took the genetic approach one step back beyond the Romantic focus upon works of literature as expressing an individual creative mind. It required a further shift towards the scientific viewpoint before works of literature could be seen as simple causal products. Given the ever-rising prestige of the natural sciences during the nineteenth century, such a shift was only a matter of time, and it duly arrived in the critical theory of Hippolyte Taine. From the 1860s on, Taine was the sole critic whose European reputation could rival that of his fellow-countryman, Sainte-Beuve.

Taine is aggressive about his scientific methodology. Considering the different periods in Western culture, he asserts:

> Here as elsewhere we have but a mechanical problem; the total effect is a result, depending entirely upon the magnitude and direction of the producing causes. The only difference which separates these moral problems from physical ones is, that the magnitude and direction cannot be valued or computed in the first as in the second.[28]

He maps out such producing causes under a tripartite division of race, milieu and moment. To uncover the influence of these three factors is to say all that can or need be said about any period of literature. As for individual works, the work is wholly determined by the psychology of its author and the psychology of the author is wholly determined by race, milieu and moment.

Taine's concept of race is curiously dated, involving 'some very general disposition of mind and soul, innate and appended by nature to the race, or acquired and produced by some circumstance acting upon the race'.[29] Certain psychological tendencies are attributed to the French in general, the British in general, the Dutch in general. As for 'some circumstance acting upon the race', Taine typically invokes the role of climate. So, for the Anglo-Saxons and their British descendants: 'Rain, wind, and surge leave room for naught but gloomy and melancholy thoughts.'[30] Such climatic explanations had been a favourite of amateur cultural theorists ever since the eighteenth century, and Taine's explanations are scarcely less amateurish. The influences of the social environment come under moment (i.e. the pervasive attitudes of the age) or milieu (i.e. the particular circumstances affecting literary production). Of the latter, Taine says:

> the *milieu*, that is to say, the general social and intellectual state, determines the species of works of art; it permits only those which are conformable to it, and suppresses other species, through a series of obstacles interposed, and a series of attacks renewed, at every step of their development.[31]

Unfortunately, Taine's focus is entirely upon general intellectual states rather than upon specific obstacles. He seems to have little sense of the material practices and institutions which are the unconscious determinants of literary production. No doubt this is why many commentators have had difficulty in separating his concept of milieu from his concept of moment. Taine's milieu is an airily homogeneous social mind, far removed from the real complications of historical power-structures. One seeks in vain for detailed analyses of the financial interests of publishers, the class complexion of audiences or the social status of authors. Empirical evidence for particular causal connections is notably lacking in this very general, very hypothetical procedure.

Taine's scientific claims are further compromised by his adherence to traditional notions of the literary canon. He justifies the higher standing of some writers over others with the argument that great authors are especially typical of their age, while the greatest authors are typical of their whole race as well as their age. Established masterpieces can thus be valued for new sociological reasons – as best serving to reveal the societies from which they have sprung. 'The more perfect a poet, the more national he is. The more he penetrates into his art, the more he has penetrated into the genius of his age and of his race.'[32] The verb 'penetrate' here suggests a similarity to Belinsky's view that the writer has special insight into current social trends; but, whatever Taine may have been thinking of, an actively aware insight is clearly not compatible with a methodology under which the writer's mind appears as simply the causal product of social influences. Modern sociological critics are more consistent in their distinction between conscious insight and unconscious determination, and more consistent in discarding the traditional genuflections towards the literary canon. Especially in the sociological criticism of the last two or three decades, the most revealing works are usually those whose very flaws and cracks enable the critic to *see through into* causal forces of which the writer was unaware.

In fact, Taine foreshadows modern sociological criticism more in his proclamations than in his practice. In practice, he remains at heart a Hegelian, not so very different from other literary historians of the nineteenth century. There is indeed something suspicious about the very directness of his analogies to the natural sciences, to mechanics and chemistry and biology. In the terminology of Louis Althusser, he has failed to conceive the object appropriate to his own science, the specific object of a sociological science. By contrast, it can be claimed – as Althusser also claims – that Marx does conceive the appropriate object. Although Marx has little to say about literature as such, he sets up the parameters within which later sociological criticism could work.

In the first place, Marx is a materialist who believes that mental consciousness is very definitely secondary to social existence. 'It is not the consciousness of men that determines their being, but, on the contrary, their social being that determines their consciousness.'[33] A Marxist approach will therefore not proceed by 'setting out from what men say, imagine, conceive . . . in order to arrive at men in the flesh', but by 'setting out from real, active men, and on the basis of their real life-process demonstrating the development of the ideological reflexes and echoes of this life-process'.[34] As for the 'subjective *human* sensibility' which appreciates music, art and literature, this is not a matter of innate senses but of socially constructed senses: '*human* sense . . . comes to be by virtue . . . of *humanised* nature', and 'the *senses* of the social man *differ* from those of the non-social man'.[35] Given this kind of secondarity, it is no longer possible to explain literary history in terms of some grand Hegelian story of unfolding consciousness or unfolding aesthetic sensibility. The true story, the engine of history, exists on the level of social practices. Consciousness and aesthetic sensibility are mere epiphenomena, with no independent continuity of their own.

Social practices impinge upon the artist in specific, constraining ways:

Raphael as much as any other artist was determined by the technical advances in art made before him, by the organisation of society and the division of labour in his locality, and, finally, by the division of labour in all the countries with which his locality had intercourse. Whether an individual like Raphael succeeds in developing his talent depends wholly on demand, which in turn depends on the division of labour and the conditions of human culture resulting from it.[36]

Marx insists upon seeing the artist as part of a production system, not as a pure and self-sufficient mind. Thus the general principles applying to the capitalist mode of production apply no less to artistic production under a capitalist system: the product is commodified and divorced from the labour of its producer. Marx also notes how technological changes affect the aesthetic possibilities available. 'The conditions necessary for epic poetry disappear', he suggests, 'when the printing press and even printing machines exist.'[37] And the conditions necessary for mythological invention are irrevocably lost with the advent of railways, locomotives and electric telegraphs: 'All mythology subdues, controls and fashions the forces of nature in the imagination and through imagination; it disappears therefore when real control over these forces is established.'[38] No effort of free will or mind can outweigh such material determinants.

Moreover, the Marxist account does not homogenise society under a single, simple *Volksgeist* or *Zeitgeist*. It emphasises conflicting interests and opposing practices, the division of labour and the division of classes. If one particular cultural pattern predominates, this is because the economically dominant class has been able to disseminate its ideology at the expense of other classes. 'The class which has the means of material production at its disposal, consequently also controls the means of mental production, so that the ideas of those who lack the means of mental production are on the whole subject to it.'[39] At the same time, claims to naturalness and universality typically attempt to camouflage the self-interest of a particular cultural pattern. The ruling class 'has to give its ideas the form of universality, and present them as the only rational, universally valid ones'.[40] Friedrich Engels provides an example of how to pierce through such camouflage in his reading of a book on Goethe by Karl Grün. Grün repeatedly grounds his assertions upon essentialist assumptions about *man*, who 'exhibits a most marked respect for "the educated estates" in general and a seemly deference towards a high aristocracy in particular', 'remains wholeheartedly attached to "circumstances of well-deserved and well-accustomed property"', and 'envies no one and gives thanks to his maker if he is left in peace'.[41] As Engels ironically points out, '"man", who, as we have already seen, is *German* by birth, is gradually beginning to turn into the spit image of a *German petty bourgeois*'.[42]

Such an approach undermines the old confidence in human consciousness far more radically than anything in Taine. Taine argues that consciousness is causally produced by social forces; but, even in his proclamations, the product still mirrors or truly fashions forth the forces behind it. By contrast, Marxist theory allows that consciousness may become quite divorced from the real material state of affairs – may become *false consciousness*:

> Ideology is a process which is indeed accomplished consciously by the so-called thinker, but it is the wrong kind of consciousness. The real motive forces impelling him remain unknown to the thinker. . . . Hence he imagines false or illusory motive forces.[43]

No longer can societies or social periods be discussed in terms of their own consciousness of themselves. As with Freud, the unconscious is at its most disturbing when what it does is entirely different to anything known by the consciousness.

It is true that Marx is still a Hegelian in his liking for large-scale stories, with large-scale divisions of class and interest. It is also true that Marx's inclination to carry all social practices back into the more solid materiality of economics is no longer fashionable. Nevertheless, Marx's sociological approach is modern and relevant today in a way that Taine's clearly is not. The 'Marxism and Literary Theory' section of Chapter 7 will describe some of the ways in which Marxism subsequently influenced literary theory.

6 Naturalism, Symbolism and Modernism

In the last three decades of the nineteenth century, Naturalism pushed the cause of an extreme realism in the novel, while Symbolism pushed the cause of an extreme idealism in poetry. Both movements began in Paris, which also gave birth to Impressionism in art during the same period. The location is surprising – considering that this was the period in which France lost its traditional predominance in Europe as a result of the 1870 Franco-Prussian War; and in which Paris lost its traditional predominance in France as a result of the crushing of the Commune in 1871. For the first time, cultural importance is linked not to political power but to loss of power, not to national success but to national failure.

The configuration itself is even more surprising. The beginnings of Naturalism are usually dated from the publication of the Goncourts' *Germinie Lacerteux* in 1864, or the publication of Zola's *Thérèse Raquin* in 1867; whereas Symbolism got under way mainly in the 1870s, with the poetry of Rimbaud and Mallarmé. In this respect, Naturalism had a very short head start. But, by and large, the two new movements ran side by side all the way through to the First World War. And yet they were opposed with all the conscious contrariety of, say, Romanticism versus Neoclassicism. How to understand this unique forked path of literary history?

One model would view the situation as an overlap between essentially successive sensibilities. After all, Naturalism was in many ways a final development of nineteenth-century Realism, while Symbolism was in many ways a first development of twentieth-century Modernism. It is also true that new literary revolutions often stimulate a final productive surge from an older sensibility, as witness Crabbe and Austen in the period of British Romanticism. However, this can hardly be the whole truth about Naturalism, which carries the excitement of a radical new vision and spreads from country to country in the characteristic manner of a literary revolution. These are not the symptoms of a sensibility on the wane. An alternative model would view the situation as a conflict between the different media of poetry and prose. The enormous popularity of the nineteenth-century novel had undermined the audience for poetry; so poetry fell back upon its own distinctive qualities, discovering or rediscovering what it alone could do supremely well. The trend to short, compressed lyrics and heightened emphasis upon linguistic texture shows poetry defining itself by opposition to prose. Such recuperation of a marginalised medium has become a familiar story in the twentieth century: thus the arrival of film compelled theatre to abandon visually realistic imitation (which film could do better), and to (re)discover its own peculiar strength of direct physical impact – as realised through 'intimate theatre' and the kinds of effect advocated by Antonin Artaud. Or, to take another famous example, the arrival of television in the mid-1950s compelled radio to abandon quiz shows, dramas and serials, and to (re)discover its own peculiar strength in the field of broadcast music. But again, this can hardly be the whole truth. There are too many examples of Naturalist and Symbolist elements mingling together in the same work. Drama, with its less clear-cut allegiances, is especially revealing here. It is impossible to categorise the later plays of Ibsen or Chekhov clearly as either Naturalist or Symbolist. Such cases demonstrate the existence of a potential bridge between the two movements, which Modernism eventually crossed over.

The third model, then, recognises that Naturalism and Symbolism are not so completely opposed as they appear. Or, more exactly, they represent different manifestations of the same underlying problematic. This problematic has to do with the development of a new relationship between literature and society, between literature and its audience. The third model is no more all-encompassing than the other two: but, given the organisation of this chapter, it is the one that calls for explanation here.

In brief, both Naturalists and Symbolists reacted against the bourgeoisie, the class which dominated the nineteenth century with its economic power and its characteristic morality. Naturalists tended to argue on behalf of the working class while Symbolists tended to adopt aristocratic poses, but the writers of both movements typically belonged in the curious new class or grouping of the *intelligentsia*. Educated but not materialistic, the *intelligentsia* might perhaps best be compared to the clergy of early medieval times. These writers had no time for the kind of realistic novel which told readers that their own real lives were fairly much in order and their own real world a nice, safe, familiar place to be. Or to put it another way, these writers regarded the cultivated but comfortable level of 'middlebrow' fiction as merely a superior form of entertainment. Naturalists and Symbolists envisaged literature as confrontational to a degree that went beyond any previous phase of literature theory. In the last few decades of the nineteenth century, the notion of challenging an audience came to be accepted as *the* defining property of literature.

As Naturalists and Symbolists turned against middle-class morality, so too they discarded the moralising presence of the author in the work. It was not the author's right or responsibility to tell an audience how to interpret or judge. Nor was the audience to be merely entertained by having its emotions excited and manipulated. Whereas Romantic literary theory had emphasised authorial expression, and Neoclassical (and Classical) literary theory had emphasised audience affect, the new movements preferred to focus upon an object which lay between author and audience. For the Naturalists, this object was the real world as represented through the text; for the Symbolists, it was the linguistic text as an object in itself. As objects, these could hardly be more different; nonetheless, they are similar in what they exclude, and the distance between them is not so difficult to cross over as might appear. It is interesting that art accomplished a similar crossover in the same period, as the realism of Courbet led on to Impressionism, thence to Post-Impressionism, and thence to the radically non-representational forms of modern art. From painting the real world, to painting the real medium of light in the real world, to painting the real medium of canvas and colours in the art-work – the trajectory is smoother than the literary trajectory but demonstrates much the same logic.

French Naturalists
(*Flaubert, Zola, the Goncourt brothers*)

Naturalism in France built upon the work of earlier nineteenth-century French novelists, who had carried realism generally further than their counterparts in other countries. Stendhal, for example, had claimed that 'a novel is a mirror passing down a road'.[1] Balzac, for all his melodramatics in practice, had nonetheless thought of himself as a kind of scientist, and was accepted as such by Taine and Zola. Flaubert was a genuine proto-Naturalist in his insistence upon recording a depressingly mundane reality, even if his obsessions over language and motif could also entitle him to be considered as a proto-Symbolist or proto-Modernist. This love of style had not disappeared even with the Goncourt brothers, whose realism extended to the recording of lower-class lives. But it disappeared with Zola, who claimed that 'the reign of the word-mongers is over'.[2] Zola stands as the Naturalist *simpliciter.*

Zola made Naturalism into arguably the first deliberate '-ism', the first literary *programme* in the modern sense of the term. The Romantics had never named themselves as a specifically contemporary group, nor had they argued their values on the basis of contemporary as opposed to eternal principles. But the historical studies of the nineteenth century encouraged literature to become self-conscious about its own revolutions. Zola, who had worked in publicity and journalism, was particularly well equipped to promote Naturalism as a literary revolution. As well as giving the movement its name, as a banner for marching under, he also positioned it strategically alongside other contemporary battalions:

> naturalism [is] the all-powerful master, giving direction to the age of which it is the very life breath. . . . It is the motive power of our productions, the pivot on which our society turns. You find it in the sciences . . . you find it in all manifestations of intelligence . . . it is renovating the arts, sculpture and especially painting.[3]

On this presentation, Naturalism in literature is not simply desirable but inevitable. Whatever the attraction of its individual products, as a movement it has the appeal of certain success.

In fact, the Naturalists did not seek to make their products attractive. In earlier nineteenth-century novels, the realistic depiction of a familiar world could stimulate a pleasurable sense of recognition in the audience. But this flavour of realism was not necessarily incompatible with unrealistic coincidences, calculated suspense, heightened emotional 'hooks', climactic dénouements and happy endings. In earlier nineteenth-century novels, the new taste for realistic depiction did not take precedence over all other tastes. But for the Naturalists, the accurate recording of reality was more than just a taste, it was an absolute principle. In Zola's words:

> We begin with the idea that nature is all we need; it is necessary to accept her as she is, without modifying her or diminishing her in any respect. . . . Instead of imagining an adventure, complicating it, and arranging a series of theatrical effects to lead to a final conclusion, we simply take from life the story of a being or group of beings whose acts we faithfully set down. The work becomes an official record, nothing more . . .[4]

With the advent of Naturalism, realism becomes a duty and a responsibility – for both author and audience.

A famous remark in one of Flaubert's letters may serve to exemplify the willed nature of this particular proto-Naturalist's devotion to duty. 'Don't you believe that this ignoble reality, the depiction of which disgusts you, also sickens my heart to an equal extent? If you knew me better, you would know that I execrate ordinary life.'[5] In writing *Madame Bovary*, Flaubert had to force himself to an accurate recording of reality; nor did he expect the novel to be exactly pleasing to his readers: 'It will make dreary reading; it will contain atrocious things of misery and sordidness.'[6] For the Goncourt brothers, their novel *Germinie Lacerteux* represented a deliberate slap in the face of the reading public:

> The public . . . loves vapid and consoling reading, adventures that end happily, imaginings which upset neither its digestion nor its serenity: this book with its sad and violent distraction is bound to challenge its habits and upset its hygiene.[7]

Zola expresses much the same attitude when, lamenting the reviewers' failure to understand *Thérèse Raquin*, he wishes only 'the deep satisfaction of having disgusted them for the right reason'.[8] The underlying assumption is that the audience's knowledge and sense of reality is inadequate and stands in need of improvement. In Zola's words: 'It seems at first that, as all the world have two eyes to see with, nothing ought to be more common than the sense of reality. However, nothing seems to be more rare.'[9] For their own good, readers must be confronted with more reality, whether they like it or not.

This is no mere sugar-coated pill along the lines of the old Horatian prescription. Readers must be in the complicated mental state of literally wanting what they do not want. In practice, such a mental state has often been created by the ambiguous operation of shock-appeal. The Naturalists discovered that the novel of sordid revelation could excite simultaneous disapproval and fascination in a middle-class readership. (And of course, the readership for Naturalist novels *was* middle-class, regardless of the lower-class lives which they took as their subject-matter.) In this respect, Naturalism actually developed its own new kind of reader-appeal – and one which has remained powerful ever since.

However, this was not the kind of appeal that could be consciously articulated or paraded around in public. The Naturalists needed some other justification for their devotion to realistic duty, and they found it in science. 'In the present day . . . the Novel has undertaken the studies and obligations of science,' said the Goncourt brothers.[10] Science was the rising tide which would carry the Naturalist novel to ultimate and inevitable success. And the novelists could draw support from the scientists in the matter of facing unpalatable facts, in being willing to accept that the world is not ordered in accordance with human wishes. Just how unpalatable such facts might be was especially apparent after the 1859 publication of Darwin's *The Origin of Species.*

From science, the Naturalists derived their characteristic methods: 'the study of separate facts, the anatomy of special cases, the collecting, classifying, and ticketing, of human data'.[11] Like scientists, the Naturalists believed in looking at all the evidence equally, seeing no reason why any particular life or social group should be considered intrinsically more important or interesting than any other. As for human behaviour, 'one and the same determinism must govern the stone in the road and the brain of man'.[12] The physiological model influenced Zola as it influenced so many nineteenth-century scientists: 'we must operate with characters, passions, human and social data as the chemist and the physicist work on inert bodies, as the physiologist works on living bodies'.[13] In his most famous essay, 'The Experimental Novel', Zola even argued that the novelist should set up characters in the same way that a scientist sets up an experiment, in order to test an hypothesis; the characters then run through their own interactions, and the novelist simply records the results. A complete parallel – and completely vitiated by the fact that a novel can never run itself in the 'hands off' manner of, say, a chemical interreaction. Zola's argument may have had short-term strategic benefits, but the Naturalists in general were on safer ground when claiming to record the real-world experiments which *nature* conducts.

No matter where the experiment takes place, the novelist as scientist does not interfere with the outcome. Moral beliefs are the likeliest source of interference, as Flaubert recognises: 'How stupid and false all works of the imagination are made by preoccupation with morality!'[14] By contrast, Flaubert asserts the common nineteenth-century view that science is wholly detached and objective: 'That's what is so fine about the natural sciences: they don't wish to prove anything.'[15] The novelist's scientific responsibility is fulfilled by a refusal to intervene; by the same token, the novelist cannot be blamed if the outcome turns out contrary to social morality. 'In the world of science an accusation of immorality proves nothing whatsoever,' declares Zola, defending *Thérèse Raquin* against accusations of immorality.[16] Or, to complete an earlier partial quotation from the brothers Goncourt: 'in the present day when the Novel has undertaken the studies and obligations of science, it can demand the liberties and freedom of science'.[17]

If Naturalist practice is promoted for its objectivity and detachment, so too with the Naturalist manner. Like the writer of a scientific report, the Naturalist novelist must avoid personal reflections and partialities. Even before the arrival of outright Naturalism, Flaubert had given clear expression to this particular requirement: 'I believe, even, that a novelist *does not have the right to express his opinion* on anything whatsoever.'[18] Zola continues in the same vein:

> You cannot imagine a chemist getting angry at nitrogen because that element is hostile to life, or tenderly sympathizing with oxygen for the opposite reason. Likewise a novelist who feels a need to become indignant against vice and to applaud virtue spoils the documents which he sets forth . . .[19]

It is not even desirable to spell out the conclusions of a Naturalist experiment: 'the works carry their conclusions within them'.[20] The majority of Naturalist novelists were politically on the left, and many of them were politically active in their own lives. But in their novels, they deliberately left it up to the audience to draw appropriate conclusions and follow through with appropriate political solutions.

The alliance with science which served Naturalism so well in its early days turned out to be of little long-term value. Extreme forms of realism did not die out with the original Naturalist movement: something very much like Naturalism has continued to surface here and there throughout the twentieth century. For faithful non-selective recording, what better example than pure stream-of-consciousness technique? For sheer assertion of reality in the face of human wishes, what better example than the *chosisme* of Robbe-Grillet?[21] But these extreme forms of realism are no longer justified by reference to science, which lost its special glamour in the early twentieth century.

French Symbolists
(*Gautier, Baudelaire, Mallarmé, Valéry*)

Whereas France came early to Realism, it came late to Romanticism. As often in literary history, this meant that French Romanticism appeared in a distinctive late version; and, as often in literary history, this distinctive late version provided the germ for a further revolution. The 'bohemian' wing of French Romanticism developed into an evolutionary bridge between Romanticism and Symbolism, a bridge that has no exact parallel in other European countries.[22] Amongst the transitional poets, Théophile Gautier and Charles Baudelaire are particularly important as formulating many of the ideas which later became constitutive of Symbolism proper.

The one crucial aspect of Romanticism rejected by Gautier and Baudelaire was the Romantic worship of Nature and the natural. According to Gautier, 'Nature is stupid, without consciousness of itself, without thought or passion . . . art is more beautiful, more true, more powerful than nature.'[23] As an avid theatregoer, Gautier preferred the spectacle of painted stage scenery to any natural scenery. Baudelaire for his part wrote in praise of cosmetics. This assertion of art as superior to Nature has a long history in French tradition, going back at least as far as the deliberate artifice and convention of the Neoclassical age. The same attitude is still visible today in the characteristic emphases of French Structuralism and Poststructuralism, as when Roland Barthes praises the blatant artificiality of wrestling at the expense of the phony naturalness of boxing.[24]

This assertion of art also affects ideas about the way poetry ought to be written. The Romantic cult of spontaneous inspiration has no appeal for Gautier, who insists that 'the word poet means literally *maker*: whatever is not well *made* does not exist'.[25] The writing of poetry involves craft and labour and calculation. Not surprisingly, the

Romantic insistence upon emotion at the expense of intellect also comes under challenge. 'The sensibility of the heart is not entirely favourable to the poetic process,' as Baudelaire puts it.[26] It is no coincidence that Gautier initiated the rediscovery of baroque poetry which, with its special kind of intelligence, was to prove so important to the Modernists (especially in English- and Spanish-speaking countries). The general trend of such thinking was to emphasise Art as a very special and distinct kind of thing. Art was to be regarded as quite separate from the writer's everyday life ('it is just as absurd to say that a man is a drunkard because he describes an orgy, or a debauchee because he tells of a debauch, as to claim that a man is virtuous because he has written a work on morality'[27]); quite separate from moral concerns ('if the poet has pursued a moral aim, he has diminished his poetic force'[28]); and quite separate from any social utility ('there is nothing really beautiful save what is of no possible use'[29]). The first of these separations parallels the Naturalistic doctrine of authorial impersonality, albeit for different reasons; the second parallels the Naturalistic doctrine of scientific non-interference, albeit for different reasons. But the third contradicts both Naturalism and all varieties of nineteenth-century social criticism. Gautier's famous slogan is 'l'art pour l'art', or 'art for art's sake'. Adopting the role of the dandy, the poet remains aloof from the practical world, from science, from progress ('that great heresy of decay'[30]), and from the mundane greyishness of bourgeois existence.

Gautier was the originator of almost all of the views described so far. But Baudelaire added a new depth to them when he developed a new way of seeing the world itself as a work of art. Whereas Gautier was in love with visual surfaces, Baudelaire was moved by the sense of an ulterior reality behind appearances. In Baudelaire's quasi-religious vision, 'this world [is] a dictionary of hieroglyphics'; visible reality is governed by 'universal *correspondence* and symbolism'.[31] This notion of a deeper, hidden level of meanings and connections was to prove enormously influential in the further development of Symbolism proper.

As regards the further development of Symbolism proper, the most significant figures are Stéphane Mallarmé and his self-declared disciple, Paul Valéry. Mallarmé is responsible for the crucial early breakthroughs; Valéry, who stands at a point where Symbolism merges into Modernism, converts gleams and flashes into fully worked-out principles. Both poets adopt Baudelaire's notion of a deeper, hidden level of meanings and connections, but apply it somewhat less to the world and somewhat more to the poem. Symbols and correspondences are present in the language and structure of the poem, regardless of whether they originate in reality.

Applied to the poem, the notion of a universal symbolism encourages the discovery of ulterior meanings on a higher level than the ordinary obvious meanings of language. At the same time, these ulterior meanings are self-generating, as in Baudelaire's vision. They are not generated by the writer in the old allegorical manner, where a higher level of meaning is nonetheless subjected to an ordinary overt level of control. As I have sought to show in another book (*Beyond Superstructuralism*, chapter 13), ulterior meanings in the symbolist mode are like the ripples spreading out around a pebble tossed into a pond; and the pebbles in this case are isolated words or verbal units cut free from the ordinary syntactical interdefinition that occurs between words combined in sentences. 'Words rise up unaided and in ecstasy,' says Mallarmé, when '[the mind] sees the words not in their usual order, but in projection (like the walls of a cave)'.[32] The process is almost akin to a form of meditation:

> When I say: 'a flower!' then from that forgetfulness to which my voice consigns all floral form, something different from the usual calyces arises, something all music, essence, and softness: the flower which is absent from all bouquets.[33]

Mallarmé also speaks of the poem as 'a kind of incantation'.[34]

Correspondences come into play between the ulterior meanings thus generated. According to Mallarmé, the poet must 'avoid[] any thought that might tend to arrange [the materials] too directly or precisely', seeking rather to 'establish a careful relationship between two images, from which a third element, clear and fusible, will be distilled and caught by our imagination'.[35] Instead of the kind of thought specified and controlled by sentences, Mallarmé advocates implied relationships which readers will have to divine for themselves. And such relationships are as it were simultaneous across a poem, overleaping the ordinary continuities and contiguities of language. Valéry expresses a similar view when defining the poetic state of mind as one in which

> well-known things and beings – or rather the ideas that represent them . . . attract one another, they are connected in ways quite differ-

ent from the ordinary; they become . . . *musicalized*, resonant, and, as it were, harmonically related.[36]

Musical analogies are popular with all Symbolist poets and critics, in so far as music can be envisaged in terms of pure relationships and harmonics. Analogies envisaged in terms of mere sound-effect would be misleading, however: Symbolist poems are generally more visual and less 'sounded' than the poems of previous eras. Mallarmé for one drew particular attention to 'a simultaneous vision of the Page', and the importance of the 'whites' or blank spaces between and around the words as printed.[37]

The new kind of poetic meaning preserves mystery by means of indirect suggestion. 'To *name* an object is largely to destroy poetic enjoyment, which comes from gradual divination,' says Mallarmé.[38] Inevitably, this makes great demands upon the reader, and Mallarmé is well aware that many readers will dismiss the new kind of poetic meaning as obscure. But he is perfectly willing to do without such readers. 'If a person of mediocre intelligence and insufficient literary experience happens to open an obscure book and insists on enjoying it, something is wrong; there has simply been a misunderstanding.'[39] Poetry thus becomes exclusive, not merely because the poet chooses to adopt an aristocratic pose towards society, but because of the very nature of the poetic medium. Perhaps the most extreme expression of Symbolist élitism occurs in an early essay by Valéry:

> We love the art of this age, complicated and *artificial* . . . and all the more as it becomes more mysterious, narrower, more inaccessible to the crowd. What matter if it be closed to the majority, if its ultimate expressions remain the luxury of a small number, provided that with the few *elect*, whose divine realm it is, it reaches the highest degree of splendour and purity![40]

What is more, the new kind of poetic meaning is unable to serve social purposes, even if it wanted to. Correspondences and relationships do not amount to assertions or messages, and cannot be put to use in the manner of assertions or messages. The type of musical structure envisaged by Mallarmé and Valéry is essentially a closed system. As Mallarmé puts it:

> our principal aim should be to make the words of a poem self-mirror-

ing (since they are sufficiently autonomous to begin with and need
no outside impression) to such an extent that no one of them will
seem to have a colour of its own, and all of them will be merely the
notes of a scale.[41]

Ultimately the poem is about itself. As for society – 'in our time the
poet can only go on strike against society', says Mallarmé.[42] There is
no social role for poetry whatsoever.

But poetry does have a role in relation to language. For Mallarmé
and Valéry, ordinary everyday language lacks the subtlety needed to
capture the true qualities of experience. The linguistic medium has
been degraded by habits of crude usage in a materialistic society.
'Language, in the hands of the mob, leads to the same facility and
directness as does money,' charges Mallarmé.[43] Valéry specifically
blames the way in which social categorisations override individual
apprehensions:

> words have passed through so many mouths, so many phrases, so
> many uses and abuses, that the most delicate precautions must be
> taken to avoid too much confusion in our minds between what we . . .
> are trying to think, and what dictionaries, authors, and, for that
> matter, the whole human race since the beginning of language, want
> us to think.[44]

On this view, the challenge for the poet is to 'draw a pure, ideal Voice'
out of 'a medium essentially practical, perpetually changing, soiled, a
maid of all work, *everyday language*'.[45] Valéry grandly states the
Symbolist ambition: 'poetry implies a decision to change the function
of language'.[46] Poetry is to be justified not as a higher form of experience or thought or feeling, but, in the first place at least, as a higher
form of language.

The intensity with which the Symbolists insisted upon the verbal
nature of poetry was something quite new. Valéry records an
exchange between Mallarmé and the painter Degas, in which Degas
complained 'Yours is a hellish craft. I can't manage to say what I want,
and yet I'm full of ideas.' To which Mallarmé replied, 'My dear Degas,
one does not make poetry with ideas, but with *words*.'[47] Valéry
himself goes even further in producing arguments for the peculiar
textuality of poetry. In an act of ordinary everyday communication, he
claims, 'I speak to you, and if you have understood my words . . . it

means that the words have vanished from your minds and are replaced by their counterpart, by images, relationships, impulses.'[48] But in poetic language, the 'concrete form takes on . . . such importance that it asserts itself and makes itself, as it were, respected'.[49] Poetry, unlike prose, 'tends to get itself reproduced in its own form: it stimulates us to reconstruct it identically'.[50] This is an argument which continues to be heard throughout the Modernist period, as does Valéry's corollary on 'the impossibility of reducing [the poet's] work to prose, of *saying* it, or of *understanding it as prose*'.[51]

Whereas a focus upon communication throws the emphasis onto sender and receiver, a focus upon textuality throws the emphasis onto the language-object as a kind of barrier between sender and receiver. As regards the sender of poetry, this means that the poet becomes relatively invisible. 'The great discovery in modern poetry', according to Mallarmé, is that 'the poet disappears'.[52] By this disappearance, the words of the poem are empowered: 'the poet's voice must be stilled and the initiative taken by the words themselves'.[53] Symbolist theory thus differs from Romantic theory, which promotes the poet's personal presence in the poem; and also from Naturalist theory, which promotes the disappearance of the novelist in order to hand the initiative over to an objectively-recorded reality. As regards the receiver of poetry, Mallarmé condemns poems which 'fail to give our minds the exquisite joy which consists of believing that we are creating something'.[54] The new kind of meaning calls for a new degree of creative input from the reader.

Valéry expresses much the same sentiment. The poet's production of the work and the reader's interpretation of the work are essentially separate; neither looks through to the experience of the other. Like Mallarmé, Valéry calls for the author to surrender control: 'An author can, no doubt, inform us of his intentions; but it is not a question of these; it is a question of what subsists, what he has made independent of himself.'[55] As for interpretation, Valéry at times goes even beyond the guided creativity envisaged by Mallarmé, and allows for an absolute creativity on the part of the reader:

> *there is no true meaning to a text* – no author's authority . . . Once published, a text is like an apparatus that anyone may use as he will and according to his ability: it is not certain that the one who constructed it can use it better than another.[56]

The logic of Symbolism thus leads through to Modernism and Post-modernism.

The language-consciousness of Symbolism also represents perhaps the earliest large-scale manifestation of the *linguistic turn* which has since become dominant in twentieth-century thinking. In linguistics, in philosophies of language, in the humanities and social sciences generally, attention has come to be increasingly focused upon the linguistic medium rather than the out-there object, upon language as the master rather than the servant of human understanding. Some of the varied directions taken by the *linguistic turn* will be examined in subsequent chapters.

British Aestheticism and Henry James
(*also Pater, Wilde*)

The art-for-art's-sake views of British Aestheticism relate to Gautier and Baudelaire rather than to Symbolism proper. In spite of their occasional radical statements, Swinburne and Pater remain under the general influence of Romanticism. By contrast, Oscar Wilde is more thoroughly and consistently radical, even if his radicalism often comes across as a form of outrage-for-outrage's-sake. Like Swinburne and Pater, Wilde stands largely outside the direct line of evolution leading through to Symbolism and Modernism, but he has many fascinating premonitions of developments in literary theory subsequent to Modernism.

The British Aesthetes share the French poets' contempt for bourgeois morality in literature. 'The sphere of Art and the sphere of Ethics are absolutely distinct and separate,' says Wilde.[57] They also dismiss all notion of imitating real life, and Wilde in particular proclaims the inferiority of Nature: 'what Art really reveals to us is Nature's lack of design, her curious crudities, her extraordinary monotony, her absolutely unfinished condition'.[58] However, their conception of art focuses not upon correspondences or relational structures, but primarily upon *style* – and even, in a hangover from Romanticism, upon *personal* style.

For Wilde, Art not only refuses to copy from real life but in some senses even creates real life. Thus it is thanks to a particular school of poets and painters that the 'wonderful brown fogs' of London have been made perceivable:

At present, people see fogs, not because there are fogs, but because poets and painters have taught them the mysterious loveliness of such effects. There may have been fogs for centuries in London. I dare say there were. But no one saw them, and so we do not know anything about them. They did not exist till Art had invented them.[59]

This paradoxical priority of culture over nature foreshadows many of the paradoxes of Structuralist and Poststructuralist thinking, more than half a century later. Even more profoundly prescient is an incidental reference to 'language, which is the parent, and not the child, of thought'.[60]

Aestheticism also involves a distinctive mode of literary criticism. Impressionist criticism (which has very little to do with Impressionist painting) begins with a profound distrust of all objectivist criteria. For Walter Pater, the founding father of Impressionist criticism, there are only individual responses to individual works. The work is relativised to the personal predilections that a reader brings to a reading: 'What is . . . this engaging personality presented . . . in a book, to *me*? . . . How is my nature modified by its presence and under its influence?'[61] It follows that critics can do no more than record honest accounts of their own experience. 'The first step towards seeing one's object as it really is, is to know one's own impression as it really is.'[62]

In his essay on 'The Critic as Artist', Wilde carries such views through to their logical conclusions. Objective description is not the purpose of criticism: the critic, like the actor interpreting a playscript, must always add his or her personality to the original text. Objective judgement is equally irrelevant. Instead, Wilde proposes that criticism should 'treat the work of art simply as a starting-point for a new creation'.[63] He even suggests that the critical form of creativity will expand as the stocks of primary creative material become exhausted: 'the subject-matter at the disposal of creation is always diminishing, while the subject-matter of criticism increases daily. There are always new attitudes of mind, and new points of view.'[64]

Changes in contemporary consciousness may be one major source of new attitudes and points of view: creative criticism 'will be always showing us the work of art in some new relation to our age'.[65] Necessarily, the author's intention gets left behind:

criticism of the highest kind . . . does not confine itself . . . to discovering the real intention of the artist and accepting that as final. . . . For when the work is finished it has, as it were, an independent life of its own, and may deliver a message far other than that which was put into its lips to say.[66]

For the purposes of creative criticism, the best kind of writing will be that which remains open-ended and available for further interpretations. 'The aesthetic critic rejects . . . obvious modes of art that have but one message to deliver, and having delivered it become dumb and sterile, and seeks rather for such modes as . . . make all interpretations true, and no interpretation final.'[67]

Every one of the statements just quoted adumbrates some theme of recent theory in the Postmodernist period. But there is a difference. Wilde's version of critical creativity is always essentially a matter of *style*. The essay on 'The Critic as Artist' is itself full of purple passages in praise of famous masterpieces. The beautifully-expressed *appreciation* became the general goal of all Impressionist criticism, and the new approach actually merged in very easily with the older Romantic 'praise of beauties' tradition. In practice, the Impressionist critics did *not* record honest accounts of their own reading responses, but competed to produce ever more fulsome phrases in honour of works already glamorised by the social cachet of established reputation.

The criticism of Henry James is roughly contemporaneous with Aestheticism. Like the Aesthetes, James draws heavily upon art for his images and points of reference; like the Aesthetes, he distrusts criticism by general or abstract principles; and like the Aesthetes, he combines in his approach both forward-looking and backward-looking elements. But whereas the Aesthetes' focus is poetic even when not specifically upon poetry, James's focus is novelistic, and the whole tenor of his criticism differs accordingly.

James is at his most backward-looking in his insistence upon the moral function of the novel – a moral function conceived in the manner of Wordsworth, Shelley and Arnold. Thus he speaks of the 'miraculous enlargement of experience' which the reader gains from a successful novel.[68] Elsewhere he speaks of morality in literature as 'simply a part of the essential richness of inspiration . . . The more a work of art feels [morality] at its source, the richer it is.'[69] Literature does not inculcate particular moral judgements, but refines and expands the imagination and sensibility in preparation for future judgement.

In other respects, James inclines towards Naturalistic beliefs. He insists that the novel should represent reality undistorted by romance or artificial plotting or effects calculated for the sake of entertainment.

> In proportion as in what [fiction] offers us we see life *without* rearrangement do we feel that we are touching the truth; in proportion as we see it *with* rearrangement do we feel that we are being put off with a substitute, a compromise and convention.[70]

Even more important is his endorsement of the Naturalistic doctrine of impersonality. Thus he approves of Turgenev's fiction where 'the drama is quite uncommented; the poet never plays chorus; situations speak for themselves'.[71] By contrast, he strongly disapproves of Trollope who

> took a suicidal satisfaction in reminding the reader that the story he was telling was only, after all, a make-believe. He habitually referred to the work in hand (in the course of that work) as a novel, and to himself as a novelist, and was fond of letting the reader know that this novelist could direct the course of events according to his pleasure.[72]

The author's visible presence is seen as undermining the reality represented.

However, James does not share the Naturalistic respect for science, and does not wish the novel to achieve impersonality in the manner of a scientific report. Instead, he develops the concept of a human filter or *reflector*, a character through whom the events of the novel can be mediated to the reader. Human interest and human significance are thus maintained even in the absence of a personal author. Such an approach opens up the many issues associated with point-of-view – issues which had scarcely risen to notice under the previous novelistic practice of merely *accompanying* a leading character from place to place. It is in his dealings with these issues that James makes his most original contribution to the criticism of the novel.

Point-of-view is an aspect of treatment, and James always insists upon the importance of treatment. '[The novelist's] subject is what is given him . . . by a process with which we have nothing to do. . . . His treatment of it, on the other hand, is what he actively gives, and it is with what he gives that we are critically concerned.'[73] To the extent that a novel is successful, it is impossible to see the treatment as separate or secondary to the subject. James may sound like a Naturalist when claiming that a novel should represent real life without artificial rearrangement, but he can also make Aestheticist-like statements to the effect that 'it is art that *makes life,* makes interest, makes importance'.[74] And he is not far behind the Symbolists in emphasising the role of conscious craft and calculation:

> A picture without composition slights its most precious chance for beauty, and is moreover not composed at all unless the painter knows *how* that principle of health and safety, working as an absolutely premeditated art, has prevailed.[75]

There is no contradiction here, only a common paradox of modern criticism. For the art and composition praised by James have their impact not upon the subject-matter but upon the treatment, not upon the story but upon the medium through which the story is presented. Even the unity of a novel appears to James as a matter of some unified perceiving consciousness rather than a matter of causally convergent events. James carries the old critical principle of unity across into a new dimension, as did the Symbolists with their conception of musical structure and correspondences. When James focuses upon the application of art to the *medium,* his thinking about the novel is moving along a track parallel to the Symbolists' thinking about poetry.

The subsequent twists and turns of point-of-view criticism constitute a whole branch of literary theory. Percy Lubbock turned Jamesian impersonality into a dogma in *The Craft of Fiction* (1921); Wayne Booth successfully challenged that dogma in *The Rhetoric of Fiction* (1961). The concept of point-of-view was complicated with crucial discriminations by both Booth and Gérard Genette. In general, recent criticism has rediscovered an interest in personal authors, but without allowing them to return to their old position of authority. If anything, the personal author has been brought under point-of-view analysis of the kind previously applied to filtering, reflecting characters. Unfortunately, point-of-view criticism is too specialised to follow up further within the scope of this book.

Modernism and the avant-garde

Modernism arrived in the second decade of the twentieth century, not by a wave of influence passed on from country to country, but almost simultaneously, as by a general change of mood. Of course, Naturalism and Symbolism had already prepared the ground, while the First World War provides an obvious explanation for the general change of mood. Perhaps *too* obvious, since the beginnings of Modernism actually preceded the outbreak of hostilities. Nonetheless, the psychological impact of 'the Great War' confirmed those beginnings in the most overwhelming way.

The First World War changed two attitudes: the Naturalist belief in science, progress and human rationality, and the Symbolist pose of aloof indifference towards the conditions of ordinary practical life. As regards science, the quantum and relativity revolutions had already undermined the model of smoothly accumulating knowledge upon which nineteenth-century science had plumed itself (although it was not until after the war that those revolutions were accepted by the scientific community as a whole). Human rationality had also been challenged by certain new movements of thought, some of which will be examined in the next chapter. But the First World War was the supreme disproof of progress and human rationality, and vividly brought home the fact that science and technology could as easily advance towards Armageddon as towards Paradise. As for the Symbolist pose of aloof indifference, it was difficult to ignore the conditions of ordinary practical life in the face of wholesale death and destruction. Reading Mallarmé nowadays, the most curiously dated feature of his thinking is the effortless leap to such bloodless abstractions as the Idea, the Eternal, the Absolute, and the purity of poetry.

In other respects, however, Naturalism and Symbolism combined and complemented one another in Modernism. Thus poetry now took on the raw material of modern urban reality which the Naturalists had previously introduced into the novel. Conversely, the novel now took on many of the characteristics of Symbolist poetry. For example, a vision of correspondences might appear within the novel's action in the form of an *epiphany,* whereby a character finds his or her chaotic chronological life suddenly redeemed by a 'vertical' perception of total meaning and simultaneous connection. Or more commonly, the novel's descriptive details become motifs and are tied together over and above the action in symbolic correspondences. In this latter case, Naturalism contributes to the extent that Naturalistic representation encourages a proliferation of free descriptive details unconstrained by necessities of story; while Symbolism gives the writer something to do with such freedom. (The later plays of Ibsen and Chekhov already manifest the logic of this complementarity.) As the raw material becomes more raw, writers look to exercise their powers on the different level of the medium.

It is by its restless experimentation with the medium that Modernism most clearly distinguishes itself as a new development. The Symbolists had challenged the adequacy of ordinary language and had set up the alternative of a new kind of meaning; but, with a few famous exceptions, they had been generally content to work within established literary forms and formats. For the Modernists, however, everything had to be subjected to critique and rethought from scratch. What moved them was indeed their sense of being modern, that is, of living in a new kind of present where the old rules and traditions no longer applied. This mentality can of course be attributed to the First World War, which made so sudden and radical a break with the past; but it should also be traced back to the Naturalists, who had asserted their own modernity in response to a sense that the foundations of the world had shifted. Similarly with the remarkable multiplication of '-isms' and manifestos characteristic of the Modernist period (Imagism, Vorticism, Futurism, Expressionism, etc.), which can be traced back to Naturalism as the first programme fully conscious of its own revolutionary aims and group principles.

One product of such thinking in the Modernist period is the very important notion of the *avant-garde*. Under this notion, literature comes to define itself not as writing of higher quality but as writing ahead of its time, writing which is more advanced than the general sensibility and linguistic practice of the age. The writer is cast in the role of explorer and pathbreaker, leading the way for others to follow. So deeply ingrained has this notion become that we are nowadays almost surprised to realise that earlier writers and their audiences did not share it. Natural and obvious as it may appear, it is in fact a comparatively recent historical development.

Modernist experimentation places very heavy demands upon the reader. Under Modernism, all literature acquires the kind of difficulty that the Symbolists had introduced into poetry. But the difficulty of Modernist writing is not merely the product of internal literary evolution. It is also a response to a larger cultural context – specifically, a spectacular growth in new forms of popular culture. The period from around the end of the nineteenth century to the First World War saw the explosive arrival of the film industry, and a vastly expanded market for newspapers and 'entertainment' fiction, fuelled by the advent of mass literacy. In the face of this new cultural force, 'literature' (in another modification of the term) defined itself by deliberate opposition to the popular, the commercial, and the entertaining. The anti-democratic tendencies of Modernism were most forcefully expressed by Ortega y Gasset: 'The new art obviously addresses itself not to everybody, as did Romanticism, but to a specially gifted minority. Hence the indignation it arouses in the masses.'[76] More than ever, literature became an élite preoccupation; but the élite in this case was not so much an élite by class as an élite by specialisation. The markers of wealth and social position counted for less than full-time devotion to art.

As for the practical conditions of literary publication, the most significant development of the Modernist period was the rise of the 'little magazines', very limited in their circulation and usually very brief in their lifespan. Poetry in particular depended upon this outlet; experimental novels might slip in through the cracks in the commercial publishing industry or appear under the imprint of small private presses. In this period, lack of popular success came to be viewed not simply as an unfortunate side-effect but as virtually a proof of serious literary commitment.

Hulme and Pound

It is useful to distinguish between two wings of Modernism, especially in relation to poetry: on the one hand, such Symbolist-Modernists as Rilke, Blok, Jiménez and Valéry; on the other hand, such avant-garde Modernists as Benn, Mayakovsky and Apollinaire. The Symbolist–Modernists retained much of the mystical orientation of earlier Symbolism, and I have already discussed the theoretical position of Valéry as the most notable critic amongst this group of writers. By contrast, the avant-garde Modernists, a slightly later generation, were typically more cynical, more ironic, more materialistic, more technically experimental. In Anglo-American literature, where writers had long lingered under the influence of Victorian morality and late Romantic emotionalism, Modernism arrived all in a jump; not surprisingly, Anglo-American Modernists tended strongly to the avant-garde side. Here I shall consider Hulme and Pound as key innovators in the Anglo-American scene, and Eliot as the most notable writer-critic of all the avant-garde Modernists.

As a poet, T. E. Hulme was involved in the founding of Imagism, although his own output was minuscule. As a philosopher, he borrowed from various contemporary European sources, especially Henri Bergson. His poetic preferences were anti-Romantic; he particularly hated 'sloppy' emotionality and vague invocations of the infinite. 'It is essential to prove that beauty may be in small, dry things.'[77] For Hulme, Romanticism appeared as the enemy because Romanticism was still very much the dominant tradition in British poetry. By way of opposition, he called his own views 'Classical', a badge also adopted by Pound and Eliot. But Hulme had no classical love of universals, and Bergson's influence propelled him towards a very non-classical irrationalism. In general, the 'Classical' badge only distracts from the real nature of Anglo-American Modernism.

The 'small, dry things' onto which Hulme wants to direct attention are concrete particulars. He thinks of poetry as making us see some individual thing exactly as the poet has seen it. 'The great aim is accurate, precise and definite description.'[78] The thing described may be trivial rather than grand, amusing rather than soul-stirring – what counts is how well it is captured in words. 'Subject doesn't matter,' says Hulme, and he proposes a description of 'the curious way in which [a woman's] skirt rebounds from her heels'.[79] This is indeed one point upon which Naturalists, Symbolists and Modernists all agree: that no subjects are *intrinsically* more literary or poetic than any others.

Accurate description may seem an unambitious goal, but according to Hulme it is extraordinarily difficult. The cause of the difficulty is ordinary language. 'Language is by its very nature a communal thing; that is, it expresses never the exact thing but a compromise – that which is common to you, me and everybody.'[80] What's more, our ordinary words are liable to become so staled with habit that they no longer stimulate us to realise their meanings in perceptual terms. 'The old [epithets] cease to convey a physical thing and become abstract counters.'[81] Hulme also extends his diagnosis to the way in which words mould our perceptions in the first place: 'Things have been classified with a view to the use I can make of them. It is this classification I perceive rather than the real shape of things. I hardly see an object, but merely notice what class it belongs to.'[82] Like Mallarmé and Valéry, Hulme is dissatisfied with ordinary language; but, in a typically British modification, his dissatisfaction has less to do with capturing transcendental glimpses than with capturing individual, concrete perceptions.

Hulme defines the poet as someone engaged in 'a terrific struggle with language'.[83] In the first place, the poet must break through the limiting categories of language in order to recover a fresh perception of the real thing. In the second place, the poet must communicate that freshness by forcing the poem's language to reproduce the very shape of the perception. The highest form of poetic activity is 'the avoidance of conventional language in order to get the exact curve of the thing'.[84] It is the peculiar role of poetry to jolt readers out of their usual bad linguistic habits. Poetry 'always endeavours to arrest you, and to make you continuously see a physical thing, to prevent you gliding through an abstract process'.[85] No matter how trivial the particular thing reproduced in a particular poem, such jolting is beneficial for the general health of our linguistic and perceptual systems.

But the poet cannot simply coin hitherto unknown words: how then are conventional words to be given freshness of meaning? The answer is metaphor. 'Visual meanings can only be transferred by the new bowl of metaphor.'[86] For Hulme, metaphor is the heart and soul of poetry, a promotion of status that has since become common in twentieth-century Anglo-American criticism. But although metaphors are so important, their effectiveness is only temporary. 'You have continually to be searching out new metaphors . . . because the visual effect of a metaphor so soon dies.'[87] A poet might once have communicated a fresh perception by saying that 'the hill is *clothed* with trees', but habitual usage has long since reduced 'clothed' to just another abstract counter, a dead metaphor. Hulme even suggests that 'every word in the language originate[d] as a *live* metaphor'.[88] His theory allows for no permanently fresh metaphors or permanently fresh poetry. Instead, language requires endless renewal in an ongoing process of displacement and replacement.

As a tireless promoter of new programmes and manifestos, Ezra Pound exemplifies the exploratory spirit of the avant-garde. 'Artists are the antennae of the race,' he announces at the head of one essay.[89] He also exemplifies the specialist perspective of the avant-garde, despairing of the British public's attachment to non-technical, man-in-the-street judgements: 'they will not have a specialist's opinion as to what art is good'.[90] He hopes for a time when 'there is such a general understanding of the fact that poetry is an art and not a pastime . . . that the amateurs will cease to drown out the masters'.[91] And in a proposal that was to prove prophetic, he asks for 'definite subsidy of individual artists, writers, etc., such as will enable them to follow their highest ambitions without needing to conciliate the ignorant *en route*'.[92]

In many respects, Pound's views resemble Hulme's. He wants poetry to be 'austere, direct, free from emotional slither'; he warns the poet to 'go in fear of abstractions'; and he emphasises the necessity of accurate description almost to the point of valuing truth in Naturalistic terms: 'bad art is inaccurate art. It is art that makes false reports'.[93] Also like Hulme, Pound believes that poetry's primary role is to maintain the health of language:

> this function [of literature] is *not* the coercing or emotionally persuading, or bullying or suppressing people into the acceptance of any one set or any six sets of opinions . . . it has to do with the clarity and vigour of 'any and every' thought and opinion. It has to do with maintaining the very cleanliness of the tools. . . . [T]he individual cannot think and communicate his thought . . . without words, and the solidity and validity of these words is in the care of the damned and despised *litterati*. [94]

Society may damn or despise its literary writers, but they perform an invisible social service of the utmost importance.

For Pound, the poet's struggle is especially against 'excessive or bloated' language; by contrast, poetry aspires to 'maximum efficiency of expression'.[95] Elsewhere he exhorts the poet to 'use no superfluous word', and states that 'great literature is simply language charged with meaning to the utmost possible degree'.[96] The idea of poetic meaning as a uniquely concentrated form of meaning is perhaps Pound's most distinctive contribution to literary theory. His important definition of the image partakes of the same idea:

> An 'Image' is that which presents an intellectual and emotional complex in an instant of time. . . . It is the presentation of such a 'complex' instantaneously which gives that sense of sudden liberation; that sense of freedom from time limits and space limits; that sense of sudden growth, which we experience in the presence of the greatest works of art.[97]

As distinct from an extended passage of description, the image has a kind of momentary intensity, like a flashbulb going off. This version of the image conditions the major movements in Anglo-American criticism over the next few decades, along with Pound's general insistence upon concentrated meaning, and the emphasis (in both Hulme and Pound) upon concrete, primarily visual presentation.

T. S. Eliot

Like Hulme and Pound, T. S. Eliot is a writer-critic who pushes the cause of his own new kind of writing. But he also inclines to a more 'catholic' form of criticism, ranging respectfully over the literature of the past. The will-to-respect is indeed a curious trait in Eliot's make-up, both as poet and as critic. As he might almost have said of himself: only those who have heterodox thoughts and radical impulses know what it means to want to escape from these things.[98] Eliot shares the usual Modernist élitism in respect of art, but whereas other Modernists like to cast themselves in the role of an élite revolutionary cadre, Eliot prefers the role of a defender of traditional hierarchical values.

Eliot's most famous single argument is his argument for authorial impersonality, against the Romantic view of poetry as self-expression. For Eliot as for Mallarmé and Valéry, the poet necessarily disappears as the language of the poem takes over. Once again, the poem's existence as a verbal artifact is seen as blocking any direct communication of experience between poet and reader:

> *If* poetry is a form of communication, yet that which is to be communicated is the poem itself. . . . The poem's existence is somewhere between the writer and the reader; it has a reality which is not simply the reality of what the writer is trying to 'express'. [Eliot's italics: he has earlier suggested that the term 'communication' may beg the question][99]

In what has become a commonplace of twentieth-century theory, Eliot also argues that the very process of verbalisation will create new experiences which even the poet could not have envisaged beforehand. 'By the time [the experience] has settled down into a poem it may be so different from the original experience as to be hardly recognisable . . . what is there to be communicated was not in existence before the poem was completed.'[100]

Eliot is particularly concerned to reject the Romantic interest in pre-existing *emotion*. 'Poetry is not a turning loose of emotion, but an escape from emotion.'[101] The only relevant kind of emotion 'has its life in the poem and not in the history of the poet'.[102] One way of getting emotion into the poem is by the projection of an independent *objective correlative*. According to Eliot's definition, an objective correlative is 'a set of objects, a situation, a chain of events which shall be the formula of that *particular* emotion; such that when the external facts, which must terminate in sensory experience, are given, the emotion is immediately evoked'.[103] Clearly, the objective correlative is an extension or close relative of the symbol: a concrete image standing for something non-concrete, representing something beyond itself.

Pre-existing thought is also ruled out of consideration. Eliot has no objection to philosophical ideas in poetry: 'the possible interests of a poet are unlimited; the more intelligent he is the better; . . . our only condition is that he turn [his interests] into poetry'.[104] But the process of 'turning into poetry' leaves truth-value behind. Eliot draws an absolute distinction between the value of philosophy as philosophy and the value of poetry as poetry. Dante's system of beliefs must be understood by the reader of Dante's poetry, 'but you are not called upon to believe them yourself'.[105]

For Eliot, emotions and thoughts are valuable in a poem not as elements in themselves, but to the extent that they enter into relationships with other emotions, other thoughts. 'For it is not the "greatness", the intensity, of the emotions, the components, but the intensity of the artistic process . . . under which fusion takes place, that counts.'[106] And not only the fusion of emotions with emotions or thoughts with thoughts, but a fusion of disparate experience across all levels and domains:

> When a poet's mind is perfectly equipped for its work, it is constantly amalgamating disparate experience; the ordinary man . . . falls in love, or reads Spinoza, and these two experiences have nothing to do with each other, or with the noise of the typewriter or the smell of cooking; in the mind of the poet these experiences are always forming new wholes.[107]

The formation of new wholes is viewed as the special business of poetry. What the poet expresses is not a personality but 'a particular medium . . . in which impressions and experiences combine in peculiar and unexpected ways'.[108]

There is a resemblance here to the Symbolist vision of correspondences and relationships, and the above quotations might well be set alongside Valéry's previously quoted description of the poetic state of mind connecting well-known things and beings in ways quite different from the ordinary. But there is also a shift of emphasis. Eliot has very little to say about the nature of the relationships to be achieved, but a great deal to say about the heterogeneity of the material to be overcome in the achieving. The essential virtue for Eliot is not mystical vision but sheer inclusiveness. He values a maximum quantity of elements brought into the poem – 'the concentration . . . of a very great number of experiences' – and regards 'variety and complexity' as a necessary feature of writing in the varied and complex state of twentieth-century civilisation.[109] The shift of theoretical emphasis corresponds to the difference between Valéry's "La Jeune Parque" and Eliot's "The Waste Land". Eliot takes pleasure in the leap between incongruous elements for its own sake – a new kind of taste which decisively separates Modernism (and Postmodernism) from Symbolism.

The medium in which the amalgamation of disparate experience takes place is not only language but also the poet's mind. The poet's mind becomes a *medium* when it serves as an essentially passive channel for elements to pass through: 'The poet's mind is in fact a receptacle for seizing and storing up numberless feelings, phrases, images, which remain there until all the particles which can unite to form a new compound are present together.'[110] It is also significant that Eliot specifies 'phrases' amongst other elements in the poet's mind. The poem is effectively 'written through' by pre-existing language. A similar suggestion is that the best parts of a poet's work 'may be those in which the dead poets, his ancestors, assert their immortality most vigorously'.[111] Taken in conjunction with a poem like 'The Waste Land', Eliot's criticism here foreshadows the later Postmodernist concept of intertextuality, where every text is a channel 'written through' by earlier texts.

In 'Tradition and the Individual Talent', however, Eliot seeks to view such channelling in a somewhat different light, as an act of homage towards the 'dead poets'. The tradition is larger than the individual talent. But this conservative twist is falsely imposed upon the situation. If the poet should be, as Eliot also claims, 'the servant of his language, rather than the master of it', then the authority of all poets is ultimately undermined.[112] It is not only the modern poets who are 'written through' by language. To the extent that language takes charge, the poet is not performing deliberate *acts,* whether of homage or of any other kind.

Elsewhere, Eliot undermines the authority of all poets in another respect:

> A poem may appear to mean very different things to different readers, and all of these meanings may be different from what the author thought he meant. . . . The reader's interpretation may differ from the author's and be equally valid – it may even be better. There may be much more in a poem than the author was aware of.[113]

So far as meaning is concerned, the poet has no special rights as the source of the poem. And what applies to individual readers also applies to whole generations: 'each generation, like each individual, brings to the contemplation of art its own categories of appreciation, makes its own demands upon art, and has its own uses for art'.[114] Eliot follows through on the consequences of this position when he accepts that 'the past should be altered by the present as much as the present is directed by the past'.[115] But to change the past in this way is certainly not very respectful. Eliot's arguments are radical in their implications, in spite of the traditionalist gloss he seeks to put upon them.

Eliot himself revises the past in the interests of the present with his famous model of the *dissociation of sensibility.* According to this model, the seventeenth century, in the poetry of the Metaphysicals, 'seems for more than a moment to gather up and to digest into its art all the experience of the human mind';[116] but Restoration and Augustan verse focuses upon thought to the exclusion of feeling; and the verse of the Age of Sentiment and the Romantics reacts by focusing upon feeling to the exclusion of thought. Or, in a slightly different version, the dissociation appears from the outset in the contrast between the 'magniloquence' of Milton (who can hardly be taken to exemplify feeling) and the intellectual cleverness of Dryden. This is less of an opposition between contents, more of an opposition between forms of discourse. Eliot, who shares the common Modernist view that the health of language is the poet's peculiar responsibility, blames both Milton and Dryden for 'injur[ing] the language'.[117]

In seeking to re-establish connection with the Metaphysicals, Eliot was undoubtedly moved by the genuine affinity existing between

Baroque and Modernist poetry. But his discussion of Marvell under-plays the disconcerting edginess of the Baroque manner and concentrates instead upon a kind of balanced wide-mindedness. Thus wit in the Metaphysical sense is said to involve 'a recognition, implicit in the expression of every experience, of other kinds of experience which are possible'.[118] Eliot goes even further in the essay 'What Is a Classic?', where he praises the virtues of 'comprehensiveness' and 'maturity'.[119] Such virtues may involve inclusiveness, but not the sheer inclusive-ness of heterogeneous material suggested in Eliot's earlier criticism or displayed in Eliot's earlier poetry. Once again, Eliot's will-to-respect leads to the blurring of an important discrimination.

Eliot's criticism is a kind of conceptual crossroads leading on to various later critical movements. In the Anglo-American world, the work of the Modernist writer-critics is only the beginning of Modernist literary theory. Similarly in Russia, where the creative revo-lution of Russian Futurism inspired the general theory of Russian Formalism. These further developments will be examined in Chapters 8 and 9.

7   New Developments in Theory

The Symbolist and Modernist poet-critics typically defined literature as a very special realm. In the face of growing forces which they felt to be hostile, they insisted upon a great difference separating their own kind of activity from all other human activities. This defensive–exclusive stance was given a new application by later critical movements developing out of Modernism. For Formalists in Russia, Cambridge Critics in Britain and New Critics in America, it was a natural next step to suppose that the criticism of literature was also a very special realm, and that their own kind of thinking was also quite different from other kinds of thinking. During the first half of the twentieth century, literary criticism was generally busy with proclamations of autonomy and the erection of barriers to interdisciplinary traffic.

Nonetheless, there were many potential connections between new developments in literary criticism and new theories appearing in philosophy, linguistics, psychology and political sociology. The new theories on the latter side frequently extended into discussions of literature. But the dominant schools of professional literary criticism disdained and dismissed such intrusions. Only in the second half of the twentieth century did the interdisciplinary barriers begin to crumble. In presenting the new theories at this stage, I am following the chronology of their appearance rather than the chronology of their much-delayed impact upon literary criticism.

Nietzsche

Nietzsche's philosophical works were written in the 1870s and 1880s, but it was only after the turn of the century that his thinking became widely known. Nietzsche follows Schopenhauer to the extent of seeing everything in human existence as driven by blind will and desire, which consciousness merely rationalises after the event. *'This world is the Will to Power – and nothing else.'* [1] But Nietzsche, more consistent and thoroughgoing than Schopenhauer, refuses to search for loopholes allowing special momentary escapes from this condition. Instead, he accepts and embraces the blind force from which Schopenhauer can only turn with abhorrence. Rejecting Schopenhauer's pessimism as the traditional philosopher's response to irrationality, Nietzsche seeks to develop a new attitude of joy – albeit a stern and tragic kind of joy.

As has been seen, Schopenhauer finds one of his most important loopholes in calm aesthetic contemplation. But Nietzsche proposes irrational drives as the basis for art. 'All kinds of ecstasy, however differently produced, have [the] power to create art.'[2] This claim features prominently in his first major work, *The Birth of Tragedy*, which seeks to overthrow the traditional view of Greek art as exemplifying qualities of purity, lucidity, poise, and formal harmony. Nietzsche does not deny the presence of such qualities in Greek tragedy, associating them with the Greek god Apollo. But he also recognises a darker side, which Classical scholars and critics had preferred to ignore. Whereas attention had been previously focused upon the audience's identification with the individual tragic protagonist (as in Schopenhauer's theory of tragedy), Nietzsche argues that the audience also, and more importantly, identifies with the chorus. 'The audience of Attic tragedy discovered *itself* in the chorus of the orchestra.'[3] And the chorus has a ritualistic role, associated with music, and expressing communal feelings, dark fears, instinctive premonitions. In this respect, the experience of Greek tragedy involves ecstasy and intoxication, a merging across boundaries, and surrender of the individual self. These qualities Nietzsche associates with the Greek god Dionysus. 'The mystical jubilation of Dionysos . . . breaks the spell of individuation and opens a path to the maternal womb of being.'[4] Nietzsche even draws an analogy to rituals of sacrifice in order to explain the audience's paradoxical delight in the pity and terror of tragedy. '[The audience] will have . . . seen . . . the tragic hero in epic clarity and beauty and yet rejoiced in his destruction.'[5] In his concern for the 'primitive' elements in Greek art, Nietzsche foreshadows what has become a major trend of modern Classical research and scholarship.

Nietzsche also foreshadows a view which has become widespread in general literary theory over the past twenty years: the view that all art is 'interested'. Schopenhauer, drawing from Kant, had asserted that aesthetic contemplation is peculiarly disinterested, peculiarly liberated from the usual urgings of selfish desire. Nietzsche ridicules such assertions:

> When our estheticians tirelessly rehearse, in support of Kant's view, that the spell of beauty enables us to view even *nude* female statues 'disinterestedly' we may be allowed to laugh a little at their expense. The experiences of artists in this delicate matter are rather more 'interesting'.[6]

Nietzsche's approach works by exposing the artist's unconfessed desires. Pointing to art as a discharge of energy, and to the absolute egotism of the artist, he asks: 'What instincts does [the artist] sublimate?'[7] Sexual and sensual urges are included as possible motives, along with a desire for success or power. Even the urge to avoid sexual urges may be seen as a form of selfish interest – and Nietzsche, with a typical undermining twist of psychology, suggests that Schopenhauer himself was 'interested' in precisely this manner.

As an interested activity, art is not superior to other human activities for the reasons advanced by Schopenhauer. But since all human activities are equally interested, it is also not inferior. Nietzsche's critique of disinterest cuts even more deeply against the kind of impersonal objectivity traditionally claimed by scientists and philosophers. 'A prejudiced proposition, idea, or "suggestion", which is generally their heart's desire abstracted and refined, is defended by them with arguments sought out after the event.'[8] What Nietzsche calls the Will to Truth is merely an offshoot of the Will to Power, a means of establishing control or mastery. In all cases, the world is constructed by will, and supposed truths about that world are constructed by acts of interpretation:

> 'truth' is not something which is present and which had to be found and discovered; it is something *which has to be created* and which *gives* its name . . . to the Will to overpower, which in itself has no purpose: to introduce truth is . . . an *active determining* – it is not a process of becoming conscious of something, which in itself is fixed and determined.[9]

Many interpretations are possible, but none can be finally validated against independent facts. 'There are many kinds of eyes . . . therefore there must be many kinds of "truths", and consequently there can be no truth.'[10] What appears as true depends upon the choice of perspective.

Nietzsche also undermines scientific and philosophical claims by the very modern strategy of challenging the linguistic categories upon which they depend. 'For all its detachment and freedom from emotion,' says Nietzsche, 'our science is still the dupe of linguistic habits' – as in its reification of energy or its construction of atoms as the ultimate 'out there' things.[11] Similarly with philosophy: the family resemblance between all Indian, Greek and German philosophising is due to an affinity between the Indo-European languages employed: 'owing to the unconscious domination and guidance of similar grammatical functions . . . it cannot but be that everything is prepared at the outset for a similar development and succession of philosophical systems'.[12] For Nietzsche, language enters into the way the world is constructed; no language ever simply reflects the already-existing structure of an already-existing world.

Above all, Nietzsche sees language as fundamentally metaphorical. To apply a word to a new situation requires the active creation of a new relation, seizing upon one potential similarity out of many possible similarities. At bottom, the 'truth' expressed in language can never be more than 'a mobile army of metaphors, metonymies, anthropomorphisms; in short a sum of human relations which become poetically and rhetorically intensified, metamorphosed, adorned'.[13] Nietzsche points to the metaphorical gendering of 'der Baum' ('tree' in German) as masculine and 'die Pflanze' ('plant') as feminine; he might equally have pointed to the metaphorical leap which carries a word from concrete to abstract senses (from the *flow* of a river to the *flow* of an argument; from the *branch* of a tree to the *branch* of a corporation). The danger, as Nietzsche sees it, is that such metaphors are liable to forget their metaphorical status. As they become 'powerless to affect the senses', so they also begin to seem 'fixed, canonic, binding'.[14] Instead of an ongoing series of creative raids, language congeals into a 'great edifice of ideas'.[15] We lose sight of the creative act which momentarily relates one individual leaf to other very different leaves, and falsely imagine that some eternal universal essence stands behind the single word 'leaf'. Such are the 'ideas' upon which science and philosophy are built.

These arguments overthrow the traditional scale by which human assertions are judged as more or less true. (Parallel Nietzschean arguments overthrow the traditional scale by which human acts are judged as more or less moral.) But another scale emerges from such overthrowing. If the world *is* the Will to Power, then assertions and acts can be judged as more or less honest and straightforward in manifesting that Will. Nietzsche despises disguised, surreptitious manifestations in which the Will to Power pretends to be something other than itself – as in the case of science. (Similarly with the Christian ethos of meekness, which Nietzsche sees as a means for the weak to gain power by persuading the strong that power is immoral.) By contrast, art and literature offer the possibility of a very direct manifestation of the Will. For art and literature do not claim to be telling truths: 'In art the lie becomes consecrated, the will to deception has good conscience at its back.'[16] Writers need submit neither to 'the facts' nor to social morality, they can create their own facts and values out of themselves. And, of course, writers delight in the creation of new metaphors. So, although literature can not be said to tell truths, it can be said to *act truly*, that is, in accordance with the real nature of the human condition. In this respect, aesthetic creation becomes a model for all human activity: 'Only as an aesthetic product can the world be justified.'[17] For reasons almost diametrically opposed to Schopenhauer's, Nietzsche also elevates art to a position of supreme importance: 'Metaphysics, morality, religion, science, – all these things are but the offshoot of [man's] will to art.'[18]

Nietzsche's highest praise goes out to literature that revels in its own free creativity:

> There are writers who, by portraying the impossible as possible, and by speaking of morality and genius as if both were merely a mood or whim, elicit a feeling of high-spirited freedom, as if man were rising up on tiptoe and simply had to dance out of inner pleasure.[19]

Mimetic writing does not display the virtues he admires: 'Art is not an imitation of nature but its metaphysical supplement, raised up beside it in order to overcome it.'[20] He also values a certain attitude on the part of the artist, a grand or noble manner, which he especially associates with Greek art. In this respect, Nietzsche is an anti-Romantic:

> there are two kinds of sufferers: on the one hand those that suffer from *overflowing vitality*, who need Dionysian art, and require a

tragic view and insight into life; and on the other hand those who suffer from *reduced vitality*, who seek repose, quietness, calm seas, and deliverance from themselves through art or knowledge, or else intoxication, spasm, bewilderment and madness. All Romanticism . . . responds to the twofold craving of the *latter*.[21]

Nietzsche has only contempt for the Romantic expression of weakly self-centred states of mind; nonetheless, his own theory is Romantic and expressive to the extent that it focuses upon the expression of the writer's creative impulse. It is no accident that the previously quoted passage in which Nietzsche ridicules the supposed disinterest of the viewer also redirects attention towards the more 'interesting' experiences of the artist. For Nietzsche, the most overwhelming experience for the receiver is a kind of identification with the artist – a surge of power in sympathy with the artist's creating will.

Freud

Unlike Nietzsche, Freud embraced no radical new *attitude* towards the irrational, but sought to retain an objective and generally scientific standpoint for his own studies. Nonetheless, his studies of the unconscious gave the irrational a new site, a new importance and a new degree of specificity. Freud saw himself as performing a third crucial decentring of the human self-image: as Copernicus had shown that the Earth is not the centre of the universe and as Darwin had shown that the human species is not the centre or purpose of evolution, so Freudian psychoanalysis would show that human consciousness is not master even within its own house, in the individual psyche.[22] Freudian psychoanalysis is unsettling, not because it recognises blind bodily instincts over which we have no control, but because it posits a kind of *thinking* about which we do not even know. The Freudian unconscious exists not merely below consciousness but as a kind of alternative to consciousness. With a will and goals of its own, it resists and seeks to outmanoeuvre our conscious will and goals.

In Freud's account, the unconscious is born when simple drives towards gratification are postponed or transposed under pressure from social constraints and the reality principle. The energy thus thwarted splits off to produce the unconscious, which constitutes the reject bin, as it were, for images and impulses now excluded by consciousness. As the mind comes to itself elsewhere, the excluded material develops its own modes of connection and laws of organisation. And the energy in the unconscious continues to seek to manifest itself, with an urge to self-expression which has no equivalent in any merely biological causality.

In so far as the unconscious is a kind of thinking, it works with meanings; in so far as it seeks to express itself, it strives to make those meanings emerge through the socially dominant level of consciously controlled meaning. Unconscious meanings thus lie in a hidden, ulterior position behind ordinary, rational meaning – not unlike the hidden ulterior meanings buried in Symbolist and Modernist poetry. And in both cases, it is impossible to read off the ulterior meanings simply by reference to some clear-cut, regular code. The analogy is particularly close when Freud discusses the psychoanalytic interpretation of dreams:

> the dream-work carries out a very unusual kind of transcription of the dream-thoughts: it is not a word-for-word or a sign-for-sign translation; nor is it a selection made according to fixed rules . . . it is something different and far more complicated.[23]

Compared with ordinary language, the modes of symbolisation are here unpredictable, open and suggestive.

Freud spells out two general processes operating in dream-symbolisation. In *displacement*, one element stands in for some other (unacceptable or taboo) element. The relation between the two separate elements is a matter of 'allusion', typically following the line of 'the most external and remote relations'.[24] In *condensation*, only one element is involved, but a fragment or part of the element represents the whole. In the standard case, this occurs when various elements are condensed together, so that a figure in a dream may combine representative parts of several real people – for example, the look of person A plus the dress of person B plus the behaviour of person C, and so on.[25] Such processes are akin to certain well-known 'irrational' processes of poetic language: in metaphor, something presented in a poem stands in for and alludes to some other thing not presented; in metonymy, something presented stands in for and alludes to some co-occurring thing (and in synecdoche, as a special case of metonymy, a component part represents the whole). However, it should be noted that *displacement* does not turn upon a relation of resemblance: on the contrary, Freud prefers to emphasise the sheer difference between the two elements. This goes against traditional accounts of metaphor, but is somewhat less in opposition to twentieth-century accounts, where the role of resemblance has been generally downplayed.

In the case of the composite dream figure representing several real people, it is clear that a single element can carry several meanings. And according to Freud, multiple and ambiguous meanings are in fact characteristic of all symbolisation in dreams. Analysing his own 'dream of the botanical monograph', for example, he discovers

> constituted 'nodal points' upon which a great number of the dream-thoughts converged, and because they had several meanings in connection with the interpretation of the dream . . . each of the elements of the dream's content turns out to have been 'overdetermined'.[26]

Overdetermination is Freud's term for the motivation of a single dream-motif by a number of different, even contradictory, meanings in the unconscious.

Many features of Freudian interpretation can be paralleled in the methods of Modernist-oriented literary critics. As will be noted in subsequent chapters, these critics typically see themselves as divining meanings which do not appear under standard linguistic codes; seek out ambiguities and multiple meanings; and regard poetic language as peculiarly condensed in a way that justifies the unfolding of vast ulterior complexes from apparently small surface details. They also find their divinations confirmed when a hypothesised symbolism applies successfully all across a poem – just as Freud finds confirmation in successful application all across a dream.

In the Postmodernist period, such parallels have been supplemented by deliberate borrowings. In particular, Postmodernist-oriented critics have noticed how often Freud's analyses focus upon linguistic phenomena. Even in his examination of dreams, where images are naturally the main elements, Freud devotes special attention to the occurrence of words – dreamed words which present themselves as charged with a strange significance. According to Freud, such words do not point to conceptual senses in the ordinary manner; rather, their meaning is a kind of connotation surrounding the physical body of the word. 'Words are frequently treated in dreams as though they were things.'[27] Interpretation thus proceeds by looking for physically related words, for sound-semblances and puns. Freud also draws upon philological research to show that the behaviour of meaning in the unconscious is analogous to the behaviour of meaning in early or archaic languages. 'Concepts are still ambivalent in dream-language, and unite within themselves contrary meanings – as is the case, according to the hypotheses of philologists, in the oldest roots of historical languages.'[28] Freud refers to an example from one particular philologist:

> in Ancient Egyptian, 'ken' originally meant 'strong' and 'weak'. . . . It was only later, by means of slight modifications of the original homologous word, that two distinct representations were arrived at of the contraries included in it.[29]

Even within the seemingly stable single word, meaning can slide between opposing poles, can be tilted across from one extreme to the other. Freud notes occasional survivals of the same tendency in modern languages: in English, for example, the word 'cleave' means both 'to adhere to' and also 'to split apart'.[30] This argument is important because it relates so closely to the deconstructive methods of post-Derridean literary interpretation, where the meaning of a single word is deliberately tilted across from one extreme to the other. In his explanation of *the uncanny* or 'unheimlich' in literature, Freud himself executes a proto-deconstructive move on the German word 'heimlich', which refers to what is homely and familiar, but also to what is hidden and kept out of sight. Drawing upon Grimm's dictionary, Freud is able to show that 'heimlich' in the second sense is actually very close to its supposed antithesis, 'unheimlich'. He concludes that what was once homely and familiar – for example, the 'home' of the mother's genitals or body – may be hidden and excluded from consciousness until it appears as dangerous and strange, i.e. uncanny.[31]

Last but not least, Freud also considers the effect of the unconscious upon ordinary linguistic utterance. The theory of parapraxes – or Freudian slips – comes into play whenever the unconscious interferes with the flow of ordinary utterance. If someone utters an irrelevant or meaningless word in place of an intended word, Freud sees the 'accident' as unconsciously motivated. So, a young man, offering to 'begleitdigen' a lady, consciously wanted to 'begleiten' (= accompany) her, but unconsciously wanted to 'beleidigen' (= insult) her.[32] At other times, the unconscious may 'speak' by refusing meanings, by producing gaps and discontinuities. In recent criticism, the interpretation of gaps and discontinuities, of what is *not* said, has become a whole art of ulterior reading.

In spite of so much promising potential, Freud's own literary applications of his theory are disappointing. His attention to language in dreams, jokes and everyday behaviour seems to diminish rather than increase when he turns to literature. Confronting a literary text, his first move is to project for analysis some extra-textual individual psyche, cither that of the author (e.g. Jensen as the author of *Gradiva*) or that of a dramatic character (e.g. Hamlet in *Hamlet*).[33] His immediate disciples pursued the same psychobiographical orientation: notably, Ernest Jones in his book on Hamlet and Marie Bonaparte in her book on Poe.

Freud's general ideas about literature are similarly disappointing. His attitude towards writers has all the condescension of the serious-minded scientist towards the escapist daydreamer:

> An artist is . . . in rudiments an introvert, not far removed from neurosis. He is oppressed by excessively powerful instinctual needs. He desires to win honour, power, wealth, fame and the love of women; but he lacks the means for achieving these satisfactions. Consequently, like any other unsatisfied man, he turns away from reality and transfers all his interest, and his libido too, to the wishful constructions of his life of phantasy.[34]

Although Freud sometimes talks of such constructions in terms of sublimation, he seems more often inclined to regard them as mere delusive trickery. '[The artist] understands how to work over his daydreams in such a way as to make them lose what is too personal about them and repels strangers . . . how to tone them down so that they do not easily betray their origin.'[35] In particular, the writer's arrested desires can be gratified through an identification with the triumphant protagonist: 'in a certain fashion he actually becomes the hero, the king, the creator, or the favourite he desired to be, without following the long roundabout path of making real alterations in the external world'.[36] To the extent that such daydreams are suitably toned down and depersonalised, readers can also enjoy the same proxy gratifications, the same relief from unwanted tensions.

Freud assumes that neither writer nor readers are conscious of the processes underlying their own gratifications or relief. This assumption allows no room for the self-proclaimed mission of Modernist writers, to challenge and disturb and promote new awareness. Not surprisingly, early Freudian critics had little influence upon Modernist-influenced critics, who took a very lofty view of the writer's role. More recent critics have taken a less lofty view, being more inclined to allocate to themselves the mission of promoting new awareness; and they have been correspondingly less reluctant to discover in a text unconscious symptoms of which neither writer nor (ordinary) readers are aware. Nonetheless, recent critics at least allow the writer to *matter,* interpreting the symptoms in the text as indicative of a widespread state of affairs in society as a whole. By contrast, Freud's approach is essentially medical, interpreting the symptoms in the text as indicative of the merely personal problems of the individual writer.

Saussure

Freudian psychoanalysis was part of a general trend, at the end of the nineteenth and start of the twentieth centuries, to extend the sway of science over whole new domains of the human world. From the standpoint of literary theory, the most relevant of the new human sciences was linguistics. Whereas nineteenth-century philology had focused upon the historical evolution of languages, in line with the overwhelming historical bent of the nineteenth century, the new study of language focused upon simultaneous relationships and formal structures in language. Structural Linguistics was launched by Ferdinand de Saussure in a course of lectures delivered from 1906 to 1911, and published from notes in 1916.

Saussure proposed a new object for linguists to study: not *parole* or the endlessly varying proliferation of actual utterances, but *langue* or the system of rules and categories which make such utterances possible. Native speakers carry the system of *langue* in their heads, just as chess players carry in their heads the system of rules for playing all conceivable games of chess. But since language is what makes human beings human, the system of *langue* must be implanted at a very early stage, before the individual is able to exercise any power of choice or control. 'A language cannot therefore be treated simply as a form of contract,' says Saussure; in *langue*, 'the linguistic sign eludes the control of our will'.[37] Even society as a whole can not make conscious decisions about *langue* – cannot, for example, decide to shift the meaning of a particular word in a particular direction. For this system of rules and categories determines all our thinking, and so cannot itself be summoned into conscious thought (at least, not under normal non-scientific circumstances). *Langue* is implanted within us, yet remains outside us – not unlike the unconscious, in Freud's theory of the human psyche.

As for the organisation of *langue*, it is structured through associative relations – again, not unlike the Freudian unconscious. Saussure unfolds the options of the system along branches of likeness and difference. In English, for example, to opt for 'hip' is to opt against 'hit', to opt for 'cat' is to opt against 'pat' – phonetically similar words, but with a decisive difference. Or, in the realm of meaning, to opt for 'hot' is to opt against 'cold', to opt for 'rise' is to opt against 'fall'. Language is full of such oppositions, as amply attested by the organisation of Roget's Thesaurus.

In the above examples, a difference – as between 'rise' and 'fall' – is built upon a common ground – of 'vertical movement', as it were. But 'vertical' itself exists by opposition to 'horizontal', 'movement' by opposition to 'stasis'. Saussure concludes that, in the total system of *langue*, 'there are only differences, *and no positive terms*'.[38] As regards meaning, this does away with the need to posit some image or representation or set of memories that the individual calls to mind as the concept of a word. (And philosophers have long struggled with the impossibility of imagining how such representations might actually look in experience.) Instead

> the concepts in question are purely differential . . . defined not positively, in terms of their content, but negatively by contrast with other items in the same system. What characterises each most exactly is being whatever the others are not.[39]

After all, could anyone understand the concept of 'rise' without also understanding the concept of 'fall'? or 'hot' without 'cold'? In Saussure's system, word meanings are empty compartments held in place by a structure of mutually supporting boundaries.

Relations of likeness and difference are not peculiar to language (in the way that true grammatical relations are: see chapter 2 of my

Beyond Superstructuralism). The human mind can apply a perspective of likeness and difference to any raw material; and the human
mind has *already* worked likeness and difference into the construction of human signs. For all human signs operate by either–or
contrasts marked upon a common ground. In traffic signals, for
example, the lights are similar in appearance and brightness, but their
variations of colour – red versus green versus amber – function as
absolute differences. The Structural Linguists' approach to *langue* is
thus potentially extensible to the entire field of human signs. In a
moment of prophecy, Saussure foretells the coming of a general semiology or science of signs, wherein 'the laws which semiology will
discover will be laws applicable in linguistics'.[40]

Marxism and literary theory
(*Engels, Lukács, Benjamin, Brecht, Adorno*)

Marxism also posits a kind of unconscious: the real relations of
production which govern human behaviour, but which are masked or
hidden from consciousness. In the first half of the twentieth century,
versions of Marxism arising outside the USSR focused upon the way
in which industrial capitalism had substituted machine-like relations
for genuine human relations. This relative shift of theoretical emphasis was accompanied by a relative shift of interest away from *Das
Capital* and towards Marx's earlier writings, away from scientific
economics and towards such socio-cultural topics as *commodity
fetishism* and the *alienation* of workers from the products of their
work. One twentieth-century theorist, the Hungarian Georg Lukács,
advanced the notion of *reification,* according to which the dominant
model of the thing-like commodity infects all human existence, until
even interpersonal relations take the form of a relation between
things. In similar vein, the German theorist Theodor Adorno
condemned the rise of *instrumental reason* or *technological reason,*
whereby human lives are brought under the sway of a means-oriented
scientificist rationalism, with no sense of ultimate human goals.
Under these more humanist versions of Marxism, the enemy was no
longer simply the ruling class, but the whole dehumanising 'system'.

At the same time, Marxist theorists began to pay more attention to
aesthetic production, including literature. But no single Marxist
perspective on literature emerged. Lukács and Adorno arrived at

almost antithetical positions, while a third position was worked out in the writings of Benjamin and Brecht. Different literary tastes led to strikingly divergent theoretical arguments.

Lukács' position was foreshadowed by Friedrich Engels, who shared a similar admiration for nineteenth-century realist novels. Engels takes it for granted that Marxists must learn to see social reality clearly in order to change it. He believes that realist novels can assist in developing clear sight, without being under any obligation to preach the desirable direction of change. Writing to Minna Kautsky in 1885, he suggests that 'the [political] purpose must become manifest from the situation and the action themselves without being expressly pointed out'.[41] And in a letter to Margaret Harkness, he goes so far as to allow that 'the realism I allude to may crop out even in spite of the author's opinions'.[42] He cites the example of Balzac, whose novels yield valuable insights into social reality in spite of the fact that Balzac's own expressed political opinions were royalist and reactionary.

Lukács turned this point of view into a fully elaborated literary theory. Naturally, the insights of the great realists can be put to practical use, but considerations of practical use must not be allowed to dominate over an initial moment of detached, aesthetic contemplation:

> a truly profound aesthetic development is not possible without regard to moral problems and feelings; in the realm of aesthetics, however, these feelings must remain contemplative . . . the problems remain problems, they 'merely' broaden man's horizon . . . without going over into practice in a direct manner.[43]

Lukács insists upon concrete 'reflection' as against abstract propaganda, and has no time for 'the notion of literature-as-illustration'.[44] The reactionary Sir Walter Scott joins the reactionary Balzac as a further example of a writer's realism triumphing over his political prejudices.

For Lukács, however, realism is more problematic than for Engels. Looking back from a twentieth-century perspective, he is compelled to confront the evolution of realism into Naturalism. This evolution appears to Lukács as an entirely unfortunate development, which he dates from the failure of the 1848 revolutions in Europe. The Naturalist copying of mere surfaces yields no insights of the kind which Lukács, as a Marxist, most values: insights into the deeper historical currents underlying a given state of society. Rejecting 'the lifeless and false objectivity of an "impartial" imitation', he thus has to insist upon a pre-shaping 'perspective' on the part of the novelist, a 'hierarchy of significance' under which some things matter more than others.[45] His distinction between realist *narration* and Naturalist *description* reinforces the point: 'Narration establishes proportions, description merely levels.'[46] By describing human beings in exactly the same way as things, the Naturalists turn human beings into inanimate 'still lives', devoid of purpose and potential.[47] According to Lukács, this is yet another manifestation of the tendency to reification.

Lukács sees Modernism as continuing the vices of Naturalism, with some further decadent features of its own. One such feature is the subjectivised point of view, presenting life as experienced within a single consciousness. Lukács objects that 'the inner life of man . . . can be truly portrayed only in organic connection with social and historical factors'.[48] In his version of Marxism, social relations are a defining property of human life, not something secondary or added on. The subjectivisation of experience is thus associated with a self-enclosed, solipsistic vision, and the typical character in Modernist literature is condemned as 'a solitary being, incapable of meaningful relationships'.[49]

Lukács also criticises the way in which Modernists link the individual with the universal by their symbolic technique – which he calls 'allegory'. When the individual merely signifies or symbolises the universal, the individual is free to become very singular and the universal is free to become very absolute and eternal. But Lukács dislikes the very singular, as in the case of the pathological or abnormal characters often favoured in Modernist literature. Such characters he considers as exemplifying mere 'morbid eccentricity'.[50] At the other extreme, he also dislikes the very absolute and eternal, as contrary to the shifting historical nature of human existence. For a Marxist, there can be no permanent *condition humaine,* valid across all epochs and all societies. His own theory of *speciality* combines the particular and the general in a more 'in-between' way. 'In realistic literature,' he claims, 'each descriptive detail is both *individual* and *typical.*'[51] Reviving the theory of 'types' proposed by Belinsky and Dobrolyubov, he asks that individual characters be selected as socially representative. Selection here does not apply to traits within the character, does not produce a stereotype where all aspects of personality are geared to some overarching concept. However, the fully-rounded character selected will exemplify, in at least some important traits, a larger trend common to a great many individuals in the society of his or her time.

Lukács also condemns what he regards as the excessive Modernist interest in formal experimentation. Although by no means indifferent to questions of form, Lukács believes that in the last instance 'content determines form', and goes on to assert that 'there is no content of which Man himself is not the focal point. However various the *données* of literature . . . the basic question is, and will remain: what is Man?'[52] To concentrate excessively upon form is to sidestep this basic question; and the consequences, once again, are liable to be dehumanising.

Whereas Lukács focuses upon content, Walter Benjamin focuses upon the medium. In his account of language, Benjamin rejects the notion of some independent mental entity merely *passing through* language: 'What is communicable in a mental entity is its linguistic entity.'[53] And the most important thing that language communicates is its own form, its own shaping power: 'all language communicates itself *in* itself'.[54] However, this form is not always one and the same – and here Benjamin parts company with the usual Symbolist or Modernist exaltation of language. For the medium, according to Benjamin, cannot be considered independently of particular conditions of production and reception, and such conditions change, historically, in relation to changing states of society and technology. Benjamin thus focuses upon the enormous differences between different ways of using language: for example, communal face-to-face communication in the case of oral story-telling as against distanced communication between private individuals in the case of printed novels. 'The birthplace of the novel is the solitary individual, who is no longer able to express himself by giving examples of his most important concerns, is himself uncounseled, and cannot counsel others.'[55] In his willingness to hypothesise very large-scale shifts in ways of seeing on the basis of very particular shifts in the conditions of production and reception, Benjamin is the first truly modern media theorist.

His most famous argument concerns the impact of modern technological developments which make it possible to reproduce the same work many times over – as in the case of film, recorded music, art reproductions and printed books. In 'The Work of Art in the Age of Mechanical Reproduction', he argues that the earliest art had a ritual or sacred value – as in the case of paleolithic drawings, primitive myths, and plays performed on special religious occasions. Art retained this *aura* even when it gradually separated off as a source of purely aesthetic, non-religious pleasure. That is, the work of art was to be approached with reverence and treated with awe, as something special and unique. But such reverence and awe have been rendered irrelevant in the modern age. Mass reproduction destroys the sense of the special and unique, allowing the work to spread out into all corners of life. 'That which withers in the age of mechanical reproduction is the aura of the work of art.'[56] The conditions of reception for films, recorded music, and art reproductions are entirely different from those for staged plays, music recitals and original paintings.

In general, Benjamin considers this a potentially positive development, especially as regards film. (As a collaboratively-produced and communally-received medium, film does not suffer from the de-socialising tendencies of which Benjamin disapproves in the case of the printed book.) In undermining the élite status of 'auratic' works of art, mass reproduction simultaneously undermines the élite status of the social class which can afford to buy and exclusively own such works. And when the work is no longer treated with reverence and awe, Benjamin believes, it becomes capable of social and critical action. 'Instead of being based on ritual, [the total function of art] begins to be based on another practice – politics.'[57] Such hopes might reasonably attach to the Soviet cinema of Eisenstein and Pudovkin, where Benjamin could see political effectivity advancing side by side with the technological exploration of the medium. However, he was not unaware of a very different development in Hollywood, where 'the film responds to the shriveling of the aura with an artificial build-up of the "personality" outside the studio'.[58] The cult of the movie-star thus appears as a recuperation of aura in a new dimension.

On the side of production, Benjamin rejects the 'outmoded concepts' of 'creativity and genius'.[59] Given the input of social and technological factors, it is impossible for the writer to sustain grand claims as sole controlling source and origin. However, it is possible to be conscious of the social and technological factors involved in one's own producing, and Benjamin calls upon the writer '*to think*, to reflect on his position in the process of production'.[60] Assuming an 'exemplary character' as producer, the writer must strive to improve the apparatus of production in a socialist direction. Whereas Engels and Lukács want to improve the reader's *understanding*, Benjamin wants to improve the writer's *practice*. And the practice of aesthetic production will be 'better the more consumers it is able to turn into producers – that is, readers or spectators into collaborators'.[61]

In his arguments on production and the conversion of consumers into collaborators, Benjamin explicitly acknowledges the influence of Berthold Brecht. Brecht's own theorising concentrates upon conditions of production and reception for the theatrical medium in which he himself worked. But since the theatre had not been redetermined by new social or technological factors in Brecht's time, his approach necessarily diverges from that of Benjamin. Whereas Benjamin examines how various media *have* changed, Brecht advances ideas on how his own particular medium *could and should be* changed.

Brecht's ideas for a new *epic theatre* represent a reaction against the established bourgeois theatre, which he saw as encouraging the audience to an unthinking empathetic involvement with the dramatic characters. Such involvement stirs the emotions, but only for as long as the play lasts. Brecht, on the other hand, wants to make the audience think – and above all, to make them aware that the situations they are watching are not be be taken for granted. He contrasts two kinds of response: for the established theatre, 'Yes, I have felt like that too – Just like me – It's only natural – It'll never change'; but for the epic theatre, 'I'd never have thought it – That's not the way – That's extraordinary, hardly believable – It's got to stop. . . .'[62] The audience must be made to realise that things could be otherwise. Such is the justification for Brecht's method of *alienation* (in a sense entirely different from Marx's use of the term) or A-effect: 'The A-effect consists in turning the object of which one is to be made aware . . . from something ordinary, familiar, immediately accessible, into something peculiar, striking and unexpected.'[63] Particular alienating devices include a non-naturalistic style of acting, narrative discontinuity, visible stage apparatus, captions and placards.

The influence of Brecht's A-effect is a part of twentieth-century theatrical history. But Brecht's theory represents something of more general importance in the history of literary theory – a first coming together of two different types of critique. On the one hand, there is the aesthetic critique, which attempts to strip away assumptions that make habitual perceptions and conventional literary forms appear natural and obvious. As already noted, this critique is characteristic of

Modernism, with its mission to challenge and disturb and promote new awareness. But there is also the political critique, characteristic of Marxism, which attempts to strip away assumptions that make established social relations and power structures appear natural and obvious. In both cases, what is needed is an unmasking, a seeing with new eyes, a shift to a higher level of critical consciousness. Brecht here foreshadows a convergence of the two types of critique which takes place under the political phase of Postmodernism, in the literary theory of the 1980s and 1990s.

Although Brecht hoped that his epic theatre would become a popular theatre, in practice his plays have always been appreciated mainly by the élite intelligentsia, the audience for Modernist literature generally. There is inevitably a paradox when the democratic principle of having audiences think for themselves requires such thinking to be forced upon audiences in despite of their own wishes. But for a wholehearted endorsement of Modernist attitudes, it is necessary to turn to the Frankfurt School and Theodor Adorno, the School's foremost representative on aesthetic matters.

The Frankfurt School took a far more cynical view of the modern media than Benjamin. Historical developments had shown how easily the new technology could be made to serve the purposes of right-wing propaganda – as in Nazi Germany – and how easily it could be assimilated to the capitalist mode of production – as in the US. The sociological and cultural researchers of the Frankfurt School had ample opportunity to observe the latter development during their long American exile. Horkheimer and Adorno's *Dialectic of Enlightenment* contains the most forceful presentation of their observations.

Under capitalist conditions, according to Horkheimer and Adorno, art becomes a species of commodity, to be passively consumed like any other industrial product. Hollywood-style movies are thus held responsible for 'the stunting of the mass-media consumer's powers of imagination and spontaneity'.[64] The experience is enervating and ultimately unfulfilling: 'Pleasure hardens into boredom because, if it is to remain pleasure, it must not demand any effort and therefore moves rigorously in the worn grooves of association.'[65] Although there are countless entertainment products from which to choose, they are all ultimately identical. The mass media generates only an illusion of distinctiveness. 'Pseudo individuality is rife: from the standardised jazz improvisation to the exceptional film star whose hair curls over her eye to demonstrate her originality.'[66] Similarly with the illusion of novelty. Although 'there is never-ending talk of ideas, novelty and surprise', yet 'the machine rotates on the same spot' and 'excludes the untried as a risk'.[67] Far from encouraging heightened critical consciousness, the modern media damp down all forms of active awareness, including political awareness.

Such vices call for redemption by an art which pushes in the opposite direction, an art which insists upon strenuous active effort on the part of the reader, and strives for distinct individuality and genuine innovation. This is virtually a definition of the Modernist avant-garde, which Adorno – himself a composer of avant-garde music – endorses wholeheartedly. Such art may be élitist; but then popular entertainment is also not a product of the people when generated by the capitalist mass media. The typically bourgeois origins of Modernist art are less important than its refusal to accept the role of a marketable commodity. In fact, Adorno places great stress upon the liberal bourgeois value of individuality as realised in the non-conforming work of art. 'Culture is the perennial claim of the particular over the general, as long as the latter remains unreconciled to the former.'[68] This is at the very opposite pole to Lukács, with his contempt for 'morbid eccentricity'. For Lukács, the capitalist system is above all a threat to genuine social interpersonal relations; for Adorno, it is a threat to genuine human individuality.

Nor does Adorno ask the artist to promote socialist goals. What he values is the pure act of rejection, as exemplified in such favoured writers as Kafka and Beckett. The autonomy of art as art is itself a message. 'The uncalculating autonomy of works which avoid popularisation and adaptation to the market involuntarily becomes an attack on [popularisation and adaptation to the market].'[69] Given the all-pervasive influence of the capitalist mass media, this is the most that can be expected under current social conditions. 'This is not a time for political art . . . politics has migrated into autonomous art.'[70] And the message of autonomy is more likely to be conveyed through form than through content: 'art's opposition to the real world is in the realm of form'.[71] Adorno has no wish to see literature commit itself to any grand vision of improved social reality.

In fact, Adorno has a general distrust of grand visions. Given the all-pervasive influence of the capitalist mass media, he believes that it is nowadays impossible to lay claim to a detached outside position, or to come up with comprehensive answers for culture and society as though one were not already fatally involved in a particular present state of culture and society. 'The choice of a standpoint outside the sway of existing society is as fictitious as only the construction of abstract utopias can be.'[72] His concept of a *negative dialectic* proposes instead an undermining strategy, whereby critical consciousness launches its attacks from within, accepting partial involvement but achieving local detachment. A similar strategy has become prominent in the subversion techniques of recent literary (and political) theory.

8   20th-Century Russian Theory

Russia, which had produced some major innovative critics in the nineteenth century, produced an even more impressive cluster of critics in the twentieth. In the fifteen years between 1914 and 1929, Russian literary theory raced through a succession of stages equivalent to a whole half-century of development elsewhere. Unfortunately, the Russian advances were closed down or closed off by the rise of Stalinism, and had almost no immediate impact outside the Slavic-speaking world. Western critics discovered the radical work of the Russian Schools only much later, only as they began to arrive at similar theoretical positions for themselves.

Russian Formalism
(*Shklovsky, Eikhenbaum, Tomashevsky, Tynyanov, Jakobson*)

The first stage in this succession of stages was Russian Formalism. The Formalists centred upon two discussion groups: the OPOJAZ group in St Petersburg, where Boris Eikhenbaum, Boris Tomashevsky, Yuri Tynyanov and especially Viktor Shklovsky were the leading figures; and the Moscow Linguistic Circle, where Roman Jakobson was the leading figure. Largely composed of university freshmen scholars, these groups had strong links with the creative movement of Futurist poetry. Both Formalists and Futurists were eager to challenge traditional assumptions and jettison traditional reverences, both sharing in the ferment of radical thinking characteristic of Russia in the years before and after the Revolution. Their reaction against Realism was especially dramatic, given the overwhelming prestige of the great Russian Realist novelists of the nineteenth century. Also significant was their strong reaction against the Russian version of Symbolism, which (like many post-French versions) had tended to a

kind of misty mysticism. By contrast, the Formalists and Futurists saw
themselves as hard-headed and clear-minded, as brushing away
cobwebs of all kinds – the most modernist of Modernists.

The Formalists hoped to make literary criticism into a science with
its own unique object of study. 'It has at last been made clear', wrote
Eikhenbaum, 'that the science of literature, not being simply part of
the history of culture, must be an independent and specific science,
one which possesses its own sphere of concrete problems.'[1] The
historical and biographical researches which had satisfied the nineteenth-century urge for hard factual rigour could not satisfy the
Formalists. (As regards biographical research, Tomashevsky put
forward the subtle argument that 'the poet considers as a premise to
his creations not his actual curriculum vitae, but his ideal biographical legend' – that is, certain kinds of poetry may indeed require a
knowledge of the poet's life, but the life as a deliberate textual
construction rather than as a factual reality.[2]) The proper object for a
literary critical science was what Jakobson called *literariness*, or that
which makes literature different from all other phenomena. Like
scientists, the Formalists sought to isolate a pure element for study,
free from all adjuncts and admixtures.

Many candidates for literariness were rejected. Literature could not
be defined by a distinctive state of feeling in the poet, nor by a distinctive subject-matter ('No nook or cranny, no activity, landscape, or
thought stands outside the pale of poetic subject matter'[3]), nor by the
use of metaphors or images as such. Instead, the Formalists located
literariness in a special use of language. Following the general trend of
French Symbolist and Modernist thinking, they set up an absolute
separation between poetic language and practical language. Practical
language is concerned with conveying something about the world, or
with self-expression, or with persuading others, or with establishing
social contact. But poetic language is not concerned with communication in any of these senses: its business is to draw attention to itself
as language. In Jakobson's formulation:

> Poeticity is present when the word is felt as a word and not a mere
> representation of the object being named or an outburst of emotion,
> when words and their composition, their meaning, their external and
> inner form, acquire a weight and value of their own instead of refer-
> ring indifferently to reality.[4]

Poetic language is language aestheticised, de-functionalised, appreciated for its own sake.

When language draws attention to itself as language, naturally it draws attention to its own materiality. This is clearly the case in poetry, and the sound-qualities of (Russian) verse were much studied by the Formalists. They were particularly interested in rhythm, which they distinguished from the independent or pre-existent pattern of metre. For the Formalists, rhythm is inescapably influenced by meaning – by boundaries between units of meaning, for example. More importantly, rhythm itself also influences meaning, deforming words and creating new emphases and interactions. 'In poetry,' claims Tynyanov, 'the meaning of words is modified by the sound.'[5] By changing the sound-qualities, the poet encourages 'secondary meanings' and 'colorations' to 'glitter through'.[6] Sound matters for the Formalists, but not because it is independent of sense. On the contrary, sound matters because, in the connection with sense, it now begins to assume power, the erstwhile subordinate taking precedence over the erstwhile master.

Many Formalists viewed rhythm as the overarching source of literariness in verse; but a different source was needed when they later turned to the study of prose fiction. Here the key to their approach was a distinction between *fabula* and *syuzhet*, between the raw narrative material of cause-and-event and the artistically treated narrative actually presented to the reader. In Tomashevsky's formulation, *fabula* is 'the action itself', while *syuzhet* is 'how the reader learns of the action'.[7] (The same essential distinction has since been cast in a bewildering variety of terms, perhaps the best known being *histoire* versus *récit* and *story* versus *plot.*) Thus the artistic treatment might involve telling events out of chronological order, or taking up special angles and points of view, or creating effects of mystery and suspense, or artistically selecting 'free motifs', i.e. incidental details not constrained by the requirements of narrative.[8] In all such cases, according to the Formalists, it is the conversion into *syuzhet* that allows art and craft and literariness to come into play. The *fabula* is merely the 'motivation', the unformed clay, possessing no aesthetic value in itself. 'The story line is nothing more than material for plot formation,' says Shklovsky.[9]

A somewhat similar view has already been noted in the criticism of Henry James; and it is evident that considerations of treatment loomed ever larger in the minds of novelists as the Age of Realism gave

way to the Age of Modernism. But the Formalists boost the importance of treatment in the prose fiction of all ages. Thus Eikhenbaum
rejects the notion that, in Schiller's play *Wallenstein*, the main character slows down the action by his individual procrastination; rather, it is
a structural and technical need to slow down the action which brings
about the character's procrastination. (The general Formalist view of
psychologising characters in literature is summed up by Tynyanov:
'we [have] outgrown the type of criticism which considers (and
judges) the heroes found in novels as living people.'[10]) In similar vein,
Shklovsky eschews the Romantic idea that Don Quixote gradually took
on a life of his own in the course of Cervantes' novel: 'The Don
Quixote type made famous by Heine and gushed over by Turgenev
was not the author's original plan. This type appeared as a result of the
novel's structure. . . .'[11] On Shklovsky's showing, the specific devices
adopted by Cervantes in order to tell his story ultimately altered his
conception of the story he had to tell. Or, as Shklovsky elsewhere puts
it: 'Yes, a [literary] task exists all right, but this task is completely
altered by the technical means at the author's disposal.'[12] Once again,
form takes a paradoxical priority over content.

The name of 'Formalist', although not self-bestowed, is thus appropriate enough. Doubtless this sounds unpromising, given that
'formalist' has been used mainly as a term of accusation and abuse in
recent years. But there is a real sense in which the Formalists can
justifiably claim to have gone beyond traditional concepts of form
and content. As Eikhenbaum writes in retrospect:

> the Formalists simultaneously freed themselves from the traditional
> correlation of 'form–content' and from the conception of form as an
> outer cover or as a vessel into which a liquid (the content) is poured.
> . . . the concept of form took on a different meaning.[13]

This different meaning follows from a recognition of how form frames
and constitutes the object that one sees. Strikingly diverse objects
may be constituted by apparently neutral or insignificant features of
technique and medium. It is in this sense that Eikhenbaum can speak
of 'form understood as content'.[14] The Formalists' attempt to isolate
literature from life indeed pits them against the politically oriented
literary theory of recent years; but their vision of how particular ways-
of-seeing are locked into particular forms is part of a much larger
movement – and one which is still with us.

The relation between forms and ways-of-seeing emerges especially in the concept of *ostranenie* (or defamiliarisation, or estrangement). Developed primarily by Shklovsky, the concept applies on several levels. Initially it applies to the way in which a literary work may refresh our real-life perceptions. According to Shklovsky, our real-life perceptions are always being dulled by habit: 'Automatization eats away at things, at clothes, at furniture, at our wives, and at our fear of war.'[15] We recognise signs instead of seeing things. But art devises unfamiliar approaches and unexpected ways of seeing in order to bring us to things as if for the first time. 'We must extricate a thing from the cluster of associations in which it is bound. It is necessary to turn over the object as one would turn a log over the fire.'[16] Shklovsky points to Tolstoy's device of describing an object without naming it, without allowing us that instant recognition and encapsulation which goes with a name. Another example from Tolstoy illustrates the device of the unfamiliar viewpoint: the scene presented from the perspective of a horse. Paradoxically, the recovery of nature proceeds by way of art.

The argument here is similar to that of T. E. Hulme, and is in fact similarly influenced by the philosophy of Bergson. But Shklovsky is interested in every kind of perceiving, not merely visual observation, and the de-automatising devices he admires go far beyond Hulme's single device of metaphor. Most significant, perhaps, are the many retarding devices which hold back easy comprehension: for example, detours, repetitions, and deformed or complicated language generally. 'We've arrived at a definition of poetry as the language of *impeded, distorted* speech.'[17] For Shklovsky, it seems, an enhanced state of perception necessarily follows from the blocking of ordinary perception. We see better when we burst out into the open after struggling through a thicket of difficulties.

But the struggle also has the effect of making us more aware of the thicket itself. This is another level of *ostranenie* – a strangeness of words and language which draws our attention to words as words and language as language. No longer working in the habitual way, the medium too is de-automatised. And on the highest level of consciousness, we become aware of the devices in a work even as they are being used. Thus Shklovsky praises *Tristram Shandy* as a novel which repeatedly throws the spotlight upon the typical techniques of novel-writing, repeatedly reminds the reader of its own novelhood. Eikhenbaum points to a similar tendency in the short stories of O. Henry:

O. Henry often enough annotates the progress of the plot, taking each instance as an opportunity for introducing literary irony, for destroying the illusion of authenticity, for parodying a cliché, for making palpable the conventionality of art, or showing how the story is put together.[18]

In such cases of *baring the device*, the work exposes its own artfulness. This is not only an apotheosis of conscious seeing, but an apotheosis of form over content. When 'the device turns upon itself', then in a very literal sense 'the realisation of the form constitutes the content of the work'.[19] *Tristram Shandy* is not about characters and events, but about its own form and the techniques of novel-writing.

Ostranenie thus counteracts not only the automatisation of real-life perceptions but also the automatisation of words and devices in literature. The Formalists recognise that unfamiliar perspectives will eventually become familiar, that unexpected distortions of language will eventually become expected. As Tomashevsky explains:

> devices are born, live, grow old, and die. To the extent that their use becomes automatic, they lose their efficacy and cease to be included on the list of acceptable techniques. Renovated devices with new functions and new meanings are required to prevent techniques from becoming mechanical.[20]

The corollary of this view is an understanding of literary evolution as an open-ended series of revolutions. In order to keep doing the same thing, literature must keep changing the means of doing it. Clearly, a relativistic approach to literary standards and values is implied, and such an approach is in fact built into the Formalist concept of *the dominant*. The dominant is the special version of literariness governing all the works of a particular genre in a particular period. But dominants differ between different genres and different periods. There is no single eternally valid version of literariness.

Such an approach is not only relativistic but also cataclysmic. That is, it does not work by gradual uni-directional growth, but by sudden sharp overthrowings and reactions. The evolution of literary language, says Tynyanov, 'cannot be understood as a planned development of tradition, but rather as colossal displacements of traditions'.[21] Reacting against an established dominant, writers may return to an earlier disestablished dominant; thus, in English literary history,

Romantic writers looked back to Renaissance and medieval writers, Modernist writers looked back to Baroque/Metaphysical writers. This is what Shklovsky calls the grandfather (or great-grandfather) to grandson line of development. Another possible line runs from uncle to nephew, when a previously marginalised genre is *canonised*, becoming a model for new literary devices. Thus, the English Romantics drew upon fairy tales, ballads, and the popular Gothic novel.

On this approach, literary evolution is also essentially autonomous, requiring no input from changes taking place in society at large. The logic of revolutions is a logic of forms, not of contents. '*The new form*', claims Shklovsky, '*makes its appearance not in order to express a new content, but rather, to replace an old form that has already outlived its artistic usefulness.*'[22] This leads to a characteristically Formalist interpretation of the Age of Realism. According to Eikhenbaum in *The Young Tolstoy*, Tolstoy's supposed realism must be understood as a new system of devices reacting against the old Romantic system. In his presentation of war, for example, Tolstoy parodies the Romantic presentation, selecting incongruous and 'messy' details of military life just as deliberately as the Romantics leave them out. Or as Shklovsky also argues: 'Every epoch has its own Index, its own list of themes forbidden because of their obsolescence. For example, Tolstoi imposes his own Index, which forbids him to write about the romantic Caucasus or about the moonlight.'[23] The realism of the nineteenth-century novelists is simply an artistic system like any other system, with no greater or lesser claim to the accurate representation of real life.

If literary evolution is not to be explained by reference to outside forces, it is also not to be explained by reference to individual geniuses. According to Eikhenbaum, 'the central problem of literary history for us is the problem of evolution outside individual personality'.[24] Shklovsky allows very little room to the heroic individual will: 'a writer's consciousness is . . . determined by literary form. The crises of a writer coincide with the crises of literary genres. A writer moves within the orbit of his art.'[25] Such a view can be seen as following from the notion of forms as ways of seeing. A whole way of seeing is obviously less likely to come under conscious individual control than the choice of some particular subject-matter or feature of style.

Propp

Formalism shifted direction in the course of the 1920s. Detaching itself from the creative revolution of Futurist poetry, it began to take its own scientific aspirations more seriously. Gradually the influence of the polemicist Shklovsky gave way to that of the more academically-minded Jakobson and Tynyanov. Jakobson, whose main career lay in linguistics, and Tynyanov, whose interests extended to social and cultural history, were no longer inclined to make aggressive claims about the absolute autonomy and distinctiveness of art. The shift was signalled by the Jakobson–Tynyanov 'theses' of 1928, which called for a more precise and systematic methodology and the investigation of 'specific structural laws'.[26]

1928 also saw the publication of Vladimir Propp's *Morphology of the Folktale,* a perfect example of scientific methodology and the investigation of structural laws. Coming from a different background, Propp introduced a new element into the Formalist picture. For Propp's object of study is the fairy tale – the very antithesis of challenging, revolutionary Modernist literature. Although the fairy tale is a non-realistic genre, its artifice is a matter of familiar and enduring *conventions,* rather than of defamiliarising Shklovskian *devices.*

Propp followed in the footsteps of an earlier Russian folklorist, Veselovsky, who had collected and studied recurring motifs in fairy tales. That motifs do recur in fairy tales is apparent on even a small acquaintance: the motif of the three wishes, for example, or the motif of the wicked stepmother. But Propp went beyond motifs to the more abstract categories which he called *functions.* Such functions "*serve as stable, constant elements in a tale, independent of how and by whom they are fulfilled.*'[27] Thus the functions of 'the dispatch and the departure on a quest' may appear in a wide range of narrative actions:

1. The king sends Ivan after the princess; Ivan departs.
2. The king sends Ivan after some marvel; Ivan departs.
3. The sister sends her brother for medicine; he departs.
4. The stepmother sends her stepdaughter for fire; she departs.
5. The smith sends his apprentice for a cow; he departs.[28]

Propp similarly reduces individual characters to a very small number of fundamental roles, which he calls *dramatis personae.*

In a suggestive and significant analogy, Propp compares this underlying level of functions and dramatis personae to the underlying grammatical level in language.

> Is it possible to speak about the life of a language without knowing anything about the parts of speech . . .? A living language is a concrete fact – grammar is its abstract substratum . . . Not a single concrete fact can be explained without the study of these abstract bases.[29]

In Propp's analysis, functions and dramatis personae are the building blocks of the fairy tale narrative in the same way that parts of speech are the building blocks of the sentence. Out of a mere thirty-one functions and seven dramatis personae, he claims to be able to assemble his entire sample corpus of one hundred Russian fairy tales.

Such assembling is impossible to demonstrate briefly, but Propp's summary overview may give a general indication of the method:

> Morphologically, a tale may be termed any development proceeding from villainy (A) or a lack (a), through intermediary functions to marriage (W*), or to other functions employed as a dénouement. Terminal functions are at times a reward (F), a gain or in general the liquidation of misfortune (K), an escape from pursuit (Rs), etc.[30]

Unlike motifs, the functions here are not elements *within* the narrative – they *are* the narrative. No other cement or glue is required: their mere contiguity is sufficient to lock them together. Propp even talks about 'the mechanical manner in which the constituents are joined'.[31] There is nothing holistic about Propp's approach: the total narrative is no more than the sequence of its side-by-side parts.

Propp also claims that this sequence is the same for all fairy tales. In any given tale, many functions will be omitted and some functions may be repeated. But such functions as are selected must keep to their relative positions. This is a bold claim (and one which Propp's followers have tended to discard), but it can be referred to the general principles of causality operating on the level of *fabula*. For example, the giving of a magical aid to the hero necessarily precedes the hero's use of a magical aid. Propp allows that his sequence of functions does not apply to later *literary* fairy tales, where the underlying chronology of events is always liable to be re-ordered in the artistic treatment.

Propp adopts the model of the natural sciences in his methodology, breaking texts down into minimal units in order to discover the rules of their reassembly. His success in making his rules apply to so much of the evidence opens up the prospect of a predictive power on the model of the natural sciences. Shklovskian Formalism can be scientific only 'after the event' (especially since the very operation of *ostranenie* precludes predictability). But Propp's rules lay out all possible morphologies for fairy tales, even those not yet encountered, even those not yet composed. This predictive power is something quite new to literary criticism. Propp's achievement, albeit in a very narrow and specialised field, represents a dream to which French Structuralism will later aspire.

Czech Structuralism
(*Mukarovsky*)

Developing directly out of Russian Formalism, the Czech version of Structuralism followed the direction of the Jakobson–Tynyanov theses rather than the direction of *Morphology of the Folktale*. Jakobson himself helped to found the Prague Linguistic Circle, the discussion group on which the movement was based. With an initial membership composed mainly of linguists, the Circle soon spread its interests to literary criticism, particularly stylistics. Czech Structuralist criticism flourished through the 1930s and into the 1940s, with Jan Mukarovsky as its most prominent individual exponent.

The Czech approach typically combines Formalist ideas on literature with the wider social perspective of linguistics. Formalist ideas include the distinction between poetic language and ordinary practical language, and the view that poetic language is focused upon language itself, rather than upon communication or reference to reality. However, the Formalist emphasis on autonomy is toned down by the recognition of a different kind of relationship to reality. For, according to Mukarovsky, 'the work of art, even when it does not overtly or indirectly contain evaluations, is saturated with values', and such values impact upon the values of our real-life living: 'the work of art as a sign acquires an indirect (figurative) tie with realities which are vitally important to the perceiver, and through them to the entire universe of the perceiver as a collection of values'.[32] This position is not unlike that of the New Critics, to be presented in the next chapter.

Czech Structuralism also takes over the Formalist idea of defamiliarisation, applying it primarily to the study of deformations and distortions in poetic language. Mukarovsky again:

> for poetry, the standard language is the background against which is reflected the esthetically intentional distortion of the linguistic components of the work, in other words, the intentional violation of the norm of the standard.[33]

Such deformations serve to make language conscious of itself, *foregrounding* the poetic utterance *as* an utterance. However, the norms against which deformations work are not simply external to the poem, as for Shklovsky. According to Mukarovsky, it is impossible for a poem to be constituted entirely of deformations: the norms of the standard language must also have a presence within the poem. Similarly with the norms of whatever poetic conventions the poem is reacting against: 'The work of art always disturbs (sometimes slightly, sometimes considerably) an aesthetic norm which is valid for a given moment of artistic development. But even in extreme cases it must also adhere to the norm.'[34] Mukarovsky thus recognises the coexistence within the text of a 'structured aesthetic' (an expected rhythm or phrasing, for example) and an 'unstructured aesthetic' (an unexpected rhythm or phrasing, for example). 'Poetry', he claims, 'is a constantly renewed and unceasing synthesis of the unstructured with the structured esthetic.'[35] The individual poem appears as a kind of dynamic oscillation between competing forces – a conception already adumbrated by Tynyanov at the end of the Formalist period in Russia.

Mukarovsky's most striking contribution, however, is his radical relativisation of the aesthetic *per se*. In this he goes far beyond the Formalists and their rejection of eternally valid routes to literariness. His argument is grounded on a distinction between the 'artifact' and the 'aesthetic object', between the words on the page and the poem as mentally constructed. In the last analysis, only the construction matters: 'the work of art exists as an "aesthetic object" located in the consciousness of an entire community'.[36] Inevitably, this confers enormous power upon the community and the predispositions which it brings to the business of construction. Mukarovsky suggests that communities in different cultural periods may construct quite different aesthetic objects on the basis of the same artifact. 'Even, for example, when a certain work in two chronologically separate periods is evaluated affirmatively and equally, the aesthetic object being evaluated is a different one in each case, and hence, in some sense, a different work.'[37] What's more, the very boundaries of what is to be construed *as* aesthetic are socially determined and immensely variable from period to period. Mukarovsky sums up his conclusions as follows:

> 1. The aesthetic is, in itself, neither a real property of an object nor is it explicitly connected to some of its properties. 2. The aesthetic function of an object is likewise not totally under the control of an individual, although from a purely subjective standpoint the aesthetic function may be acquired (or, conversely, lost) by anything, regardless of its organization. 3. Stabilizing the aesthetic function is a matter for the collective. . . . Hence any given distribution of the aesthetic function in the material world is tied to a particular social entity.[38]

It has to be said that Mukarovsky was never entirely happy about these conclusions, and continued to search for objective aesthetic criteria in spite of them. Nonetheless, it is his argument for relativisation that carries conviction.

Bakhtin and his circle
(*also Voloshinov, Medvedev*)

In the years around 1930, Stalinism effectively extinguished the Formalist movement in Russia. The Formalists had begun to turn away from their original proclamations of literary autonomy – willingly (in the case of Tynyanov) or unwillingly (in the case of Shklovsky). But their new-found social interests were still nowhere near enough to satisfy the dominant political regime. What is more, Stalinism had now developed its own literary agenda in the form of Socialist Realism. Of Socialist Realism, it is sufficient to say that at best it corresponds to Lukácsian realism, with a similar but cruder emphasis upon content, social history and socially significant 'types'; at worst, it inclines to propaganda, idealised role models, and a 'revolutionary romanticism' which is anything but realistic.

Stalinism also extinguished another movement which flourished briefly and brightly at the end of the 1920s: the Bakhtin circle. The circle included Mikhail Bakhtin, Pavel Medvedev and V. N. Voloshinov. (It has long been rumoured that Bakhtin himself was

largely responsible for the works brought out under his friends'
names; but since the issue remains unsettled, I shall here refer simply
to the titular authors, Medvedev and Voloshinov.) The members of
the Bakhtin circle defined a stance in opposition to the Formalists
when they proclaimed a political, Marxist-oriented approach to literature and language. But at the same time, their distinctive brand of
Marxist-oriented politics was anti-hegemonic and anti-authoritarian.
Such views were not popular under the increasingly hegemonic,
increasingly authoritarian version of Marxism espoused by Stalin.

The Bakhtinian case on language underlies the Bakhtinian case on
literature. In *Marxism and the Philosophy of Language,* Voloshinov
launched an all-out attack on the Structural Linguistics of Saussure.
Saussure's emphasis upon *langue* as a single socially-instituted
system of rules and categories seemed to bear down crushingly upon
the individual language-user. The particular utterances of *parole*
appear as mere selections out of a socially-predetermined catalogue
of ready-made meanings. But Voloshinov argues that the most important part of meaning is created by the particular circumstances that
condition the particular utterance. He takes the example of two
people sitting in a room; both look up at the window and see that it
has begun snowing again; both feel sick and tired of a winter that has
gone on too long (and both know that they share the same feeling);
and one utters the word 'Well!' No dictionary will furnish the meaning
of this 'Well!' It expresses, Voloshinov suggests, an attitude of 'indignation and reproach moderated by a certain amount of humour'.[39]
Such an attitude is no mere overtone but the very root of the meaning.
'*The situation enters into the utterance as an essential constitutive part
of the structure of its import.*'[40]

Two features are significant here. In the first place, the kind of
meaning being promoted is attitudinal and evaluative, not descriptive
or referential. The two people in the situation share a set of assumptions, a larger world-view that lies behind the particular utterance. In
the second place, the speaker reaches out towards the state of mind of
the 'other', anticipating a certain response. '*The word is oriented
towards an addressee,* toward *who* that addressee might be.'[41]
According to Voloshinov and Bakhtin, even a speaker who appears to
be wholly focused upon an objective subject-matter is always also
glancing sidewards at a potential addressee. In this respect, language
is intrinsically *dialogical,* engaged in a form of dialogue regardless of
whether any response is actually forthcoming. Bakhtin imagines a

dialogue from which the words of the second speaker have been omitted:

> The second speaker is present invisibly, his words are not there, but deep traces left by these words have a determining influence upon all the present and visible words of the first speaker . . . each present, uttered word responds and reacts with its every fibre to the invisible speaker, points to something outside itself, beyond its own limits. . . .[42]

The 'other' is mentally *internalised* by the speaker and can be seen as a presence within the utterance, even without the support of any further evidence.

This approach to language is given a literary application in Bakhtin's *Problems of Dostoevsky's Poetics*, which appeared in 1929, the same year as *Marxism and the Philosophy of Language*. Bakhtin sees Dostoevsky's novels in terms of competing, interreacting voices, where each voice takes account of the probable evaluations of others whilst striving to assert its own evaluations:

> In Dostoevsky, consciousness never gravitates towards itself but is always found in intense relationship with another consciousness. Every experience, every thought of a character is internally dialogic, adorned with polemic, filled with struggle . . . it is accompanied by a continual sideways glance at another person.[43]

And this is valid not only for character in relation to character, but also for narrator in relation to reader. Bakhtin's analysis of the narrator in *Notes From Underground* is particularly acute. The Underground Man is always seeking to express 'his complete indifference to the other's opinion and the other's evaluation'; he 'anticipates the other's response' because 'he fears most of all that people might think he is repenting before someone, that he is asking someone's forgiveness, that he is reconciling himself to someone else's judgement or evaluation'; but 'precisely in this act of anticipating the other's response and in responding to it he again demonstrates . . . his own dependence on this other'.[44] Paradoxically, the attempt to assert autonomy *against* the other only supplies further proof of the interpersonal nature of human life and language.

Dostoevsky's characters assert their own world-views not only in relation to other characters, not only in relation to the reader, but even in relation to the author. As is known from his journalistic writings, Dostoevsky himself espoused reactionary political opinions; in his novels, however, quite contrary world-views manage to have their say almost in spite of the author. The fact that Dostoevsky certainly disapproved of Ivan Karamazov (in *The Brothers Karamazov*) and Peter Verkhovensky (in *The Devils*) does not prevent those two characters from making their attitudes sound convincing. In such novels, claims Bakhtin, 'the character is treated as ideologically authoritative and independent; he is perceived as the author of a fully weighted ideological conception of his own, and not as the object of Dostoevsky's finalizing artistic vision'.[45] The author's voice does not provide a superior encompassing point of view, but competes on a par with the other voices in the novel. For Bakhtin, this is the mark of the *polyphonic novel* (and also the *dialogical novel* : Bakhtin coins many terms with similar meanings but slightly different inflections).

By contrast, the *monological novel* makes the author's point of view supreme. In Tolstoy's novels, according to Bakhtin,

> the author neither argues with his hero nor agrees with him. He speaks not with him, but about him. The final word belongs to the author, and that word – based on something the hero does not see and does not understand, on something located outside the hero's consciousness – can never encounter the hero's words on a single dialogical plane.[46]

Whereas Dostoevsky's characters can always 'render *untrue* any externalizing and finalizing definition of them',[47] Tolstoy's characters lack ultimate independence vis-à-vis the author.

This may or may not be fair to Tolstoy, but there is no doubt that Bakhtin pinpoints Dostoevsky's peculiar virtues very precisely. However, Bakhtin shifted his ground in the long essays that he wrote during the 1930s. Now the claims about dialogism are applied to the novel in general, while monologism is attributed to other forms and genres. Thus poetry is seen as dominated by the single voice of a poetic style, which overrides any individual speakers. 'The world of poetry, no matter how many contradictions and insoluble conflicts the poet develops within it, is always illumined by one unitary and indisputable discourse.'[48] Bakhtin is especially savage on epic poetry, which he associates with the assertion of a unifying national myth. He condemns not only the separate language of epic poetry, but also the removed temporal setting: 'epic time itself, in its entirety, is an "absolute past", a time of founding fathers and heroes, separated by an unbridgeable gap from the real time of the *present day*'.[49] Completed and closed off in the past, epic narrative refuses to interreact with the living reality of the present-day reader.

By contrast, the novel – even as written by Tolstoy – contains many voices. There are the different voices of the speaking characters, the different voices of narrators within the text, the different voices of 'reproduced' letters or journals, and the different voices assumed by the author in addressing the reader. As regards the address to the reader, Bakhtin argues that the novel has never developed any single, established, instantly recognisable manner comparable to that of epic poetry. Many authorial manners are in fact borrowings from non-fictional discourses: the discourse of the historian, for example, or the travel-writer, or the moral essayist. And such borrowings may often involve parody or irony, as when Fielding adopts the life-history-of-a-great-criminal mode, or Sterne makes play with the mode of the friend-to-friend chat, or Joyce slips into the mode of medieval rhetoric. In this respect, 'the novel parodies other genres . . . it exposes the conventionality of their forms and their language'.[50]

It is because the novel is so open to outside influences that Bakhtin can present it as a kind of anti-genre: 'The novel . . . is essentially not a genre; it must imitate (rehearse) some extra-artistic genre.'[51] And the outside influences to which the novel is open include even the most recent sources and contemporary developments. The novel displays 'an indeterminacy, a certain semantic openendedness, a living contact with unfinished, still-evolving contemporary reality'.[52] One might cite the incorporation of newspaper headlines in the novels of Dos Passos, or of 'reproduced' data printouts in modern science-fiction novels.

When Bakhtin extends the dialogical principle to all novels, he harks back to another aspect of the case on language presented in *Marxism and the Philosophy of Language*. The speaker who anticipates answers and seeks to assert a personal world-view looks towards the future; but the words that are used in such assertion already have pasts of their own. Words can never be innocent because they are imprinted with the world-views which they have been previously used to assert. In a sense, all utterance is in a condition resembling indirect reported speech ('She said that she hoped he could . . .'), where the reporting speaker superimposes a further attitude confirming or contesting the attitude imprinted on the words by their original speaker. As Voloshinov puts it: 'Each word . . . is a little arena for the clash and crisscrossing of differently oriented social accents.'[53] As a pertinent example, one might consider the phrase 'political correctness', and current attempts to contest the particular world-view which has been imprinted by a certain kind of pejorative usage into that phrase.

Naturally, the strongest attitude with which a word is charged will have been imprinted by many speakers on many occasions. In this respect, Bakhtin's new emphasis falls upon social confirmation, rather than upon the essentially individual self-assertion of Dostoevskyan voices. But such confirmation is still a matter of actual particular utterances and not of some predetermined system for society as a whole. And in this respect, the new emphasis remains as far as ever away from the Saussurean conception of a homogeneous *langue* for all speakers of, say, French or Russian. Each different interest group within society will have its own sub-language or speech genre, influenced by factors of class, profession, generation, geographical region, etc. What is more, the same speaker will enter into different speech genres at different times: at one time, perhaps, 'the light and casual causerie of the drawing room where . . . the basic differentiation . . . is that between men and women'; at another time, the genre of 'conversation between husband and wife, brother and sister'; at another time, the genre of verbal exchanges which occur when 'a random assortment of people gathers – while waiting in a line or conducting some business'.[54] Bakhtin's linguistic ideal is a decentralised state of competing sub-languages, a state which he describes as *polyglossia*.

Sub-languages of this kind can speak even in the novels of a Tolstoy. Tolstoy's characters may not assert themselves as autonomous consciousnesses in the manner of Dostoevsky's characters, may fail to outleap the consciousness of their author. But the sub-language of their utterance can still assert itself as the proclamation of the particular world-view of a particular social interest group. The novel thus becomes an interaction of competing languages rather than competing characters, leaving behind the obvious plane of action and events. 'Characteristic for the novel as a genre', says Bakhtin, 'is not the image of a man in his own right, but a man who is precisely the *image of a language*.'[55]

This approach had been to some extent foreshadowed by the Formalists. Tynyanov had pointed to the two very different languages upon which Russian literary language is founded (the 'low' source of Russian vernacular versus the 'high' source of Church Slavonic), and had suggested that a competition between different kinds of discourse is often the dynamic upon which poems are built. Even earlier, Eikhenbaum had launched the Formalist investigation of *skaz* (a Russian term for a style of writing in which the author's literary idiom is partly overridden by a narrator's oral idiom), and had suggested that a competition between two different kinds of discourse was the real subject-matter of Gogol's short story 'The Overcoat'. Such ideas followed from the Formalists' intense interest in language and their relative lack of interest in 'organic' unity. (As Shklovsky had said, 'the unity of a work of literature is more likely than not a myth'.[56]) But such ideas were inevitably compromised by the fundamental Formalist separation of literary language from practical language.

The remarkable feature of the Bakhtinian approach is that it inverts the impact of Symbolist- and Modernist-oriented criticism, whilst maintaining the same predominant interest in language. For Bakhtin, the dividing-line between literary language and practical language is erased in favour of multiple dividing-lines between different kinds of practical language; and these different kinds of practical language are carried across into literature. Since the different kinds of practical language involve competing attitudes and world-views, hence competing ideologies and political positions, it follows that competing ideologies and political positions are also carried across into literature. Literature is thus tied on to social reality – by way of its language(s) rather than by way of its content. But not all forms of literature are tied on equally. Bakhtin values the novel because of its unique capacity to internalise competing discourses; by contrast, poetry is far less permeable to outside languages. The exclusive language of poetry, which made it the representative form of literature under the Symbolist- and Modernist-oriented approach, becomes a reason for its relative marginalisation under the Bakhtinian approach.

In the long run, however, Bakhtin tends to re-focus his claims about the novel onto a somewhat different genre of prose fiction; for it is Menippean satire which best exemplifies the competition of discourses, where different manners of writing are imitated, parodied and juxtaposed. Compared with the novel (as ordinarily understood), Menippean satire is very much concerned with the play of languages and world-views, very little concerned with character creation or psychological consistency. Menippean satire flourished as a distinct genre in Classical and Renaissance times, impacted upon the novel in the eighteenth century, was largely submerged during the nineteenth century, and re-emerged as a tendency within the novel in the twentieth century (e.g., Joyce's *Ulysses*). One of the greatest works associated with the genre is Rabelais's *Gargantua and Pantagruel,* and this text becomes Bakhtin's main literary point of reference in the third phase of his critical career.

But Bakhtin also has a non-literary point of reference in the third phase of his career: the historical phenomenon of carnival. During the medieval period (and diminishingly through subsequent centuries), the custom of carnival allowed 'time out' from normal rules and proprieties. 'Carnival celebrated temporary liberation from the prevailing truth and from the established order; it marked the suspension of all hierarchical rank, privileges, norms, and prohibitions.'[57] Such liberation, according to Bakhtin, was conceptual as well as behavioural:

> All things that were once self-enclosed, disunified, distanced from one another by a noncarnivalistic hierarchical worldview are drawn into carnivalistic contacts and combinations. Carnival brings together, unifies, weds, and combines the sacred with the profane, the lofty with the low, the great with the insignificant, the wise with the stupid.[58]

Carnival for Bakhtin represents a joyful state of flux and transgression, change and relativity.

Bakhtin sees carnival in Rabelais and Rabelais in carnival. In *Rabelais and His World,* he moves between his two main points of reference with no apparent shift of gear. This is indeed a 'sociological poetics', as originally proposed by Medvedev in *Formalism and Marxism.* Here literature is not explained as the mere surface product of underlying socio-political causes; the literary and socio-political realms are on a par. In fact, Bakhtin interprets the historical phenomenon of carnival in much the same way that he and many other twentieth-century critics interpret a literary text: by an unfolding or opening out of *significances.* He is not interested in the story of how the practice of carnival evolved over the centuries; he is interested in the *principle* of carnival and what it *stands for*. Seizing upon a particular focal phenomenon, he extends its relevance more and more widely by analogy and generalisation. Moreover, his socio-political values are much the same as his literary values: he favours multiplicity and proliferation and even (as in the above quotation) the unification of opposites. Permanent revisions of the class-structure do not feature strongly on his agenda.

Bakhtin's methodology thus textualises the socio-political realm even as it politicises the literary realm. This same double-sided convergence has since become a common feature of literary theory in the 1980s and 1990s – amongst American New Historicists, for example, and British Cultural Materialists. The Cultural Materialists are more specifically foreshadowed by Bakhtin's attempt to discover sites of genuine political resistance in traditional manifestations of popular culture (though they would not necessarily agree that carnival is such a site). Last but not least, Bakhtin harks ahead to more recent ways of talking about 'the body' when he discusses the emphasis upon supposedly degraded bodily functions in *Gargantua and Pantagruel*. For example: 'the grotesque body has no façade, no impenetrable surface, neither has it any expressive features. It represents either the fertile depths or the convexities of procreation and conception. It swallows and generates, gives and takes.'[59] For Bakhtin, the body is not a physical fact but a construction; and 'the grotesque body' is just one of several possible ways in which bodies may be constructed.

After the publication in 1929 of the original edition of *Problems of Dostoevsky's Poetics,* Bakhtin was unable to publish any of his writings until 1963. His book on Rabelais, completed by 1941, came out in Russian only in 1965. By the time his writings were translated in the late 1960s, literary theory in the West was beginning to arrive independently at ideas which Bakhtin had worked out over a quarter of a century earlier. But even belatedly, his influence was considerable, especially when Postmodernist literary theory began to move into its political phase.

9 Anglo-American Criticism, 1900–60

In the twentieth century, Britain and the United States led the way in a massive development of the 'lit crit' industry, as universities for the first time became the overwhelmingly dominant site of literary theory and literary criticism. The 'man of letters' critic, publishing articles and reviews in general magazines and newspapers, virtually ceased to exist in the Anglo-American world. Writer-critics, though still important, were numerically swamped by university and college professionals, just as the 'little magazines' of the avant-garde, though still important, were numerically swamped by the enormous multiplication of specialist academic journals. Not surprisingly, teaching concerns came to the forefront: for academics, their relationship to students was far more immediate than their relationship to creative writers. Unlike the old 'man of letters' critics, the new professionals no longer moved in the same social circles as the writers of their time.

As noted at the start of Chapter 5, university chairs of literature and language started to appear in the nineteenth century, but with a focus upon the scholarly determination of historical and philological facts. The appreciation of literature could be left to look after itself. But in Britain, around the turn of the century, professors of a different breed began to be appointed: notably, George Saintsbury, Walter Raleigh and Arthur Quiller-Couch. Influenced by the Impressionist criticism of the Aesthetes, these professors adopted a deliberate subjectivism, and sought to communicate the sheer enthusiasm of their response to literature. A famous phrase from a French writer of the same period best sums up the nature of this kind of criticism, which 'relates the adventures of [one's] soul amongst masterpieces'.[1]

At the same time, a push for English studies was building up on a different level: the level of Working Man's Colleges, institutes, and eventually, government-run schools. With the move to mass education towards the end of the nineteenth century, new avenues of education were opened up to whole new segments of the population. But one traditional element in education at this level was becoming increasingly difficult to justify: 'the Classics'. Latin and Greek could no longer be viewed as the Renaissance had viewed them – as a means of accessing vital information and exemplary thinking. Scientific progress had left the Classics behind. In the schools of the ruling classes, the retention of the Classics might be motivated by a tacit class-politics, in that familiarity with Latin and Greek remained the distinguishing mark of the 'gentleman'. But intellectually and explicitly, the Classics could be justified only as a separate humanising element in education, only as a *counterbalance* to scientific knowledge and thinking.

Naturally, the class motive didn't apply in the case of mass education: of what use was a distinguishing mark if everyone could possess it? Stripped of this motive, the weakness of the intellectual justification became glaringly obvious. If humanisation was the goal, why waste so much time in merely *learning the languages* of Latin and Greek? The reading of literature in one's own language seemed to offer a much more quickly ingested counterbalance to scientific knowledge and thinking. English studies thus rose to prominence as a kind of 'poor man's classics'. And in relation to the 'poor man', it was felt to be especially advantageous that the humanising element in his education should also inspire in him a patriotic sense of the common British heritage, thereby overriding his working-class background.

The idea of literature as something to be *taught* was an entirely new twist. At first, it was not at all clear exactly how the teaching ought to be done. For purposes of acculturation, students were expected to read widely and remember a great deal (including the rote memorisation of long passages of poetry). But they could hardly be expected to say anything much *about* literature in either of the two established modes: the scholar's mode of discovering historical facts or the writer's mode of setting up literary ideals in the light of personal practice. Instead, students were expected to show how literature had *rubbed off on them,* by producing well-written essays full of literary graces and stylistic virtues. Assessment struggled to measure the quality of the writing rather than the quality of the statements.

This pedagogy can be understood in relation to its social origins, but it was clearly lacking in real intellectual content. For many years, English studies remained a subject in search of a discipline – in search of replicable procedures, rigorous thinking and assessable results. In the end, it was the universities that elaborated the required intellectual content, drawing heavily upon the concepts of Modernism. The turn to Modernism may seem surprising in view of the fact that English studies, with its promotion of heritage, British values and general positive-mindedness, had hitherto taken a very different tack to twentieth-century literature. But not so surprising, perhaps, in view of the larger fact that significant literary theory has always ultimately reflected the literary practice of its own historical period. In Britain during the 1920s and 1930s, the elaboration of the new theory went hand in glove with a movement to include works of twentieth-century literature as fit objects of study. However, the original rationale for English studies was never simply superseded, and the subsequent story of literary theory (in Britain, if not the US) reveals an ongoing contest between that rationale and the incompatible concepts of Modernism.

Richards and Empson

The source of the new theory was one particular British university – Cambridge. The study of English literature arrived late at Cambridge, which had always plumed itself (to the disgust of William Wordsworth) upon its scientific and mathematical achievements. The key figure in launching the new theory also came from an unexpected intellectual background. I. A. Richards began his career in philosophy and psychology, and even as a literary theorist continued to draw upon concepts derived from those disciplines.

At the same time, Richards' tastes inclined towards Modernist poetry, and he was one of the earliest advocates of Eliot's 'The Waste Land'. Like the Modernists, he fought against the rising tide of popular commercialised entertainment, which he associated especially with the appeal to stock responses. 'Against these stock responses the artist's internal and external conflicts are fought, and with them the popular writer's triumphs are made.'[2] In *Practical Criticism,* he blames stock responses as perhaps the greatest influence leading students astray in their interpretations and evaluations of poetry. Like the Modernists, he thinks of literature as having a duty to challenge and unsettle established habits of response. 'Nearly all good poetry is disconcerting.'[3]

Richards' theory of poetry is based upon a theory of language which was first spelt out in *The Meaning of Meaning*, a book co-authored with C. K. Ogden in 1923. Richards' theory of language is essentially a theory of two languages, the *scientific* or *symbolic* as opposed to the *emotive*.

> The symbolic use of words is *statement:* the recording, the support, the organization and the communication of references. The emotive use of words is a more simple matter, it is the use of words to express or excite feelings and attitudes.[4]

Richards understands scientific or symbolic language very much according to the ideal proposed for all language by British philosophy in the period of Logical Atomism and Logical Positivism. (The essential rationale of these movements is described in chapter 8 of my *Beyond Superstructuralism*.) 'In the scientific use of language,' says Richards, 'not only must the references be correct for success, but the connections and relations of references to one another must be of the kind which we call logical.'[5] Having wholly surrendered statement, reference and logic to scientific language, Richards then sets about clearing a quite separate patch of ground for poetry. And he goes on to argue that the entirely emotive function of poetry is every bit as important as the entirely referential function of science; they are 'both necessities, and neither can be subordinated to the other'.[6] Just how drastically Richards has polarised the situation can be seen in a comparison with what one might call the 'obvious' view, that poetic language and scientific language are comparatively rare extremes, and the overwhelming mass of ordinary language lies somewhere in the middle.

Richards' notion of emotive language is far removed from any kind of neo-Romanticism. He is not interested in 'the poet . . . unpacking his heart in words',[7] and does not think of poetry as involving any special intensities of emotion beyond everyday experience. '[Poetry] is made up of experiences of exactly the same kinds as those that come to us in other ways.'[8] The difference is that 'as a rule the experience is more complex and, if we are successful, more unified'.[9] What matters is the multiplying and interrelating of emotions rather than the sheer qualitative pitch of their emotionality.

In making complexity a criterion of good poetry, Richards agrees with Eliot, but with a stronger quantificational emphasis. This emphasis derives from Richards' extra-literary background: from a psychology which analyses experience into large numbers of separate impulses, and from an ethics which places value upon the satisfaction of as many impulses as possible. (In British philosophy, this greatest-satisfaction-of-the-greatest-number kind of arithmetic is especially associated with the name of Jeremy Bentham, a name invoked approvingly by Richards.) According to Richards, 'the most valuable states of mind . . . are those which involve the widest and most comprehensive co-ordination of activities and the least curtailment, conflict, starvation and restriction'.[10] The peculiar importance of poetry is that poets possess an exceptional capacity for experiencing many simultaneous impulses which more ordinary people would find incompatible. In a successful poem, a state of balance and poise is achieved without sacrificing one impulse for the sake of another. 'This balanced poise, stable through its power of inclusion, not through the force of its exclusions . . . is a general characteristic of all the most valuable experiences of the arts.'[11]

Such poise also takes in a wide coverage across very different kinds of impulse. Thus Richards talks of 'the extraordinary heterogeneity of the distinguishable impulses', even to the extent of 'opposed' impulses.[12] Naturally this conditions the kind of unity to be expected in poetry. Although Richards revives the Romantic terminology of 'organic unity', his concept of unity is very different from that of the Romantics, let alone Aristotle. Particularly illuminating is the way in which he rewrites Coleridge:

> In place of 'the power by which one image or feeling is made to modify many others and by a sort of *fusion to force many into one*', I have used phrases which suggest that it is the number of connexions between the many, and the relations between these connexions, that give the unity – in brief, that the co-adunation is the inter-relationship of the parts.[13]

For all his talk of 'reconciliations', Coleridge ultimately adheres to a Kantian notion of synthesis whereby the many are *fused* into a real oneness. By contrast, Richards' notion is a matter of impulses merely playing off one another, adding further overtones to one another. In the process, which Richards calls 'interinanimation', the many remain many, in spite of the countless linkages between them.

In fact, it would be difficult for Richards to conceive of any truly synthetic unity, given the atomistic principles of his psychology. How could separate emotive impulses unify into a single emotive impulse? Without rising to the level of thought and understanding, only balances and reconciliations are possible. Paradoxically, Richards comes to a version of unity very similar to that which the mystically-inclined Symbolists handed down to the Modernists, even though his own almost behaviouristic approach is at the very opposite extreme to mysticism. This version of unity is exemplified in 'The Waste Land', where 'the items are united by the accord, contrast, and interaction of their emotional effects'.[14] Richards converges even more closely with the Symbolist–Modernist view when he claims that the ideas in 'The Waste Land' combine into a coherent whole because they are arranged like musical phrases.

A similar convergence from radically different starting-points occurs over the issue of truth in poetry. Eliot in particular, and the Symbolists and Modernists in general, rejected the notion that a poem possesses a truth-value with which the reader must agree or disagree. Richards similarly denies that 'we can wrench the sense free from the poem' or 'screw it down in a prose paraphrase'; and he insists that poetry 'tells us, or should tell us, nothing'.[15] This view is carried to an extreme in the doctrine of poetic 'pseudo-statements'. On Richards' definition, a pseudo-statement 'is a form of words which is justified entirely by its effect in releasing or organising our impulses and attitudes'.[16] Sentences in poetic language may seem to be saying things about the world in the same way as sentences in scientific language; however, their only real business is to get our emotional attitudes into better internal shape.

According to Richards, the release and organisation of emotional attitudes is essential for psychological health. Modern science has eradicated the pseudo-statements by which earlier generations lived:

> Countless pseudo-statements - about God, about the universe, about human nature . . . about the soul, its rank and destiny – pseudo-statements which are pivotal points in the organization of the mind, vital to its well-being, have suddenly become . . . impossible to believe.[17]

The factual statements of science can not substitute for these lost pseudo-statements. Richards attributes the mental diseases of the modern age to 'the strain imposed by the vain attempt to orient the mind by belief of the scientific kind alone'.[18] But the pseudo-statements of poetry can transfer to the mind of the reader the poem's own balance and poise. Richards endorses Matthew Arnold's critique of science and his hopes for the high redeeming role of poetry: 'poetry . . . will remake our minds'.[19] But whereas Arnold's focus is public and social, Richards' is private and inward. When a balance of emotional attitudes is transferred to the mind of the reader, as by a successful tragedy, then 'all is right here and now in the nervous system'.[20]

Richards' borrowings from psychology were not of long-term importance. Subsequent Anglo-American critics did not employ his terminology of 'impulses', nor did they focus discussion upon the reader's receiving mind. But the general scientific bent of his approach was highly influential. Whereas criticism in the aftermath of Aestheticism had tended to gushing phrases in praise of indefinable Beauty, Richards adopted a no-nonsense, look-at-the-evidence tone. Such a tone doubtless appealed to the cynical tough-mindedness of the post-war generation. It was no longer enough to stimulate attitudes by sympathetic feeling; the critic must refer, objectively, to specific observables. Richards thus directs criticism into a *scientific* use of language, even as he proclaims *emotive* language as the proper domain of poetry.

Yet Richards is not interested in descriptions of how readers do *in fact* respond to poems. His specific observables are not simple facts, but facts-of-value. He is interested in what specific elements make one poem valuable and superior to other poems. This curious combination of description-plus-judgement launches Anglo-American criticism along a different trajectory from that of Russian Formalism and Czech Structuralism. The combination is especially striking in *Practical Criticism*. In this book, Richards reports on students' responses to previously unseen poems presented without contextual background. The methodology is scientific to the extent that all extraneous influences have been removed, as in a laboratory experiment. But Richards then goes on to analyse the students' responses in the light of how they *should* have responded. And his conclusions are correspondingly judgemental: namely, that intelligent people (such as students) have a lamentable tendency to think very highly of bad poems, whilst remaining blind to the merits of good poems.

As has been pointed out often enough since, Richards' 'experiment' is a classic case of the methodology redefining the object under study. It is by no means obvious that all background knowledge ought to be excluded as extraneous to the appreciation of a poem. Nor is it obvious that reliable evaluations are to be expected in relation to a single sample poem of only a dozen or so lines. Nevertheless, Richards' version of practical criticism held out the promise of an objective assessment procedure requiring strenuous intellectual skills of the kind that had been previously lacking in English studies. It was not long before Cambridge took the lead in introducing practical criticism into university examinations; and it was not long before the practical criticism orientation shed an influence over critical thinking in general. Soon it began to seem quite natural that literature should be appreciated only in 'pure' and decontextualised form, quite natural that it should be judged and justified only on the basis of very close inspection of very short passages of text.

But although Richards' version of practical criticism promoted close reading, he did not himself provide a replicable procedure for carrying out that activity. Such was the contribution of his pupil at Cambridge, William Empson. Using Empson's procedure, it became possible to show a great deal going on within a tiny compass for almost any sample of poetic language. In fact, Empson suggested that any small portion of a longer text carries within itself a miniature reflection of the whole, as microcosm to macrocosm. This belief continued to underpin almost all Anglo-American criticism over the following decades.

In his famous *Seven Types of Ambiguity*, Empson stretches 'ambiguity' to cover, not merely the alternative dictionary senses of a word but 'any verbal nuance, however slight, which gives scope for alternative reactions to the same piece of language'.[21] The discovery of ambiguities is the opening gambit in his procedure. Consider the following analysis of a sentence uttered by Macbeth immediately prior to the murder of Banquo:

> . . . Light thickens, and the Crow
> Makes Wing to th' Rookie Wood.

According to Empson

> *Rooks* live in a crowd and are mainly vegetarian; *crow* may be either another name for a *rook*, especially when seen alone, or it may mean the solitary Carrion crow. This subdued pun is made to imply here that Macbeth, looking out of the window, is trying to see himself as a murderer, and can only see himself as in the position of the *crow*; that his *day* of power, now, is closing; that he has to distinguish himself

from the other *rooks* by a difference of name, *rook-crow*, like the kingly title, only; that he is anxious, at bottom, to be at one with the other *rooks*, not to murder them; that he can no longer, or that he may yet, be united with the rookery; and that he is murdering Banquo in a forlorn attempt to obtain peace of mind.[22]

Not only does the word 'Crow' have two senses, but those two senses have opposing conceptual implications: isolation and violence in the *Carrion crow* sense, community and peaceful living in the *rook* sense. In the former sense, 'Crow' stands in a relation of contrast with 'Rookie'; in the latter sense, a relation of similarity. It is upon the basis of these two possible relations that Empson erects his network of varied thematic connections.

The successive steps of the total procedure can now be set out. In the first step, the individual word is liberated from the ordinary reductive interdefinition operating between grammatical parts of speech, and is opened up to its full potential of meaning and implication. In the second step, this potential is cross-related to the potential of other words, with a view to discovering relations which can be turned into alternative meanings on a semi-propositional level. The first step generates the necessary material for the second, and the second step provides a retrospective justification for the first. There is an evident resemblance to the old double movement of symbols and correspondences in Symbolist thinking, but this new procedure is a matter of linguistic strategy rather than of mystical vision.

The kind of meaning that Empson pursues is not ordinary sentence meaning, nor any version of logical meaning; nonetheless, it is unfolded out of the cognitive senses of a word and requires considerable intellectual effort on the part of the interpreter. Richards' claim that poetry produces a purely emotive response is unacceptable to Empson, and he eventually rejects the entire emotive-versus-cognitive distinction.[23] This rejection was subsequently upheld by the New Critics when they took over Empson's interpretative procedure. Richards' focus upon attitudes continued to remain important (as in the above example from Empson), but not his focus upon mere emotional impulses.

In other respects, Empson's views differ from those which later became standard under the hegemony of the New Critics. His sixth and seventh types of ambiguity, in particular, push forward into more radical territory than the New Critics were prepared to explore. Thus, an ambiguity of the sixth type 'occurs when a statement says nothing, by tautology, by contradiction, or by irrelevant statements; so that the reader is forced to invent statements of his own and they are liable to conflict with one another'.[24] This allows room for the *reader* to engage in extra-textual activity clearly exceeding what is 'in' the text. An ambiguity of the seventh type, on the other hand, points towards the *writer* and the unconscious processes underlying production. 'The total effect is to show a fundamental division in the writer's mind.'[25] The seventh type of ambiguity serves to open up the writer to Freudian psychoanalysis. This psychoanalytical dimension is well exemplified in Empson's 'reading' of the mind of Charles Dodgson, the real human being behind the Lewis Carroll pseudonym.[26] Empson refuses to respect the New Critics' 'Intentional Fallacy' (see p. 192), which leads to an exclusion of biographical interests.[27] For Empson, an ambiguity opens up many possibilities for speculation, possibilities which do not stop short at the boundaries of the text.

Empson's speculations also spread out into socio-politics. Empson differs from most Modernist-influenced critics in drawing no strong distinction between poetic language and ordinary language. So, in *The Structure of Complex Words,* he examines the play of senses in certain key words, which are shaped by general social usage before ever entering into poetry: such words as 'wit' (in Pope's 'Essay in Criticism'), 'all' (in *Paradise Lost*), 'fool' (in *King Lear*) and 'sense' (in *The Prelude*). Under his examination, this play of senses reveals insights into the way of thinking prevalent in society at the time, which further relates to the political structures operating in society at the time. Empson is very much aware that a word 'may signal to the reader what he is meant to be taking for granted', and that 'our language is continually thrusting doctrines on us'.[28]

Perhaps the key factor behind Empson's more radical tendencies is that his interest in multiplicity of meaning does not involve an interest in evaluating individual poems. Describing the kind of criticism in which he is interested, he remarks that 'to assess the value of the poem as a whole is not the primary purpose of this kind of criticism'.[29] So far as value is concerned, he suggests that 'the selection of meanings is more important to the poet than their multitude'.[30] This leaves him free to explore contradictions in the writer's psyche, or contradictions in the writer's society, which clearly do not enhance the quality of the individual poem *as a poem.* Such explorations are impossible for the New Critics, who seek to correlate the value of a poem with the quantity of meaning it 'contains'. In his more radical tendencies, Empson points the way forward beyond the New Critics to Postmodernist literary theory.

Leavis and the Leavisites

Whereas Empson most strongly represents the Modernist – and potentially Postmodernist – wing of Anglo-American criticism, F.R. Leavis most strongly represents the continuing push for English studies. Although Leavis appeared as an advocate of Modernist poetry at the start of his career, the promotion of new writing was always of less concern for him than the promotion of a new role for English studies. The Leavisite movement – which may be taken to include Q. D. Leavis, Derek Traversi, L. C. Knights and many others – was a movement zealously focused upon a specific teaching mission. It addressed itself to an audience concerned about possible developments in educational institutions rather than to an audience concerned about possible developments in creative writing. In Britain and the Commonwealth, literature was for many years taught according to Leavisite principles, especially at the school level.

Not that Leavis does not share important principles with other critics of the Modernist period: in particular, the principle that what matters is the text as distinct from the writer's life or beliefs or society; and the principle that, within the text, what matters most of all is language. Leavis insists that the writer has a special role in maintaining the general health of language, and consistently refers his approval of individual writers to the quality of their language. 'A novel, like a poem, is made of words,' he states; 'there is nothing else we can point to. We talk of a novelist as "creating characters", but the process of "creation" is one of putting words together.'[31] The Leavisite distrust of characters treated as though they were independent beings was most famously expressed by L. C. Knights in 'How Many Children Had Lady Macbeth?'[32] In this essay, Knights argues that textual characters do not exist in the same way as real people in the real world, and it is a mistake to ask real-world questions about them. Knights' argument encapsulates a view common to many twentieth-century schools of criticism.

In similar vein, Leavis objects to critics like Samuel Johnson who, he claims, are never happy until they have discovered a thought which can be stated independently of the literary work's own words. Johnson's failure is that 'he couldn't come to terms with the use of language, not as a medium in which to put "previously definite" ideas, but for exploratory creation'.[33] Leavis himself values writers who think – 'intelligent' is one of his favourite words of praise, whereas 'emotional' is usually a term of condemnation – but he values the kind of tentative, ongoing thinking which explores and develops on the way through a narrative. Discussing Lawrence's *Women in Love*, for example, he asserts that 'an experimental process of exploring, testing, and defining does seem really enacted, dramatically, in the "tale"; so little are we affected as by any doctrine formulated in advance'.[34] Remembering the final outcome of *Women in Love*, we might perhaps agree that, although Lawrence often loads a great deal of undigested doctrine into his novels, yet he often doesn't seem to know the ultimate 'Moral' in advance.

But even when he shares Modernist principles, Leavis tends to give them a distinctive twist. Although he believes that writers have a duty to maintain the health of language, he does not envisage this role in terms of advancing new possibilities or opening new paths. For Leavis, healthy literary language must be grounded in a strong relation to the spoken idiom of the writer's society. The emphasis is upon preservation rather than experimentation. In fact, Leavis manifests a general distrust of writing which is on the fringe or marginal to the overall norms of society, and has no time for the exploration of purely personal forms of sensibility. Thus Wordsworth is praised for 'his essential sanity and normality', while Lawrence is given the accolade of being 'normal, central and sane to the point of genius'.[35] This is the view of the writer as social representative, not as rebel or outsider or misfit.

Nor do Leavis's claims for the importance of text and language ever approach Formalism. According to Leavis, 'a serious interest in literature' should not confine itself 'to the scrutiny of the "words on the page" in their minute relations', but should involve 'an interest in man, society and civilization'.[36] There is always an extra-linguistic standard against which the writer's language must be measured. An early statement in *New Bearings* is revealing:

> [The poet is a poet] because his interest in his experience is not separable from his interest in words; because, that is, of his habit of

> seeking by the evocative use of words to sharpen his awareness of his
> ways of feeling, so making these communicable.[37]

In effect, a poet carries language back into the earliest stages of apprehension, articulating experience in a way that is peculiarly close to the
source, peculiarly sincere and authentic. But the aim is still to capture
something which exists before language. For language to usurp the
priority of content appears to Leavis a condemnable inversion; and he
condemns it most vociferously in Joyce's *Work in Progress*.[38]

Diverging from the main thrust of Modernism, Leavis's criticism
allies itself with the traditional side of T. S. Eliot and the traditional
side of Henry James; but above all it harks back to the social and critical position of Matthew Arnold. For Leavis as for Arnold, literary
education matters because of the state that modern industrialised
civilisation has got itself into. Nostalgic for a more 'organic' state of
community which supposedly survived until the latter part of the
seventeenth century, Leavis despises the 'vacuity that technological-
Benthamite civilisation is creating and establishing in this country'.[39]
He views the twentieth century as a time of 'standardization, mass-
production and levelling-down', when 'civilization is coming to mean
a solidarity achieved by the exploitation of the most readily released
responses'.[40] Such exploitation is seen as located especially in the
'day-dreaming' appeal of mass-market film and fiction, which 'tends,
not to strengthen and refresh the addict for living, but to increase his
unfitness by habituating him to weak evasions, to the refusal to face
reality at all'.[41]

However, Leavis does not imagine that the 'organic' community of
the past can be simply recovered in the present. In present conditions, the survival of civilised values depends upon an all-important
élite. 'The important works of to-day, unlike those of the past, tend to
appeal only at the highest level of response, which only a tiny minority can reach'.[42] It is the teaching mission of Leavisite criticism to

> restor[e] to this country an educated public that shall be intelligent,
> conscious of its responsibility, qualified for it and influential – such a
> public as might affect decisively the intellectual and spiritual climate
> in which statesmen and politicians form their ideas, calculate, plan
> and perform.[43]

In an extraordinary inflation of status, literary criticism thus comes to claim guardianship over a whole culture's 'emotional hygiene' and 'spiritual health'.[44]

Hygiene and health are not promoted by the mere reading of literature, but by the critical activity of *judging* literature. According to Leavis, 'the literary-critical judgement is the type of all judgements and valuations belonging to . . . the collaboratively created human world'.[45] The application of the evaluative faculty to literature thus exercises and enhances our powers of judgement generally, quite over and above any particular verdicts on particular texts. In Leavis's view, it is our powers of judgement which stand most desperately in need of enhancement in the current state of civilisation. 'Discrimination is life, indiscrimination is death.'[46] Indeed, the ability to judge properly becomes an almost religious attainment: 'our judgements ought to come from an impersonal centre in us'.[47] This resembles the value that Matthew Arnold attributed to critical disinterest, as rising above the merely personal promptings of the ego. Leavis follows through on a claim which was always implicit in Arnold: that not only literature but *literary criticism* may serve as a contemporary substitute for traditional religion.

Not surprisingly, Leavis's criticism is overwhelmingly concerned with evaluative 'placings': of certain authors above or below other authors; of certain texts above or below other texts; of certain parts of a text above or below other parts of the same text. This activity sometimes involves 'fine' and 'subtle' discriminations (to borrow two of Leavis's own favoured terms of praise), but it also often involves some notoriously intemperate exaggerations. Especially notorious are Leavis's *canons*, which construct a 'tradition' out of a very small number of authors, whilst violently dismissing all other claimants. Thus the scathing reference to 'the ruck of Gaskells and Trollopes and Merediths' who are excluded from 'the great tradition' of the English novel.[48]

No doubt the pedagogical orientation of Leavisite criticism is partly responsible, concentrating attention upon the small number of books which can be set for school or university courses, as distinct from the large number of books which a true enthusiast might be expected to read. But there is also no doubt that Leavis likes *strong* judgements for their own sake – as suggested in a revealing incidental reference to 'that sense of absoluteness which seems necessary to a robust culture'.[49] Strong judgements represent, as it were, the maximum assertion of the evaluative faculty in a world overrun with indiscrimination and standardisation. For Leavis fears not merely the 'debased' quality but also the sheer quantity of mass-market fiction: 'the modern [reader] is exposed to a concourse of signals so bewildering in their variety and number that . . . he can hardly begin to discriminate'.[50] Faced with a 'perpetual avalanche of print',[51] the critic takes a stand by demonstrating a general power of saying No. As a form of evaluative criticism, this is at the very opposite extreme to the Romantic 'praise of beauties' or the Aestheticist 'appreciation'.

Judgement is not only the overall goal but also the opening move in Leavis's methodology. The kind of interpretation and unfolding favoured by Empson and the New Critics has only a secondary role. The Leavisite critic sifts the details of the text mainly in order to justify a judgement which has already been made. And such justification typically involves appealing to the sympathetic reader to participate in an experience: 'The form of a judgement is "This is so, isn't it?"'[52] Although Leavis quotes copiously, his quotations are often left to stand for themselves, unanalysed, as witnesses to their own value. Leavis does not appear to share the belief of other twentieth century critics, that value can be *proved* by hard demonstrable evidence.

Evaluation as an act also precedes any theoretical setting up of evaluative criteria. Leavis rejects all *a priori* standards:

> so far from valuing being a matter of bringing . . . an array of fixed and definite criteria to the given work, every work that makes itself felt as a challenge evokes, or generates, in the critic a fresh realization of the grounds and nature of judgement.[53]

Nonetheless, it has often been noted that certain standards recur consistently throughout Leavis's criticism. Thus Leavis approves of the concrete as opposed to the abstract; the natural as opposed to the artificial; the life-enhancing as opposed to the nihilistic; and the maturely responsible as opposed to the playfully humorous. These standards remain inflexible regardless of the implicit goals or grounds of a particular work. (Milton, Sterne, Auden and Flaubert are just a few of the writers who stand no chance under Leavis's unargued preferences.) It is illuminating here to continue a quotation begun earlier:

> The form of a judgement is 'This is so, isn't it?', the question asking for confirmation that the thing *is* so, but prepared for an answer in

the form, 'Yes, but – ', the 'but' standing for corrections, refinements, precisions, amplifications.[54]

Leavis's version of criticism as a 'collaborative' enterprise encourages disagreement within a larger frame of common assumptions, but is not prepared for an answer which disagrees about assumptions.

There is one further preference which recurs throughout Leavis's criticism: a preference for writers who 'place' and discriminate. Leavis admires in literature much the same virtues that he admires in criticism. If it is the critic's business to form canons of literature, so it is the creative writer's business to form canons of life. 'The creative drive in [the writer's] art *is* a drive to clarify and convey his perception of relative importances.'[55] Thus in Dickens's *Little Dorrit,* Leavis comments favourably upon the way in which each character 'invit[es] us to make notes on his or her distinctive "value" in relation to the whole'.[56] Although not interested in characters as lively autonomous beings, Leavis is very much interested in the novelist's comparing, contrasting, weighing and placing of the different moral values which characters represent.

The exercise of discrimination is also required in relation to language. When Leavis praises a writer's use of language, he is often thinking of a particularly precise choice and selection amongst possible words. Leavis sees discriminations everywhere; and where he sees them, he regards them as moral acts in their own right. Indeed, such acts constitute a kind of bridge between form and morality. Leavis is not simply a moralist in the old way: as already noted, he is hostile to moral messages of the kind that can be viewed independently of the work of art. When he asserts that Jane Austen does not 'offer an "aesthetic" value that is separable from moral significance', he is not simply dismissing aesthetic value.[57] Rather, he is subordinating both the writer's handling of form *and* the writer's moral beliefs to the writer's powers of evaluative discrimination. Hence the curious Leavisite discourse which imports the term 'moral' into seemingly inappropriate contexts: which talks about moral organisation or moral structure, for example; or refers to the 'moral tradition' of 'the English language'.[58] For Leavis, there is a moral dimension to the process of comparing and weighing between different elements in a structure, and a moral dimension to the process of choosing and selecting amongst possible words.

The New Criticism: Southern phase
(*Ransom, Tate*)

With the growth of the Leavisite movement, criticism in the UK shifted into a very distinctively British channel. In the course of the 1930s and 1940s, the general Modernist momentum which had been developing through Eliot, Richards and Empson passed across to the US. Until this time, twentieth century American criticism had tended towards scholarly and historical studies (especially with the foundation of the Modern Languages Association) and towards the discussion of great moral ideas (under the banner of 'the New Humanism'). Arising in the Southern states, the New Critics reacted against such approaches – as had that Southern critic of an earlier century, Edgar Allan Poe. This upsurge of critical activity was related to an upsurge in creative activity, the so-called Southern Renaissance, most famously represented by William Faulkner. Two poets prominent in the Southern Renaissance, John Crowe Ransom and Allen Tate, were also responsible for launching the New Criticism.

For Ransom and Tate, literary criticism was initially tied in with social criticism. As leading proselytisers for the Fugitive and Agrarian programmes, Ransom and Tate rejected the industrial, urban and technological ethos which had dominated American culture since the victory of the Northern states in the Civil War. Calling for a return to rural community living, they sought to revive the values of 'the old South'. In its early phase, the New Critical approach to poetry was part and parcel of a wider belief in a less goal-directed, more 'aesthetic' way of life.

In typical Modernist manner, Ransom and Tate set up poetry in opposition to science. Science is seen as a useful tool, giving us practical control over our environment. But such control is achieved at the cost of abstraction and generalisation, at the cost of losing sight of the full, individual things of the world. By science, says Ransom, 'we know the world only as a scheme of abstract conveniences'.[59] By focusing too exclusively upon scientific knowledge, modern society jeopardises other more important values necessary to human well-being.

Poetry gives us an alternative form of knowledge. It does not merely stimulate emotions: both Ransom and Tate attack Richards on this point, and both are particularly hostile to Romanticism and what Ransom disparages as 'heart's-desire poetry'.[60] But the poetic form of knowledge has no practical purpose. 'Poetry', says Tate, 'finds its true usefulness in its perfect inutility.'[61] Coining slogans in what was to become a characteristic New Critical style, Tate dismisses 'the Doctrine of Relevance' (i.e. the belief that poetry must be socially or politically useful), 'the heresy of the will' (i.e. the preference for functionalistic, goal-directed ways of thinking) and 'the fallacy of communication' (i.e. the assumption that a poem is merely a channel for passing ideas from poet to reader).[62] In opposition to this last 'fallacy', he proposes a view of 'the work of literature as a participation in communion'.[63] Such a view has profound implications for the role of poet and the role of reader.

As against the abstract conveniences of science, Ransom argues for a poetry which will recover the fullness and concrete particularity of 'the world's body'. Like Hulme, he lays great stress upon images: 'The image . . . is marvellous in its assemblage of many properties, a manifold of properties.'[64] Ransom allows that poems may contain logical arguments, but these are merely the bare bones, of no poetic value in themselves. It is the incremental 'texture' which 'peculiarly qualifies a discourse as poetic'.[65] Such texture includes lively local details, connotations, images, metaphors, ambiguities, word-play. What is ornament or irrelevance from a logical point of view is the essential value and meaning from a poetic point of view.

Tate focuses specifically upon the full quantity of meaning within a poem. A poem, he argues, offers up all the *extension* (= the denotation, the set of objects referred to as under a scientific definition) and all the *intension* (= the connotation, the associated qualities and properties and attitudes) in the meanings of its words. Like Ransom, Tate does not exclude the logical or scientific kind of meaning, but he demotes and effectively swamps it under a far larger proliferation of intensive meanings. Under Tate's covering term *tension,* all kinds of meaning in a poem are on a par. By happy chance, the ordinary sense of *tension* also suggests those states of opposed meaning which New Critics increasingly delighted to discover in poetry.

This focus upon meaning is simultaneously a focus away from effects. For Ransom, the attempt to propagate affective responses is just as un-aesthetic as the attempt to propagate ideas or moralities. The popular view that the writer has designs upon the public 'denies the autonomy of the artist as one who interests himself in the artistic object in his own right, and likewise the autonomy of the work itself as existing for its own sake'.[66] This is a characteristic Modernist stance, which well accords with the difficult, complex nature of Modernist poetry. In the face of such poetry, readers must be encouraged to learn to understand something which exists beyond themselves, beyond their own untutored responses.

Ransom also offers the following general argument against affective criticism:

> There may be a feeling correlative with the minutest alteration in an object, and adequate to it, but we shall hardly know. What we do know is that the feelings are grossly inarticulate if we try to abstract them and take their testimony in their own language. Since it is not the intent of the critic to be inarticulate, his discriminations must be among the objects.[67]

For the sake of critical precision and critical objectivity, the critic is obliged to 'cite the nature of the object rather than its effects upon the subject'.[68] The supposed error of citing effects upon the subjectivity of the reader later became known, in W. K. Wimsatt's famous phrase, as the Affective Fallacy.

Kenneth Burke

Although both Ransom and Tate were poet-critics, the further development of the New Criticism carried the movement out of the hands of creative writers and into the hands of university professionals. In an essay published in 1937, Ransom himself anticipated and welcomed this trend: 'Criticism must become more scientific, or precise and systematic, and this means that it must be developed by the collective and sustained effort of learned persons – which means that its proper seat is in the universities.'[69] But as the theoretical principles of the New Criticism were narrowed and standardised under the academic hegemony of the 1940s and 1950s, even Ransom's own position came to appear a little off-centre. Other early individual figures were left still further out in the cold. In the case of Yvor Winters, an early association with the New Criticism was probably always misleading, for Winters never agreed with the fundamental tenets of the movement. R. P. Blackmur, on the other hand, contributed significantly to the Southern phase, as the most 'aesthetically minded' of all New Critics and closest in spirit to the original

Symbolists. However, Blackmur's distinctive approach diverged from the mainstream in the 1940s and 1950s. More divergent again was the approach of Kenneth Burke, who not only grew beyond his early affiliations to the New Criticism, but leaped far ahead in the direction of Poststructuralism and Postmodernism.

Burke is at his most New Critical in his focus upon ulterior symbolic meanings. His practical analyses typically start from images or clusters of images which he gathers and links up across a text. But Burke does not value a multiplicity of interconnected symbolic meanings simply for its own aesthetic sake. He is concerned with the way in which such meanings *act* upon the lives of writer and readers. 'The poem is designed to "do something" for the poet and his readers . . . and we can make the most relevant observations about its design by considering the poem as the embodiment of this act.'[70] From the very first, Burke differs from the New Critical orthodoxy in refusing to limit discussion to the text as an autonomous object or 'verbal icon'.[71]

Burke proposes a cathartic action for literature, as in the Aristotelian theory of tragedy (see p. 14). Literature serves to cure and cleanse and purge. 'The Rime of the Ancient Mariner' is thus explained by Coleridge's need to cleanse himself of a sense of guilt over his drug addiction and his failings as a husband. Redemption from guilt is indeed the fundamental motive in Burke's account. Guilt is universal because we are all involved in recurrent offences against the symbolic meanings of the world in which we live. In tribal cultures, there were methods of purging away symbolic offences. For example, the killing of an animal, though necessary for the survival of the tribe, was commonly followed by rites to cancel the wrong that had been done to the animal's spirit. But the modern culture of science and technology not only encourages us to commit symbolic offences on a vastly expanded scale, but has no place for rituals of purification. What we need is 'a set of symbolic expiations . . . to counteract the symbolic offences involved in purely utilitarian actions'.[72] In his writings of the 1930s and 1940s, Burke suggests that a poem may be used by both writer and readers as a means of purging personal problems and social anxieties.

In the course of the 1950s, Burke's emphasis shifts. He becomes less interested in literature and more interested in language generally. He draws attention to the forms of action operating in all language and all symbol-systems (now taking 'symbol' in the philosophical or linguistical sense, rather than the literary sense). Pointing to 'the necessarily *suasive* nature of even the most unemotional scientific nomenclatures', he insists that neutral naming or disinterested description is always an illusion.[73] Action as persuasion is shown to operate socially, involving 'the ways in which the members of a group promote social cohesion by acting rhetorically upon themselves and one another'.[74] Although such persuasion is over and above the communication of literal meaning, it is clearly not symbolic meaning as understood by the New Critics. Rather it is an ideological freight with which all words are loaded. 'In the selection of terms for *de*scribing the scene, one automatically *pre*scribes the range of *acts* that will seem "reasonable', "implicit", or "necessary".'[75]

Acts of social persuasion may be specific to particular groups, but there are also certain very general directives which follow from the nature of language itself. According to Burke, the invention of language is also the invention of the negative, since only language enables us to think in terms of *what is not*; and the invention of the negative leads to the development of negative moral commandments or *thou-shalt-nots*. These are responsible for our general state of guilt, since it is impossible for us to abide by our own moral commandments. In another argument, the invention of language is also the invention of categories for dividing up reality; and those categories lead to the development of hierarchical structure, one category always appearing higher than another. (This is Burke's non-binary version of the later Poststructuralist argument that one pole of an opposition always dominates over the other.) Hierarchical structures are responsible for our upward-and-onward aspirations; 'goaded by the spirit of hierarchy',[76] we are always driven to carry things through to unbalanced planet-endangering extremes. But, for better or worse, such consequences of language are inescapable. As Burke muses: 'how fantastically much of our "Reality" could not exist for us, were it not for our profound and inveterate involvement in symbol systems.'[77] Like the theorists of a later generation, Burke believes that human reality is fundamentally language-constituted.

Burke also foreshadows later theorists in the role of cultural critic. His earlier ritual-based perspective, though never superseded, becomes increasingly subordinated to a socio-political perspective. Yet this socio-political perspective in no way undermines his primary focus upon language. On the contrary: Burke sees the structures of language as directly embodied in socio-political structures – most obviously in so far as the hierarchy of categories reappears in the hierarchy of classes. In the last analysis, 'vocabularies [are] not words alone but the social textures, the local psychoses, the institutional structures, the purposes and practices that lie behind those words'.[78] Social and textual analysis are inextricable.

The New Criticism: hegemonic phase
(*Brooks, Penn Warren, Wimsatt, Wellek*)

Following the end of the Second World War, the college population in the United States expanded dramatically, and literary studies shared in this expansion. Suddenly, vast new quantities of subject-matter were required: subject-matter for lectures, for essays and assignments, for postgraduate theses. The 'close reading' techniques of the New Criticism filled the gap by enabling students and academics to say far more on any given text than had ever been said previously. Now it became possible to present non-obvious interpretations without the qualification of specialist historical or philological knowledge, and to assert value-judgements without the qualification of exceptionally wide reading. In fact, although the New Critics proclaimed the importance of evaluation, their judgements typically arose as the product of their interpretations, to the extent that the value of a poem often seemed directly proportional to the amount of interpretation it could sustain. Not since the time of Fulgentius had criticism been so devoted to the business of sheer interpretation.

The techniques of close reading were disseminated by one enormously influential text: *Understanding Poetry* (1938), a teaching primer by Cleanth Brooks and Robert Penn Warren. Brooks and Penn Warren had themselves been involved in the Southern phase of the New Criticism, but their migration to larger Northern universities signalled the start of a period during which the New Criticism extended its sway across the whole of the US. The once-marginal movement became the established orthodoxy of the 1940s and 1950s, dominating all critical thinking and teaching. During this later hegemonic phase, the theorising of New Critical principles passed into the hands of such critics as René Wellek and W. K. Wimsatt, who had no associations with the original Southern group but may be categorised as New Critics by virtue of intellectual affiliation. In what follows, however, I shall refer most often to Cleanth Brooks: not as necessarily the best or most profound of these critics, but as the most central and most representative.

The most powerful and productive strategy of New Critical close reading follows the two-step movement developed by Empson. In the first step, words in a poem are seen as having an unusual fulness of meaning, thus allowing the critic to open up all their dictionary senses and all their qualitative connotations. As Brooks puts it, 'the word, as the poet uses it, has to be conceived of, not as a discrete particle of meaning, but as a potential of meaning, a nexus or cluster of meanings'.[79] In the second step, the yield of meaning from one word (or small group of words) is cross-related to the yield from other words, simultaneously back and forth across the poem. In the course of this process, meaning drifts ineluctably from the particular to the general. Under New Critical assumptions about the nature of poetic language, a particular item of clothing typically comes to represent the general principle of clothing – the principle of putting-on-for-outward-show, for example.[80] The particular is taken to stand for or symbolise its own properties or connotations.

This orientation towards higher-level symbolisation clearly corresponds to the linguistic possibilities which Symbolist and Modernist poets discovered and consciously exploited. The New Critics do not always speak of 'symbols' in such cases, often preferring to reserve the term for only the most emphatic examples. However, their distinctive discourse of 'image' and 'theme' works to produce much the same results. In the hegemonic period, this distinctive discourse came to seem entirely natural and innocent. But in fact, the conceptualisation underlying the terms 'image' and 'theme' directs attention along very specific tracks, and automatically predisposes the critic to a certain kind of interpretation.

Images depend upon language that is concrete and particular; and the New Critics firmly insist that the language of poetry must be in the first place concrete rather than abstract. One of Brooks's critical tenets is that '*the general and the universal are not seized upon by abstraction, but got at through the concrete and the particular.*'[81] However, this is not the concretion and particularity of an extended physical description of scene or action. As in Pound's original definition (see p. 119), the term 'image' suggests an instantaneous explosion, an isolated point expanding outwards. And not only outwards, to visual and sensory associations, but also upwards, to more general conceptual ideas. This upwards movement is the movement of symbolic signifying.

At the same time, the ideas thus generated are also in a point-like state. They are not new ideas developed through a continuous train of thought or argument, but existing ideas touched upon, summoned to mind. Brooks prefers to talk of 'attitudes' rather than 'ideas', and describes a poem as 'a structure of "gestures" or attitudes'.[82] Or, to put it another way, these are ideas in the shape of 'themes': brief evocations which can be introduced at strategic moments here and there across a poem, much like the themes in a piece of music. To talk about a poem's themes of Life or Death or Art or Nature does not mean that the poem makes propositional assertions on such topics.

Inevitably, such themes tend to organise themselves oppositionally: thus, Life versus Death, Life versus Art, Art versus Nature. As in Roget's Thesaurus, general ideas in the form of abstracted qualities can almost always be seen as falling on one or other side of some universal dividing-line. Finding oppositional themes within a single poem, the New Critics interpret them as *contradictions* or *paradoxes,* indicative of a conflict of attitudes. For Brooks and the New Critics, the overcoming of such conflict is the main business of poetry: 'contrasts to be harmonized and differences to be reconciled constitute the very stuff of poetry'.[83] And the greater the contrasts or contradictions overcome, then the greater the poem.

The overcoming is achieved on the way through the poem, as initially opposing attitudes are gradually complicated and shown to involve or contain elements of one another. By the end of the poem, the conflict has been mediated, and order and stability have been re-established – as at the end of a Shakespearian tragedy. There is in this a kind of moral message, where order and stability feature as ultimate positive values. Although the New Critics disbar outright moral statements from poetry, their interpretative strategy typically produces a high yield of moral implication (differing in this respect from Empson's original version). It is not difficult to see how the emphasis upon order and stability relates to the conservative social politics of the earlier Southern phase of the New Criticism. Respecting and balancing all points of view, the poem arrives at a final state of stasis, thus confirming the general New Critical principle that poetry does not lead on to action – least of all, radical political action.

Certain key terms take on special senses in the light of the New

Critical interpretative strategy. Such is the case with the much-favoured term *irony*. According to Robert Penn Warren:

> the poet . . . proves his vision by submitting it to the fires of irony . . . in the hope that the fires will refine it. In other words, the poet wishes to indicate that his vision has been earned, that it can survive reference to the complexities and contradictions of experience.[84]

Clearly, this is irony along the line of Eliot's principle of wit and Richards' principle of inclusiveness. The ironic poem is wide-minded and aware of alternative positions; it does *not* simply undermine one position on behalf of another, as in the everyday application of the term. In his reading of irony in Pope's *The Rape of the Lock*, Brooks displays a common New Critical tendency when he refuses to see a simple one-way deflation of Arabella, perceiving instead a more equal competition between alternative perspectives. As Ransom had earlier said: 'a poem is, so to speak, a democratic state, whereas a prose discourse . . . is a totalitarian state'.[85]

The same tendency influences New Critical dealings with metaphor, another term that plays a vital role in New Critical thinking. Again, the New Critics reject the old notion that a metaphor comprises an overt level of figurative meaning and an underlying level of real meaning, the latter being understood as continuous with the surrounding context. Instead the two levels of meaning are placed very much on a par. In Wimsatt's words: 'in understanding imaginative metaphor we are often required to consider not how B [real meaning] explains A [figurative meaning], but what meanings are generated when A and B are confronted or seen in the light of each other'.[86] It should be noted that a metaphor's figurative meaning, which typically appears in a striking isolated image, benefits from the New Critical focus upon precisely such images; conversely, the underlying 'real' meaning gains no special advantages from its continuity with a surrounding context.

Another key term in the New Critical lexicon is *organic unity*. However, this conception of unity is 'organic' only in Richards' peculiar sense, involving no synthesis or fusion but rather a multiplicity of cross-relations in which nothing is lost or sacrificed. Brooks again:

> the principle of unity . . . unites the like with the unlike. It does not unify them, however, by the simple process of allowing one connota-

tion to cancel out another nor does it reduce the contradictory attitudes to harmony by a process of subtraction. . . . It is a positive unity,
not a negative; it represents not a residue but an achieved harmony.[87]

Not surprisingly, the analogy to the unity of a piece of music comes
often to the fore.

The New Critics are also fond of a new analogy to drama: 'the structure of a poem resembles that of a play'.[88] The idea here is that the
different conflicting attitudes engendered in a poem resemble the
different conflicting attitudes of dramatic characters. In the development of a poem as in the development of a play, these attitudes are
brought to a final state of balance or resolution. In drawing this
analogy, however, the New Critics ignore the most obvious unifying
factor in the development of a play – the story or causal action. In a
play, the resolution of conflicting attitudes (if it occurs at all) is determined by what *happens* between characters. But the New Critical
model has no place for this kind of unity, which Aristotle considered
'organic'. Here there are only cross-relations between *attitudes*, spun
out in a vacuum. Paradoxically, the New Critics' overwhelming
concern for unity is a concern to recover new kinds of unity after the
strongest and most obvious kinds of unity have already been left
behind.

If the direction of the New Critical enterprise is positively defined
by such terms as 'image', 'theme', 'paradox', 'irony' and 'organic
unity', it is also negatively defined by such famous taboos as 'the
heresy of paraphrase' and 'the Intentional Fallacy'. The taboo on
paraphrase, as argued by Brooks, follows from the belief that there is
no separate value in the content of a poem, such as could be retained
in a prose rendition. The value of a poem is indissolubly bound up
with its form. The taboo on paraphrase is thus equivalent to the principle that form and content are or ought to be inseparable:

> in poetry that is truly poetry, form and content have merged so thor-
> oughly that to try to detach the content so as to speak of it separately
> represents a violation of the poem and threatens to reduce the 'form'
> to a kind of rhetorical husk or envelope.[89]

The old simplistic notion of content as something contained or
wrapped up in a form is the target of many New Critical attacks.

In defeating this notion, the New Critics manage to promote their own preferred kind of structure – 'a structure of meanings, evaluations, and interpretations'.[90] This kind of structure overcomes the dichotomy of form and content because it is genuinely intermediate between form and content. On the one hand, it is formal in so far as it is entirely a matter of relationships, never rising to the level of propositional ideas or causal action. On the other hand, it is also contentual in so far as the relationships operate between attitudes and carry moral implications. Here indeed is a form-like version of content and a content-like version of form. However, it is by no means obvious that this specialised kind of structure is present in all poetry, or that it represents the only alternative to the old simplistic notion.

The irrelevance of authorial intentions had been suggested by several earlier critics in the Cambridge–New Critical tradition, but it was an article on 'The Intentional Fallacy' by W. K. Wimsatt and Monroe Beardsley which gave the taboo its decisive formulation. According to Wimsatt and Beardsley, if the poet succeeded in realising an intention, 'then the poem itself shows what he was trying to do'; if the poet did not succeed, then 'the critic must go outside the poem – for evidence of an intention that did not become effective in the poem'.[91] Such external evidence is taken to include journals, letters and consultation with the poet in person. Wimsatt and Beardsley have no difficulty in demonstrating that all of these sources are inadequate as guides to what was going on inside the poet's head. They conclude that 'the design or intention of the author is neither available nor desirable as a standard for judging the success of a work of literary art'.[92]

The interesting thing here is that, if the knowledge of an intention required a knowledge of what was going on inside someone's head, we would be equally incapable of hypothesising intentions in real life. How could we tell that the carpenter intended to drive the nail into the wood (when the hammer missed)? or that the pedestrian intended to cross the road (when she drew back at the last minute)? In fact, we hypothesise intended doings in such situations by drawing upon our general social assumptions about human practices and human purposes. But the application of general social assumptions has already been ruled out under the New Critical insistence that readers must empty their minds of all presuppositions and prejudices before engaging with the pure isolated text. And the notion of the text as an *intended doing* has already been ruled out under the New Critics' refusal to think of literature as *affective*, as trying to produce certain responses in readers.

Wimsatt and Beardsley's essay focuses not upon the intention to produce certain responses but upon the intention to mean certain meanings – specifically, meanings in the form of allusions (e.g., Eliot's allusions to other poems, Donne's allusions to astronomical beliefs). Such allusions are higher-order meanings much like the symbolic significances so prevalent in New Critical interpretation generally. It is in relation to higher-order meanings that issues of intention become genuinely problematic. How does the critic decide whether a particular phrase is intended as an allusion, whether a particular sunflower is intended as a symbol of Life? A conservative approach to such issues would undoubtedly eliminate vast quantities of New Critical interpretation. But the Intentional Fallacy frees the critic from worrying about intentions. 'The poem . . . is detached from its author at birth and goes about the world beyond his power to intend about it or control it'.[93] The Intentional Fallacy is a necessary component in the general strategy of New Critical interpretation.

The strategy of New Critical interpretation was always especially appropriate to Symbolist and Modernist poems, to the new mode of meaning which Symbolist and Modernist poets consciously exploited. But the same strategy could be made to apply to every kind of poem: it was only necessary to view all concrete language in terms of images, only necessary to focus upon the isolated points of words (or small groups of words) at the expense of connected propositions and causal actions. Such wider application became increasingly common as the New Criticism rose to hegemonic status. Once again, Cleanth Brooks is exemplary: his 1939 volume *Modern Poetry and the Tradition* down-grades the Romantics and Victorians in order to elevate the Modernists (and Metaphysicals); but his 1947 volume *The Well-Wrought Urn* argues for the same essential characteristics in poetry of all periods, including Milton, Pope, Gray, Wordsworth, Keats and Tennyson.

The goal for criticism, as propounded in the latter book, is to develop 'an instrument . . . which may be used in the service, not of Romantic poetry or of metaphysical poetry, but of *poetry*.'[94] No longer associated with a particular 'push' of practising poets, the New Critics now claim to have discovered a single language common to all poetry, underlying historical differences. And even common to all literature – from the time of Mark Schorer's essays 'Technique as Discovery' and

'Fiction and the "Analogical Matrix"' (1948 and 1949 respectively), the same strategy is increasingly applied to prose novels. In the high period of its dominance, the New Criticism assumes a professional air of impartial universality and takes on the mentality of an established orthodoxy.

Myth criticism and Northrop Frye

Even in its heyday, the New Criticism did not pass unchallenged. One persistent source of challenge was the Neo-Aristotelian Chicago School, led by R. S. Crane. Like the New Critics, the Chicago critics opposed earlier forms of criticism oriented towards ideas and morality, or towards biography and historical background. But they followed Aristotle in asserting the differences between genres and the primary importance of causal action. Naturally this led them to condemn the New Critical preference for intensive study of very short passages and the New Critical insistence upon language as the ground of all virtues. In their view, the New Critics' pursuit of essential common characteristics reduced the variety of literature to the single genre of the Modernist lyric. But in spite of some effective hits, as in Elder Olsen's essay on 'William Empson, Contemporary Criticism, and Poetic Diction', the Chicago critics remained only a minor irritant to the dominant orthodoxy.[95]

More successful in the long run was the movement of Myth Criticism. The theoretical underpinnings for this type of criticism were worked out by Carl Jung, Freud's renegade disciple. Jungian psychoanalysis posits the existence of a collective unconscious which lies deeper than the personal unconscious, and which is identical for all human beings. 'We mean by collective unconscious, a certain psychic disposition shaped by the forces of heredity.'[96] Here are to be found the archetypes, which Jung describes as follows: 'The primordial image, or archetype, is a figure – be it a demon, a human being, or a process – that constantly recurs in the course of history and appears wherever creative fantasy is freely expressed.'[97] Jung's ideas made an early appearance in the work of a British critic, Maud Bodkin, whose *Archetypal Patterns in Poetry* was published in 1934. But Myth Criticism only began to develop a head of steam when taken up by a number of American critics in the late 1940s and early 1950s: Richard Chase, Leslie Fiedler, Philip Wheelwright and Francis Fergusson.

Chase and Fiedler, in particular, directed critical attention towards nineteenth century American fiction, which proved a fertile hunting-ground for mythical archetypes.

The Myth Critics had their own obvious reasons for focusing upon causal action rather than upon language. After all, the same mythical narrative may be realised in many different linguistic formats. For less obvious reasons, they also tended to emphasise the variety of genres – perhaps partly because the nature of nineteenth century American fiction prompted a recognition of the special standards of the romance, as distinct from the standards of the realistic novel. Another characteristic emphasis has to do with the kind of effect appropriate to myth: a response of simple awe and wonder, quite unlike the taste for sophisticated irony encouraged by the New Criticism. In fact, this latter emphasis converged with a more general pro-Romantic trend in America during the 1950s, when critics such as Harold Bloom, Geoffrey Hartmann and M. H. Abrams began to promote Milton, Blake and Shelley over and above the Metaphysicals. (Again, a solitary British figure foreshadows this trend: G. Wilson Knight, writing in the 1930s and 1940s.)

But Myth Criticism still derives from the Modernist matrix. No less than the New Critics, the Myth Critics are concerned to divine a higher (or deeper) level of signifying hidden behind a literal surface signifying. It is the units of interpretation which have changed: no longer single words or small groups of words, but larger figures, created beings and whole narrative sequences. Moreover, the hidden significances are no longer static 'themes' of the order of Art or Life or Death, but involve a newly dynamic dimension of working-out. On Fiedler's definition, archetypes 'at once define and *attempt to solve* what is most permanent in the human predicament [my italics]'.[98] The idea that archetypes solve problems corresponds to Jung's original claim that archetypes have genuine cognitive value. But such working-out can only be attributed to the whole human race, not to the individual poem or poet.

Myth Criticism began to overtake the New Criticism when Northrop Frye's *Anatomy of Criticism* appeared in 1957. Frye, a Canadian critic, not only enlarged enormously upon the work of previous Myth Critics, but shifted conceptions as to the very nature and task of literary criticism. At the same time, his approach was less strictly Jungian than that of his predecessors. American Myth Critics had already tended to skim over Jung's claim to locate the collective unconscious in the inherited architecture of the brain; now Frye argued that arche-types are revealed no less clearly in literature than in the mythology of pre-literate societies. Very rarely does Frye adduce evidence from anthropology or Jungian psychoanalysis. What is more, his approach derives almost equally from another ultimate source in the *Poetics* of Aristotle (though *not* by way of the Chicago Neo-Aristotelians). 'In literary criticism,' he asserts, 'myth means ultimately *mythos*, a struc-tural organizing principle of literary form.'[99] *Mythos* is the Aristotelian term for an action or plot; and just as different kinds of *mythos* define different genres for Aristotle, so too for Frye. In Frye's criticism, concepts of archetype are very close to concepts of genre – and vice versa.

Frye reverses the New Critics' homogenisation of genres and their tendency to localise analysis upon very short passages of language. But he continues, and even accentuates, their insistence upon the autonomy of literature. 'Pure literature, like pure mathematics, contains its own meaning,' he asserts, drawing a favourite analogy.[100] Like the New Critics, he downplays consideration of historical context, author's intention, moral ideas and real-world reference. Such concerns are overridden by the Jungian notion of internally-implanted, universally-existing archetypes – and in this respect at least, Frye is a thoroughgoing Jungian. Particularly important is his rejection of real-world reference, which translates into a radical chal-lenge to realism and realistic fiction. The New Critics had also under-cut the value of realism, but Romantic or late-Romantic poetry had been the main target of their hostility. Now, however, the battle-lines are redrawn: with Frye's focus upon large-scale narratives, the princi-ple of the autonomy of literature comes into direct conflict with the realist novel.

In this new battle, one strategy is the strategy of taxonomic re-clas-sification. Frye confines the value of realism to a single genre of prose fiction, and recognises other genres governed by other values. Earlier Myth Critics had already put the non-realist *romance* on a par with the realist *novel*; Frye now adds the *anatomy* and the *confession*. The 'low mimetic prejudice' of expectations appropriate to the realist novel can only lead to misunderstanding when applied to a romance like Maturin's *Melmoth the Wanderer,* or a confession like Hogg's *Confessions of a Justified Sinner,* or an anatomy like Walton's *The Compleat Angler.* Frye also draws attention to the multiple criteria required for such hybrids as the romance-anatomy (e.g., *Moby Dick*),

the novel-anatomy (e.g., *Tristram Shandy*), and the romance-confes-
sion (e.g., De Quincy's *Confessions of an English Opium Eater*). As
often, the creation of new categories for thought enables what had
been previously unnoticed or unvalued to emerge into the open light
of day.

What is more, Frye undermines the value of realism even within the
genre of the realist novel. Even here, the narrative is always ultimately
archetypal. Frye suggests that we can discover the essential shape of a
novel's narrative by backing away to a position at which its local
details become unimportant: 'If we "stand back" from a realistic novel
such as Tolstoy's *Resurrection* or Zola's *Germinal,* we can see the
mythopoeic designs indicated by those titles [i.e. a story of resurrection, and a story of birth and growth].'[101] Whereas novel-oriented
critics have typically viewed romances as mere early steps along the
road to realism, Frye views realist novels as mere transpositions of
romance into a context of everyday life. Defining displacement as 'the
adjusting of formulaic structures to a roughly credible context', he
argues that 'the novel was a realistic displacement of romance, and
had few structural principles peculiar to itself'.[102] In Frye's theory,
novels are never allowed to make primary contact with our own real
world, and truthful reflection of that world is never allowed to become
a criterion in its own right. Instead, realism is seen as a matter of 'realistic' impression, a patina of seemingly plausible details thrown over
the primary imaginative reality of the archetype.

The same logic also discounts truthful reflection of the writer's own
experience. 'To dissolve art back into the artist's experience is like
scraping the paint off a canvas in order to see what the "real" canvas
looked like before it assumed its painted disguise.'[103] Archetypal
material comes from beyond individual experience, and produces
itself through the writer as through a conduit. 'He is responsible for
delivering [the poem] in as uninjured a state as possible.'[104] The
degree to which the writer is conscious of what thus produces itself is
of no concern to the critic.

But Frye allows the literary work to open out in one direction –
towards other literature. 'Poetry can only be made out of other
poems; novels out of other novels.'[105] The principle of the autonomy
of literature applies not to individual works but to the total field of
literature as a whole: 'myth criticism pulls us away from "life" toward
a self-contained and autonomous literary universe'.[106] This is Frye's
own characteristic emphasis, which did not appear in earlier versions

of Myth Criticism. Frye is at his least Jungian – and most Aristotelian – when he associates his archetypes with literary influences and even literary conventions. For Frye, all literature is equally conventional, though only unfamiliar conventions are noticed as such. The sole relevant distinction is between a deeper or shallower use of convention:

> For the serious mediocre writer convention makes him sound like a lot of other people; for the popular writer it gives him a formula he can exploit; for the serious good writer it releases his experiences or emotions from himself and incorporates them into literature, where they belong.[107]

Frye does not share the general Modernist belief that the primary duty of literature is to disturb established habits of thought and expression.

The plausibility of Frye's theoretical assertions rests ultimately upon his ability to demonstrate an internal logic by which differentiated possibilities are generated within the total field of literature. And this is in fact the most impressive feature of his criticism. Literature, he claims, 'is organized by huge containing conceptions which establish the literary societies and the family resemblances among large groups of writers'.[108] Typically, he distinguishes a set of logical possibilities – often four in number – on a given conceptual dimension: for example, a set of four primary narrative movements, 'first, the descent from a higher world; second, the descent to a lower world; third, the ascent from a lower world; fourth, the ascent to a higher world'.[109] He arrives at a characterisation of particular works by permutating the possibilities available on various dimensions. Literature thus appears as 'a complication of a relatively restricted and simple group of formulas'.[110] Unfortunately, no brief sample can serve to convey the mutually reinforcing nature of the system as a whole, which is its strongest suit. Frye needs to be tasted in sizeable quantities – at a minimum, one of the four 'essays' in *Anatomy of Criticism*.

The ideal of understanding as a complication of simple formulas is of course a scientific ideal, and Frye often draws a parallel between criticism and science.

> Everyone who has seriously studied literature knows that the mental process involved is as coherent and progressive as the study of

science. A precisely similar training of the mind takes place, and a similar sense of the unity of the subject is built up.[111]

The key term here is 'unity': it is science's initial assumption of comprehensive coherence that Frye has in mind, not science's practical methodology of empirical observation. Whereas Aristotle approached literary genres with a view to describing such particular species as happened to exist, Frye's approach is considerably more abstract and a priori. His assumption of comprehensive coherence commits him to the claim that the possibilities he describes are indeed the *only* possibilities.

If all of literature is a unity, then its many different parts are all complementary and necessary to the whole. Judgements of better or worse become irrelevant. Frye thus dismisses evaluation from his taxonomic poetics: 'Criticism as knowledge is one thing, and value-judgements informed by taste are another.'[112] Nonetheless, it is clear that value-judgements – even if not by Frye himself – have already constructed the field which he denominates as 'literature'. Although his tastes are less strenuously highbrow than those of the New Critics, nonetheless, his 'undiscriminating catholicity' does not extend to popular or lowbrow writings – or at any rate, he noticeably fails to mention them. He also introduces a new evaluative criterion of his own when he exalts certain works, such as Joyce's *Ulysses,* which manage to incorporate a maximum number of different taxonomic categories. This somewhat inconsistent criterion seems to derive from the New Critics and their preference for a maximum number of different or contrasting elements within the individual poem.

The strength of Myth Criticism in the period following the publication of *Anatomy of Criticism* was a North American phenomenon, which had virtually no echo in Britain. Starting from the same sources, British and North American criticism had come to a point of wide divergence. In this period, British criticism turned with renewed interest to prose fiction – but under the generally pro-realist orientation of the Leavisites. In North America, Frye's influence prepared the ground for the importation of French Structuralism, which can be seen as a more *absolute* form of systematic, taxonomic poetics.

10 Phenomenological Criticism in France and Germany

In the first half of the twentieth century, while Russia, England and the US surged ahead with new forms of Modernist-oriented criticism, French and German literary theory remained strangely in the doldrums. In France, the institutional teaching of literature was dominated by the *explication de texte*, a kind of close reading commentary which paid great attention to line-by-line linguistic features without ever rising to any larger theoretical insights. Germany continued its strong nineteenth-century tradition of historical scholarship and grand evolutionary hypothesis. (The most impressive evolutionary hypothesis was presented in Erich Auerbach's *Mimesis*, covering the linguistic representation of reality across the whole of Western literary history.) However, there were significant stirrings in both countries around the mid-century, especially associated with the phenomenological perspective in philosophy.

Phenomenology in its first phase is linked to the name of Edmund Husserl. Husserl's philosophy turns upon the idea of *acts of consciousness*. Consciousness is not a mirroring (with all the attendant problems of duplicated entities, the thing-out-there versus the image-in-here), but an intending or attending, a willing and grasping. Such a perspective ties in with many well-known experiments in Gestalt psychology: for example, the mental switch which converts a picture of two faces into a picture of a vase, and vice versa. According to Husserl, all consciousness is directed at a target, and we are not only aware of doing the directing but aware of the kind of directing that we are doing. After all, it is virtually impossible to confuse the seeing of a tree with the remembering of a tree, no matter how similar the respective tree-images.

The goal of this philosophy is to understand what is involved in the different kinds of directing, the different types of grasp. Clearly, we can only achieve such understanding from the inside, from within our own subjective lived experience. But Husserl assumes that the philosopher's mind can rise and comprehend its own acts of consciousness from above. His methodology even calls for the setting aside of all such practical cares and interests as are inspired by the real existence of the objects that consciousness targets. In Husserlian Phenomenology, consciousness is potentially superior to its own acts.

The contrary applies in the case of Existentialism. This second phase of phenomenology (now appropriately spelt with a small 'p') was launched by another German philosopher, Martin Heidegger. Heidegger denies the possibility of rising and comprehending from above. The objects that consciousness targets are targeted precisely because of our existing cares and interests, including our bodily wants. 'Thrown' into particular bodies at a particular location in historical time, we are condemned to look out from a starting-point which we did not choose but cannot leave behind. Above all, we come to consciousness in a world where everything is already shaped by human cares and interests, where everything already appears in its relevance to human purposes. No effort of consciousness can ever recover a pure, objective state of the world; we can never return to basics and think our way up on rational principles. Our horizons are inescapably time-bound, predetermined by the whole of human history that has come before us.

And yet we are also free – towards the future. Although our starting point is given, our acts of consciousness, like our physical acts, are under our own direction. Indeed, our acts of consciousness open up a far greater freedom than our physical acts; through them, we can even make and create ourselves. Laying the stress upon *acts* rather than upon *consciousness*, Heidegger arrives at an ethics of choosing and willing and reaching towards the future. Whereas Husserlian Phenomenology is mainly concerned with how we may know the world, Existentialism is mainly concerned with how we should live in it.

Poulet and the Geneva School

The Geneva School of criticism originated in Francophone Switzerland in the 1930s, with the writings of Marcel Raymond and Albert Béguin. But it was only when Georges Poulet published his first book in 1949 that the school began to develop its full philosophical orientation. This was the period when Existentialist ideas were spreading into France; however, it is what the Existentialists share in common with Husserl that is relevant to an understanding of the Geneva critics. Specifically, their approach seeks to characterise the essential kind of grasp that a writer directs towards reality.

Poulet terms this essential grasp the *cogito*. Examining such metaphysically fundamental features as a writer's way of structuring space and time, he comes up with some extraordinarily deep differences. Amongst mid-nineteenth-century American writers, for instance, Emerson

> pursues in time a reflection of experience that only takes place outside of time, contrary to time, in the moment.
> [His] work . . . therefore . . . applies itself to destroying time, before summoning up in the void of time the positive reality of the moment.[1]

In Hawthorne, on the other hand,

> the present moment . . . is meager and quickly dismantled . . . existence is formed of the perpetual swallowing up of what has just been lived[2]

while Whitman's thought

> is nothing, except that infinite receptivity which is the quality proper to shores; it depends entirely on an exterior universal phenomenon which, by overrunning it, gives it animation and existence. This phenomenon is time. Whitman's present is essentially the collecting place of that movement which is duration.[3]

The extreme abstraction in these quotations is typical. It matters little what particular objects or particular contents are written about; any object may equally serve to reveal the kind of grasp that a writer directs towards reality. In Poulet's own retrospective words:

> All literature was philosophy for me. . . . No matter what sort of text I read, at the instant I began to sense the effect of a concept in it, I found the same origin in almost each line and the same course running from this source.[4]

Most of all, Poulet favours those moments when the writer's *cogito* becomes its own object, in an act of self-directed thought.

Looking through to the writer's *cogito,* Poulet and the Geneva critics largely ignore the verbal medium of the text. Formal and material features are only obstacles to their special quest. Nor are they interested in the individual qualities of individual works, or the generic qualities appropriate to specific genres. Their focus is entirely upon the *oeuvre,* upon all the writings attributable to a given *cogito,* including fragments and juvenilia. As J. Hillis Miller in his early Geneva phase puts it: 'all the works of a single writer form a unity, a unity in which a thousand paths radiate from the same centre'.[5] By postulating such a centre, the Geneva critics can justify even their deepest plunges below the textual surface.

But the exploration of the writer's *cogito* is not the same as an exploration of the writer's life. Biography has little relevance for the Geneva critics. After all, a writer's everyday behaviour reveals only personality traits – not fundamental metaphysical acts of consciousness. The Geneva critics keep their eyes upon the literary evidence because only the literary evidence can serve their purposes. In Poulet's words: 'it is not the biography which explicates the work, but rather the work which sometimes enables us to understand the biography'.[6] Nor do the Geneva critics have much use for a writer's own self-descriptions or philosophical formulations. For the *cogito* is not thought which the writer knows as object; it is that which *conditions* the writer's act of thinking.

The critic, on the other hand, must know the *cogito* as object in order to talk about it. But before this can happen, the critic must first reproduce empathetically the writer's original act. As in all phenomenology, acts of consciousness can be understood only from within. Poulet describes the process as a kind of self-surrender to an alien consciousness: 'I am on loan to another, and this other thinks, feels, suffers, and acts within me'.[7] Viewed in this light, literary criticism appears as a very intuitive business, to the point where the critic becomes almost another creative artist.

The Geneva School may seem outdated to contemporary eyes. Their empathetic approach harks all the way back to Romantic criticism (and it is no coincidence that their tastes also incline towards Romantic and neo-Romantic writers). Amongst twentieth-century critics, they are exceptional in their indifference to the verbal medium of the text. However, their interest in ways-of-seeing is a typical twentieth-century interest, and their fondness for describing ways-of-seeing on a very high level of metaphysical abstraction has remained an abiding tendency of literary theory ever since. It is perhaps not so surprising that critics whose careers began in the Geneva School, such as J. Hillis Miller and (to a lesser extent) Paul de Man, later shifted across into Deconstructionism without great difficulty.

From Ingarden to Iser

Phenomenological ideas were applied in a different way by critics based at the University of Constance (Konstanz) in southern Germany. Under the banner of Reception Aesthetics, the Constance School focused attention not upon the writer's but upon the reader's acts of consciousness. Since the school's two main proponents worked along different dimensions and came under different influences, I shall deal with them in separate sections: first, Wolfgang Iser, then Hans-Robert Jauss.

Iser draws upon the ideas of Roman Ingarden, who draws directly upon Husserl. Ingarden, a Polish philosopher and aesthetician, outlined a Phenomenological theory of the literary work in two major books published in the 1930s. In this theory, the focus is upon the active construction of fictional worlds by the reader. Verbal meanings guide and channel the reader's creative acts of consciousness – on the way to a target that lies beyond verbal meanings. Ingarden regards the level of language as essentially a means towards a further level of projected objects: 'I cannot reduce the literary work of art . . . to mere language. . . . I relate to the human beings presented in a work of art.'[8] Although not real, fictional human beings (and fictional scenes, and fictional actions) have objective existence, in the sense that any number of readers can project them on any number of occasions. They are projected *from* the mind of the reader, but they are not simply *in* the mind of the reader. It should be noted that, in Husserlian Phenomenology, real-world human beings, scenes and actions are similarly projected *from* the mind of the perceiver – through the guidance and channelling of perceptual sense-data.

However, there is one significant difference. Apprehended perceptually, real human beings, scenes and actions exist in a state of full concrete individuality. But fictional human beings, scenes and actions exist only in terms of a limited number of epithets:

If, e.g., a story begins with the sentence: 'An old man was sitting at a table,' etc., it is clear that the represented 'table' is indeed a 'table' and not, for example, a 'chair'; but whether it is made of wood or iron, is four-legged or three-legged, etc., is left quite unsaid and therefore – this being a purely intentional object – *not determined.*[9]

Even the addition of further epithets can never particularise in the manner of sense-data. For example, the old man may be described as 'thin' and 'grey-haired', but exactly how thin? exactly what shade of grey? Words by their very nature are general and schematic. At the same time, though, the literary work encourages us to imagine states of full concrete individuality. We imagine a character in a novel as we do not ordinarily imagine a real person named in a history book; we imagine a scene in a novel as we do not ordinarily imagine a real locale discussed in a handbook on urban planning. *Spots of indeterminacy* arise wherever the reader's justifiable impulse to imagine surpasses the evidence actually provided.

Ingarden thus recognises a further creative activity on the part of the reader: an activity of *concretisation.* 'On his own initiative and with his own imagination [the reader] "fills out" various places of indeterminacy with elements chosen from among many possible or permissible elements.'[10] One proof that such activity takes place might be found in our common reaction on seeing the movie after reading the book: 'Oh, that wasn't the way I imagined Mrs X.' And yet the physical appearance of the actor playing the character may be perfectly compatible with such evidence as the text provides. The act of filling out spots of indeterminacy is both necessary and yet free, prompted and yet uncontrolled.

Following a typical line of Phenomenological thinking, Ingarden envisages the construction of a fictional world as an experience developing progressively through time. This is very different from most Modernist-oriented criticism, which tends to view all literary works as simultaneously and spatially present, on the model of the short lyric.[11] According to Ingarden, the reader is fully and vividly aware of details only at – or immediately after – the actual point of reading. Further behind lies the hinterland of 'the parts already read, which sink into the "past" of the work'; while up ahead, 'certain "coming" events announce themselves in outline; sometimes several possibilities announce themselves at once'.[12] This *double horizon* of memory and anticipation corresponds to the Husserlian philosophy of human experience in general. Ingarden also notes that the reader's past acts of construction may undergo retrospective revision in the light of new information appearing in the present: 'from the point of view of the "later" phase (the phase being read), the parts of the work which the reader already knows . . . often present themselves in another form from the one in which they showed themselves . . . when they were being read'.[13]

Although Iser began publishing in the 1950s, his most significant writings belong to the 1970s. In the different literary climate of this later period, Ingarden's ideas are redirected to new purposes. Iser concentrates especially upon the reader's temporal progression through a text, which he describes as 'a moving viewpoint which travels along *inside* that which it has to apprehend'.[14] This progression is seen as involving retrospective revisions far more drastic than anything in Ingarden's theory. Whereas Ingarden emphasises the steady accumulation of a fictional world, Iser argues that 'the act of recreation is not a smooth or continuous process, but one which, in its essence, relies on *interruptions* of the flow to render it efficacious'.[15]

Iser describes the text as an 'appeal structure' which sets up blanks and gaps for the reader to fill in. This involves concretisation, as described by Ingarden; but Iser casts a wider net and includes every kind of connection – between sentences, between actions – which the reader is encouraged to supply. 'The blanks . . . indicate that the different segments of the text *are* to be connected, even though the text itself does not say so.'[16] The reader actively participates in creating 'good form' and 'gestalt groupings' – just as, in visual perception, our minds join up lines in a drawing which don't actually meet.

Such active participation is necessary in order to involve the reader in a learning process of adjusting, correcting and overcoming mistakes. Connections made or anticipated are always liable to be undone later on in the text. Discussing Fielding's *Joseph Andrews*, Iser argues that 'the problems thus aroused are necessary to entangle [the reader] in the configurative meaning he is producing; only when this happens, can the effect of the novel really begin to work on the reader'.[17] According to this argument, Fielding encourages in the reader a sense of superior comprehension which is then deliberately undermined. Such undermining is for Iser the distinguishing mark of literature: 'expectations are scarcely ever fulfilled in truly literary texts'.[18] His conception of literature is strenuous and educative; popular fiction he dismisses with contempt.

Not surprisingly, Iser especially values the kind of twentieth-century text which overthrows what the reader ordinarily takes for granted. Defamiliarisation here becomes a temporal sequence (as in so many Postmodernist narratives); the work offers the illusion of a conventional framework before frustrating and defeating it. 'What at first seemed to be an affirmation of our assumptions leads to our own rejection of them.'[19] This is in effect a whole new level of reader activity, over and above the level of connection and concretisation. The reader is prompted to a rethinking and reframing which is not laid down as such in any of the verbal meanings of the text. Such prompting depends ultimately upon a free act of the reader; it can never amount to explicit compulsion or control (as when readers of Postmodernist narratives remain merely baffled).

As in all theories of defamiliarisation, this rethinking and reframing reflects back upon the reader's own consciousness. 'The significance of the work', says Iser, 'does not lie in the meaning sealed within the text, but in the fact that that meaning brings out what had previously been sealed within us.'[20] What matters in the end is not the construction of a fictional world, but the sudden light cast by the failure of such construction upon the reader's own habitual assumptions and conventional frameworks. The interaction between reader and text has its most important effect in something that is *done* to the reader. In this respect, Iser's approach is oriented towards reader response in a way that Ingarden's isn't.

Nonetheless, Iser's approach differs considerably from that of the later American Reader-Response critics. He is concerned with what a text can do to a reader, not with what a reader can do to a text. Admittedly, he allows considerable individual variation on the level of connection and concretisation: 'one text is potentially capable of several different realizations, and no reading can ever exhaust the full potential, for each individual reader will fill in the gaps in his own way'.[21] From Iser's point of view, the specific details of connection and concretisation are unimportant, provided that readers can come to an identical awareness of the conventional frameworks upon which they had been relying. What Iser can *not* allow to readers is the right to create new meanings by supplementing the text with their own individual presuppositions and predispositions. Presuppositions for Iser are either conventional assumptions of the kind that will be overthrown in the process of reading, or they must be left behind before reading begins. Iser's 'implied reader' is an ideal figure, whose endless capacity for acts of consciousness seems curiously divorced from particular desires and personal forms of interest.

From Gadamer to Jauss

The main influence upon Jauss was Hans-Georg Gadamer, who himself followed Heidegger. Together, Heidegger and Gadamer represent a major revolution in the German tradition of hermeneutics. As has been seen, the original version of hermeneutics advanced by Schleiermacher made enormous claims for empathy, calling upon the interpreter to step across into the alien perspective of the author and the author's historical time. With modifications, this version lasted throughout the nineteenth century. But such stepping across is impossible under the principles of Existentialist philosophy, where the subjective end of every act of consciousness is inescapably tied to the particular location into which the subject has been 'thrown'. One can only ever look out from one's own perspective in one's own historical time. The interpreter is no less time-bound than the author being interpreted.

Gadamer does not regard this historicality as a limitation. Certainly, an interpreter brings to the reading of a text the prejudices of her/his own historical period; but then, if the interpreter brought nothing at all, understanding could hardly even begin. Understanding, on the Existentialist view, is more than a mere passive registering of meanings – it involves grasps and *acts* of consciousness. And in grasping, as Gadamer points out, we must be always anticipating ahead, always projecting forward on the basis of our prejudices. 'Legitimate prejudices' spread out the field on which a meaning can appear. Such preconceptions and prejudices may undergo revision in the course of further reading; but without them, we are not actively engaging with the text at all.

Gadamer's case is that we have to be interested in order to understand – in a double sense of the term 'interested'. Can we ever really grasp a meaning without *caring* about it? To understand, in Gadamer's hermeneutics, is to discover an application to our own concerns, to realise how the meaning can mean for us. 'To understand a text always means to apply it to ourselves.'[22] Understanding here is a kind of recognition – the kind of recognition that occurs when one suddenly makes sense of something in terms of one's own experience.

This relation of meaning to one's own experience is not self-centred, but a necessary feature of understanding as an interaction between two poles. To claim to leave oneself out of the account is merely to allow one's personal concerns and prejudices to rule in secret. 'A person who imagines that he is free of prejudices . . . experiences the power of the prejudices that unconsciously dominate him.'[23] By contrast, a person who is aware of being prejudiced at least puts those prejudices at risk, exposing them to challenge. Although there is no escape from the determinations of the past, we can still be free towards the future. 'All that is asked,' says Gadamer, 'is that we remain open to the meaning of the other person or of the text.'[24] It is not necessary to recover the other's pure original meaning, but rather to enter into a genuine conversation, a free play of question and answer. A genuine conversation with a historical text will ultimately illuminate both past and present. Drawing upon the phenomenological notion of the *horizon* as 'the range of vision that includes everything that can be seen from a particular vantage point', Gadamer describes such illumination as a *fusion of horizons*.[25]

An example (not from Gadamer) may serve to illustrate here: the example of Marxist interpretations of Marx. In this case, interpretations have always been very *interested* indeed. The urgent need to apply Marx's writings to strategies for action under current conditions has naturally outweighed the objectivist goal of recovering Marx's original historical meaning. From Lukács to Sartre to Althusser to Eagleton, interpretations have shifted with each new input from each new interpreter. But this does not mean that interpreters have simply overridden Marx with their own prejudices. On the contrary, the discovery of Marx has often opened their eyes with the force of a revelation. Marxist interpretations of Marx illustrate very clearly the kind of conversation that can take place between the stimulus of a text and the prejudices of later interpreters. Over and again, the end product has been an illumination that surpasses both stimulus and prejudices taken separately. So long as changing social conditions continue to produce changing inputs on the side of the interpreter, there is no reason why interpretations of Marx might not continue to move onward indefinitely.

Gadamer's relativising of interpretation has had a general influence upon literary theory. But in Gadamer's own hermeneutics, the radicalism of this relativising was somewhat muted by a concept of *tradition.* According to Gadamer, a conversation with past texts is possible because the past is not a total stranger to us. Although our own perspective is determined by the socio-historical conditions into which we are 'thrown', those conditions have been built upon past conditions and contain within themselves the inheritance of past perspectives. We can never leap into the state of mind of a medieval Christian, for example, because we can never clear from our minds the deposits of the last five hundred years of human history; but by the same token, the continuity of tradition guarantees that at least something of the medieval Christian way of thinking has been laid down in our own way of thinking. Being locked into a tradition is an empowerment to the extent that it enables us to come to an agreement with the past. But it does not empower us to open up a profound disagreement with the past – to subject the past to a radical critique. There are conservative implications in the concept of tradition, as Gadamer's critics have been swift to point out.

Gadamer's ideas were taken up and reapplied by his student Hans-Robert Jauss. Jauss brought the Constance School to general attention with a polemical lecture delivered in 1967, subsequently published under the title 'Literary History as a Challenge to Literary Theory'. As the title suggests, Jauss was essentially a literary historian, not a literary critic like Iser. His major concern was to rejuvenate on new principles the once-powerful German tradition of literary history.

Jauss's new principles involve a new site for literary history. Traditional literary historians had related the literary work to its origins – that is, to the social and cultural conditions which supposedly shaped the author's mind at the time of writing. Such an approach went with the belief that the work exists in full and final form as it leaves the author's hands. But Jauss, following Gadamer, insists upon a further stage of production, in the interaction that takes place between work and audience. The work attains full existence only when creatively constituted by its readers. 'The historical life of a literary work is unthinkable without the active participation of its addressees.'[26] The audience spreads out the field upon which the work can appear. Jauss thus calls for a literary history of readers, which will focus upon reception rather than production.

Naturally, a history of readers will recognise the very different creative contributions made by different historical audiences. There is no eternal bedrock of human nature of the kind upon which Aristotle and the Neoclassical critics relied. Jauss coins the phrase *horizon of expectations* to characterise the specific norms and assumptions brought to bear by the audience of a specific period – norms and assumptions derived from previous literary encounters and socio-cultural determinations generally. A literary work may 'satisf[y], surpass, disappoint, or refute the expectations of its first audience'.[27] But the first audience is not the end of the story. Subsequent audiences with different horizons of expectation may generate different interactions, produce different works. 'A literary work is not an object that stands by itself and that offers the same view to each reader in each period. It is not a monument that monologically reveals its time-less essence.'[28] Jauss thus proclaims the possibility of ongoing, developing meanings for a work. It is the literary historian's task to trace the history of such meanings, rather than to recover a single original meaning as created by a first audience.

By re-siting literary history, Jauss draws in the wider social context at a new point. When traditional literary history focuses upon production, the causal sequence inevitably runs from the very general to the very particular: from, say, national economic conditions to national culture to an individual author to an individual piece of writing produced by that author. On this sequence of explanation, all pieces of writing in a given period ought to be very much alike. But such is not the case. General social conditions are not so directly reflected in individual works. Literature is 'variously permeable of events in historical reality', says Jauss; 'in the fullness of its forms, [it] allows itself to be referred back only in part and not in any exact manner to concrete conditions of the economic process'.[29] But audiences are another matter. It seems reasonable to suppose that the norms and assumptions imprinted upon a great many minds through a great many previous literary encounters will be far more typical of society at large, far less specialised than the individual work of the individual writer.

In fact, Jauss's history of readers allows for considerable variation in how a literary work relates to its period. Some works may be very much of their time, fully confirming the audience's expectations; others may be so far out of step as to be wholly baffling in their own time, only becoming readable with the arrival of a new horizon of expectations. Most interesting of all, some works may unsettle norms and expectations to just such a degree that the reader, entering into a conversation with the text, comes out changed. 'The experience of reading can liberate one from adaptations, prejudices and predica-ments of a lived praxis in that it compels one to a new perception of things.'[30] Whereas traditional literary history views literature only as a product, Jauss's model makes room for the 'socially formative function of literature'.[31] In the total field of socio-cultural determinations, literature can be a cause as well as an effect.

If audiences bring their own horizons of expectation, so too does the literary historian, looking back over past periods. Jauss rejects the 'historical objectivism' of the interpreter 'who, supposedly bracketing himself, nonetheless raises his own aesthetic preconceptions to an unacknowledged norm and unreflectively modernizes the meaning of the past text'.[32] Like Gadamer, he insists that the historian's own norms and assumptions must be taken into the account and used productively. Also like Gadamer, he suggests that the past is not a total stranger to us because our own horizon has been in some sense built upon earlier horizons. 'If the original horizon of life in an earlier time were not always already contained within our own, later, horizon, historical understanding would not be possible.'[33] But the 'conversation with the past' is necessarily a two-way process. For Jauss, the purpose of reconstructing a past horizon of expectations is to illuminate the present. 'One's own expectations will be corrected and expanded through the experience of the other.'[34] The light is cast back equally upon the interpreter, who cannot remain neutral and uninvolved.

In practice, however, Jauss is more of a historical objectivist than his statements might indicate. And in one respect at least, he raises his own twentieth-century preconceptions to an unacknowledged norm. That is, he values a work precisely to the extent that it distances itself from the prevailing horizon of expectations. Without elevating Modernist qualities as such, he nonetheless measures all literature against a Modernist ideal of challenging and unsettling accepted assumptions. Works 'fulfilling the expectations prescribed by a ruling standard of taste' are associated with popular culture, which is dismissed as '"culinary" or entertainment art'.[35] Looking back later on his 1967 lecture, Jauss himself admits 'the flagrant modernism of this earliest paradigm for a reception aesthetic'.[36] However, his later attempts to set up positive *pleasure* as an alternative literary value have been far less influential than his original position.

De Beauvoir and two predecessors
(*also de Staël, Woolf*)

While women writers had long struggled against the odds, a growing number of women writers came to the fore in the nineteenth and first half of the twentieth centuries. But the business of criticism and theory remained firmly in male hands: men continued to set the standards and judge the results. Nonetheless, some determined voices managed to prepare the way for the great explosion of feminist criticism which began at the end of the 1960s – voices such as those of Germaine de Staël (Madame de Staël), Virginia Woolf and, of course, Simone de Beauvoir. These three novelist-critics were spokeswomen for specific movements in their time: de Staël introduced Romanticism to France, Woolf wrote important manifestos for Modernism, and de Beauvoir was wholly committed to Existentialism. But their involvement with such movements did not save them from the experience of being marginalised as women. Even the enormously successful de Staël was always aware of pressures with which no male Romantic writer ever had to contend. The three women thus share something in common which transcends their Romantic, Modernist and Existentialist perspectives. For this reason, I have chosen to discuss them together, carrying the two earlier figures across to de Beauvoir's chronological moment – a moment of particular importance in the history of feminism.

De Staël attempts to advance the cause of women in both political criticism and literary criticism. Discarding long-established judgements, she insists upon evaluating societies according to the way they treat women. Greek culture is condemned for suppressing and excluding one half of the human race. Not surprisingly, she is in favour of progress, as tending overall towards increasing civilisation and an improved status for women. But she is well aware that revolutions driven mainly by men are not necessarily beneficial for women. Although a supporter of the Republican cause, she observes a short-term cultural decline due to 'the grossness of certain people's ideas during the [French] Revolution'.[37] Nor had the Revolution significantly improved the position of women writers: 'in monarchies, women [who set their minds upon literary celebrity] have ridicule to fear; in republics, hatred'.[38]

In *Literature Considered in its Relation to Social Institutions*, de Staël relates literature to social manners, and social manners to political institutions. 'No one', she suggests, 'has adequately analyzed the moral and political causes that modify the spirit of literature.'[39] At the same time, she recognises a reverse influence of literature upon customs and laws. She is especially interested in the development of literary forms appropriate to the post-Revolutionary state of French society. Tragedy and comedy, for example, can no longer be expected to function as under a monarchical regime. Although she allows that 'tragedy concerns unchanging feelings', she argues that 'it is nevertheless altered, as are all products of the human mind, by social institutions and the customs that rest upon them'.[40]

Her advocacy of Romanticism is complicated for the same reasons as her advocacy of Republicanism. No doubt it says much about de Staël's marginal position in her own society that she could set herself outside the French cultural tradition and identify with what she called 'the North' (primarily Germany). But, as has often been noted, her version of Romanticism includes Sentimental and even Neoclassical tendencies. Above all, she downplays those elements in Romanticism potentially inimical to the interests of women: viz, the glorification of Nature and the natural; the harking back to a more savage past; and the cult of the solitary (male) hero. De Staël's version of Romanticism is mild in literary terms; but in socio-political terms, it is strong in its sense of a distinctively female perspective.

Woolf is a strong Modernist as well as a strong feminist. As a Modernist, she lays great weight upon aesthetic and formal virtues, upon harmony and unity. In two famous essays, 'Modern Fiction' and 'Mr Bennett and Mrs Brown', she condemns the Naturalist novelists' obsession with the recording of external material details. But this does not make her any the less aware of how mere practicalities influence the actual business of writing. 'Intellectual freedom depends upon material things,' she asserts; and 'material circumstances' are always 'against the likelihood that [a work of genius] will come from the writer's mind whole and entire. . . . Dogs will bark; people will interrupt; money must be made; health will break down.'[41] Sharing the very lofty Modernist view of the writer's vocation, she attends to the conditions under which a writer must operate – precisely because unfavourable conditions will prevent the achievement of such a vocation.

Naturally, the conditions for women writers have always been particularly unfavourable. Woolf notes the practical effects of financial dependence upon a father or husband, of exclusion from the higher levels of the education system, and of restriction to a narrow range of 'feminine' experience. Even to secure a private space for writing, a 'room of one's own', has been no trivial matter for women writers. Woolf also draws attention to the invisible psychological obstacles which make it difficult for a woman to regard writing as a vocation. 'The world did not say to [the woman writer] as it said to [male writers], Write if you choose; it makes no difference to me. The world said with a guffaw, Write? What's the good of your writing?'[42] Even the topics of women's writing are not taken seriously in a world dominated by male values. 'This is an important book, the critic assumes, because it deals with war. This is an insignificant book because it deals with the feelings of women in a drawing-room.'[43]

The woman writer is thus thrown into a defensive posture from the very outset – with dangerous consequences for her art. *Jane Eyre* is Woolf's prime example of a novel flawed by an impulse to fight against anticipated criticism: 'it is clear that anger was tampering with the integrity of Charlotte Brontë the novelist'.[44] The woman writer in a male-dominated world is always liable to be 'saying this by way of aggression, or that by way of conciliation' – and thereby 'thinking of something other than the thing itself.'[45] The typical Modernist objection to pushing a cause or preaching a message is visible here; and it is in relation to such pushing or preaching that Woolf at one point even makes the claim that 'it is fatal for anyone who writes to think of their sex . . . anything written with that conscious bias is doomed to death'.[46]

However, Woolf does not believe that a writer's sex is something to be generally transcended. On the contrary, she insists upon the importance of writing *as a woman,* and, in many essays on past and forgotten women writers, begins the necessary work of constructing a feminine tradition. Most radically of all, she suggests a fundamental distinction between male language and female language. The standard male sentence, she claims, is not suitable for adoption by the woman writer: 'the weight, the pace, the stride of a man's mind are too unlike her own for her to lift anything substantial from him successfully'.[47] Similarly as regards the overall structure of a book: 'There is no reason to think that the form of the epic or of the poetic play suit a woman any more than the [male] sentence suits her.'[48] Only the novel is young enough not to have been wholly constructed by men out of their own needs and for their own uses. In one particularly prophetic moment, she even suggests that 'the book has somehow to be adapted to the body'.[49] With a Modernist's interest in form and language, Woolf manages to draw fundamental formal and linguistic distinctions of a kind which no male Modernist ever contemplated. Her suggestions launch the debate on *écriture fémi-nine* – a separate women's writing – which has continued to reverber-ate all the way through to current-day feminist theory.

De Beauvoir introduces a new phase of feminist thinking – a phase in which the most entrenched social assumptions are subjected to general theoretical critique. De Beauvoir's own theoretical input derives from her background in Existentialist philosophy. Although the more specifically Existentialist elements in her work often appear dated nowadays, Existentialism offered a uniquely effective tool for opening up a deeper level of feminist analysis in the late 1940s, when *The Second Sex* was written. For, as has been seen, Existentialist philosophy envisages the subject as a pure power of consciousness, always ultimately free towards the future. Such consciousness has no inbuilt biological essence, no inescapable personality or character traits of the kind that might be typed as masculine or feminine. By virtue of its very purity, the Existentialist version of subjecthood is necessarily the same for every human individual.

According to Jean-Paul Sartre, de Beauvoir's lifelong partner and philosophical mentor, every human individual is ethically responsible for maintaining his or her own freedom towards the future. But de Beauvoir sees that women are in a fundamentally different situation from that of men. The freedom of women is reduced by pervasive social forces which consciousness can hardly grasp, let alone shrug off. The root of the problem goes far deeper than the obvious legal and institutional controls which restrict women's lives. The root of the problem is that women are taught to see themselves as something less than full subjects. 'It is required of woman that in order to realise her femininity she must make herself object and prey, which is to say that she must renounce her claims as a sovereign subject.'[50] The consciousness of women is colonised from within.

Women see themselves as less than full subjects in so far as they are made to think of themselves as 'the Other'. In Existentialist philoso-phy, Otherness is the category that consciousness applies in the attempt to contain the freedom of someone else's consciousness. Sartre for one spends a great deal of time describing the subject's vain struggles to reduce other individuals to the status of the Other. But in society as a whole, this status has already been effectively imposed upon minority groups – including women (as the only minority which is also a numerical majority). De Beauvoir points to a profound asymmetry between man and woman: 'she is defined and differentiated with reference to man and not he with reference to her. . . . He is the Subject, he is the Absolute, she is the Other.'[51] A man thinks of his point of view as the natural, normal, human point of view, whereas a woman is taught to consider her point of view as somehow special and peculiar, determined by her sex. A woman who wishes to define herself 'must first of all say: "I am a woman"'; but 'a man never begins by presenting himself as an individual of a certain sex'.[52]

The Other is secondary and inessential, but at the same time also strangely necessary. 'Once the subject seeks to assert himself, the Other, who limits and denies him, is none the less a necessity to him: he attains himself only through that reality which he is not.'[53] The generalised idea of woman thus becomes a repository for all those qualities which the male subject wishes to exclude from himself. 'She is passivity confronting activity, diversity that destroys unity, matter as opposed to form, disorder against order.'[54] Above all, woman is set up as Nature in contradistinction to (male) consciousness.[55] Men have determined the destiny of woman 'not according to her interests, but rather with regard to their own projects, their fears, and their needs'.[56] As with other 'minorities' cast in the role of the Other, woman becomes by her very exclusion an object of simultaneous fear and fascination.

De Beauvoir uses literary analyses to exemplify her wider social claims. In Part III of *The Second Sex,* her focus is upon the ways in which male writers have represented women – the 'feminist critique' approach, as Elaine Showalter calls it. De Beauvoir discovers that the apparent importance of female characters in literature is illusory, since female characters exist always in relation to male projects, fears and needs, rather than as subjects in their own right. 'Woman is an eminently poetic reality since man projects into her all that he does not resolve to be.'[57] Woman serves in the roles of 'treasure, prey, sport and danger, nurse, guide, judge, mediatrix, mirror', and 'is so necessary to man's happiness and to his triumph that it can be said that if she did not exist, men would have invented her'.[58] Such roles are not only varied but incompatible, pointing to the essential ambivalence of male representations. That which is incomprehensible as the Other inevitably appears under contradictory polarities. 'She is an idol, a servant, the source of life, a power of darkness; she is the elemental silence of truth, she is artifice, gossip, and falsehood; she is healing presence and sorceress; she is man's prey, his downfall.'[59] De Beauvoir's insight into the sources of such contradictory polarities have fuelled feminist criticism (and Postcolonialist criticism) down to the present day.

Women writers can aspire to create more adequate representations in the future; but de Beauvoir is disappointingly negative on women writers of the past. Her attitude is shaped by certain universalist assumptions about the role of literature:

> the individuals who seem to us most outstanding, who are honoured with the name of genius, are those who have proposed to enact the fate of all humanity in their personal existences, and no woman has believed herself authorized to do this.[60]

For de Beauvoir, the very greatest writing must transcend the limitations of gender in order to arrive at *the human condition* – the kind of underlying metaphysical condition about which Existentialist philosophers love to talk. Unlike Woolf, she has no interest in a separate woman's tradition, and her Existentialist emphasis upon pure consciousness rules out any notion that the book must be adapted to the body. She does not consider the possibility that her heroic conception of the writer's role (as exemplified in the discourse of 'outstanding' and 'genius') might be merely a male conception, to which women could develop an alternative of their own. *The Second Sex* is remarkable for working out a theoretical feminist perspective even before feminism as a movement had come into existence; but it belongs very much to the earlier phase of feminist thinking, when rights were grounded in claims to sameness rather than difference.

11   French Structuralism

The Structuralism of the 1950s and 1960s had its centre in Paris, although several of its most famous practitioners – including the Bulgarian Todorov and the Lithuanian Greimas – were not in fact French by birth. The movement rose to prominence as a reaction against Sartre's version of Existentialism, which had also had its centre in Paris. For a short period at least, enormous energy and excitement were generated by this new French phase of Structuralism (which, for brevity's sake, I shall henceforth refer to simply as 'Structuralism'). Yet the energy and excitement did not come from association with any particular creative revolution, in the usual manner of previous critical upheavals. No writer-critics featured amongst the major proponents of Structuralism, and only Roland Barthes kept close company with creative writing circles. The Structuralist upheaval demonstrated forcefully what Fryean Myth Criticism had perhaps indicated rather more weakly: that the enterprise of literary theory and criticism had now grown to such size that it could develop by its own momentum, independently of the creative writers.

But Structuralist literary theory was influenced by an outside force of a different kind: the rising force of the social or human sciences. As has been noted, the logic of Modernism encouraged Modernist-oriented critics to keep the social sciences at a distance. But in the 1950s and 1960s, Modernism was no longer a powerful immediate influence, while Postmodernism had not yet achieved recognition as a major new development. At this juncture, the Structural Linguistics of Saussure and the Structural Anthropology of Lévi-Strauss were able to strike a chord – and effectively the same chord, since Structural Anthropology had already been shaped by Structural Linguistics. An entirely new cast of mind was thus introduced into literary theory. The Structuralists had no interest in promoting a particular literary movement, nor in promoting the importance of literature in general, nor in discovering what makes one individual piece of writing work better than another. Such evaluative concerns come naturally to the writer-critic, but not to the social scientist.

At the same time, the conjunction of literary theory and the social sciences required a significant shift on the part of the latter. The social sciences could make little contribution to literary theory so long as they based themselves upon empiricist ideals, involving the statistical analysis of vast quantities of observational data. Traditionally, such ideals have always been strong in Anglo-American countries. But Saussure's Structural Linguistics and Lévi-Strauss's Structural Anthropology offered a more abstract, more purely mathematical approach. On this approach, the social scientist seeks to set up models for explaining the facts *from behind*, rather than patiently accumulating evidence in the hope that some more general theory will eventually suggest itself. A Structuralist critical text typically shows its science in its logic and concepts and diagrams; but not necessarily in its referencing of evidence, which may seem fairly casual by Anglo-American standards.

The ideal of explaining the facts *from behind* is especially pertinent to the facts of experience. When Lévi-Strauss attempts to explain the myths of South American Indian tribes, he does not gather interpretations from the tribespeople themselves – for the underlying explanation is precisely what they themselves are unable to know. Similarly in relation to literature. The models proposed by Structuralists are based upon logical necessity, and cannot be proved or disproved by appealing to the reader's experience. In the words of Gérard Genette, the essential structures 'are at the heart of the work, no doubt, but as its latent armature, as a principle of objective intelligibility, accessible only, through analysis and substitutions, to a sort of geometrical mind that is not consciousness'.[1] Nor does Structuralist literary criticism aim to enhance or expand the reading experience. When American New Critics bring forth underlying patterns in a text, their tacit goal is to encourage a fuller appreciation, a more comprehensive experience on the part of the reader. No such mission moves the Structuralist critics: they keep strictly to the scientific business of description and explanation.

The overall Structuralist methodology is what gives the movement its unity. Beyond this, Structuralist literary criticism postulates a number of different conceptual objects requiring different forms of approach. In what follows, it will be necessary to recognise such differences as occurring not only between different writers, but also between different writings by the same writer.

Paradigmatic structural relations
(*Jakobson, Lévi-Strauss*)

Like so many schools of twentieth-century literary theory, Structuralism is founded upon concepts of language. But Structuralists do not consider literary language as a special version of language which diverges from ordinary language, or advances ahead of ordinary language, or redeems the inadequacies of ordinary language. Unlike Modernists, Formalists and New Critics, they focus upon *analogies* between literature and ordinary language. In the words of Roland Barthes: 'the literary work thereby offers structuralism the image of a structure perfectly homological . . . to the structure of language itself'.[2] This is not to say that literature is written in ordinary language, but that the structures of ordinary language (as our first and foremost coding system) set the pattern for all other cultural coding systems – of which literature is one. Although linguistic models are central for Structuralist theorists, the fact that literature works through words matters rather less to them than to Modernists, Formalists or New Critics.

Structuralist literary theory borrows its linguistic models from Structural Linguistics, especially as promulgated by Roman Jakobson. As already noted, Jakobson had been a Russian Formalist in his earlier career; and in spite of the differences, Structuralist literary theory draws more heavily upon Russian Formalism than upon any other critical movement. Jakobson also had an indirect influence upon Structuralist literary theory by way of Lévi-Strauss, whose Structural Anthropology was inspired by contact with Jakobson in the 1940s. Last but not least, Jakobson himself returned to the study of literature in his later career, and some of his later essays can be counted as classics of Structuralist literary analysis.

As a linguist, Jakobson followed Saussure in claiming that a linguistic unit must be defined not in itself but by its structural relations with other units. One kind of structural relation has already been considered in the 'Saussure' section: the kind of relation which Saussure called *associative* but which subsequent linguists have preferred to call *paradigmatic*. This is the relation which keeps words distinct by their differences: thus 'hot' fixes a distinct semantic concept by virtue of a contrast against 'cold', 'rise' by virtue of a contrast against 'fall'. Such relations can be considered as existing abstractly in the mutually interdependent system of *langue*, but they can also be considered as implicitly invoked by a particular word in an actual utterance. If someone says 'The helicopter rose slowly through the clouds', the semantic unit 'rise' presupposes other semantic units which could have been selected but were not: in the first place, 'fall', and then, further back, 'move horizontally', 'remain stationary', and so on. But if someone says 'The helicopter rose slowly through the clouds', then another kind of structural relation is also brought into play – the relation between different words set side by side in a sentence. Clearly the meanings of 'helicopter' and 'slowly' have a bearing on the meaning of 'rise'. In this case, there are differences but no contrasts, differences involving complementary parts of speech under the rules of syntax. Saussure calls such relations *syntagmatic*.

Jakobson in his later career puts forward the argument that, in poetry as opposed to prose, contrastive relations of the paradigmatic kind are typically superimposed upon side-by-side relations of the syntagmatic kind. He suggests that when we read along the sequence of a poem, we discover 'striking symmetries and antisymmetries, balanced structures, efficient accumulation of equivalent forms and salient contrasts'.[3] To grasp the full import of this argument, it is necessary to examine the particular conception of paradigmatic relations which Jakobson developed in his linguistics, and, more especially, his phonetics.

In general, a contrastive relation is a difference built upon a similarity. Thus, the sound of 'cat' and the sound of 'pat' are similar but differ in their initial consonant; and 'sat', 'bat', and 'fat' differ again. Saussure went no further than this. But Jakobson breaks down the single sound of a consonant or vowel into a simultaneous multiplicity of *distinctive features*. These more abstract features make it possible to discriminate similarities and differences on a hierarchy of separate levels. Thus, the sound of a 'p' and the sound of a 't' are similar to the extent that both are 'diffuse' (i.e. backwardly flanged in the mouth), but differ to the extent that a 'p' is 'grave' (i.e., peripherally constricted in the mouth) whereas a 't' is 'acute' (i.e., centrally constricted in the mouth). On each separate level, according to Jakobson, there are just two options. This is the smallest possible case of mutually interdefining units, the atomic form of structural relations.

Jakobson's theory of *distinctive features* makes the binary principle central to all subsequent Structuralist thinking.

Applying this conception of paradigmatic relations to poetry, Jakobson directs his attention first upon formal effects. For instance, any poem written in iambic metres relies upon a binary alternation between stressed and unstressed syllables. In reading the poem, we must emphasise and equalise the stresses as against the absences of stress. Even a more subtly modulated reading is still far removed from the way we read the randomly graded stresses of prose. Other formal effects are also patterned by similarities and contrasts: for example, rhyme (where a difference of sound is built upon a similarity of sound); refrains and repetitions; and grammatical parallelisms and inversions.

The binary principle is even more important when Jakobson turns to effects of meaning, as he does in an essay co-written with Lévi-Strauss on Baudelaire's 'Les Chats'. As a Structural Anthropologist, Lévi-Strauss had already discovered fundamental binary oppositions in various manifestations of primitive thinking: oppositions between nature and culture, the high and the low, the raw and the cooked, etc. (For a critique of Lévi-Strauss's methods generally, see my *Beyond Superstructuralism*, chapter 15.) Similar oppositions are unearthed when Lévi-Strauss and Jakobson join forces over Baudelaire's poem: oppositions between the animate and the inanimate, the sensual and the intellectual, the lover and the knower, spatio-temporal limits and the dissolution of boundaries, numbered days and eternity, the active and the passive, dark and light, extrinsic and intrinsic, the empirical and the mythological, the metaphorical and the metonymical. Baudelaire's poem is seen as struggling to resolve or mediate these contrary categories of human thought.

The quest for binary oppositions is characteristic of most Structuralist literary criticism – and also characteristic of American New Criticism, as noted in Chapter 9. Unlike the New Critics, Structuralists do not habitually launch off from concrete images, nor do they incline to view the struggle between contrary categories as a matter of *moral* dilemma. Their approach postulates a kind of abstract thinking underlying a surface of concrete language and individual emotions. Nonetheless, the similarities of interpretive technique are significant. As in the case of the essay by Jakobson and Lévi-Strauss, the similarities tend to emerge most strongly when Structuralist critics operate over the New Critics' own favoured territory: that is, poetry, and in very short samples.

Another influential argument from Jakobson deploys the paradigmatic–syntagmatic distinction in another way. This is the argument which connects paradigmatic relations to metaphor and syntagmatic relations to metonymy. (It may be noticed that Jakobson's interest in metaphor-versus-metonymy resurfaces as an opposition in Baudelaire's poem, just as Lévi-Strauss's preoccupation with culture-versus-nature has a habit of resurfacing in the South American myths that he interprets.) In conducting this particular argument, Jakobson thins out paradigmatic relations to a simple principle of similarity (rather than a contrastive difference built upon a similarity); and thins out syntagmatic relations to a simple principle of contiguity (rather than a syntactical complementarity built upon – or expressed through – side-by-side contiguity). The principles of similarity and contiguity, he claims, are the two fundamental dimensions along which the human mind operates.

He finds evidence for this claim in the two different forms of aphasia or speech loss. In cases where the principle of contiguity is disordered, the aphasic loses the power of syntagmatic combination and is typically incapable of seeing a sentence as anything more than a 'word-heap'. In cases where the principle of similarity is disordered, the aphasic loses the power of paradigmatic selection and is typically incapable of understanding the meaning of a word considered in isolation. In either form, the loss of one dimension leads to an overextended use of the other. The 'contiguity disorder' aphasic, who retains the power of paradigmatic selection, tends to jump between words related by similarity, substituting, for example, *fire* for *gaslight*. The 'similarity disorder' aphasic, who retains the power of syntagmatic combination, tends to jump between words related by contiguity, substituting, for example, *smoke* for *pipe* (associating on the basis of such common sentence combinations as *he smoked a pipe*).

These two kinds of jump lead Jakobson to the concepts of metaphor and metonymy. In literature, a jump based on similarity, as between *gaslight* and *fire*, would be termed a metaphor, while a jump based on contiguity, as between *pipe* and *smoke*, would be termed a metonymy. (It may be noted, however, that literary metaphors are not limited to the special kind of similarities involved in paradigmatic word selection, and that literary metonymies are not limited to the specifically linguistic contiguities involved between words co-occurring in sentences.) Jakobson also draws upon evidence to show that 'similarity disorder' aphasics are typically unable to jump to the metaphorical meanings of metaphors, which they try to take literally. 'Metaphor is alien to the similarity disorder,' he states, 'and metonymy to the contiguity disorder.'[4] Far from being just two possible devices in poetry, metaphor and metonymy come to exemplify the two fundamental dimensions along which the human mind operates.

As a claim about metaphor, this corresponds to the widespread claim of Modernist critics and New Critics, that metaphor is not a mere matter of ornament but a whole way of thinking. Like these critics, Jakobson associates metaphor with poetry – in particular, Romantic and Symbolist poetry. But the role given to metonymy is entirely original with Jakobson himself. Holding to his logic of grand antithesis, Jakobson does not associate metonymy with poetry at all, but with realist novels – as the extreme opposite to poetry in the field of literature. 'Following the path of contiguous relationships, the Realist author metonymically digresses from the plot to the atmosphere and from the characters to the setting in space and time. He is fond of synecdochic details.'[5] In other words, realist novels digress from the large-scale essentials of narrative to details that are contiguously present in the same scene; move between details on the basis that one thing is located alongside another; and often narrow to 'close-ups' on some representative detail when conveying important action. (In the last case, the part stands for the whole in the manner of *synecdoche*.) It follows that realist novels can not justify their workings simply by reference to reality: in their own way, they are just as figured and constructed as poetry. Such a view is very much in accord with the general trend of Structuralist literary theory.

Structuralist narratology
(*Greimas, Bremond, Todorov, Barthes*)

Jakobson's interest in short samples of poetry involves a small-scale focus, as does his interest in the local details of 'realistic' fiction. But because Structuralists are concerned with linguistic analogies rather than the actual language of texts, they are also able to take a much larger focus. Perhaps the most striking and distinctive area of Structuralist literary analysis is the area of narratology, dealing with whole narratives, most commonly in prose. (The same approach can also be applied to verse epics, films, comics, etc.) Narratology examines a dimension which American New Critics almost entirely ignore: the dimension of syntagmatic relations.

Of the most prominent theorists associated with Structuralist narratology, A.-J. Greimas and Claude Bremond are wholly narratologists; Tzvetan Todorov is a narratologist in many essays and in his *Grammaire du Décaméron*; while Barthes is an out-and-out narratologist only in one long essay, 'The Structural Analysis of Narrative'. These theorists are all concerned with narrative as raw story, as an underlying material of actions and events. One other prominent theorist not discussed here is Gérard Genette, who has concentrated upon the way in which a story is treated in the telling. Although his achieved results are arguably more substantial than those of his fellow narratologists, Genette's goals are less ambitious and lie somewhat outside the main Structuralist project.

For Structuralist narratologists, the most important linguistic analogy is the analogy between the structure of a narrative and the syntax of a sentence. 'A narrative is a long sentence,' says Barthes, 'just as every constative sentence is in a way the rough outline of a short narrative.'[6] On this analogy, the overall articulation of a story obeys certain conventional rules in the same way that the articulation of a sentence obeys the rules of syntax. Just as the different parts of speech in a sentence do not follow one another merely according to the sequence of thoughts occurring in the speaker's mind, so the units of action and event in a story do not follow one another merely in imitation of some external happenstance in the real world. The grammarian's goal is to set forth a simple system of rules which, by permutation and recursive application, can account for all the complexities of all possible sentences – and the Structuralist narratologists aim to do the same for narrative.

This conventionalist approach to narrative has already been encountered in Propp, whose *Morphology of the Folktale* represents the strongest single influence upon Structuralist narratology. But whereas Propp was content to suggest a general similarity between the building blocks of a sentence and the building blocks of a fairy tale, the narratologists are in search of something much more specific. Typically, they relate characters or substantive agents to nouns, and actions to verbs. 'We shall understand narrative better if we know that the character is a noun, the action a verb,' claims Todorov.[7] They are also eager to incorporate a parallel to adjectives, suggesting that qualities or descriptive features are attributed to a character in the same way that adjectives modify a noun. This not only extends the linguistic analogy, but follows from the narratologists' attempt to carry the application of their models beyond fairy tales to all forms of narrative. The attribution of qualities to individuals may matter little in an action-oriented genre operating with stock characters, but it becomes enormously important in modern novels, where a great deal of time is spent in constructing static situations and individual psychological cases.

The most complicated model is put forward in Greimas's *Structural Semantics.* Greimas recognises a small number of fundamental relations between what he calls *actants*: subject versus object, sender versus receiver, and the options of helper or opponent. The relation between subject and object resembles the relation between the subject noun and the direct object noun in a sentence like: '*The knights* sought *the Holy Grail.*' The relation between sender and receiver resembles the relation between the subject noun and the indirect object noun in a sentence like: '*Eve* gives *Adam* an apple.' (When grammarians have attempted to define a category of content for the indirect object, they have typically come up with such terms as Greimas proposes: receiver or beneficiary. The relations between subject, direct object and indirect object are strangely fundamental to our way of thinking the world – strangely, because it is difficult to say why the world itself should require just these relations.) As for the options of helper or opponent, Greimas sees these *actants* as furthering or hindering the subject's movement towards the object, and compares them to adjectivalised participles modifying the noun subject. With a little straining, this might be illustrated in a sentence like: 'The *dragon-fighting, magically aided* knights sought the Holy Grail'.

In attempting to apply their models to all forms of narrative, the narratologists also find it necessary to recognise a more internal dimension of story. In most modern novels, the reader not only watches events but shares the characters' attitudes towards events – anticipating, believing, making choices. Events are here virtual or potential, not yet actual. The narratologists take this dimension into account by drawing upon an analogy to the grammatical moods of the verb. In the indicative mood, we simply state 'X happened', but other moods allow us to express more complex attitudinal and evaluative relations to X: 'X should happen', 'X must happen', 'X might happen', 'if X were to happen', and so on. Todorov thus allows for events which exist under such ontological modes as being feared, being predicted, being hoped for, being renounced. Bremond goes so far as to view narrative as a matter of alternative pathways or binary choices facing the individual character at successive point after point. On this view, what does not happen is as much a part of the story as what does – yet another application of the basic Saussurean principle that a selected item has meaning by virtue of its relation to non-selected alternatives.

In general, the narratologists seek to explain at a deeper and more abstract level than Propp, as Propp himself had sought to explain at a deeper and more abstract level than Veselovsky. According to Greimas, Propp 'renounces analysis too early . . . at an insufficient level of formalization'.[8] Greimas's own analysis of the marriage or wedding function shows how a particular content can be broken down into more fundamental elements: 'The wedding . . . is not a simple function, as Propp's analysis supposes, but a contract, passed between the sender, who offers the object of the quest to the receiver, and the subject-receiver who accepts it.'[9] Here, the key element of the contract is clearly applicable to a far wider range of events than weddings alone. By this further step of abstraction, Greimas is able to include a great many kinds of narrative which do not end in fairy-tale weddings. It should also be noted that Greimas's *actants*, as mentioned above, are not individual characters but abstract principles prior to individual characterisation – such that several *actants* may eventually be realised in the one character.

This further step of abstraction may be compared to the further step of abstraction taken by Jakobson when he breaks down the sound of a 'p' into *distinctive features,* which may be present or absent in other consonantal sounds. The consequences in both cases are also comparable. In the first place, there is a reduction in the number of elements required: almost all narratologists find Propp's thirty-one functions excessive. In the second place, there is an increase in logical necessity: almost all narratologists find Propp's functions *ad hoc* and arbitrary. And in the third place, there is a move to binary systemati-sation, which always tends to become more available with increasing abstraction. (Consider the series *ultramarine – blue – coloured,* where only the last term immediately suggests a contrasting term, *colourless;* or the series *dog – mammal – organic creature,* where only the last term immediately suggests a contrasting term, *inorganic object.*) In Bremond's model, it is at a very abstract level that the choices facing a character appear as binaries rather than as choices between several options. And in Greimas's model, the opposition of subject *versus* object assumes a binary equality of status which has no parallel in the grammatical relation between a subject noun and a direct object noun. Although they may focus initially upon syntagmatic relations, the narratologists ultimately share the general Structuralist partiality for seeing in binaries.

Binarism has a special importance for Greimas, who calls for further explanation here. Greimas's model is influenced as much by Lévi-Strauss's analyses of primitive mythology as by Propp's analysis of fairy tales, and like Lévi-Strauss, he actually seeks to *derive* narratives from an underlying level of binary thinking. Lévi-Strauss himself does this in a single direct leap between levels, picking out items from a narrative without regard for sequence or contiguity, and tabulating them under oppositional columns. Thus the myth of Asdiwal is shown to contain references to things that are *high* which can be set against references to things that are *low*, and references to *land* which can be set against references to *water*.[10] However, the method does not seek to account for the vast quantities of narrative pudding set around these conceptual plums. In fact, there is very little difference between the strategy which Lévi-Strauss applies to a narrative myth and the strategy which he and Jakobson apply to a non-narrative poem like Baudelaire's 'Les Chats'.

Greimas on the other hand seeks to derive narratives from binary thinking by way of a great many intermediate stages, so that the final structure is determined in all respects. His goal is to pass 'from system to process', converting binary concepts in static relations into concrete people and events in dynamic relations.[11] It is impossible to give an account of all the stages of conversion involved, but, roughly speaking, he proceeds by way of a kind of logic, then by way of a kind of grammar.

The logical stages employ what Greimas calls the *semiotic square*. The semiotic square sets static binary concepts in motion by playing upon an imbalance between two different forms of binary opposition. For example: the polarised opposite to *male* is *female*, but the logical opposite is *non-male* – which takes in not only the socially standardised category of *female* but all versions of sexuality which do not fall under the socially standardised category of *male*. Similarly, *non-female* is the logical opposite of *female*. But now *non-female* stands in polarised opposition to *non-male*. Compared with the original opposition of *male* versus *female*, the opposition of *non-female* versus *non-male* includes rather than excludes, is wide-minded rather than narrow-minded – and to that extent embodies an improved or at least higher understanding. What Greimas has discovered here is a new kind of dialectic by which one concept can be made to give birth to further concepts, over and over again.

As for the grammatical stages, they progress gradually from logical grammar to narrative grammar. Greimas draws upon a parallel between the polemical dynamic of conflicting, interacting concepts and the narrative dynamic of struggling, interacting human beings. Thus the logical conjunction of subject + object may be converted into Perceval + Grail, and Perceval + Grail may be converted into Perceval's action of picking up the Holy Grail. It is when abstract *actants* are given human embodiment that logical operations become narrative doings. 'Deep grammar, which is of a conceptual nature, in order to be able to produce stories . . . where human or personified actors would accomplish tasks, undergo tests, reach goals . . . must first . . . receive an *anthropomorphic . . .* representation.'[12] At the same time, values enter into the picture – after all, one cares about human agents in a special way that does not apply to abstract concepts. But still these human agents are not yet particular characters, and these doings are not yet particular actions. In Greimas's model, even surface narrative grammar is at least as deep as the level of Propp's functions. Further steps of concretisation and particularisation have to be fed in before the narrative is fully realised in the form we finally read.

This is all far more theoretically thorough and rigorous than anything in Lévi-Strauss. However, it may be doubted whether the practice lives up to the promise. Greimas offers two main applications of his model, to the novels of Georges Bernanos and to a short story by Maupassant. He discovers life versus death and truth versus lie as the fundamental oppositions underlying the novels of Bernanos, while the Maupassant short story is traced back to oppositions of life versus death and peace versus war. But there is surprisingly little grammatical explanation of narrative in these analyses, which treat the texts almost as if they were poems. In particular, the convenient but non-grammatical concept of an *anti-subject* eases the way for binary oppositions between subject and anti-subject. In the end, Greimas's practice does not differ from Lévi-Strauss's practice as much as might have been expected.

Such practical disappointments are not uncommon with the narratologists generally. Todorov's *Grammaire du Décaméron* represents
perhaps the most successful application of a model, but then
Todorov's model is notably less formalised and systematised than
those of Greimas and Bremond. The narratologists are at their best in
putting forward programmes and proposals; their empirical results
often seem to fall short of their lofty scientific aspirations.

Structuralism as a poetics
(*Todorov, Barthes*)

But if the narratologists' results are often disappointing, this is *not*
because they fail to bring forth fresh interpretations of individual
texts, in the manner of, say, the New Critics. Such a goal is simply
irrelevant to all Structuralists. 'The critical task', says Barthes, 'is . . .
not to "discover" in the work or the author something "hidden",
"profound", "secret" which hitherto passed unnoticed.'[13] The
Structuralists' goal is to develop a general theory of literature, and
individual cases are important only as serving to test whether that
theory can be applied successfully. New insights into an individual
text are of no concern to them, just as new insights into an individual
falling object are of no concern to the physicist seeking to test a
general theory of gravity.

Barthes describes this approach as *the science of literature*; Todorov
reverts to an older term and calls it a *poetics*. As in the poetics of
Aristotle and Frye, the object of study is literature as a total system,
interdefining and essentially self-sufficient. For such study, the properties which a work shares with other works are what matter, rather
than the properties which make a work unique. Concepts of convention and concepts of genre inevitably come to the fore, as with
Aristotle and Frye. Todorov in particular develops the Structuralist
analysis of genre.

It has already been noted that Frye's approach is more abstract and
a priori than that of Aristotle, and Todorov's approach is more
abstract and *a priori* yet again. According to Todorov, Frye is still
excessively concerned with *historical genres,* that is, observable clus-
terings of past texts. Although Frye arrives at his genres by permutating features in varying combinations, he picks and chooses in such a
way as to avoid combinations which do not correspond to any observ-

able clustering. But Todorov looks at 'what literature *can* be rather than what it *is*'.[14] Following the general Structuralist principle that relations precede substances, he draws up a system of dividing lines and creates *theoretical genres*. He is not in the least perturbed by the fact that some of his theoretical categories may as yet be entirely unoccupied.

Todorov's most impressive work in genre analysis appears in his book on *The Fantastic*. As he describes it, *the fantastic* involves the supernatural, but differs from *the uncanny* on the one hand (where the supernatural is eventually reduced by a physical explanation) and from *the marvellous* on the other (where the supernatural is simply accepted as a feature of the imagined world). In the genre of *the fantastic*, the supernatural remains problematical, and the reader is kept endlessly hovering between belief and disbelief. Todorov asserts the existence of this genre in spite of the fact that he can find hardly any texts to fit his definition all the way through. However, the Postmodernist period has discovered a taste for ontological uncertainties and inconclusive endings, and one could probably list a number of examples of *the fantastic* since the time of Todorov's writing. In this respect, Todorov's *theoretical genres* have a potential predictive power of the kind to which scientific Structuralism has always aspired.

The genres described in *The Fantastic* demonstrate another difference from Frye. As noted earlier, Frye claims to eschew value-judgements in setting up his system, but remains always within the boundaries of 'literature' as traditionally constituted. By contrast, Todorov readily extends his interests to the modern genres of popular entertainment: to science fiction as a sub-genre of *the marvellous*; to ghost stories; to detective, spy and thriller novels. In his own words, 'today there is no longer any reason to confine to literature alone the type of studies crystallized in poetics'.[15] Such inclusiveness is typical of the Structuralists in general. As befits their claim to the role of scientists, they are comparatively unconstrained by the usual evaluative preference in favour of 'literature'.

Genres are viewed as social codes governing individual texts in the same way that *langue* as a social code governs individual acts of *parole*. 'For us,' says Barthes, 'a text is speech which refers to language, a message which refers to a code, a performance which refers to a competence.'[16] To make sense of a detective novel, we must understand the kind of game being played, the responses that are called for. A detective novel does not 'refer' us to reality (as Todorov points out, the game of guess-the-murderer runs completely contrary to real-world likelihood); it 'refers' us to a special set of rules which are signalled by the very look of the book (title and cover), by the style of the writing, by certain opening conventions. If it was necessary to read through a book in order to place it in the detective genre, it would not have been a detective novel that we had read. Barthes extends the same argument to many fields:

> however familiar, however casual may today be the act of opening a novel or a newspaper or of turning on the television, nothing can prevent that humble act from installing in us, all at once and in its entirety, the narrative code we are going to need.[17]

For Structuralists, even a metaphor is not simply a poetic act but also a signal of poetry, 'because, in using it, the text signifies its adherence to literature or one of its subdivisions'.[18]

Clearly, the codes of literature and its genres involve a higher-order signifying over and above the ordinary signifying of language. A certain kind of meaning on the level of certain characters and events conveys the further message *I am a detective novel*; a metaphorical kind of meaning conveys the further message *I am poetry*. The codes which concern Structuralists are analogous to, but separate from, the code of ordinary language. And in fact, such codes even diminish the powers that one might otherwise attribute to ordinary language. For on the Structuralist argument, it is impossible to arrive at a poetic experience merely by putting word-meanings together in the ordinary way. A poem must be typed *as* poetry in order to be read poetically.

To the extent that such codes are the ultimate object which Structuralists study, their focus is neither upon individual texts nor upon all texts, but upon the capacities which enable us to make sense of *any* text. The science of literature, according to Barthes, 'cannot be a science of the contents of works . . . but a science of the *conditions* of content'.[19] Jonathan Culler, the critic mainly responsible for introducing Structuralist ideas into America, pushes the point furthest when he argues that critics should

> cease thinking that [their] goal is to specify the properties of objects in a corpus and concentrate instead on the task of formulating the

internalized competence which enables objects to have the properties they do for those who have mastered the system.[20]

In the last analysis, the system of codes is a socio-cultural phenomenon. Like *langue,* it exists in the minds of all the members of a
community, both writers and readers (including those who never
actually exercise their reading capacities). Texts are the only practicable evidence for discovering the codes, but the codes themselves
occupy a very different kind of site.

Barthes

Roland Barthes is the chameleon figure amongst Structuralists. He
has already featured in the discussions of Structuralist poetics and
Structuralist narratology (and his *On Racine* might well have featured
in the discussion of Structuralist binarism). In this section I shall be
looking at two characteristic Structuralist themes most famously
formulated by Barthes, and two diverging tendencies within
Structuralism both strikingly embodied in Barthes. I shall not be
looking at the further chameleon change which overtakes Barthes in
his fully Poststructuralist phase of the 1970s; however, I shall draw
upon such transitional works as 'The Death of the Author' (1968) and
S/Z (1970) for specific arguments which remain largely constant
between Structuralism and Poststructuralism.

One of Barthes's recurring themes is indeed the death of the author
– the impossibility of continuing to believe that the author
'*nourish[es]* the book, which is to say that he exists before it, thinks,
suffers, lives for it, is in the same reiation of antecedence to his work
as a father to his child'.[21] Barthes's argument against the traditional
view is in many ways a stronger assertion of claims already advanced
by Eliot and the New Critics: namely, that the text means what it
means regardless of authorial intentions, that authors discover what
they are going to write only in the process of writing it, and that
creativity is never under conscious control anyway. Like Eliot and the
New Critics, Barthes sees the power of language as overriding the
power of the author. 'To write is . . . to reach that point where only
language acts, "performs", and not "me".'[22] What makes Barthes's
argument stronger is that, from the Structuralist point of view, the
author is overridden not only by language but by all the other higher-

order codes of literature and its genres. The author becomes as never before a mere channel for larger socio-cultural forces.

A second recurring theme in Barthes is the argument against realism. Barthes here reasserts a claim first advanced by the Russian Formalists: that is, that realism is itself a system of literary devices, reacting against other earlier systems. Or in Barthes's own words, 'what we call "real" (in the theory of the realistic text) is never more than a code of representation (of signification)'.[23] Literature never accesses the reality of the real world: the *reality effect* is merely a further level of artifice.

Barthes is able to give a clearer account of this reality effect than the Formalists because he is able to draw upon Structuralist concepts of higher-order signifying. Considering a passage in Flaubert's short story "A Simple Heart", he argues that details of the setting – a barometer and a pyramidal heap of boxes and cartons on top of a piano – appear realistic only because they are unintelligible in terms of the basic codes of narrative. 'The pure and simple "representation" of the "real" . . . appears as a resistance to meaning.'[24] We take it that such details come from reality precisely because we see no other reason why they should be described. And yet, as Barthes points out, there is no genuine denotation here. It makes absolutely no difference whether Flaubert was remembering a particular room or borrowing from other texts or simply inventing. Paradoxically, the details only *connote* denotation, only convey an aura of real-world reference. 'Just when these details are reputed to *denote* the real directly, all that they do – without saying so – is *signify* it.'[25] Working through a higher-order code, even above the basic codes of narrative, the barometer and pyramidal heap of boxes and cartons mean nothing except: *we are the real.*

Barthes disapproves of the reality effect not because it is artificial but because it disguises its artifice, because the details do their special kind of signifying 'without saying so'. If literature can never be true to the real world or to the author's real nature, it can at least be true to its own untruth. Of all French Structuralists, Barthes is the most emphatic opponent of *the alibi of the natural,* and the most ardent advocate of flaunting artifice as artifice, sign as sign. Literature is not only 'fundamentally, constitutively unrealistic', but should embody '*the very consciousness of the unreality of language*'.[26] Barthes's favourite motto refers to the open conventionality of classical Greek theatre: *larvatus prodeo,* or 'I advance pointing to my mask.'

Whereas Barthes's anti-authorial and anti-realist themes carry through into his fully Poststructuralist phase of the 1970s, his period as a leading semiologist belongs entirely to the heyday of Structuralism, in the mid-1960s. It is in this period that he preaches the coming of a general science of signs as predicted by Saussure. Language-like models are extended to all kinds of cultural phenomena – to styles of furniture, clothing fashions, photographs, advertisements, TV shows, etiquette and food rituals. And almost everything turns out to be a cultural phenomenon: even a glass of wine is not natural or innocent, but carries a social meaning, affirms a social ideology. The human world is revealed as a total forcefield crisscrossed by waves of signification, typically organised in binary contrasts. (In Anglo-American countries, for example, the social meaning of wine is opposed to the social meaning of beer.) Everywhere, we see and taste and hear only through the meanings which society has already implanted in us – just as we experience a detective novel only through the idea of a detective novel.

Barthes expounds many individual cultural insights in *Mythologies* (1957), but it is in *Elements of Semiology* (1964) and *The Fashion System* (1967) that the grand scientific programme comes to the fore. The whole human world is revealed as a text, to be read under symbolic techniques of the kind originally developed for literary texts. In this sense, semiology represents an apotheosis of the methods of Structuralist literary criticism. But at the same time, literature itself sinks back to the status of just another wave in the general forcefield. In the comprehensive scientific analysis of culture, literature is on a par with movie posters and advertisements for spaghetti.

However, Barthes also acts as advocate for a very different cause – the cause of avant-garde writing. As already noted, Barthes was unusual amongst Structuralists in his close personal association with contemporary writers, specifically the *Nouveau Roman* group in his earlier career and the *Tel Quel* group in his later career. Even in the years when he was putting forward the most ambitiously scientific claims on behalf of semiology, he continued to put forward claims on behalf of avant-garde writing. And the latter claims naturally involve the avant-garde mission of disturbing socially established assumptions – precisely the kind of implanted ideas which are the object of semiological analysis. The divergence is glaring: either an all-encompassing net of conventional meanings, or the special status of a form of literature which claims to escape from that net.

Corresponding to this divergence, Barthes offers two divergent accounts of critical method. On the one hand, the critic stands outside and above the text, employing a language which is higher, more abstract and more scientific than the language of the text itself. 'Criticism . . . is a second language, or a *meta-language* (as the logicians would say), which operates on a first language (or *language object*).'[27] Or on the other hand, the critic can only respond to the text on its own level, employing a similar literary language with similar creativity. In this latter account, the notion of 'mak[ing] the work into a language-object and science into a meta-language' is dismissed as an 'illusory privilege'.[28] Barthes's ambivalence arises out of the different roles into which he steps at different times.

Eventually, the ambivalence is resolved against the meta-language option, and the 'euphoric dream of scientificity' is dropped.[29] Along with the Poststructuralists in general, Barthes eventually comes to concentrate upon ways of escaping from the net, or dissolving the net entirely. Compared with the full scope of Poststructuralist theory, the particular escape route associated with avant-garde literature is narrow and limited; nonetheless, the earlier avant-garde side of Barthes's thinking clearly indicates the shape of future developments. Even in its heyday, even in the person of its most famous polemicist, Structuralism contains an internal contradiction and the seeds of the next revolution.

Epilogue: Into the Postmodernist Period

The beginning of the Postmodernist period can be dated to the two crucial years of 1967 and 1968. With no world wars or obviously cataclysmic events, society changed inwardly, people started to think in a different way. One aspect of the difference was the anti-scientific mentality which can be traced to the counter-cultural upheaval of 1967. Another aspect was the alternative politics which can be traced to the demonstrations and new political formations of 1968. Students and universities were at the forefront of both developments, which also led to changes in educational practices and teaching relationships. Structuralism lost its appeal on two counts: both as a scientific cause, and because the vision of society as a totally predetermined forcefield seemed incapable of theorising political action against the social status quo.

Around the same time – both before and after 1967–8 – literature also moved into a Postmodernist mood. Postmodernist literature relates to Modernist literature in the sense of continuing the same general goal of challenging and disturbing established habits of thought. But it is post- or beyond Modernism in the sense that the challenge has now become much more radical. Whereas Modernist writers aimed to reinvigorate perception which had been deadened by habit, and language which had been staled by clichés, Postmodernist writers now questioned the very nature of perception and the very nature of language. No longer is it sufficient to clear out the mediating passages so that the subject may gain better knowledge of the object. For Postmodernists, both subject and object are caught up within the passages, and knowledge in the traditional sense is out of the question.

The new literary theory is influenced by Postmodernist writing, but the influence does not run all one way. In the Romantic period or the Symbolist period, it is possible to say that theory follows where creative practice leads. But this is no longer true in the latter half of the twentieth century. Poststructuralist theory develops out of Structuralist theory by its own internal momentum. In the hands of philosophers (or anti-philosophers) such as Derrida and Deleuze, Poststructuralist arguments were not initially directed towards literature at all. The new theory has its own goals, which are never merely subordinated to those of the writers. In the Postmodernist period, the relation between literary practice and literary theory is more of an equal partnership, where either can draw ideas from the other.

As well as mutual influence, there is also a convergence of activities. On the one side, Postmodernist writers do not simply create characters or communicate experiences: they reflect upon language and literature and the very writing of the text they are writing. Their distinctively Postmodernist activity is an activity of *critique* – which inevitably approaches the activity of theorists and critics. On the other side, theorists and critics do not simply talk *about* a text as object, but extend it, produce it, and make its language generate further meanings. Postmodernist literary theory drops the impersonal, objectivist discourse of Structuralism and takes on, to a greater or lesser degree, the figurative style and manner of creative writing.

At this point, a brief terminological clarification becomes necessary. *Postmodernism* is the commonly accepted term for describing the general sensibility and also the literature from the late 1960s to the present. The literary theory of the whole period can therefore be described as *Postmodernist,* in the same way that the literary theory which comes under the Modernist sensibility and relates to Modernist literature can be described as *Modernist.* At the same time, the initial 'textual' phase of the new theory can also be described as *Poststructuralist,* in that it both develops from and reacts against Structuralism. But the situation becomes complicated when, in the late 1970s, a distinctively different 'political' phase both develops from and reacts against this initial 'textual' phase. For many commentators, myself included, it seems inappropriate to continue to apply the name *Poststructuralist* to the latest phase. Unfortunately, the term which has often been used to replace it is *Postmodernist* – so that *Postmodernist* in one sense comes to be defined almost in opposition to *Poststructuralist.* It seems that two terms are doing duty where three are needed: a term for each of the two phases, plus an overarching term for the new tendency as a whole. However, the distinction between the two phases will not be an issue in this brief epilogue, and I shall henceforth refer, cumbersomely but comprehensively, to *Postmodernist–Poststructuralist* literary theory.

Postmodernist–Poststructuralist literary theory still follows the *linguistic turn* of the twentieth century. More specifically, it still relies upon the general Structuralist vision of a vast hinterland of *langue* lying behind any individual utterance of *parole*. But the relation between *langue* and *parole* is completely inverted. In the Structuralist model, *langue* is a static, mutually-supporting system where one category of meaning is propped up by leaning against another; and it is this system which fixes a stable meaning for any given word in an individual utterance. But in Postmodernist–Poststructuralist theory, it is not *langue* that controls *parole* but *parole* that destabilises *langue*. Starting from a particular word or words in a particular utterance, the new theory sets up a movement which spreads out more and more widely from one tiny corner across the entire system. Barthes (in the final Poststructuralist phase of his career) furnishes the perfect image when he suggests that 'the structure can be . . . "run" (like the thread of a stocking)'.[1] A mutually supporting system is stable only so long as all of its categories hold up together. If one falls, there is no limit to the ongoing collapse.

The destabilising movement depends upon a new way of looking at language – specifically, a new way of finding contrary implications hidden inside a single word. If a word is not homogeneous but contains contraries within itself, it can no longer be defined by the boundaries which separate it from other contrasting words. The boundaries fail and meaning disseminates outwards. There is a degree of resemblance here to the procedure of Empson and the New Critics, who also opened words up to all their potentialities of meaning. But whereas Empson and (especially) the New Critics sought to gather in a full hoard, a richness of meaning, Postmodernist–Poststructuralist theorists concentrate upon the emptiness, the failure to mean, the hole in the stocking. Language ultimately undoes itself, subverts itself from within. Such self-subversion is the real message revealed by a Postmodernist–Poststructuralist reading.

No doubt, the apparent resemblance to New Critical procedure helped to make the new theory acceptable to American critics – as did the apparently familiar starting-point of a close reading technique applied to an individual text. But although a Postmodernist–Poststructuralist reading may begin with words in an individual text, it spreads rapidly out across language and signifying in general. There is no claim that the meanings unfolded have been packed or stored inside the text as such. The supposed unity of the individual text is dismissed, and the boundaries circumscribing that unity are dissolved as easily as any other boundaries. On the principle of intertextuality, all text is continuous.

A Postmodernist–Poststructuralist reading may also move outside the text – all text – in order to make contact with social reality. In its 'political' phase especially, the new theory is scornful of any attempt to quarantine text as a world apart, to maintain literary theory as a politics-free zone. However, this is still not a move outside of signifying in the most general sense, for social reality itself now appears as a realm of meanings. The Structuralists had extended the concept of signifying to cover all kinds of cultural phenomena; the new theory continues the extension, but under a dynamic, politicised vision where meanings are seen as struggling for predominance one against the other. The logic of this vision has already been partly sketched out in the section on Bakhtin. To see the world politically is indeed to see behaviour not as natural, nor as local and individual, but as representative of a larger pattern. On this vision, all social practices, discourses and institutional formations signify, and their significances involve assumptions which preserve or subvert existing power-structures.

In order to make contact with social reality, it is necessary to interpret words in a slightly different way. Whereas Modernist interpretation evolved the concept of the symbol, Postmodernist–Poststructuralist theory requires the concept of the trace. To put it crudely: the concept of the symbol suggests an active pointing towards a higher-order significance; but the trace is merely a mark that is left behind as the imprint of some outside force. One common form of trace is the gap or lacuna, a visible hollow or absence relative to a surrounding level of meaning, just as a footprint is a visible hollow relative to a surrounding level of ground. In texts, the effect of political power often reveals itself as a repression or exclusion of what *should* have been present. The concept of the trace here approaches the concept of the symptom, as a form of material signifying. But not so purely material as the symptom in Marx and Freud, where signifying soon comes to a halt in some solid imprinting cause. In Postmodernist–Poststructuralist theory, the cause of the footprint is itself a footprint, a further significance, so that the process of interpretation continues on indefinitely.

Along with social reality, the new theory also reintroduces value-judgements into the consideration of literature. Not aesthetic judgements, however, but political judgements of the kind appropriate to social reality. Positive value generally attaches to the subversion of existing power-structures, negative value to their preservation. Nor are Postmodernist–Poststructuralist theorists interested in asserting the value of literature at large. Outside of Postmodernist writing, they tend to see literary texts as bearing a very strong imprint of everything that is or was politically wrong with the societies which produced them. One role for Postmodernist–Poststructuralist theory is to stand guard against the reproduction of undesirable ideologies through literature.

Another move outside the text leads in the direction of the reader. Postmodernist–Poststructuralist theory welcomes exactly what the New Critics once sought to banish under the warning label of 'the Affective Fallacy': that is, the influence upon a reading of the reader's own personal prejudices and desires. Such influence can be banished only if one supposes that the text 'contains' an original meaning independently of the reader. But for Postmodernist–Poststructuralist theory, the text is a mere collection of marks upon the page until the reader makes it signify – and makes it signify through the channels of her/his own prejudices and desires. A similar argument as regards prejudices has already been encountered in Gadamer. Given that all meaning is essentially added on, the goal of any reading must be to *produce* meaning; and more meaning can be produced by allowing one's own pleasure-oriented or politically-oriented desires to engage, openly and consciously, with the text. Those who claim to 'respect' the text are merely less open and conscious about the role of their own desires. Even a strategic wrenching of the text, or a reading *against the grain* of the text's explicit message, is no more than a logical continuation of what all readers do already.

The empowerment of the reader is simultaneously the empowerment of the critic, who stands in as the reader's representative. The relation of critic to text is no longer that of knower to known. Producing meanings on the text's own level, the critic operates as a *doer* rather than a *knower* – and certainly not a detached or impartial knower. The critic is involved alongside the Postmodernist writer in fighting exactly the same battle against the same conservative forces in literature and politics. If the text does not explicitly subvert established assumptions, then the critic takes over the task on its behalf. In this respect too, critical and creative activity become almost indistinguishable.

By helping to produce *political* meanings, the theorist or critic can hope to make a particular kind of intervention in her/his own social reality. In the Postmodernist period, grand blueprints for future states of society have vanished from the agenda. Grand blueprints must be formulated from a position wholly detached from one's own society – and we no longer believe in the possibility of such detachment. Instead, the new politics relies upon small leverage-points which can be used to initiate a widening destabilisation from within. Literary texts are precisely such leverage-points. Although literature may occupy a relatively tiny space in the total system of contemporary society, literary theorists and critics can lay claim to a crucial political role – the kind of role once claimed by political philosophers and political scientists.

So much for a brief overall impression of literary theory in the Postmodernist period. The true picture – even on the level of simplification attempted elsewhere in this book – is infinitely more complicated. Derrida's emphases differ from Foucault's emphases; American Deconstructionism and Reader-Response theory are half in and half out of the new perspective; Feminist literary theory and Postcolonial literary theory have their own twists and turns and revolutions. My limited purpose here has been to provide a connecting link between the theory of the past and the theory of the last thirty years. It will be my aim to paint a more adequate picture of that last thirty years in a sequel to this book.

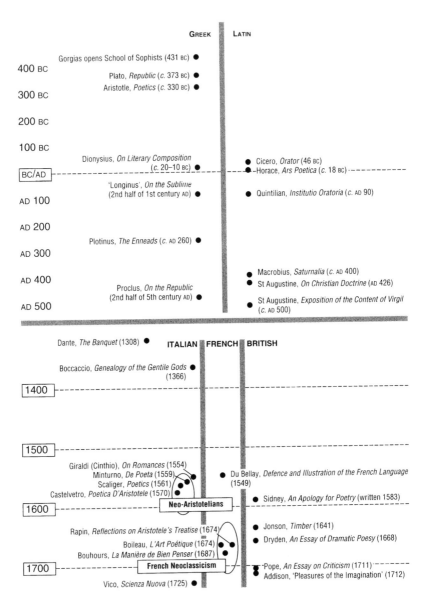

GREEK | LATIN

Gorgias opens School of Sophists (431 BC) ●

400 BC

Plato, *Republic* (*c.* 373 BC) ●

Aristotle, *Poetics* (*c.* 330 BC) ●

300 BC

200 BC

100 BC

Dionysius, *On Literary Composition*
(*c.* 20–10 BC) ●

BC/AD

● Cicero, *Orator* (46 BC)
● Horace, *Ars Poetica* (*c.* 18 BC)

'Longinus', *On the Sublime*
(2nd half of 1st century AD) ●

AD 100

● Quintilian, *Institutio Oratoria* (*c.* AD 90)

AD 200

Plotinus, *The Enneads* (*c.* AD 260) ●

AD 300

AD 400

● Macrobius, *Saturnalia* (*c.* AD 400)
● St Augustine, *On Christian Doctrine* (AD 426)

Proclus, *On the Republic*
(2nd half of 5th century AD) ●

AD 500

● St Augustine, *Exposition of the Content of Virgil*
(*c.* AD 500)

Dante, *The Banquet* (1308) ● | **ITALIAN** | **FRENCH** | **BRITISH**

Boccaccio, *Genealogy of the Gentile Gods* ●
(1366)

1400

1500

Giraldi (Cinthio), *On Romances* (1554)
Minturno, *De Poeta* (1559)
Scaliger, *Poetics* (1561)
Castelvetro, *Poetica D'Aristotele* (1570)

● Du Bellay, *Defence and Illustration of the French Language*
(1549)

● Sidney, *An Apology for Poetry* (written 1583)

Neo-Aristotelians

1600

Rapin, *Reflections on Aristotele's Treatise* (1674)
Boileau, *L'Art Poétique* (1674)
Bouhours, *La Manière de Bien Penser* (1687)

● Jonson, *Timber* (1641)
● Dryden, *An Essay of Dramatic Poesy* (1668)

French Neoclassicism

1700

● Pope, *An Essay on Criticism* (1711)
● Addison, 'Pleasures of the Imagination' (1712)

Vico, *Scienza Nuova* (1725) ●

Time Chart 1

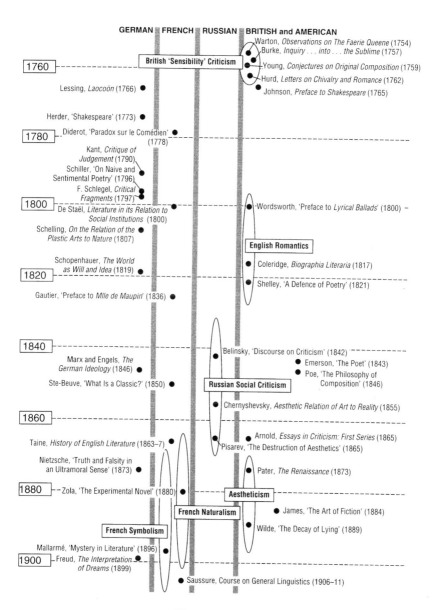

GERMAN FRENCH RUSSIAN BRITISH and AMERICAN

Warton, *Observations on The Faerie Queene* (1754)
Burke, *Inquiry . . . into . . . the Sublime* (1757)

British 'Sensibility' Criticism

1760

Young, *Conjectures on Original Composition* (1759)
Hurd, *Letters on Chivalry and Romance* (1762)
Johnson, *Preface to Shakespeare* (1765)

Lessing, *Laocoön* (1766) ●

Herder, 'Shakespeare' (1773) ●

1780 Diderot, 'Paradox sur le Comédien' ●
(1778)
Kant, *Critique of
Judgement* (1790)
Schiller, 'On Naive and
Sentimental Poetry' (1796)
F. Schlegel, *Critical
Fragments* (1797)

1800 De Staël, *Literature in its Relation to
Social Institutions* (1800)
Schelling, *On the Relation of the* ●
Plastic Arts to Nature (1807)

● Wordsworth, 'Preface to *Lyrical Ballads*' (1800) –

English Romantics

Schopenhauer, *The World
as Will and Idea* (1819) ●

● Coleridge, *Biographia Literaria* (1817)

1820

● Shelley, 'A Defence of Poetry' (1821)

Gautier, 'Preface to *Mlle de Maupin*' (1836) ●

1840

Belinsky, 'Discourse on Criticism' (1842)

Marx and Engels, *The
German Ideology* (1846) ●

● Emerson, 'The Poet' (1843)
● Poe, 'The Philosophy of
Composition' (1846)

Ste-Beuve, 'What Is a Classic?' (1850) ●

Russian Social Criticism

● Chernyshevsky, *Aesthetic Relation of Art to Reality* (1855)

1860

Taine, *History of English Literature* (1863–7) ●

● Arnold, *Essays in Criticism: First Series* (1865)
Pisarev, 'The Destruction of Aesthetics' (1865)

Nietzsche, 'Truth and Falsity in
an Ultramoral Sense' (1873) ●

● Pater, *The Renaissance* (1873)

1880 Zola, 'The Experimental Novel' (1880) ●

Aestheticism

French Naturalism

● James, 'The Art of Fiction' (1884)

French Symbolism

● Wilde, 'The Decay of Lying' (1889)

Mallarmé, 'Mystery in Literature' (1896) ●

1900 Freud, *The Interpretation* ●
of Dreams (1899)

● Saussure, *Course on General Linguistics* (1906–11)

Time Chart 2

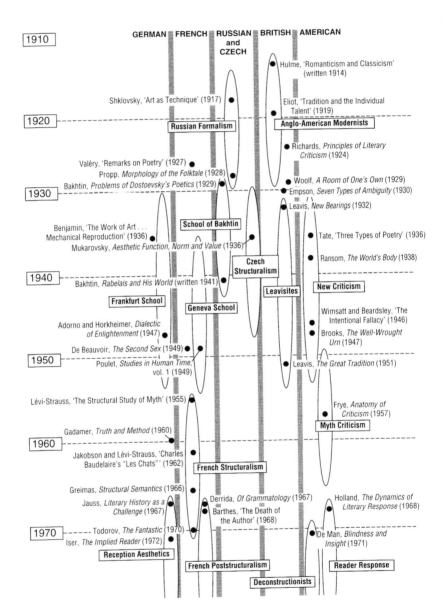

GERMAN   FRENCH   RUSSIAN   BRITISH   AMERICAN
                  and
                  CZECH

1910

Hulme, 'Romanticism and Classicism'
(written 1914)

Shklovsky, 'Art as Technique' (1917)

Eliot, 'Tradition and the Individual
Talent' (1919)

1920

Russian Formalism   **Anglo-American Modernists**

Richards, *Principles of Literary
Criticism* (1924)

Valéry, 'Remarks on Poetry' (1927)
Propp, *Morphology of the Folktale* (1928)
Bakhtin, *Problems of Dostoevsky's Poetics* (1929)

Woolf, *A Room of One's Own* (1929)
Empson, *Seven Types of Ambiguity* (1930)

1930

Leavis, *New Bearings* (1932)

School of Bakhtin

Benjamin, 'The Work of Art . . .
Mechanical Reproduction' (1936)
Mukarovsky, *Aesthetic Function, Norm and Value* (1936)

Tate, 'Three Types of Poetry' (1936)

**Czech
Structuralism**

Ransom, *The World's Body* (1938)

1940

Bakhtin, *Rabelais and His World* (written 1941)

Leavisites   **New Criticism**

Frankfurt School

Geneva School

Wimsatt and Beardsley, 'The
Intentional Fallacy' (1946)

Adorno and Horkheimer, *Dialectic
of Enlightenment* (1947)

Brooks, *The Well-Wrought
Urn* (1947)

De Beauvoir, *The Second Sex* (1949)

1950

Poulet, *Studies in Human Time,*
vol. 1 (1949)

Leavis, *The Great Tradition* (1951)

Lévi-Strauss, 'The Structural Study of Myth' (1955)

Frye, *Anatomy of
Criticism* (1957)

Myth Criticism

Gadamer, *Truth and Method* (1960)

1960

Jakobson and Lévi-Strauss, 'Charles
Baudelaire's "Les Chats"' (1962)

French Structuralism

Greimas, *Structural Semantics* (1966)
Jauss, *Literary History as a
Challenge* (1967)

Derrida, *Of Grammatology* (1967)
Barthes, 'The Death of
the Author' (1968)

Holland, *The Dynamics of
Literary Response* (1968)

1970

Todorov, *The Fantastic* (1970)
Iser, *The Implied Reader* (1972)

De Man, *Blindness and
Insight* (1971)

Reception Aesthetics

French Poststructuralism   **Reader Response**

Deconstructionists

Time Chart 3

Glossary

Actant   In the terminology of A.-J. Greimas, an actant is a fundamental role or agency in the underlying structure of a narrative. Greimas's six possible actants – subject and object, sender and receiver, helper and opponent – are very abstract, and may ultimately surface as human characters, animals, objects or places.

Affective fallacy   The affective fallacy is the supposed error of describing and evaluating a literary work on the basis of its affect, that is, the feelings which it produces in its readers. The 'fallacy' was named by Wimsatt and Beardsley, but expresses a general New Critical principle. Criticism, it is argued, should not be a description of merely subjective responses, nor should interpretation and judgement be subordinated to the statistically most common responses of a majority of readers. In general, the New Critics emphasised intellectual effort on the part of the reader, and were inclined to consider the deliberate stimulation of the reader's emotions as characteristic of popular culture rather than literature.

Alienation effect   Brecht's alienation effect or A-effect is designed to discourage the members of an audience from losing themselves in the realistic illusion of a play, and to prevent them from identifying emotionally with the experience of the characters. Brecht wants the audience to think critically about the social and political conditions *behind* the characters' experience; and he wants them to refer such thinking to the social and political conditions of *their own* real lives. The alienation effect may work by sudden interruptions, switches of level, deliberate artificialities, etc.

Allegory   involves a further level of meaning which can be consistently understood as the 'message' behind a story. This message is the story's underlying *raison d'être*; general concepts have been as if 'clothed' in concrete actions and individual characters. In many works of allegory, general concepts are allowed to show through at certain points, as when a forest is named 'Perplexity' or a character is named 'Innocent'.

In Romantic literary theory, allegory came to feature as the negative pole of a contrast between allegory and symbol. Allegory was condemned as predetermining its concrete particulars by general meanings, while symbols were praised as developing *towards* general meanings *from* concrete particulars. Allegory was also condemned as being translatable into simple cut-and-dried concepts, while symbols were praised as being open-ended and emotionally suggestive. Since the time of the Romantics, allegory has often appeared as a kind of failed or clumsy symbolism, rather than as a mode of writing with its own historical rationale.

The prestige of the symbol was at its height in the period of Symbolism and Modernism; more recent Structuralist and Poststructuralist thinking has cast doubt on whether concrete particulars *ever* truly precede general concepts. The contrast has thus lost its edge, and the symbol is no longer granted automatic superiority.

Avant-garde   The notion of the avant-garde becomes important under a Modernist conception of the role of literature. The avant-garde writer explores ahead, opens up possible paths for others to follow, and experiments with new ways of seeing or thinking or using language.

Belles-lettres   translates as 'beautiful letters' or 'fine writing'. In the Renaissance and Neoclassical periods, 'belles-lettres' defined the domain of serious aesthetic writing, as distinct from scientific or philosophical writing. When the term 'literature' subsequently took over the larger part of this domain, 'belles-lettres' came to be applied to the small remaining part which the new term did not cover – namely, to 'fine writing' which is not imaginative in content, as in the case of stylishly written essays.

Canon (or *kanon*)   In one sense, a canon is a list of works that are accepted as genuine – thus, the Shakespeare canon is the list of works indisputably written by Shakespeare. In a wider sense, a canon is a list of works that are accepted as major literature, indisputably worthy of study. British Leavisites and American New Critics were very active in setting up canons of this latter kind; and subsequent British and American critics have since been very active in pulling them down.

Carnival In medieval (and sometimes later) communities, carnival time was a brief period of permitted popular anarchy, when institutional hierarchies were overturned and official doctrines subjected to laughter. Bakhtin extends the principle of carnival to many cultural forms, including literary forms, where alternative voices are liberated against a dominant ideological system.

Catharsis (or *katharsis*) is the emotionally cleansing effect of tragedy. According to Aristotle, strong feelings of pity and terror which would be undesirable in ordinary life have therapeutic benefits when released in response to a fictional representation. Catharsis may work by 'using up' our free-floating irrational emotions or by making us more capable of dealing with similar emotions in ordinary life. (The exact manner of cleansing is still under dispute.)

Characteristic In German literary theory of the Romantic period, 'the characteristic' is the unique individual essence or 'thusness' of a thing, the distinctive flavour which makes it interesting.

Classical, Classic, Classicism A *classic* is any work of lasting excellence, a lofty standard against which later works are measured. *The Classics* are all the works of Greek and Roman literature (which have indeed lasted, and against which later works have often been measured). Confusingly, the adjective 'classical' can point towards either concept; even more confusingly, it can also point towards the properties associated with either concept. In relation to a *classic*, 'classical' suggests the property of centrality as against marginality; in relation to *the Classics*, it suggests the Greek and Roman virtues of proportion and symmetry, restraint and self-control, logic and clarity.

The term 'Classicism' applies to any movement which aspires to reproduce the Greek and Roman virtues. However, Classicism has also come to represent the polar opposite of Romanticism, and has sometimes been adopted (as by Eliot, Hulme and Pound) mainly to indicate hostility towards Romanticism, rather than to indicate affinity with Greek and Roman literature or its supposed virtues.

Cogito is short for Descartes's *cogito ergo sum* ('I think therefore I am'). In contemporary usage, 'the cogito' refers to the subjective centre of consciousness, especially when viewed as the necessary and fundamental ground for all explanation and understanding. The Geneva critics seek to identify and empathise with a writer's distinctive 'cogito' as the necessary and fundamental ground for understanding the writer's work as a whole.

Condensation   is the process which occurs when, according to Freud, many unconscious meanings converge onto a single image or element in a dream. A single dreamed person may be a composite of several different people, for example, or a single dreamed word may pun upon several different words. Such *overdetermined* images or elements have to be unpacked at great length in psychoanalytical interpretation.

Connotation   *See* 'Denotation versus connotation'.

Correspondences (also, in French, '*correspondances*')   are hidden echoes, recurrences, resemblances, linkages. Baudelaire's initial vision looked through to a mystical level of correspondences in reality itself. Later French Symbolist poets extended the vision to hidden echoes and linkages in literature and their own writings.

Decorum   is 'fittingness' in any one of a great many applications. For the sake of decorum, action and speech must fit the character; style and diction must fit the subject-matter; tone must fit the theme and genre; and emotional effects must be appropriate to the audience. (It would be inappropriate to inflict scenes of vulgarity or violence upon a well-bred audience!) Behind the concept of decorum lies one of the oldest of all critical principles; and Wordsworth was surely fighting against the tide when he tried to write grandly and solemnly about swollen ankles.

In the hands of Horace and the Neoclassical critics, however, decorum takes on a special slant, promoting the general norm at the expense of local particularity. Thus, the behaviour of an old man must be *consistently* grave, and a king must *always* speak in an elevated style (no momentary private expletives!). Donne's use of scientific words in a love lyric would not be 'decorous', and nor would the occasional perverse acts of goodness exhibited by Dostoevsky's most immoral characters. In practice, the concept of decorum tends to exclude erratic or centrifugal tendencies.

Defamiliarisation (or *'ostranenie'*) According to Shklovsky, our everyday perceptions are dulled by habitual stereotypes; it is the writer's task to make us see things as if for the first time by approaching them from an unfamiliar angle (by way of an unfamiliar point of view, for example, or through an unfamiliar use of language). Since words play a major role in the stereotyping process, such defamiliarisation also unsettles words from their grooves and gives them new vitality.

Denotation versus connotation The denotation of a word is its strict definitional meaning, such as might be pinned down in a dictionary. Thus the denotation of 'wine' requires little more than the concepts of *grape-juice* and *fermented* – the necessary and sufficient criteria for picking out examples of wine amongst all other phenomena. By contrast, the connotations of a word are the qualities, associated contexts, attitudes and emotional responses which surround the definitional meaning. Thus the connotations of 'wine' might typically include deep rich colours, drinking rituals and revelry, desirable happiness or damnable drunkenness, etc.

Dialogism, dialogic, dialogical In the linguistics of Bakhtin and Voloshinov, all language is imprinted with the ideological world-views of particular speakers and social groups; at the same time, every verbal utterance derives from other utterances and is directed towards other utterances. Language is thus caught up in a continual process of negotiation and contestation between incompatible world-views. Such a process resembles the negotiation and contestation in a dialogue, where neither party can be wholly in charge and neither party can know the outcome in advance.

This concept of dialogism is applied by Bakhtin in his claims for the dialogical or dialogic novel. In a dialogical novel, different voices are allowed to speak and assert their own world-views, even against that of the author. Bakhtin prefers this kind of novel to what he calls the monological or monologic novel, where the author's world-view is always ultimately in charge.

Bakhtin uses the term *polyphonic novel* almost interchangeably with 'dialogical novel'.

Diegesis versus mimesis In Plato's contrast between diegesis and mimesis, mimesis refers to dialogue and dramatic presentation, while diegesis refers to the kind of narrating where the author takes on responsibility for putting things into words. 'Mimesis' here is not merely copying, as in the broader sense of the term (q.v.), but the peculiarly direct form of copying that occurs when the words of a literary work reproduce what already exists as words.

More recently, narratologists have given diegesis a new emphasis in their discriminations of diegetic level. A novel's primary diegesis is the level of its main story; occurrences involving the narrator of that story exist on an extradiegetic level; while sub-stories narrated or reproduced by characters within that story exist on a hypodiegetic level.

Displacement   is the process which occurs when, according to Freud, the unconscious mind transfers meaning from an original object onto a substitute object, usually in order to evade censorship. When a particular person is linked to forbidden feelings, for example, that person may appear in a dream as some other associated person, or as some associated article of clothing or accessory.

Écriture féminine   refers to the ideal of a distinctive and separate women's writing which does not obey the norms of traditional male-dominated writing. According to Hélène Cixous, who coined the term, '(l)'écriture feminine' becomes possible when women write from their bodies and their sexuality. However, bodies and sexuality should here be understood in terms of how bodies and sexuality are *lived* and not in terms of how they are determined biologically. Cixous, for one, allows that a biological male such as Genet is capable of writing '(l)écriture féminine'.

Einfühlung   is equivalent to 'empathy' in the strict sense: that is, an effort of *feeling into* some subjectivity other than one's own. Reader and critic may *feel into* the subjectivity of a represented character or an author or even a whole Zeitgeist (q.v.); a poet may *feel into* the subjectivity of a swooping falcon or a cloud. In German Romantic theory, such inner empathetic identification produces a more profound understanding than mere outside knowledge.

Fabula* versus *syuzhet   The fabula is the raw material of story, the events considered in terms of 'out there' cause and effect. The syuzhet is story as cast into a particular treatment, in the form actually presented to the reader. In this form, events may be chronologically rearranged, shown from a particular point of view, dramatised in detail or told in summary, etc. The distinction, originally made by the Russian Formalists, has since appeared in a great many variants, of which the most widely accepted are perhaps 'histoire' or 'story' for *'fabula'*, as opposed to 'récit' or 'plot' for *'syuzhet'*. (Unfortunately, there are other variants which use the same terms in different roles.)

Fancy versus imagination   Prior to the Romantic period, imagination was viewed in much the same light as fancy, that is, as the product of wit (q.v.) and invention. But the Romantics, wishing to distinguish their own kind of imagining from Baroque and Neoclassical imaginings, reduced fancy to the negative pole of a contrast between fancy and imagination. Fancy now became the work of conscious playful whimsy and shallow daydream, while imagination was taken to involve deeper vision and the serious apprehension of inner truths. Coleridge specifically condemned fancy as the mere ability to link things by external connections. Although imagination no longer looms so large in literary theory, fancy has never recovered from the lowly position to which the Romantics condemned it.

Function   For Propp and later narratologists, a function is a minimal unit of narrative action, pared down to its most general features. The narratological goal is to account for a vast range of narratives by combining and permutating from a very small stock of functions.

Genre   is a term for a distinguishable species or type of literary work. The distinguishing characteristics may include recurring kinds of form or content or attitude or effect upon the reader/audience. Genre distinctions have been posited on many different scales and levels: for example, drama, novel, lyric; tragedy, comedy, satire; epigram, sonnet, elegy; pastoral, picaresque novel, Gothic novel; science fiction, swords-and-sorcery, Utopian fiction. Some of these later narrower types might be more often described as sub-genres.
   The idea that works grow naturally into certain separate species seemed obvious to Aristotle; shifting the emphasis, Neoclassical critics expected the author to choose a genre and abide by its rules; while Romantics, Realists and Modernists dismissed the whole notion of genres when they dismissed the rules. In the second half of the twentieth century, genre theory has resurfaced in Frye's Myth Criticism and French Structuralism. Todorov makes a distinction

between historical genres as *actual* species in the history of literature, versus theoretical genres as *possible* species within the system of literature.

Horizon, horizon of expectations   Phenomenological and Existentialist philosophers have used the term 'horizon' to convey the limits of what can be seen from a particular living position. Gadamer and Jauss are especially interested in how one's position within history inevitably governs the available possibilities of understanding, response and judgement. Jauss coins the term 'horizon of expectations' to describe the field of assumptions spread out by an audience in a given historical period, the field upon which all literary works in that period must appear.

Imagination   *See* 'Fancy versus imagination'.

Intentional fallacy   Famously formulated by Wimsatt and Beardsley, the 'intentional fallacy' sums up a common New Critical view, that an author's intention cannot and should not be a criterion for interpreting or evaluating the literary work. As regards interpretation, Wimsatt and Beardsley claim that the meanings of a work are generated by independent processes of language over which an author has no control. As regards evaluation, they claim that the actual achievement of a work may be judged without reference to what the author was 'trying' to achieve. (Not surprisingly, New Critical evaluation does not recognise strongly different goals for different forms of literature.) Wimsatt and Beardsley are primarily concerned to prevent reliance upon external biographical evidence; they assume that intentions hypothesised on the internal evidence of the work cannot be anything very different from the work itself.

Intertextuality   Although Kristeva launched the use of the term, the vision of intertextuality is deeply woven into all Poststructuralist thinking. Under this vision, no text can be considered in isolation, because every text echoes, alludes to, and is ultimately constituted by other previous texts. This is not a matter of the sources that inspired the writer, but arises out of the citational nature of language in general. In order to 'mean' at all, the text cannot help but bounce off other meanings, cannot help but invoke previous linguistic contexts and systems of meaning.

Irony   is a way of pulling down a perspective by pretending to adopt it. In verbal irony, the attitude overtly expressed is undercut by the reader's understanding that the author really holds a very different attitude. In dramatic and situational irony, the perspective assumed by a particular character or narrator is undercut by real facts about the situation known (or becoming known) to the audience or reader. In cosmic irony, the whole human perspective is undercut, as in Shakespeare's *Troilus and Cressida* or the novels of Hardy.

Irony traditionally involves an extreme difference, often an outright reversal, between the perspective overtly expressed and the real understanding conveyed. However, a much wider application of 'irony' became popular in the Modernist period. For Modernist-oriented critics, all perspectives are relative and every perspective needs to be undercut by a recognition of alternative perspectives. In this case, irony is not a matter of switching across from a false perspective to a real understanding, but a matter of juggling between several possible perspectives, all partially valid but none wholly true.

Langue versus parole   'Langue' describes the total system of rules and categories which enable the speaker of a language to produce and understand individual utterances. The system precedes the individual utterances in the same way that the rules and categories for chess must be known before one can play a particular game of chess. By contrast, 'parole' describes the actual individual utterances. The sum total of all utterances which have ever been uttered is still not as large as – is not even on the same level as – the potential system for making utterances. 'Langue' is implanted without the speaker's conscious choice or volition; conscious choice and volition come into play only in relation to 'parole', when the speaker decides and selects from amongst the possibilities that 'langue' offers.

Literariness   sums up the special properties which make a text 'literary' and therefore distinct from all non-literary texts. In proposing 'literariness' as the primary concern for critics, the Russian Formalists were seeking to draw literary studies away from historical, psychological and philosophical studies.

Meta-language   is a supposedly higher level of language which enables one to look down and say things *about* language on the ordinary level.

Metaphor   works by identifying two entities normally considered as separate, so that a word or phrase for the one is used in place of a word or phrase for the other. Metaphoric identification depends upon a relation of similarity, though not necessarily a similarity that was ever apprehended before. The reader is compelled to leap to such a relation when the word or phrase as used fails to agree in any literal way with its surrounding verbal context.

In the traditional conception, a metaphor was a simile with the 'like' or 'as if' deleted: 'my heart is like a wheel' → 'my heart is a wheel', 'their love was as if blossoming' → 'their love was blossoming'. But for the Romantics and especially the Modernists, the best metaphors enable us to think what could not be otherwise thought; and the reader is not merely led across to an implicit meaning, but acquires new insight through a two-way interreaction between the implicit meaning (or *tenor*) and the literal meaning (or *vehicle*). One argument in support of the Modernist view is that so many of the meanings in present-day language are in fact the dead residues of metaphors: for example, 'branch' in the sense of *subsidiary office*, or 'grasp' in the sense of *comprehend conceptually*. Such once-living metaphors have made it possible to think what could not have been thought otherwise.

Metonymy   identifies two entities which typically occur together, and replaces a word or phrase for the one with a word or phrase for the other. Such co-occurrence can take many forms, as when 'crown' is used to mean *king*, or 'the press' is used to mean *journalism*, or 'the White House' is used to mean *the President of the USA*. Association by closeness and contiguity is the principle of metonymy, whereas metaphor associates by similarity across a distance.

Mimesis   is the Greek word for imitation, a central concept in Aristotelian and Neoclassical literary theory. Literature is mimetic in so far as it reproduces or copies something external to itself. Any work which is not purely abstract is to some degree mimetic: but the concept applies better to narrative works than to lyric poems; and applies best of all to narrative works presenting plausible real-world-like actions and people. However, the concept of *mimesis* does not involve photographic realism in the modern sense. The recording of actually observed details is unimportant for Aristotle and the Neoclassical theorists; what matters is the kind of plausibility which makes sense to the human understanding.

See 'Diegesis versus mimesis' for a second more specialised sense of the term 'mimesis'.

Objective correlative   On T. S. Eliot's original definition, an objective correlative is an object, scene or situation which both embodies and evokes a particular emotion. Eliot's approval of objective correlatives is consistent with the general Modernist disapproval of any attempt to communicate emotion directly from poet to reader. As taken up by later critics, an objective correlative is neither exactly the cause of an emotion (the fictitious monster that frightens the reader) nor the representation of an emotion (the frightened state of the monster's fictitious victim), but something more akin to the symbol of an emotion. Eliot's own poetry provides examples: in *Four Quartets,* it is clear that 'the moment in the draughty church at smokefall' and 'the smell of grapes on the autumn table' embody a particular past emotional mood for the poet, and seek to evoke an answering emotional mood in the reader.

Ostranenie   *See* 'Defamiliarisation'.

Overdetermination   *See* 'Condensation'.

Paradigmatic versus syntagmatic   Following Saussure, Structural linguists and Structuralist literary critics have distinguished two kinds of relation relevant to the meaning of any uttered word. On the one hand, a word as uttered in a sentence relates *syntagmatically* to the words which come before and after it: thus, 'sat' combines with 'the cat' and 'on the mat'. On the other hand, the meaning of 'sat' is already determined by its difference from alternative words which could have been but were not chosen in its place – words like 'stood', for example, or 'ran' and 'leaped'. The relations between such optional alternatives are described as *paradigmatic,* and are understood in terms of contrasts and similarities. Thus the meanings of 'sat' and 'stood' are contrasted but similar within an overarching concept of bodily stance; while the concept of bodily stance is itself contrasted but similar to the concept of bodily movement.

Parole   *See* 'Langue versus parole'.

Patronage   was the main source of support for many writers in the

Classical, medieval, Renaissance and Neoclassical periods. In return for bestowing gifts (often not *directly* financial) upon the writer, the patron could claim first call upon the writer's services and could expect to be honoured in the writer's works and dedications. As the 'backer' of an admired writer, the patron benefited by a general enhancement of social prestige. Corporate sponsorship is a close contemporary parallel, when companies support artistic productions for the sake of a positive public image which ultimately redounds to the credit of their balance-sheets.

Perspicuity   is transparency of language, where readers can readily see through to the meaning. Perspicuity was highly valued in the Neoclassical period.

Poetic justice   punishes the bad and rewards the good in the ultimate outcome of a narrative.

Point-of-view   refers to the angle or vantage from which the events of a narrative are presented. Questions of point-of-view turn upon who sees or who thinks or who tells what happens. Historically, such questions became important when authors first began to manipulate sharply distinct possibilities: consciously choosing to present through the experience of character A or the experience of character B, or through authorial overview, or through a limited narrator, or through an unthinking 'camera-eye', etc.

Polyglossia   is Bakhtin's term for describing the coexistence of many diverging socio-ideological languages within a single official language culture. In one sense, all speakers of English or Russian speak the same language; but in another sense, the meanings mean differently for different social groups according to their different backgrounds, interests and ideological perspectives. Bakhtin emphasises and values these divergences.

'Heteroglossia' has a similar meaning when applied to society and language at large. However, Bakhtin also sometimes applies 'heteroglossia' and 'polyglossia' to the diversity of voices within a literary work, in which case the meanings of both terms move closer to the meaning of 'polyphony'. (*See under* 'Dialogism, dialogic, dialogical'.)

Polyphonic novel   *See* 'Dialogism, dialogic, dialogical'.

Reality effect   describes an impression of the real produced under the special conventions of realistic literature. Theorists who use this term do not accept that a work can ever make contact with a reality existing simply outside of literary conventions.

Rhetoric   refers to the means of persuasion by which a speaker or writer can seek to influence a listener or reader. In Classical, medieval and Renaissance times, the possible means of persuasion were studied and cultivated as a valuable skill. Later, when the scientific age promoted the ideal of a message which should stand by itself and justify itself, rhetoric tended to appear as a kind of cheating. More recently, the rhetorical dimension has recovered its importance under the Postmodernist perspective, which sees all language as seeking to persuade, no message as standing simply by itself.

Semiotic square (also 'semiotic rectangle')   In Greimas's semiotic theory, contrary concepts (such as life versus death, nature versus culture) are made to give birth to further concepts by an unfolding of the 'semiotic square'. Whereas the unfolding of Hegel's dialectic resolves oppositions by synthesis into a single concept, Greimas's less 'resolving' process continues to generate oppositional pairs.

Semiotics and semiology   The science of signs was named 'semiology' by Saussure and 'semiotics' by the American philosopher C. S. Peirce. Originally, the difference of terms corresponded to a profound difference between the French approach and the Anglo-American approach. However, the approaches have since run together – to the detriment of Peirce, whose underlying philosophical perspective has almost wholly disappeared from view. By way of consolation, Peirce's term 'semiotics' is now the more popular term of the two.

Sublime   Inspiring a feeling of awe rather than a mere appreciation of beauty, the sublime is associated with vastness, power and mystery. Or to put it another way: whereas the beautiful is safely possessed in the apprehension of the beholder, the sublime overpowers the beholder with a sense of something exceeding her or his own capacities. The concept of the sublime rose to great prominence in the eighteenth century, when the appeal of this kind of emotional response appeared in very sharp contrast to the Neoclassical taste for charming and delicate forms of beauty.

Symbol   A symbol is anything which stands for something else. In language, for example, the physical marks on the page stand for a meaning, as when the letters 'r'-'o'-'s'-'e' stand for the idea of a rose. However, a literary symbol specifically involves a meaning beyond the ordinary linguistic meaning, as when the idea of a rose stands in turn for natural beauty or heavenly perfection or unfolding love. The movement of signifying is as if continued in a vertical direction over the same spot.

Contemporary ways of thinking about literary symbols are above all conditioned by the practice of Symbolist and Modernist writers, who elevated the symbol to a new level of importance in literature. In this practice, a symbol is typically grounded upon a vivid concrete image (hence the affinity between discussion of images and discussion of symbols). The properties of the concretion – the velvety rich colour, the multifoliate petals of the rose – are brought out with an intensity which seems to exceed and point beyond ordinary linguistic meaning. In this respect, a symbol tends to operate by a kind of hyper-concretion, whereas allegory tends to operate by a thinness or patchiness of concretion.

See 'Allegory' for further aspects of the contrast between allegory and symbol, and for further implications of the term 'symbol'.

Synecdoche   replaces the name of the whole with the name of the part (e.g. 'motor' or 'wheels' to mean *car*) or the name of the part with the name of the whole (e.g. 'the law' to mean *an individual police officer*). Since part and whole necessarily co-occur, synecdoche is commonly regarded as a special case of metonymy (q.v.).

Syntagmatic   *See* 'Paradigmatic versus syntagmatic'.

Syuzhet   *See* '*Fabula* versus *syuzhet*'.

Taste   refers to the ability to appreciate and discriminate, especially in so far as this ability is developed and cultivated. Almost everyone has a spontaneous liking for sweet foods, but most people probably have to 'acquire a taste' for red wine. Taste was an important concept in the Neoclassical period, when cultivated appreciations were at a premium.

Tenor   *See* 'Metaphor'.

Touchstones   are very short quotes from very great literature, which can be brought to mind as standards when evaluating other (lesser) works. The idea originated with Matthew Arnold, who proposed several touchstones of between one and four lines in length.

Trope   A trope is any figure of speech where words are used with a non-literal twist of meaning – as in metaphor (q.v), metonymy (q.v.), irony (q.v.), simile, hyperbole. The term featured centrally in all handbooks of rhetoric from Classical to Renaissance times, then fell from favour when rhetoric was disparaged as a mere collection of tricks and devices. It has recently undergone a minor revival in association with Postmodernist notions of self-conscious play and deliberate artifice. (*See also* 'Rhetoric'.)

Unities   The 'three unities' or 'unities' were developed by the Italian Aristotelian critics and became rigid prescriptions for all drama in the Neoclassical period. The unity of action ruled that narrative action should be coherent and convergent; the unity of time ruled that the duration of events represented should not extend beyond twelve hours (or sometimes, twenty-four hours); the unity of place ruled that the settings represented should not extend beyond the rooms of a single building (or sometimes, rooms within a single town).

Aristotle had strongly insisted upon unified action in tragedy and had made a passing suggestion about restricting the time-span of events. However, it was the Italian Aristotelians who directed the unity of action specifically to exclude sub-plots (never an issue in Greek tragedy), and who developed a whole new rationale for the unity of time. This new rationale was less concerned with the aesthetic virtue of concentration than with the maintenance of realistic illusion under the special conditions of theatrical representation. Since an audience actually experiences the passing of real time as they watch a play, will they not lose belief in the representation if it contradicts their experience? Similarly with the unity of place (which Aristotle had never even suggested): since an audience actually observes real space as they watch the stage, will they not lose belief in the representation if it contradicts their observation? Neoclassical theorists could not allow for jumps in space and time because they did not recognise the possibility of discontinuities in representation – discontinuities which enable an audience to restart with a new framing of space and time.

Vehicle *See* 'Metaphor'.

Verisimilitude (also 'vraisemblance') is the term used by Neo-classical critics to specify the kind of resemblance to reality which they expected of a literary work. This was not a realism of small observed details, as in the realistic novel, but involved principles of probability operating on a fairly large scale.

When used more recently in the nineteenth and twentieth centuries, the term *does* apply to more modern notions of realism – but with an emphasis upon mere semblance and illusion. In this usage, the implications of 'verisimilitude' are similar to the implications of 'reality effect' (q.v.).

Vernacular A vernacular is the everyday language spoken within a given local community – as distinct from forms of language which are 'proper', high-flown, imported or specially preserved.

Volksgeist refers to the distinctive spirit common to a whole people or race. Cf. the comments on 'Zeitgeist'.

Wit in its original sense referred to the intellect and its activity, with no suggestion of humour. For Elizabethan and Metaphysical poets, wit meant inventive ingenuity, especially in leaping to 'conceits'. In the Restoration and Augustan periods, the term was applied to a sharp and clever deftness, especially in verbal expression. During this latter period, wit also became increasingly associated with humorous effect, but still remained a term of high praise. Even when amusing, wit was not shallow or trivial, as in the usual modern sense. T. S. Eliot attempted a Modernist revival of the old non-humorous sense when he pointed to the many-sided awareness involved in Metaphysical wit, the sudden perception of connections between apparently incongruous items.

Zeitgeist refers to the distinctive spirit common to a whole age. The critic is typically expected to empathise with this spirit as though empathising with the mood and perspective of a single mind. Not surprisingly, the concept of the *Zeitgeist* tends to efface social and cultural conflict under an assumption of homogeneity.

Notes

Notes to Chapter 1: Literary Theory in Classical Times

1. Theophrastus, frag. 65, in D. A. Russell, *Criticism in Antiquity* (Berkeley, CA: University of California Press, 1981) pp. 203–4.
2. Gorgias, 'A Defence of Helen', in D. A. Russell and M. Winterbottom (eds), *Ancient Literary Criticism* (Oxford: Clarendon Press, 1972) p. 6.
3. Ibid., p. 7.
4. At least this is what Plato attributes to Protagoras. See Plato, *Cratylus*, 386, in *The Dialogues of Plato*, vol. III, trans. B. Jewett (Oxford: Clarendon Press, 1953) p. 43.
5. The practical examples are taken from Cicero's *De Oratore*, 3.157, 3.168 and 3.167 respectively.
6. Plato, *Republic*, in Russell and Winterbottom, *Ancient Literary Criticism*, p. 71.
7. Ibid., p. 61.
8. See Plato, *Phaedrus (and Letters VII and VIII)*, trans. Walter Hamilton (Harmondsworth: Penguin, 1973) pp. 95–9. Derrida's discussion occurs in the 'Plato's Pharmacy' section of *Dissemination*, trans. Barbara Johnson (London: Athlone Press, 1981).
9. Plato, *Republic*, p. 63.
10. Ibid., p. 72.
11. Ibid., p. 73.
12. Ibid., p. 67.
13. Plotinus, *The Enneads*, trans. Stephen McKenna (London: Faber and Faber, 1969) pp. 422–3.
14. Proclus, 'On the *Republic*', in Russell, *Criticism in Antiquity*, p. 199, p. 200.
15. Aristotle, *Poetics*, ch. 4, in *Classical Literary Criticism*, trans. T. S. Dorsch (Harmondsworth: Penguin, 1965) p. 35.
16. Aristotle, *Physics*, in *Loeb Aristotle*, vol. IV, trans. Philip H. Wicksteed and Francis M. Cornford (London: Heinemann, 1957) pp. 121–3.
17. Ibid., p. 173.
18. Aristotle, *Poetics*, in *Classical Literary Criticism*, ch. 15, p. 51; ch. 2, p. 33.
19. Ibid., ch. 25, p. 69.
20. Ibid., ch. 9, pp. 43–4.
21. Ibid., ch. 24, p. 68; ch. 25, p. 73.
22. Ibid., ch. 25, p. 72
23. Ibid., ch. 15, p. 51.
24. Ibid., ch. 4, p. 36.
25. Ibid., ch. 8, p. 43.
26. Ibid., ch. 7, p. 42.

27. Ibid., ch. 13, p. 48.
28. See ibid., ch. 6.
29. See ibid., ch. 13.
30. Ibid., ch. 13, p. 47.
31. Horace, *Epistle* 2.1, ll. 158–9, in Russell and Winterbottom, *Ancient Literary Criticism*, p. 276.
32. Horace, *Ars Poetica*, ll. 306–8, in *Classical Literary Criticism*, pp. 89–90.
33. Ibid., ll. 189–92, p. 85.
34. Ibid., ll. 86–7, p. 82.
35. Ibid., ll. 154–5, p. 84.
36. Ibid., ll. 409–10, p. 93.
37. Ibid., ll. 292–4, p. 89.
38. Ibid. ll. 386–8, p. 92.
39. Ibid., ll. 317–8, p. 90.
40. Ibid., l. 134, ll. 131–4, p. 83.
41. Ibid., ll. 333–4, p. 90; ll. 343–4, p. 91.
42. Longinus, *On the Sublime*, Preface, in *Classical Literary Criticism*, p. 99.
43. Ibid., ch. 17, p. 127.
44. Callimachus, frag. 65, cited in George A. Kennedy (ed.), *The Cambridge History of Literary Criticism*, vol. 1 (Cambridge: Cambridge University Press, 1989) p. 202.
45. Longinus, *On the Sublime*, ch. 33, in *Classical Literary Criticism*, p. 143.
46. Ibid., ch. 9, p. 109.
47. Ibid., ch. 7, p. 107.
48. Ibid.
49. Longinus, *On the Sublime*, ch. 38, in Russell and Winterbottom, *Ancient Literary Criticism*, p. 496.
50. Longinus, *On the Sublime*, ch. 42, in *Classical Literary Criticism*, p. 153.

Notes to Chapter 2: Literary Theory in the Middle Ages

1. John of Garland, *De Arte Prosayca, Metrica, et Rithmica*, in James J. Murphy, *Rhetoric in the Middle Ages* (Berkeley: University of California Press, 1974) p. 179.
2. Geoffrey of Vinsauf, *Poetria Nova*, trans. Margaret F. Nims, in Alex Preminger, O. B. Hardison, Jr, and Kevin Kerrane (eds), *Classical and Medieval Literary Criticism* (New York: Frederick Ungar, 1974) p. 388.
3. Fulgentius, *The Exposition of the Content of Virgil*, trans. O. B. Hardison, in Preminger, Hardison and Kerrane (eds), *Classical and Medieval Literary Criticism*, p. 333.
4. Ibid., p. 338.
5. See ibid., p. 339.
6. Ibid., p. 335.
7. Some scholars have questioned the authorship of the 'Epistle to Cangrande'. But even if written by another hand, it conforms to the general spirit of Dante's own arguments in the *Convivio*.
8. Dante Alighieri, *The Banquet of Dante Alighieri*, trans. Elizabeth Price Sayer (London: George Routledge, 1887) p. 48.
9. Ibid.

10. Ibid., p. 49.
11. Giovanni Boccaccio, *Boccaccio on Poetry: Being the Preface and the Fourteenth and Fifteenth Books of Boccaccio's Genealogia Diorum Gentilium*, trans. Charles Osgood (Princeton: Princeton University Press, 1930) p. xvii.

Notes to Chapter 3: The Rise and Fall of Neoclassicism

1. Dante Alighieri, *De Vulgari Eloquentia*, I, 16, and I, 19, trans. A. G. Ferrers Howell and Philip H. Wicksteed, in Preminger, Hardison and Kerrane, *Classical and Medieval Literary Criticism*, p. 429.
2. Joachim du Bellay, *La Deffence et Illustration de la Langue Françoyse*, in Margaret W. Ferguson, *Trials of Desire: Renaissance Defenses of Poetry* (New Haven: Yale University Press, 1983) p. 27.
3. Giovambattista Giraldi Cinthio, *On the Composition of Romances*, in Harold Bloom (ed.), *The Art of the Critic*, vol. II (New York: Chelsea House, 1986) p. 135.
4. Torquato Tasso, *Discourses on the Heroic Poem*, Book 1, in Bloom, *The Art of the Critic*, p. 403.
5. Sir Philip Sidney, *An Apologie for Poetry*, in D. J. Enright and Ernst de Chickera (eds), *English Critical Texts: 16th Century to 20th Century* (London: Oxford University Press, 1962) p. 31.
6. Ibid., p. 8.
7. Ibid., p. 10.
8. Ibid., p. 16.
9. Ibid., p. 19.
10. Sperone Speroni, cited in Baxter Hathaway, *The Age of Criticism: The Late Renaissance in Italy* (Ithaca: Cornell University Press, 1962) p. 159.
11. Lodovico Castelvetro, *Poetica d'Aristotele vulgarizzata et sposta* (*On the Poetics*), ch. IX, in Bloom, *The Art of the Critic*, vol. II, p. 223.
12. See Bernard Weinberg, 'Castelvetro's Theory of Poetics', in R. S. Crane (ed.), *Critics and Criticism* (Chicago: University of Chicago Press, 1952) p. 362.
13. Lodovico Castelvetro, *Poetica d'Aristotele vulgarizzata et sposta*, in Bernard Weinberg, *A History of Literary Criticism in the Italian Renaissance*, vol. I (Chicago: University of Chicago Press, 1961) p. 504.
14. H. B. Charlton, *Castelvetro's Theory of Poetry* (Manchester: Manchester University Press, 1913) p. 84.
15. Ibid.
16. Michel de Montaigne, *The Essays of Michel Eyquem de Montaigne*, trans. Charles Cotton (Chicago: Encyclopaedia Britannica, 1952) p. 114.
17. Samuel Johnson, *The History of Rasselas* (Oxford: Oxford University Press, 1977) pp. 28–9.
18. Samuel Johnson, 'Life of Cowley', in *Selections from Samuel Johnson, 1709–84* (London: Oxford University Press, 1962) p. 374.
19. Samuel Johnson, 'Preface to Shakespeare', in *Yale Edition of the Works of Samuel Johnson*, vol. VII (New Haven: Yale University Press, 1968) p. 62.
20. Alexander Pope, 'An Essay on Criticism', ll. 48–50, in *The Poems of Alexander Pope* (London: Methuen, 1965) p. 145.
21. Ibid., ll. 133–5, p. 148.

22. Nicholas Boileau-Despréaux, *Critical Reflections on some Passages out of Longinus*, in Scott Elledge and Donald Schier (eds), *The Continental Model* (Ithaca: Cornell University Press , 1970) p. 276.
23. David Hume, 'Of the Standard of Taste', in *Essential Works of David Hume* (New York: Bantam Books, 1965) pp. 453–4. Jaundice affects the perception of colour.
24. Nicholas Boileau-Despréaux, *L'Art Poétique*, trans. Ernest Dilworth, in Hazard Adams (ed.), *Critical Theory since Plato* (New York: Harcourt Brace Jovanovich, 1992) p. 242.
25. Dominique Bouhours, *The Conversations of Aristo and Eugene*, in Elledge and Schier, *The Continental Model*, p. 164.
26. Pope, 'An Essay on Criticism', l. 68, p. 146.
27. René Rapin, *Reflections of Aristotle's Treatise of Poesy*, Book I, Section 39, in Elledge and Schier, *The Continental Model*, p. 295.
28. Pope, 'An Essay on Criticism', l. 288, p. 153.
29. Ibid., l. 155, p. 149.
30. Ben Jonson, *Timber, or Discoveries*, no. 647, in Michael J. Sidnell, *Sources of Dramatic Theory, I: Plato to Congreve* (Cambridge: Cambridge University Press, 1991) p. 194.
31. See ibid., no. 125.
32. John Dryden, 'Heads of an Answer to Rymer', in *John Dryden: Selected Criticism* (Oxford: Clarendon Press, 1970) p. 145.
33. John Dryden, 'An Essay of Dramatic Poesy', in *John Dryden: Selected Criticism*, p. 25.
34. Ibid., p. 48.
35. Ibid., p. 50; and John Dryden, 'A Defence of An Essay of Dramatic Poesy', p. 92.
36. Ibid., p. 50.
37. John Dryden, 'Preface to *Secret Love*', in *The Works of John Dryden*, vol. II, ed. Sir Walter Scott and George Saintsbury (Edinburgh: T. & A. Constable, 1882–3) p. 420.
38. John Dryden, 'Preface to *Fables, Ancient and Modern*', in *John Dryden: Selected Criticism*, p. 296.
39. Samuel Johnson, *Lives of the English Poets*, vol. I (Oxford: Oxford University Press, 1905) p. 212.
40. Johnson, *The History of Rasselas*, p. 27.
41. Johnson, 'Preface to Shakespeare', p. 67.
42. Ibid., p. 66.
43. Samuel Johnson, *The Rambler*, 37, in *Yale Edition of the Works of Samuel Johnson*, vol. III, p. 205.
44. Johnson, 'Preface to Shakespeare', p. 76.
45. Ibid., p. 77.
46. Edward Young, 'Conjectures on Original Composition', in Edward Young, *The Complete Works: Poetry and Prose*, vol. II (Hildesheim: Georg Olms, 1968) p. 564.
47. Ibid., pp. 557–8.
48. Ibid., p. 552.
49. Ibid., p. 564.
50. Ibid., p. 555.
51. Ibid., p. 557.
52. Ibid.

53. Joseph Warton, *Essay on the Genius and Writings of Pope*, in Oliver F. Sigworth (ed.), *Criticism and Aesthetics: 1660–1800* (San Francisco: Rinehart Press, 1971) pp. 293–4.
54. Ibid., p. 292.
55. Thomas Warton, *Observations on the Fairy Queen of Spenser*, in Sigworth, *Criticism and Aesthetics*, p. 369.
56. Richard Hurd, *Letters on Chivalry and Romance*, XII, in Sigworth, *Criticism and Aesthetics*, p. 383.
57. Ibid., VII, p. 378.
58. Edmund Burke, *A Philosophical Enquiry into the Origin of our Ideas of the Sublime and Beautiful*, I, 7 (London: Routledge & Kegan Paul, 1958) p. 39.
59. Ibid., II, 2, p. 57.
60. Ibid., II, 3, pp. 58–9.
61. Ibid., II, 4, p. 62.
62. Ibid., V, 5, p. 170.
63. Ibid., V, 5, p. 172.
64. Giambattista Vico, *Scienza Nuova* (1725 edition), Book III, Section 5, in *Vico: Selected Writings*, trans. Leon Pompa (Cambridge: Cambridge University Press, 1982) p. 143.
65. Vico, *Scienza Nuova* (1744 edition), Book IV, Section II, 2, in *Vico: Selected Writings*, p. 223.
66. See Denis Diderot, 'A Letter on the Blind', in Beatrix L. Tollemache, *Diderot's Thoughts on Art and Style* (New York: Burt Franklin, 1971). The same volume also contains a translation of 'A Letter on the Deaf and Dumb'.
67. Denis Diderot, 'The Paradox of Acting', in Adams, *Critical Theory since Plato*, p. 365.
68. Ibid., p. 371.
69. See Dorval's argument in 'Entretiens sur Le Fils Naturel', which suggests interesting premonitions of Antonin Artaud. 'Entretiens sur Le Fils Naturel' appears in Denis Diderot, *Oeuvres Ésthetiques* (Paris: Éditions Garnier, 1968).
70. See Denis Diderot, 'On Dramatic Poetry', in Bernard F. Dukore, (ed.), *Dramatic Theory and Criticism* (New York: Holt, Rinehart & Winston, 1974) p. 293.
71. Diderot, 'The Paradox of Acting', p. 369.
72. Cited in René Wellek, *A History of Modern Criticism, 1750–1950*, vol. I (London: Jonathan Cape, 1955) p. 50.
73. Gotthold Ephraim Lessing, *Laocoön: Nathan the Wise: Minna von Barnhelm*, ed. William A. Steel (London: Dent, 1930) p. 55.
74. Ibid., pp. 64–5, p. 55.
75. Ibid., p. 56.

Notes to Chapter 4: Romantic Literary Theory

1. Samuel Taylor Coleridge, *Biographia Literaria*, vol. II, ch. XIV (London: Oxford University Press, 1954) p. 11.
2. Johann Gottfried Herder, 'The Origin of Language', in *J. G. Herder on Social and Political Culture*, trans. F. M. Barnard (Cambridge: Cambridge University Press, 1969) p. 165.

3. Johann Gottfried Herder, 'Shakespeare', in H. B. Nisbet (ed.), *German Aesthetic and Literary Criticism: Winckelmann, Lessing, Hamann, Herder, Schiller, Goethe* (Cambridge: Cambridge University Press, 1985) p. 165.
4. Cited in Wellek, *A History of Modern Criticism, 1750–1950* vol. I, p. 197–8; also footnote on p. 318.
5. Herder, 'Shakespeare', p. 167.
6. Friedrich Schiller, 'On Naive and Sentimental Poetry', in Nisbet, *German Aesthetic and Literary Criticism*, p. 196.
7. Friedrich Schiller, *On the Aesthetic Education of Man*, trans. Elizabeth M. Wilkinson and L. A. Willoughby (Oxford: Clarendon, 1967) p. 31.
8. G. W. F. Hegel, *The Philosophy of Fine Art*, trans. F. P. B. Osmaston (London: G. Bell & Sons, 1920) p. 103.
9. Ibid., p. 105.
10. Ibid., p. 110.
11. Cited in Wellek, *A History of Modern Criticism*, vol. II, p. 46.
12. Coleridge, *Biographia Literaria*, vol. I, ch. XII, p. 202.
13. Ibid., ch. IV, p. 59.
14. Immanuel Kant, *The Critique of Judgement*, 'Analytic of the Beautiful', §2, trans. James Creed Meredith, in David Simpson (ed.), *German Aesthetic and Literary Criticism: Kant, Fichte, Schelling, Schopenhauer, Hegel* (Cambridge: Cambridge University Press, 1984), p. 37.
15. Johann Wolfgang von Goethe, 'Didactic Poetry', trans. Ellen von Nardroff and Ernest H. von Nardroff, in John Gearey (ed.), *Goethe: Essays on Art and Literature* (New York: Suhrkamp, 1986) p. 194.
16. J. W. von Goethe, 'On Interpreting Aristotle's *Poetics*', in Gearey, *Goethe: Essays on Art and Literature*, p. 199.
17. Schiller, *On the Aesthetic Education of Man*, p. 157.
18. Ibid.
19. J. W. von Goethe, Letter to Zelter, 29 January 1830, cited in Wellek, *A History of Modern Criticism*, vol. I, p. 216.
20. Arthur Schopenhauer, *The World as Will and Representation*, vol. I, §38, trans. E. F. J. Payne (New York: Dover, 1966) p. 198.
21. Ibid., vol. I, §36, p. 187.
22. August Wilhelm Schlegel, *On Dramatic Art and Literature*, Lecture 22, in R. A. Foakes (ed.), *Romantic Criticism: 1800–1850* (London: Edward Arnold, 1968) p. 58.
23. Ibid., p. 59. For both Schlegels, 'Romantic' refers to a tendency in art which extends beyond what we now call the 'Romantic period'.
24. Coleridge, *Biographia Literaria*, vol. II, ch. XIV, p. 10.
25. Ibid., vol. II, ch. XIV, p. 11.
26. Ibid., vol. II, ch. XV, p. 14; Samuel Taylor Coleridge, *Shakespearean Criticism*, vol. I (London: Dent, 1930) p. 5.
27. Coleridge, *Shakespearean Criticism*, vol. II, p. 36.
28. Quoted by Eckermann in *Conversations of Goethe with Eckermann*, trans. John Oxenford, in Adams, *Critical Theory since Plato*, p. 531.
29. F. W. J. Schelling, *Concerning the Relation of the Plastic Arts to Nature*, trans. Michael Bullock, in Simpson, *German Aesthetic and Literary Criticism*, p. 153–4.
30. Samuel Taylor Coleridge, *The Statesman's Manual*, in I. A. Richards (ed.), *The Portable Coleridge* (Harmondsworth: Penguin, 1977) p. 388.

31. A. W. Schlegel discusses poetry as a 'thinking in images' in his *On Dramatic Art and Literature*, vol. I.

32. Cited in Wellek, *A History of Modern Criticism*, vol. I, p. 184.

33. Ibid.

34. Friedrich Schegel, *Literary Notebooks, 1797–1801*, ed. Hans Eichner (London: Athlone Press, 1957) p. 173.

35. Cited in Wellek, *A History of Modern Criticism*, vol. II, pp. 8–9.

36. Ibid., vol. I, p. 189.

37. Ibid., vol. II, p. 8.

38. Ibid., vol. II, p. 308.

39. Ibid., vol. II, p. 305.

40. Martin Redeke, *Schleiermacher: Life and Thought* (Philadelphia: Fortress, 1973) p. 176.

41. William Wordsworth, 'Preface to *Lyrical Ballads*', in *Wordsworth's Literary Criticism*, ed. W. J. B. Owen (London: Routledge & Kegan Paul, 1974) p. 74, p. 76.

42. Ibid., p. 71.

43. See Coleridge, *Biographia Literaria*, vol. II, ch. XX, p. 83.

44. Ibid., vol. II, ch. XX, p. 77.

45. Ibid., vol. II, ch. XXII, p. 116.

46. Wordsworth, 'Preface to *Lyrical Ballads*' and 'Essay, Supplementary to the Preface: 1815', in *Wordsworth's Literary Criticism*, p. 81, p. 211.

47. John Keats, Letter to John Hamilton Reynolds, 3 February 1818, in Enright and Chickera, *English Critical Texts: 16th Century to 20th Century* (London: Oxford University Press, 1962) p. 257.

48. John Keats, Letter to Richard Woodhouse, 27 October 1818, in ibid., p. 258.

49. Percy Bysshe Shelley, 'A Defence of Poetry', in *Complete Works*, vol. VII (New York: Gordian Press, 1965) p. 135.

50. Ibid., p. 117, p. 137.

51. Ibid., p. 118.

52. Ibid.

53. Coleridge, *Biographia Literaria*, vol. II, ch. XIV, p. 12.

54. Wordsworth, 'Preface to *Lyrical Ballads*', p. 72.

55. Ibid., p. 85.

56. Wordsworth, 'Essay upon Epitaphs, II', in *Wordsworth's Literary Criticism*, p. 141.

57. Wordsworth, 'Appendix to Essays upon Epitaphs', in *Wordsworth's Literary Criticism*, p. 165.

58. Shelley, 'A Defence of Poetry', p. 135.

59. Ibid., p. 138.

60. Ibid., p. 138.

61. Charles-Augustin Sainte-Beuve, 'On Sainte-Beuve's Method', in Francis Steegmuller and Norbert Guterman, (eds), *Sainte-Beuve: Selected Essays* (London: Methuen, 1965) pp. 281–2.

62. Charles-Augustin Sainte-Beuve, *Pensées et Maximes*, in Richard M. Chadbourne, *Charles-Augustin Sainte-Beuve* (Boston: Twayne, 1977) p. 104.

63. Ibid.

64. Charles-Augustin Sainte-Beuve, *Portraits Contemporains*, in Chadbourne, *Charles-Augustin Sainte-Beuve*, pp. 97–8.

65. Ralph Waldo Emerson, *The Complete Works*, vol. III (Boston: Houghton Mifflin, 1903–4) p. 196.
66. Ibid., vol. VIII, p. 54.
67. Ralph Waldo Emerson, 'The Poet', in Eric W. Carlson (ed.), *Emerson's Literary Criticism* (Lincoln: University of Nebraska Press, 1979) p. 30.
68. Ibid., p. 33.
69. Ibid., p. 40.
70. Edgar Allan Poe, 'The Poetic Principle', in Robert L. Hough, (ed.), *Literary Criticism of Edgar Allan Poe* (Lincoln: University of Nebraska Press, 1965) p. 38.
71. Poe, 'The Philosophy of Composition' and 'Marginalia', in Hough *Literary Criticism of Edgar Allan Poe* , p. 21, p. 57.

Notes to Chapter 5: Social Theories of the 19th Century

1. Vissarion Belinsky, 'Review of Lermontov's Poetry', in Herbert E. Bowman, *Vissarion Belinski, 1811–1848* (New York: Russell & Russell, 1969) p. 129.
2. Vissarion Belinsky, 'On the Russian Story and the Stories of Gogol', trans. Linda Gordon, in George J. Becker (ed.), *Documents of Modern Literary Realism* (Princeton: Princeton University Press, 1963) p. 42.
3. Ibid., p. 74
4. Vissarion Belinsky, 'Discourse on Criticism', in Ralph E. Matlaw (ed.), *Belinsky, Chernyshevsky, and Dobrolyubov: Selected Criticism* (New York: Dutton, 1962) p. xi.
5. Vissarion Belinsky, 'Literary Reveries', in Bowman, *Vissarion Belinsky, 1811–1848*, p. 61.
6. Vissarion Belinsky, 'Review of Turgenev', in Bowman, *Vissarion Belinsky, 1811–1848*, p. 197.
7. Belinsky, cited in R. H. Stacy, *Russian Literary Criticism: A Short History* (Syracuse: Syracuse University Press, 1974) p. 52.
8. N. G. Chernyshevsky, *Selected Philosophical Essays* (Moscow: Foreign Languages Publishing House, 1953) p. 366.
9. Nikolay Dobrolyubov, *Selected Philosophical Essays*, trans. J. Fineberg (Moscow: Foreign Languages Publishing House, 1948) p. 236.
10. N. A. Dobrolyubov, 'When Will the Real Day Come', in Matlaw, *Belinsky, Chernyshevsky, and Dobrolyubov*, p. 177.
11. Dobrolyubov, *Selected Philosophical Essays*, p. 291.
12. Matthew Arnold, 'The Function of Criticism', in *Lectures and Essays in Criticism* (Ann Arbor: University of Michigan Press, 1962) p. 275. This sense of the term 'Philistine' was popularised by Arnold himself.
13. Matthew Arnold, *Culture and Anarchy* (Cambridge: Cambridge University Press, 1960) p. 49.
14. Matthew Arnold, 'Literature and Science', in *Selected Poetry and Prose* (New York: Holt, Rinehart & Winston, 1953) p. 336.
15. Ibid.
16. Ibid., p. 338.
17. Ibid., p. 343.
18. Matthew Arnold, 'Maurice de Guérin', in *Lectures and Essays in Criticism*, p. 33.
19. Arnold, *Culture and Anarchy*, p. 49.

20. Matthew Arnold, 'Preface to First Edition of *Poems*', in *On the Classical Tradition* (Ann Arbor: University of Michigan Press, 1960) p. 4. For 'provinciality', see especially 'The Literary Influence of Academies', in *Lectures and Essays in Criticism*, pp. 245–9.

21. Matthew Arnold, 'The Study of Poetry', in *Selected Poetry and Prose*, pp. 301–2.

22. Arnold, 'The Function of Criticism', p. 270.

23. Ibid.

24. Arnold, *Culture and Anarchy*, p. 73.

25. Matthew Arnold, 'Wordsworth', in *Selected Poetry and Prose*, p. 289.

26. Arnold, 'The Study of Poetry', p. 308.

27. Ibid.

28. Hippolyte Taine, *History of English Literature*, vol. I, trans. H. Van Laun (London: Chatto & Windus, 1899) p. 13.

29. Ibid., p. 9.

30. Ibid., p. 24.

31. Hippolyte Taine, *The Philosophy of Art* (London: H. Baillière, 1865) p. 98.

32. Hippolyte Taine, *La Fontaine et ses Fables*, cited in Sholom J. Kahn, *Science and Aesthetic Judgement* (Westport: Greenwood Press, 1970) p. 75.

33. Karl Marx and Friedrich Engels, *On Literature and Art* (Moscow: Progress Publishers, 1976) p. 41.

34. Ibid., p. 43.

35. Ibid., p. 127.

36. Ibid., pp. 177–8.

37. Ibid., p. 84.

38. Ibid., p. 83.

39. Ibid., p. 70.

40. Ibid., p. 72.

41. Ibid., p. 365.

42. Ibid.

43. Engels, in ibid., p. 65.

Notes to Chapter 6: Naturalism, Symbolism and Modernism

1. Stendhal, *Scarlet and Black*, trans. M. R. B. Shaw (Harmondsworth: Penguin, 1953) p. 93. Stendhal uses the phrase as an epigraph to the novel's thirteenth chapter, attributing it to the fictitious 'Saint-Réal'.

2. Émile Zola, *The Experimental Novel and Other Essays*, trans. Belle M. Sherman (New York: Haskell House, 1964) p. 94.

3. Émile Zola, 'Naturalism in the Theatre', in Becker, *Documents of Modern Literary Realism*, p. 203.

4. Ibid., p. 207.

5. Gustave Flaubert, Letter to Laurent-Pichat, 2 October 1856, in Becker, *Documents of Modern Literary Realism*, p. 94.

6. Gustave Flaubert, Letter to Louise Colet, 1 February 1852, in Becker, *Documents of Modern Literary Realism*, p. 91.

7. Edmond and Jules de Goncourt, Preface to *Germinie Lacerteux*, in Becker, *Documents of Modern Literary Realism*, p. 118.

8. Émile Zola, Preface to the Second Edition of *Thérèse Raquin*, trans. L. W. Tancock (Harmondsworth: Penguin, 1962) p. 19.

9. Zola, *The Experimental Novel and Other Essays*, p. 212.

10. Goncourt brothers, Preface to *Germinie Lacerteux*, p. 119.

11. Zola, *The Experimental Novel and Other Essays*, p. 168.

12. Émile Zola, 'The Experimental Novel', in Becker, *Documents of Modern Literary Realism*, p. 171.

13. Ibid., p. 172.

14. Gustave Flaubert, Letter to Louise Colet, January 1854, in Becker, *Documents of Modern Literary Realism*, p. 94.

15. Gustave Flaubert, Letter to Louise Colet, 31 March 1853, in Becker, p. 93.

16. Zola, Preface to the Second Edition of *Thérèse Raquin*, p. 22.

17. Goncourt brothers, Preface to *Germinie Lacerteux*, p. 119.

18. Gustave Flaubert, Letter to George Sand, 5–6 December 1866, in Becker, *Documents of Modern Literary Realism*, p. 95.

19. Zola, 'Naturalism in the Theatre', p. 208.

20. Zola, 'The Experimental Novel', p. 180.

21. It is interesting that Robbe-Grillet's writing has gradually shifted from a *chosiste* focus upon the impenetrability of *objective* things to a focus upon the impenetrable *text* as a thing. This is essentially the same trajectory that was noted at the start of this chapter.

22. The qualification 'European' is necessary here. As has already been noted, there is a parallel in the US, and for similar reasons.

23. Théophile Gautier, *Salon of 1837* (my trans. from the French), cited in P. E. Tennant, *Théophile Gautier* (London: Athlone Press, 1975) p. 21.

24. See Roland Barthes, 'The World of Wrestling', in *Mythologies*, trans. Annette Lavers (St Albans: Paladin, 1973).

25. Théophile Gautier (my trans.), cited in Tennant, *Théophile Gautier*, p. 24.

26. Charles Baudelaire, *Baudelaire as a Literary Critic*, trans. Lois Boe Hyslop and Francis E. Hyslop, Jr (University Park, PA: Pennsylvania State University Press, 1964) p. 166.

27. Théophile Gautier, 'Preface' to *Mademoiselle de Maupin*, trans. F. C. de Sumichrast (Boston: Brainard, 1900) p. 73.

28. Baudelaire, *Baudelaire as a Literary Critic*, p. 131.

29. Gautier, 'Preface' to *Mademoiselle de Maupin*, p. 82.

30. Baudelaire, *Baudelaire as a Literary Critic*, p. 122.

31. Ibid., p. 88, p. 167.

32. Stéphane Mallarmé, *Mallarmé: Selected Prose Poems, Essays and Letters*, trans. Bradford Cook (Baltimore: Johns Hopkins Press, 1956) p. 33.

33. Ibid., p. 42.

34. Ibid., p. 43.

35. Ibid., p. 40.

36. Paul Valéry, *The Art of Poetry*, trans. Denise Folliot (London: Routledge & Kegan Paul, 1958) p. 59. Valéry developed most of his ideas in essays written in the 1920s, but much of the material is recycled almost verbatim in his 1939 essay 'Poetry and Abstract Thought'. Since this later essay is the most widely available of his writings in English, I have generally preferred it as a source of quotation.

37. Stéphane Mallarmé, 'Preface to "Un Coup de Dés"', in *Mallarmé*, trans. Anthony Hartley (Harmondsworth: Penguin, 1965) p. 210, p. 209.

38. Mallarmé, *Mallarmé: Selected Prose Poems, Essays and Letters*, p. 21.
39. Ibid., pp. 21–2.
40. Valéry, *The Art of Poetry*, p. 323.
41. Mallarmé, *Mallarmé: Selected Prose Poems, Essays and Letters*, p. 93
42. Ibid., p. 22.
43. Ibid., pp. 42–3.
44. Valéry, *The Art of Poetry*, p. 56
45. Ibid., p. 81.
46. Ibid., p. 208.
47. Ibid., p. 63.
48. Ibid., p. 64.
49. Ibid., p. 65.
50. Ibid., p. 72.
51. Ibid., p. 98.
52. Mallarmé, *Mallarmé: Selected Prose Poems, Essays and Letters*, p. 101.
53. Ibid., p. 40.
54. Ibid., p. 21.
55. Valéry, *The Art of Poetry*, p. 158.
56. Ibid., p. 152.
57. Oscar Wilde, 'The Critic as Artist', in *The Works of Oscar Wilde* (London: Collins, 1948) p. 987. In this and other quotes from the same critical dialogue, the assertion is actually made by Gilbert, who represents Wilde's views.
58. 'The Decay of Lying', in *The Works of Oscar Wilde*, p. 909. Again, in this and other quotes from the same dialogue, the assertion is actually made by Wilde's spokesperson, Vivian.
59. Ibid., p. 925.
60. Wilde, 'The Critic as Artist', p. 962.
61. Walter Pater, *The Renaissance: Studies in Art and Poetry* (London: Collins/Fontana) pp. 27–8.
62. Ibid., p. 27.
63. Wilde, 'The Critic as Artist', p. 968.
64. Ibid., p. 994.
65. Ibid., p. 973.
66. Ibid., p. 968.
67. Ibid., p. 970.
68. Henry James, *Henry James: Literary Criticism*, ed. Leon Edel, vol.: *French Writers, Other European Writers, Prefaces to the New York Edition* (New York: Library of America, 1984) p. 242.
69. Ibid., p. 157.
70. Ibid., vol.: *Literary Criticism: Essays on Literature, American Writers, English Writers*, p. 58.
71. Ibid., vol.: *French Writers . . ,* p. 983.
72. Ibid., vol.: *Essays on Literature . . ,* p. 1343.
73. Ibid., vol.: *French Writers . . ,* p. 918.
74. Henry James, Letter to H. G. Wells, 10 July 1915, in Percy Lubbock (ed.), *The Letters of Henry James*, vol. II (London: Macmillan, 1920) p. 508.
75. James, *Henry James: Literary Criticism*, vol.: *French Writers . . ,* p. 1107.
76. José Ortega y Gasset, *The Dehumanization of Art and Other Essays on Art, Culture, and Literature* (Princeton: Princeton University Press, 1968) p. 6.
77. T. E. Hulme, *Speculations* (London: Routledge & Kegan Paul, 1936) p. 131.

78. Ibid., p. 132.
79. Ibid., p. 137, p. 136.
80. Ibid., p. 132.
81. Ibid., pp. 134–5.
82. Ibid., pp. 158–9.
83. Ibid., p. 132.
84. Ibid., p. 137.
85. Ibid., p. 134. See also p. 166. As with many of the statements in the essay 'Romanticism and Classicism', this statement re-occurs with almost identical phrasing in the essay 'Bergson's Theory of Art'.
86. Ibid., p. 135.
87. Ibid., p. 151.
88. Ibid., p. 152.
89. Ezra Pound, *Literary Essays of Ezra Pound* (London: Faber & Faber, 1954) p. 58.
90. Ibid., p. 48.
91. Ibid., p. 10.
92. Ibid., p. 225.
93. Ibid., p. 12, p. 5, p. 43
94. Ibid., p. 21.
95. Ibid., p. 21, p. 56.
96. Ibid., p. 4, p. 23.
97. Ibid., p. 4.
98. I have here adapted Eliot's assertion that 'only those who have personality and emotions know what it means to want to escape from these things'. This gambit conveniently enables one to both have one's cake and eat it, as several critics have pointed out. See T.S. Eliot, 'Tradition and the Individual Talent', in *Selected Essays* (London: Faber & Faber, 1951) p. 21.
99. T.S. Eliot, *The Use of Poetry and the Use of Criticism* (London: Faber & Faber, 1964) p. 30.
100. Ibid., p. 138.
101. Eliot, 'Tradition and the Individual Talent', p. 21.
102. Ibid., p. 22.
103. T. S. Eliot, 'Hamlet', in *Selected Essays*, p. 145.
104. T. S. Eliot, 'The Metaphysical Poets', in *Selected Essays*, p. 288.
105. T. S. Eliot, 'Dante', in *Selected Essays*, p. 257.
106. Eliot, 'Tradition and the Individual Talent', p. 19.
107. Eliot, 'The Metaphysical Poets', p. 287.
108. Eliot, 'Tradition and the Individual Talent', p. 20.
109. Ibid., p. 21; Eliot, 'The Metaphysical Poets', p. 289.
110. Eliot, 'Tradition and the Individual Talent', p. 19.
111. Ibid., p. 14.
112. T. S. Eliot, *To Criticize the Critic* (London: Faber & Faber, 1965) p. 133.
113. T. S. Eliot, 'The Music of Poetry', in *On Poetry and Poets* (London: Faber & Faber, 1957) pp. 30–1.
114. Eliot, *The Use of Poetry and the Use of Criticism*, p. 109.
115. Eliot, 'Tradition and the Individual Talent', p. 15.
116. T. S. Eliot, 'Andrew Marvell', in *Selected Essays*, p. 293.
117. Ibid., p. 301.
118. Ibid., p. 303.

119. T. S. Eliot, 'What Is a Classic?', in Frank Kermode (ed.), *Selected Prose of T. S. Eliot* (London: Faber & Faber, 1975), p. 127, p. 116.

Notes to Chapter 7: New Developments in Theory

1. Friedrich Nietzsche, *The Will to Power*, in *The Complete Works of Friedrich Nietzsche*, ed. Oscar Levy, vol. XV (New York: Gordon Press, 1974) p. 432.
2. Friedrich Nietzsche, *The Twilight of the Idols*, in *The Complete Works*, vol. XVI, p. 66.
3. Friedrich Nietzsche, *The Birth of Tragedy*, in *The Birth of Tragedy and the Genealogy of Morals*, trans. Francis Golffing (New York: Doubleday Anchor, 1956) p. 54.
4. Ibid., p. 97.
5. Ibid., p. 132.
6. Nietzsche, *The Genealogy of Morals*, in *The Birth of Tragedy and the Genealogy of Morals*, pp. 238–9.
7. Nietzsche, *The Will to Power*, p. 150.
8. Friedrich Nietzsche, *Beyond Good and Evil*, in *The Complete Works*, vol. XII, pp. 9–10.
9. Nietzsche, *The Will to Power*, pp. 60–1.
10. Ibid., p. 50.
11. Nietzsche, *The Genealogy of Morals*, p. 179.
12. Nietzsche, *Beyond Good and Evil*, p. 29.
13. Friedrich Nietzsche, 'Truth and Falsity in an Ultramoral Sense', in *The Complete Works*, vol. II, p. 180.
14. Ibid., p. 180.
15. Ibid., p. 182.
16. Nietzsche, *The Genealogy of Morals*, p. 290.
17. Nietzsche, *The Birth of Tragedy*, p. 42. See also p. 143.
18. Nietzsche, *The Will to Power*, p. 289.
19. Friedrich Nietzsche, *Human, All Too Human*, trans. Marion Faber with Stephen Lehmann (Lincoln: University of Nebraska Press, 1984) p. 11.
20. Nietzsche, *The Birth of Tragedy*, p. 142.
21. Nietzsche, *The Joyful Wisdom* ('*La Gaya Scienza*'), in *The Complete Works*, vol. X, pp. 332–3. It should be remembered that the scope of the term 'Romantic' tends to be narrower in German than in English.
22. See Sigmund Freud, *Introductory Lectures on Psychoanalysis*, Lecture XVIII, in *The Standard Edition of the Complete Psychological Works of Sigmund Freud*, ed. James Strachey, vol. XVI (London: Hogarth, 1958) p. 285.
23. Ibid., lecture XI, in vol. XV, p. 173.
24. Ibid., p. 174.
25. Ibid., p. 171.
26. Sigmund Freud, *The Interpretation of Dreams*, in *The Standard Edition*, vol. IV, p. 283.
27. Ibid., p. 295.
28. Sigmund Freud, 'The Claims of Psycho-Analysis to Scientific Interest', in *The Standard Edition*, vol. XIII, p. 176.

29. Sigmund Freud, *Introductory Lectures on Psychoanalysis*, lecture XI, in *The Standard Edition*, vol. XV, p. 179.
30. Ibid.
31. See Sigmund Freud, 'The Uncanny', in *The Standard Edition*, vol. XVII, pp. 219–52.
32. Freud, *Introductory Lectures on Psychoanalysis*, lecture II, in *The Standard Edition*, vol. XV, p. 33.
33. See Sigmund Freud, *Delusions and Dreams in Jensen's 'Gradiva'*, in *The Standard Edition*, vol. IX; 'Psychopathic Characters on the Stage', in vol. VII; and *The Interpretation of Dreams*, in vol. IV, pp. 264–6.
34. Sigmund Freud, 'The Paths to the Formation of Symptoms', in *The Standard Edition*, vol. XI, p. 376.
35. Ibid.
36. Sigmund Freud, 'Formulations on the Two Principles of Mental Functioning', in *The Standard Edition*, vol. XII, p. 224.
37. Ferdinand de Saussure, *Course in General Linguistics*, trans. Roy Harris (London: Duckworth, 1983) p. 71.
38. Ibid., p. 118.
39. Ibid., p. 115.
40. Ibid., p. 16.
41. Friedrich Engels, Letter to Minna Kautsky, 26 November 1885, in Karl Marx and Friedrich Engels, *On Literature and Art* (Moscow: Progress Publishers, 1976) p. 88.
42. Friedrich Engels, Letter to Margaret Harkness, April 1888, in *On Literature and Art*, p. 91.
43. Georg Lukács, in Bela Kiralyfalvi, *The Aesthetics of György Lukács* (Princeton: Princeton University Press, 1975) p. 116.
44. Georg Lukács, *Writer and Critic and Other Essays*, trans. Arthur Kahn (London: Merlin, 1970) p. 40; and *The Meaning of Contemporary Realism*, trans. John and Necke Mander (London: Merlin, 1963) p. 119.
45. Lukács, *The Meaning of Contemporary Realism*, p. 33, p. 34.
46. Lukács, *Writer and Critic and Other Essays*, p. 127.
47. Ibid., p. 140.
48. Georg Lukács, *Studies in European Realism* (London: Merlin, 1972) p. 8.
49. Lukács, *The Meaning of Contemporary Realism*, p. 24.
50. Ibid., p. 31.
51. Ibid., p. 43.
52. Ibid., p. 19.
53. Walter Benjamin, *Reflections*, trans. Edmund Jephcott (New York: Schocken, 1986) p. 316.
54. Ibid.
55. Walter Benjamin, *Illuminations*, trans. Harry Zohn (London: Collins/Fontana, 1973) p. 87.
56. Ibid., p. 223.
57. Ibid., p. 226.
58. Ibid., p. 233.
59. Ibid., p. 220.
60. Benjamin, *Reflections*, p. 236.
61. Ibid., p. 233.
62. Berthold Brecht, *Brecht on Theatre*, trans. John Willett (London: Methuen, 1978) p. 71.

63. Ibid., p. 143.
64. Max Horkheimer and Theodor Adorno, *Dialectic of Enlightenment*, trans. John Cumming (London: Allen Lane, 1973) p. 126.
65. Ibid., p. 137.
66. Ibid., p. 154.
67. Ibid., p. 134.
68. Theodor Adorno, 'Culture and Administration', in *Telos*, XXXVII (Fall 1978) p. 97.
69. Theodor Adorno, 'Commitment', in Andrew Arato and Eike Gebhardt (eds), *The Essential Frankfurt School Reader* (Oxford: Blackwell, 1978) p. 314.
70. Ibid., p. 318.
71. Theodor Adorno, *Aesthetic Theory*, in Hazard Adams and Leroy Searle (eds), *Critical Theory Since 1965* (Tallahassee: Florida State University Press, 1986) p. 232.
72. Theodor Adorno, *Prisms*, trans. Samuel and Sherry Weber (London: Neville Spearman, 1967) p. 31.

Notes to Chapter 8: 20th-Century Russian Theory

1. Boris Eikhenbaum, 'Concerning the Question of the "Formalists"', in Christopher Pike (ed.), *The Futurists, the Formalists and the Marxist Critique* (London: Ink Links, 1979) pp. 50–1.
2. Boris Tomashevsky, 'Literature and Biography', in Ladislav Matejka and Krystyna Pomorska (eds), *Readings in Russian Poetics: Formalist and Structuralist Views* (Ann Arbor: Michigan Slavic Publications, 1978) p. 52.
3. Roman Jakobson, *Language in Literature* (Cambridge, MA: Belknap Press, 1987) p. 369.
4. Ibid., p. 378.
5. Cited in Victor Erlich, *Russian Formalism: History–Doctrine* (The Hague: Mouton, 1969) p. 213.
6. See Yuri Tynyanov, 'The Meaning of the Word in Verse', in Matejka and Pomorska, *Readings in Russian Poetics*.
7. Boris Tomashevsky, 'Thematics', in Lee T. Lemon and Marion J. Reis (eds) *Russian Formalist Criticism: Four Essays* (Lincoln: University of Nebraska Press, 1965) footnote on p. 67.
8. See Tomashevsky, 'Thematics'.
9. Viktor Shklovsky, *Theory of Prose*, trans. Benjamin Sher (Elmwood Park: Dalkey Archive Press, 1990) p. 170.
10. Yuri Tynyanov, 'Rhythm as the Constructive Factor in Verse', in Matejka and Pomorska, *Readings in Russian Poetics*, p. 126.
11. Shklovsky, *Theory of Prose*, p. 80.
12. Ibid., p. 179.
13. Boris Eikhenbaum, 'The Theory of the Formal Method', in Matejka and Pomorska, *Readings in Russian Poetics*, p. 12.
14. Ibid., p. 13.
15. Shklovsky, *Theory of Prose*, p. 5.
16. Ibid., p. 61.
17. Ibid., p. 13.
18. Boris Eikhenbaum, 'O. Henry and the Theory of the Short Story', in Matejka and Pomorska, *Readings in Russian Poetics*, p. 255.

19. Shklovsky, *Theory of Prose*, p. 153.
20. Tomashevsky, 'Thematics', p. 95.
21. Tynyavov, 'The Meaning of the Word in Verse', p. 144.
22. Shklovsky, *Theory of Prose*, p. 20.
23. Ibid., p. 191.
24. Ekhenbaum, 'The Theory of the Formal Method', p. 33.
25. Shklovsky, *Theory of Prose*, p. 171.
26. Yuri Tynyanov and Roman Jakobson, 'Problems in the Study of Literature and Language', in Matejka and Pomorska, *Readings in Russian Poetics*, p. 79.
27. Vladimir Propp, *Morphology of the Folktale*, trans. Laurence Scott, rev. Louis A. Wagner (Austin: University of Texas Press, 1968) p. 21.
28. Vladimir Propp, 'Fairy Tale Transformations', in Matejka and Pomorska, *Readings in Russian Poetics*, p. 94.
29. Propp, *Morphology of the Folktale*, p. 15.
30. Ibid., p. 92.
31. Propp, 'Fairy Tale Transformations', p. 96.
32. Jan Mukarovsky, *Aesthetic Function, Norm and Value as Social Facts*, trans. Mark E. Suino (University of Michigan Press: Ann Arbor, 1979) p. 83, p. 75.
33. Jan Mukarovsky, 'Standard Language and Poetic Language', in Paul L. Garvin (ed.), *A Prague School Reader on Esthetics, Literary Structure, and Style* (Washington: Georgetown University Press, 1964) p. 18.
34. Mukarovsky, *Aesthetic Function, Norm and Value as Social Facts*, p. 35.
35. Jan Mukarovsky, 'The Esthetics of Language', in Garvin, *A Prague School Reader*, p. 69.
36. Jan Mukarovsky, 'Art as a Semiotic Fact', in Ladislav Matejka and Irwin R. Titunik (eds), *Semiotics of Art* (Cambridge, MA: MIT Press, 1976) p. 8.
37. Mukarovsky, *Aesthetic Function, Norm and Value as Social Facts*, p. 61.
38. Ibid., p. 18.
39. V. N. Voloshinov, *Freudianism: A Marxist Critique*, trans. I. R. Titunik (New York: Academic Press, 1976) p. 99.
40. Ibid., p. 100.
41. V. N. Voloshinov, *Marxism and the Philosophy of Language*, trans. Ladislav Matejka and I. R. Titunik (New York: Seminar Press, 1973) p. 85.
42. Mikhail Bakhtin, *Problems of Dostoevsky's Poetics*, trans. Caryl Emerson (Minneapolis: University of Minnesota Press, 1984) p. 197.
43. Ibid., p. 32.
44. Ibid., p. 229.
45. Ibid., p. 5.
46. Ibid., p. 71.
47. Ibid., p. 59.
48. Mikhail Bakhtin, *The Dialogic Imagination: Four Essays*, trans. Caryl Emerson and Michael Holquist (Austin: University of Texas Press, 1981) p. 286.
49. Ibid., p. 218.
50. Ibid., p. 5.
51. Mikhail Bakhtin, *Speech Genres and Other Late Essays*, trans. Vern W. McGee (Austin: University of Texas Press, 1986) p. 132.
52. Bakhtin, *The Dialogic Imagination*, p. 7.
53. Voloshinov, *Marxism and the Philosophy of Language*, p. 41.
54. Ibid., p. 97.
55. Bakhtin, *The Dialogic Imagination*, p. 336.

56. Shklovsky, *Theory of Prose*, p. 180.
57. Mikhail Bakhtin, *Rabelais and His World*, trans. Helene Iswolsky (Bloomington: Indiana University Press, 1984) p. 10.
58. Bakhtin, *Problems of Dostoevsky's Poetics*, p. 123. Bakhtin incorporated many of his later ideas on carnival into the much-expanded 1963 version of this book – which is the version available in English translation.
59. Bakhtin, *Rabelais and His World*, p. 339.

Notes to Chapter 9: Anglo-American Criticism, 1900–60

1. Anatole France, 'The Adventures of the Soul', trans. Ludwig Lewisohn, in Adams, *Critical Theory since Plato*, p. 656.
2. I. A. Richards, *Principles of Literary Criticism* (London: Routledge & Kegan Paul, 1960) p. 203.
3. I. A. Richards, *Practical Criticism* (London: Routledge & Kegan Paul, 1929) p. 254.
4. C. K. Ogden and I. A. Richards, *The Meaning of Meaning* (London: Routledge & Kegan Paul, 1949) p. 149.
5. Richards, *Principles of Literary Criticism*, p. 268.
6. Ibid., p. 282.
7. I. A. Richards, *Coleridge on Imagination* (London: Routledge & Kegan Paul, 1962) p. 208.
8. Richards, *Principles of Literary Criticism*, p. 78.
9. Ibid., p. 17.
10. Ibid., p. 59.
11. Ibid., p. 248.
12. Ibid., p. 250.
13. Richards, *Coleridge on Imagination*, pp. 84–5.
14. Richards, *Principles of Lterary Criticism*, p. 290.
15. Richards, *Practical Criticism*, p. 191; Ogden and Richards, *The Meaning of Meaning*, p. 158.
16. I. A. Richards, *Poetries and Sciences* [a re-issue of *Science and Poetry*] (London: Routledge & Kegan Paul, 1970) p. 60.
17. Ibid.
18. Richards, *Principles of Literary Criticism*, p. 280.
19. Richards, *Coleridge on Imagination*, p. 229.
20. Richards, *Principles of Literary Criticism*, p. 246.
21. William Empson, *Seven Types of Ambiguity* (Harmondsworth: Penguin, 1961) p. 1.
22. Ibid., pp. 19–20.
23. See especially William Empson, *The Structure of Complex Words* (London: Chatto & Windus, 1964) pp. 1–15.
24. Empson, *Seven Types of Ambiguity*, p. 176. It must be admitted that Empson does not hold very tightly to his definition when he goes on to actual discussion of this or any other type.
25. Ibid., p. 192.
26. See the chapter 'Alice in Wonderland: The Child as Swain', in William Empson, *Some Versions of Pastoral* (London: Chatto & Windus, 1968).

27. Empson marshals his counter-arguments especially in his introduction to an edition of Coleridge. See William Empson and David Pirie (eds), *Coleridge's Verse: A Selection* (London: Faber, 1972).
28. Empson, *Seven Types of Ambiguity*, p. 4; *The Structure of Complex Words*, p. 39.
29. William Empson, 'Verbal Analysis', *Kenyon Review*, XII, (1950), p. 597.
30. Empson, *Seven Types of Ambiguity*, p. 7.
31. F. R. Leavis, *Anna Karenina and Other Essays* (London: Chatto & Windus, 1967) p. 228.
32. Reprinted in L. C. Knights, *Explorations* (London: Chatto & Windus, 1963).
33. F. R. Leavis, *The Common Pursuit* (Harmondsworth: Penguin, 1962) p. 130.
34. F. R. Leavis, *D. H. Lawrence: Novelist* (Harmondsworth: Penguin, 1968) p. 187.
35. F. R. Leavis, *Revaluation* (London: Chatto & Windus, 1969) p. 174; F. R. Leavis, *For Continuity* (Cambridge: Minority Press, 1933) p. 152.
36. Leavis, *The Common Pursuit*, p. 200.
37. F. R. Leavis, *New Bearings* (London: Chatto & Windus, 1961) p. 13.
38. F. R. Leavis, *The Critic as Anti-Philosopher*, ed. G. Singh (London: Chatto & Windus, 1982) p. 123. *Work in Progress* was Joyce's working title for the book which eventually became *Finnegans Wake*.
39. F. R. Leavis, *English Literature in our Time and the University* (London: Chatto & Windus, 1969) p. 24.
40. Leavis, *New Bearings*, p. 214.
41. F. R. Leavis and Denys Thompson, *Culture and Environment* (London: Chatto & Windus, 1964) p. 100.
42. Leavis, *New Bearings*, p. 15.
43. Leavis, *English Literature in our Time and the University*, pp. 29–30.
44. F. R. Leavis, *The Living Principle: 'English' as a Discipline of Thought* (London: Chatto & Windus, 1977) p. 75.
45. F. R. Leavis, *Nor Shall My Sword* (London: Chatto & Windus, 1972) p. 98.
46. F. R. Leavis, 'Catholicity or Narrowness', *Scrutiny*, XII, (1944–5), p. 292.
47. Leavis, *The Common Pursuit*, p. 226.
48. F. R. Leavis, *The Great Tradition* (London: Chatto & Windus, 1962) p. 15.
49. Leavis, *New Bearings*, p. 91.
50. Leavis, *For Continuity*, p. 31.
51. Leavis, *New Bearings*, p. 213.
52. Leavis, *The Living Principle*, p. 35. Much the same formula appears in several places in Leavis's writings.
53. Leavis, *English Literature in our Time and the University*, p. 50.
54. Leavis, *The Living Principle*, p. 35.
55. Leavis, *The Critic as Anti-Philosopher*, p. 115.
56. F. R. Leavis and Q. D. Leavis, *Dickens the Novelist* (Harmondsworth: Penguin, 1972) p. 287. Dickens was a late entry to the Leavis pantheon of English novelists, having been largely excluded in *The Great Tradition*.
57. Leavis, *The Great Tradition*, p. 7.
58. Ibid., p. 18.
59. John Crowe Ransom, *The World's Body* (Port Washington: Kennikat, 1964) p. x.
60. Ibid., p. ix.
61. Allen Tate, *On the Limits of Poetry: Selected Essays: 1928–1948* (New York: Swallow Press, 1948) p. 113.
62. See ibid., p. 11, p. 77, p. 113.

63. Allen Tate, *The Man of Letters in the Modern World: Selected Essays: 1928–1955* (New York: Meridian, 1955) p. 18.
64. Ransom, *The World's Body*, p. 115.
65. John Crowe Ransom, *The New Criticism* (Norfolk, CT: New Directions, 1941) p. 220.
66. Ransom, *The World's Body*, p. 343.
67. John Crowe Ransom, 'Criticism as Pure Speculation', in Morton D. Zabel (ed.), *Literary Opinion in America* (New York: Harper & Bros, 1951) p. 641.
68. Ransom, *The World's Body*, p. 342.
69. Ibid., p. 329.
70. Kenneth Burke, *The Philosophy of Literary Form* (Berkeley: University of California Press, 1973) p. 89.
71. The phrase 'verbal icon' is another coinage from William K. Wimsatt.
72. Kenneth Burke, *Permanence and Change* (Berkeley: University of California Press, 1984) p. 74.
73. Kenneth Burke, *Language as Symbolic Action* (Berkeley: University of California Press, 1968) p. 45.
74. Kenneth Burke, *A Rhetoric of Motives* (Berkeley: University of California Press, 1969) p. xiv.
75. Kenneth Burke, 'Dramatism' in Lee Thayer, (ed.) *Communication: Concepts and Perspectives* (Washington: Spartan Books, 1967) p. 341.
76. Kenneth Burke, *The Rhetoric of Religion* (Berkeley: University of California Press, 1961) p. 40.
77. Burke, *Language as Symbolic Action*, p. 48.
78. Burke, *Permanence and Change*, p. 182.
79. Cleanth Brooks, *The Well-Wrought Urn* (London: Dennis Dobson, 1949) p. 192.
80. The implicit allusion here is to Brooks's analysis of clothing imagery in *Macbeth*, presented in the second chapter of *The Well-Wrought Urn*.
81. Cleanth Brooks, 'The Formalist Critic', in K. M. Newton (ed.), *Twentieth-Century Literary Theory* (Basingstoke: Macmillan Education, 1988) p. 45.
82. Brooks, *The Well-Wrought Urn*, p. 191.
83. Cleanth Brooks, *A Shaping Joy* (London: Methuen, 1971) p. 96.
84. Robert Penn Warren, 'Pure and Impure Poetry', in *Selected Essays* (London: Eyre & Spottiswoode, 1964) p. 29.
85. Ransom, 'Criticism as Pure Speculation', p. 646.
86. W. K. Wimsatt, Jr, *The Verbal Icon* (Lexington: University of Kentucky Press, 1967) p. 127. I. A. Richards makes essentially the same point in his *The Philosophy of Rhetoric* (New York: Oxford University Press, 1965) p. 100.
87. Brooks, *The Well-Wrought Urn*, pp. 178–9.
88. Ibid., p. 186.
89. Cleanth Brooks, *Modern Poetry and the Tradition* (Chapel Hill: University of North Carolina Press, 1965) p. xxvi.
90. Brooks, *The Well-Wrought Urn*, p. 178.
91. Wimsatt, *The Verbal Icon*, p. 4.
92. Ibid., p. 3.
93. Ibid., p. 5.
94. Brooks, *The Well-Wrought Urn*, p. 200.
95. Olsen's essay is reprinted in R. S. Crane (ed.), *Critics and Criticism* (Chicago: University of Chicago Press, 1952).

96. Carl Gustav Jung, 'Psychology and Literature', in *Modern Man in Search of a Soul*, trans. W. S. Dell and Cary F. Baynes (London: Routledge & Kegan Paul, 1933) p. 197.
97. Carl Gustav Jung, 'On the Relation of Analytical Psychology to Poetry', trans. R. F. C. Hull, in David H. Richter (ed.), *The Critical Tradition: Classic Texts and Contemporary Trends* (New York: St Martin's Press, 1989) p. 665.
98. Leslie Fiedler, *No! in Thunder* (New York: Stein & Day, 1960) p. 299.
99. Northrop Frye, *Anatomy of Criticism* (Princeton: Princeton University Press, 1957) p. 342.
100. Ibid., p. 351.
101. Ibid., p. 140.
102. Northrop Frye, *The Secular Scripture* (Cambridge, MA: Harvard University Press, 1976) p. 36. p. 38.
103. Northrop Frye, *Fearful Symmetry* (Princeton: Princeton University Press, 1969) p. 326.
104. Frye, *Anatomy of Criticism*, p. 98.
105. Ibid., p. 97.
106. Northrop Frye, *Fables of Identity* (New York: Harcourt, Brace & World, 1963) p. 38
107. Northrop Frye, *The Educated Imagination* (Montreal: CBC Enterprises, 1963) p. 17.
108. Northrop Frye, *The Stubborn Structure* (London: Methuen, 1970) p. 53.
109. Frye, *The Secular Scripture*, p. 97.
110. Frye, *Anatomy of Criticism*, p. 17.
111. Ibid., pp. 10–11.
112. Ibid., p. 28.

Notes to Chapter 10: Phenomenological Criticism in France and Germany

1. Georges Poulet, *Studies in Human Time*, trans. Elliott Coleman (Baltimore: Johns Hopkins Press, 1956) p. 323.
2. Ibid., p. 326.
3. Ibid., p. 342.
4. Georges Poulet, 'The Self and Other in Critical Consciousness', *Diacritics*, vol. II (1972) p. 47.
5. J. Hillis Miller, *Charles Dickens: The World of his Novels* (Cambridge, MA: Harvard University Press, 1958) p. ix.
6. Georges Poulet, 'Criticism and the Experience of Interiority', in Richard Macksey and Eugenio Donato (eds), *The Structuralist Controversy: The Languages of Criticism and the Sciences of Man* (Baltimore: Johns Hopkins University Press, 1972) p. 61.
7. Ibid., p. 60.
8. Roman Ingarden, *Selected Papers in Aesthetics* (Washington: Catholic University of America Press, 1985) p. 178.
9. Roman Ingarden, *The Literary Work of Art*, trans. George G. Grabowicz (Evanston: Northwestern University Press, 1973) p. 249.
10. Roman Ingarden, *The Cognition of the Literary Work of Art*, trans. Ruth Ann Crowley and Kenneth R. Olson (Evanston: Northwestern University Press, 1973) p. 53.

11. The classic statement of the Modernist-oriented view is Joseph Frank's widely reprinted essay 'Spatial Form in Modern Literature' (first published in *Sewanee Review*, LIII, 1945).

12. Ingarden, *The Cognition of the Literary Work of Art*, p. 103.

13. Ibid., p. 104.

14. Wolfgang Iser, *The Act of Reading* (London: Routledge & Kegan Paul, 1978) p. 109.

15. Wolfgang Iser, *The Implied Reader* (Baltimore: Johns Hopkins University Press, 1974) p. 288.

16. Iser, *The Act of Reading*, pp. 182–3. See also Wolfgang Iser, *Prospecting* (Baltimore: Johns Hopkins University Press, 1989) p. 34.

17. Iser, *The Implied Reader*, p. 44

18. Ibid., p. 278.

19. Ibid., p. 290.

20. Iser, *The Act of Reading*, p. 157.

21. Iser, *The Implied Reader*, p. 280.

22. Hans-Georg Gadamer, *Truth and Method*, trans. William Glen-Doepel (London: Sheed & Ward, 1979) p. 359.

23. Ibid., p. 324.

24. Ibid., p. 238.

25. Ibid., p. 269.

26. Hans-Robert Jauss, *Towards an Aesthetic of Reception*, trans. Timothy Bahti (Brighton: Harvester, 1982) p. 19.

27. Ibid., p. 25.

28. Ibid., p. 21.

29. Ibid., p. 12.

30. Ibid., p. 41.

31. Ibid., p. 40.

32. Ibid., p. 29.

33. Hans-Robert Jauss, *Question and Answer: Forms of Dialogic Understanding*, trans. Michael Hays (Minneapolis: University of Minnesota Press, 1989) p. 198.

34. Ibid., p. 208.

35. Jauss, *Towards an Aesthetic of Reception*, p. 25.

36. Jauss, *Question and Answer*, p. 224, p. 226.

37. Germaine de Staël, *An Extraordinary Woman: Selected Writings of Germaine de Staël*, trans. Vivian Folkenflik (New York: Columbia University Press, 1987), p. 189.

38. Ibid., p. 201.

39. Ibid., p. 173.

40. Germaine de Staël, 'Literature Considered in its Relation to Social Institutions', in Adams, *Critical Theory since Plato*, p. 453.

41. Virginia Woolf, 'A Room of One's Own', in *A Room of One's Own and Three Guineas* (Harmondsworth: Penguin, 1993), p. 97, p. 47.

42. Ibid., p. 48.

43. Ibid., p. 67.

44. Ibid., p. 66.

45. Ibid., p. 67.

46. Ibid., p. 94.

47. Ibid., p. 68.

48. Ibid., p. 70.

49. Ibid.
50. Simone de Beauvoir, *The Second Sex*, trans. H. M. Parshley (Harmondsworth: Penguin, 1974) p. 599.
51. Ibid.
52. Ibid., pp. 15–16.
53. Ibid., pp. 148–9.
54. Ibid., pp. 97–8.
55. Ibid., p. 150.
56. Ibid., pp. 139–40.
57. Ibid., pp. 182–3.
58. Ibid., p. 186.
59. Ibid., pp. 151–2.
60. Ibid., p. 625.

Notes to Chapter 11: French Structuralism

1. Gérard Genette, 'Structuralism and Literary Criticism', trans. Alan Sheridan, in David Lodge (ed.), *Modern Criticism and Theory: A Reader* (London: Longman, 1988) p. 70.
2. Roland Barthes, *The Rustle of Language*, trans. Richard Howard (Oxford: Blackwell, 1986) p. 6.
3. Roman Jakobson, *Language in Literature*, p. 127.
4. Ibid., p. 109.
5. Ibid., p. 111.
6. Roland Barthes, *Image–Music–Text*, trans. Stephen Heath (New York: Hill & Wang, 1988) p. 84.
7. Tzvetan Todorov, *The Poetics of Prose*, trans. Richard Howard (Oxford: Blackwell, 1977) p. 119.
8. A.-J. Greimas, *Structural Semantics*, trans. Daniele McDowell, Ronal Schleifer and Alan Velie (Lincoln: University of Nebraska Press) p. 202.
9. Ibid., p. 226.
10. See Claude Lévi-Strauss, *Structural Anthropology 2*, trans. Monique Layton (Harmondsworth: Penguin, 1978) p. 163.
11. A.-J. Greimas and J. Courtés, *Semiotics and Language: An Analytical Dictionary*, trans. Larry Crist et al. (Bloomington: Indiana University Press, 1982) p. 9.
12. A.-J. Greimas, *On Meaning*, trans. Paul J. Perron and Frank H. Collins (London: Frances Pinter, 1987) p. 70.
13. Roland Barthes, *Critical Essays*, trans. Richard Howard (Evanston: Northwestern University Press, 1972) pp. 258–9.
14. Todorov, *The Poetics of Prose*, p. 33.
15. Tzvetan Todorov, *Introduction to Poetics*, trans. Richard Howard (Brighton: Harvester, 1981) p. 71.
16. Roland Barthes, *The Semiotic Challenge*, trans. Richard Howard (New York: Hill & Wang, 1988) p. 224.
17. Barthes, *Image–Music–Text*, pp. 116–17.
18. Todorov, *Introduction to Poetics*, p. 24. Todorov is here describing Parry's claim on oral poetry, but he goes on to widen the claim to literature generally.

19. Roland Barthes, *Criticism and Truth*, trans. Katrine Pilcher Keuneman (London: Athlone Press, 1987) p. 73.
20. Jonathan Culler, *Structuralist Poetics* (London: Routledge & Kegan Paul, 1975) p. 120.
21. Barthes, *Image–Music–Text*, p. 145.
22. Ibid., p. 143.
23. Roland Barthes, *S/Z*, trans. Richard Miller (New York: Hill & Wang, 1974) p. 80.
24. Roland Barthes, *The Rustle of Language*, trans. Richard Howard (Oxford: Blackwell, 1986) p. 146.
25. Ibid., p. 148.
26. Barthes, *Critical Essays*, p. 160.
27. Ibid., p. 258.
28. Barthes, *The Rustle of Language*, p. 7.
29. Roland Barthes, interviewed in 'Réponses', *Tel Quel*, 47 (Autumn 1971) p. 97.

Notes to Epilogue: Into the Postmodernist Period

1. Roland Barthes, *Image–Music–Text*, trans. Stephen Heath (New York: Hill & Wang, 1988) p. 147.

Further Reading

GENERAL SURVEYS AND HISTORIES

From the Greeks to the Present
Blamires, Harry, *A History of Literary Criticism* (London: Macmillan, 1991); covers the whole history of literary criticism, with a mainly British focus.
Groden, Michael, and Martin Kreisworth, *The Johns Hopkins Guide to Literary Theory and Criticism* (Baltimore: Johns Hopkins University Press, 1994); encyclopaedic coverage of both movements and individual figures.
Hayden, John O., *Polestar of the Ancients* (London: Associated University Presses, 1979); deals with Plato, Aristotle, Horace, Longinus, Sidney, Dryden, Johnson, Arnold.
Magill, Frank N., *Critical Survey of Literary theory*, 4 vols (Englewood Cliffs: Salem Press, 1987); a valuable first port of call for short sharp accounts of individual figures.
Wimsatt, William K., Jr, and Cleanth Brooks, *Literary Criticism: A Short History* (London: Routledge & Kegan Paul, 1970); a survey with a strong New Critical bias: use with caution!

From the 18th Century
Eagleton, Terry, *The Function of Criticism: From the Spectator to Post-Structuralism* (London: Verso, 1984); a selective but illuminating account, starting from the eighteenth century.
Parrinder, Patrick, *Authors and Authority: A Study of English Literary Criticism in its Relation to Culture, 1750–1900* (London: Routledge & Kegan Paul, 1977).
Wellek, René, *A History of Modern Criticism, 1750–1950*, 8 vols (London: Jonathan Cape, 1955–92); a work of massive scholarship, still the best guide to pre-1900 literary theory. New Critical preferences and personal debates tend to come to the fore in the post-1900 volumes.

The 20th Century
Borklund, Elmer, *Contemporary Literary Critics* (Byfleet: Macmillan, 1982); brief encapsulations of individual twentieth-century critics.
De Beaugrande, Robert, *Critical Discourse: A Survey of Literary Theorists* (Norwood, NJ: Ablex, 1988); individual figures described largely by quotation from their own texts.
Eagleton, Terry, *Literary Theory: An Introduction*, 2nd edition (Oxford: Blackwell, 1997).

Fokkema, D. W, and Etrud Kunne-Ibsch, *Theories of Literature in the 20th Century* (London: Hurst, 1977); covers Russian Formalism, Czech Structuralism, French Structuralism, Marxist theories, Reception Theory.

Jefferson, Ann, and David Robey (eds), *Modern Literary Theory: A Comparative Introduction* (London: Batsford, 1986); covers Formalism, New Criticism, Structuralism, Marxist theory, psychoanalytical theory.

Lentricchia, Frank, *After the New Criticism* (London: Athlone Press, 1980); takes in Frye, Poulet, Heidegger, the French Structuralists and others.

Makaryk, Irena R. (ed.), *Encyclopedia of Contemporary Literary Theory* (Toronto: University of Toronto Press, 1993); recommended for encyclopaedic coverage of twentieth-century movements and individual figures.

Newton, K. M., *Interpreting the Text* (London: Harvester Wheatsheaf, 1990); includes New Criticism, Reception Theory and twentieth-century hermeneutics.

Selden, Raman, and Peter Widdowson, *A Reader's Guide to Contemporary Literary Theory*, 3rd edition (Hemel Hempstead: Harvester Wheatsheaf, 1993); excellent generally, and especially good on the European schools.

Stamiris, Yiannis, *Main Currents in Twentieth-Century Literary Criticism* (Troy, NY: Whitston, 1986).

RECOMMENDED IN RELATION TO SPECIFIC CHAPTERS

Chapter 1: Literary Theory in Classical Times

Grube, G. M. A., *The Greek and Roman Critics* (London: Methuen, 1965).

Kennedy, George A. (ed.), *The Cambridge History of Literary Criticism*, vol. 1: *Classical Criticism* (Cambridge: Cambridge University Press, 1989).

Russell, D. A., *Criticism in Antiquity* (Berkeley: University of California Press, 1981).

Chapter 2: Literary Theory in the Middle Ages

Rollinson, Philip, *Classical Theories of Allegory and Christian Culture* (Brighton: Harvester, 1981).

Chapter 3: The Rise and Fall of Neoclassicism

Damrosch, Leopold, Jr, *The Uses of Johnson's Criticism* (Charlottesville: University Press of Virginia. 1976).

Engell, James, *Forming the Critical Mind: Dryden to Coleridge* (Cambridge, MA: Harvard University Press, 1989); Neoclassical and Sensibility critics, leading up to the Romantics.

Hathaway, Baxter, *Marvels and Commonplaces: Renaissance Literary Criticism* (New York: Random House, 1968); a briefer version of the material in *The Age of Criticism.*

Hathaway, Baxter, *The Age of Criticism: The Late Renaissance in Italy* (Ithaca: Cornell University Press, 1962); a large-scale scholarly work.

Hume, Robert D., *Dryden's Criticism* (Ithaca: Cornell University Press, 1970).

Miller, Cecilia, *Giambattista Vico: Imagination and Historical Knowledge* (New York: St Martin's Press, 1993).

Montgomery, Robert L., *Terms of Response: Language and Audience in 17th and 18th Century Theory* (University Park, PA: Pennsylvania State University Press, 1992).

Saisselin, Rémy G., *The Rule of Reason and the Ruses of the Heart* (Cleveland: Case Western Reserve University Press, 1970); topics and individual critics in French Neoclassicism, alphabetically arranged.

Chapter 4: Romantic Literary Theory

Abrams, M. H., *The Mirror and the Lamp* (New York: Oxford University Press, 1953).

Chadbourne, Richard M., *Charles-Augustin Sainte-Beuve* (Boston: Twayne, 1977).

Jackson, James R., *Method and Imagination in Coleridge's Criticism* (London: Routledge & Kegan Paul, 1969).

McCloskey, Mary, *Kant's Aesthetic* (Basingstoke: Macmillan, 1987).

Owen, W. J. B., *Wordsworth as Critic* (London: Oxford University Press, 1969).

Schulzel, Earl J., *Shelley's Theory of Poetry: A Reappraisal* (The Hague: Mouton, 1966).

Chapter 5: Social Theories of the 19th Century

Bowman, Herbert E., *Vissarion Belinsky, 1811–1848* (New York: Russell & Russell, 1969).

Jump, J. P., *Matthew Arnold* (London: Longmans, 1965).

Moser, Charles A., *Esthetics as Nightmare: Russian Literary Theory, 1855–70* (Princeton: Princeton University Press, 1989).

Stacy, R. H., *Russian Literary Criticism: A Short History* (Syracuse: Syracuse University Press, 1974); carries through to Russian Formalism.

Chapter 6: Naturalism, Symbolism and Modernism

Austen, Allen, *T. S. Eliot: The Literary and Social Criticism* (Bloomington: Indiana University Press, 1971).

Gilman, Margaret, *Baudelaire as Critic* (New York: Octagon, 1971).

Ince, W. N., *The Poetic Theory of Paul Valéry: Inspiration and Technique* (Leicester: Leicester University Press, 1970).

Schwartz, Sanford, *The Matrix of Modernism* (Princeton: Princeton University Press, 1985).

Chapter 7: New Developments in Theory

Bottomore, Tom, *The Frankfurt School* (London: Tavistock, 1984).

Eagleton, Terry, *Marxism and Literary Criticism* (London: Methuen, 1976).

Jay, Martin, *Adorno* (Glasgow: Fontana/Collins, 1984).

Harris, Roy, *Reading Saussure* (London: Duckworth, 1987).

Kofman, Sarah, *The Childhood of Art*, trans. Winifred Woodhull (New York: Columbia University Press, 1988); the best introduction to Freud on literature and art.

Sim, Stuart, *Georg Lukács* (New York: Harvester Wheatsheaf, 1994).

Young, Julian, *Nietzsche's Philosophy of Art* (Cambridge: Cambridge University Press, 1992).

Chapter 8: 20th-Century Russian Theory

Bennett, Tony, *Formalism and Marxism* (London: Methuen, 1979).

Danow, David K., *The Thought of Mikhall Bakhtin: From Word to Culture* (New York: St Martin's Press, 1991).

Dentith, Simon, *Bakhtinian Thought* (London: Routledge, 1995); also includes selections in translation.

Jameson, Fredric, *The Prison-House of Language* (Princeton: Princeton University Press, 1972); excellent on Russian Formalism.

Selden, Raman (ed.), *The Cambridge History of Literary Criticism*, vol. 8: *From Formalism to Poststructuralism* (Cambridge: Cambridge University Press, 1995).

Chapter 9: Anglo-American Criticism 1900–60

Baldick, Chris, *Criticism and Literary Theory, 1890 to the Present* (London: Longmans, 1996).

Baldick, Chris, *The Social Mission of English Criticism: 1848–1932* (Oxford: Clarendon, 1983); invaluable insights into the socio-political background.

Balfour, Ian, *Northrop Frye* (Boston: Twayne, 1988).

Bilan, R. P., *The Literary Criticism of F. R. Leavis* (Cambridge: Cambridge University Press, 1979).

Leitch, Vincent, *American Literary Criticism from the Thirties to the Eighties* (New York: Columbia University Press, 1988); very readable, recommended.

Norris, Christopher, *William Empson and the Philosophy of Literary Criticism* (London: Athlone Press, 1978).

Smith, Jerome P., *I. A. Richards' Theory of Literature* (New Haven: Yale University Press, 1969).

Webster, Grant, *The Republic of Letters* (Baltimore: Johns Hopkins University Press, 1979).

Chapter 10: Phenomenological Criticism in France and Germany

Holub, Robert C., *Reception Theory: A Critical Introduction* (London: Methuen, 1984).

Keefe, Terry, *Simone de Beauvoir: A Study of her Writings* (London: Harrap, 1983).

Lawall, Sarah N., *Critics of Consciousness* (Cambridge, MA: Harvard University Press, 1968); on the Geneva School.

Magliola, Robert E., *Phenomenology and Literature: An Introduction* (West Lafayette: Purdue University Press, 1977).

Palmer, Richard E., *Hermeneutics: Interpretation Theory in Schleiermacher, Dilthey, Heidegger, and Gadamer* (Evanston: Northwestern University Press, 1969).

Chapter 11: French Structuralism

Jameson, Fredric, *The Prison-House of Language* (Princeton: Princeton University Press, 1972).

Selden, Raman (ed.), *The Cambridge History of Literary Criticism*, vol. 8: *From Formalism to Poststructuralism* (Cambridge: Cambridge University Press, 1995).

Culler, Jonathan, *Structuralist Poetics* (London: Routledge & Kegan Paul, 1975).

Rylance, Rick, *Roland Barthes* (Hemel Hempstead: Harvester Wheatsheaf, 1994).

Scholes, Robert, *Structuralism in Literature: An Introduction* (Hew Haven: Yale University Press, 1974).

READERS AND ANTHOLOGIES OF PRIMARY SOURCE MATERIAL

General

Adams, Hazard (ed.), *Critical Theory since Plato*, revised edition (Fort Worth: Harcourt Brace Jovanovich, 1992); the most comprehensive collection of classic texts in a single volume.

Davis, Robert Con, and Laurie Finke (eds), *Literary Criticism and Theory: The Greeks to the Present* (New York: Longmans, 1989).

Richter, David H. (ed.), *The Critical Tradition: Classic Texts and Contemporary Trends* (New York: St Martin's Press, 1989).

Selden, Raman (ed.), *The Theory of Criticism: From Plato to the Present: A Reader* (London: Longman, 1988); a well chosen selection of short extracts.

20th Century

Lodge, David (ed.), *20th Century Literary Criticism: A Reader* (London: Longman, 1972).

Lodge, David (ed.), *Modern Criticism and Theory: A Reader* (London: Longman, 1988).

Newton, K. M. (ed.), *Twentieth-Century Literary Theory* (London: Macmillan, 1988).

Readers and Anthologies for Harder-to-Locate European Periods

Medieval

Preminger, Alex, O. B. Hardison and Kevin Kerrane, Jr. (eds), *Classical and Medieval Literary Criticism* (New York: Frederick Ungar, 1971); also recommended for its excellent introductions to individual figures.

Harold Bloom (ed.), *The Art of the Critic*, vol. I (New York: Chelsea House, 1985).

Renaissance and Neoclassical (Italian and French)

Bloom, Harold (ed.), *The Art of the Critic*, vol. II (New York: Chelsea House, 1986).

Elledge, Scott, and Donald Schier (eds), *The Continental Model* (Ithaca: Cornell University Press, 1970).

Romantic (German)

Hardison, O. B. (ed.), *Modern Continental Literary Criticism* (London: Peter Owen, 1964); selections from German Romanticism, Sainte-Beuve, Taine, Marx and Engels, Symbolism.

Nisbet, H. B. (ed.), *German Aesthetic and Literary Criticism: Winckelmann, Lessing, Hamann, Herder, Schiller, Goethe* (Cambridge: Cambridge University Press, 1984).

Simpson, David (ed.), *German Aesthetic and Literary Criticism: Kant, Fichte, Schelling, Schopenhauer, Hegel* (Cambridge: Cambridge University Press, 1984).

Wheeler, Katherine M. (ed.), *German Aesthetic and Literary Criticism: The Romantic Ironists and Goethe* (Cambridge: Cambridge University Press, 1984).

Naturalism (European)

Becker, George J. (ed.), *Documents of Modern Literary Realism* (Princeton: Princeton University Press, 1963).

Russian Formalism

Bann, Stephen, and John E. Boult (eds), *Russian Formalism: A Collection of Articles and Texts in Translation* (Edinburgh: Scottish Academic Press, 1973).

Garvin, Paul L. (ed.), *A Prague School Reader on Estheties, Literary Structure, and Style* (Washington: Georgetown University Press, 1964).

Lemon, Lee T., and Marion J. Reis (eds), *Russian Formalist Criticism: Four Essays* (Lincoln: University of Nebraska Press, 1965).

Matejka, Ladislav, and Krystyna Pomorska (eds), *Readings in Russian Poetics: Formalist and Structuralist Views* (Ann Arbor: Michigan Slavic Publications, 1978).

Pike, Christopher (ed.), *The Futurists, the Formalists and the Marxist Critique* (London: Inks Links, 1979).

[Other anthologies may be located in the notes for individual chapters]

Index

A-effect, 142, 247
Abrams, Murray H., 195
Académie française, 40, 45
accentual metre, 32
actant, 227–8, 230, 247
Addison, Joseph, 48–9
  'The Pleasures of the Imagination', 48
Adorno, Theodor, 137, 143–5
  Dialectic of Enlightenment, 144
Aeschylus, 2
Aestheticism, Aesthetes, 109–11, 113,
  166, 172
Affective Fallacy, 184, 242, 247
'against the grain' (reading), 242
Age of Faith, 22
agon, 1
Agrarian program, 182
Alexander of Macedon (the Great), 18,
  42
alexandrine, 40
alibi of the natural, the, 235
alienation, 64, 137, 142, 247
allegory, 24–8, 64, 139, 247–8
  vs symbolism, 64, 71, 80, 248, 260
Althusser, Louis, 93, 209
anatomy (as a genre), 196–7
anti-subject, 230
aphasia, 224–5
Apollinaire, Guillaume, 116
appreciation, the (as mode of criticism),
  72, 74, 111, 166, 180
a priori, 36, 43, 47–8, 180–1, 199, 231
Ariosto, Ludovico, 33, 36; *Orlando
  Furioso*, 33
Aristophanes, 2
Aristotelianism, xii, 33, 36–9, 41, 43, 47,
  53, 185, 194, 196, 197, 261
Aristotle, 2, 4, 10–18, 23, 33–4, 36–9, 41,
  43, 47, 48, 53, 68, 70, 72, 170, 185,

191, 196, 197, 199, 210, 231, 249,
  253, 256, 261
  Rhetoric, 4
  Poetics, 10–18, 33, 36, 38
  rediscovery of *Poetics*, 36
Arnold, Matthew, 87–90, 111, 171,
  178–9, 261
  'The Study of Poetry', 90
art-for-art's-sake, 109
Artaud, Antonin, 97, 268 f.69
associative relations, 136, 221
Athenaeum, 61
Athens, 6, 10
Atticism, 18
Auden, W. H., 180, 181
Auerbach, Erich, *Mimesis* 200
Austen, Jane, 96, 181
avant-garde, 115, 116, 118, 144, 166,
  236, 237, 248

Bakhtin, Mikhail, 57, 157–65, 241, 249,
  251, 258
  Problems of Dostoevsky's Poetics,
    159–60, 165, 280n.58
  Rabelais and his World, 164–5
Balzac, Honoré de, 81, 82, 98–9, 138
  La Comédie Humaine, 82
baring the device, 150–1
baroque, 39, 40, 44–5, 81, 124, 152, 253
Barthes, Roland, 103, 219, 221, 226, 231,
  232–3, 234–7, 240
  Mythologies, 103, 236
  'Introduction to the Structural
    Analysis of Narrative', 226
  On Racine, 234
  'The Death of the Author', 234
  S/Z, 234
  Elements of Semiology, 236
  The Fashion System, 236

Baudelaire, Charles, 104–5, 109, 223, 224, 229
  'Les Chats', 223, 229
Beardsley, Monroe, 192–3, 247, 254
  'The Intentional Fallacy' (with W. K. Wimsatt), 192–3, 254
Beaumont, Francis and John Fletcher, 46
beauties, praise of (as mode of criticism), 72, 74, 111, 180
Beauvoir, Simone de, 213, 216–18
Beckett, Samuel, 144
Béguin, Albert, 201
Belinsky, Vissarion, 84–5, 86, 92, 139
belles-lettres, 30–1, 248
Bembo, Pietro, 31
Benjamin, Walter, 137, 140–2, 143
  'The Work of Art in the Age of Mechanical Reproduction', 141
Benn, Gottfried, 116
Bentham, Jeremy, 170, 178
Bergson, Henri, 117, 150
Bernanos, Georges, 230
binaries, binarism, 186, 222–3, 228–30, 234, 236
biographical approach, 78–9, 134, 147, 175, 254
Blackmur, R. P., 184–5
Blake, William, 195
Blok, Alexander, 116
Bloom, Harold, 195
Boccaccio, 28, 29, 31–2, 34
  Decameron, 22
  Genealogy of the Gentile Gods, 28
Bodkin, Maud, Archetypal Patterns in Poetry, 194
Boileau, Nicholas, 41, 43–4, 46, 53
  'L'Art Poétique', 44
Bonaparte, Marie, 134
Booth, Wayne, The Rhetoric of Fiction, 113
Bouhours, Dominique, 41, 44
Brandes, Georg, 91
Brecht, Berthold, 138, 142–3, 247
Bremond, Claude, 226, 228, 231
Brontë, Charlotte, Jane Eyre, 215
Brooks, Cleanth, 187–9, 190, 191–2, 193, 282
  Understanding Poetry (with Robert Penn Warren), 187

Modern Poetry and the Tradition, 193
  The Well-Wrought Urn, 193, 282n.71
Brunetière, Ferdinand, 91
Burke, Edmund, 53–5, 58
Burke, Kenneth, 185–7
Byron, George Gordon, Lord, 60

Cambridge Critics, 125, 168–76, 192
Campion, Thomas, 32
canon, 18, 92, 128, 152, 179, 181, 248, 249
Canterbury Tales, 22, 30
Carlyle, Thomas, 79, 80
Castelvetro, 36, 38–9, 41, 50
Castiglione, Baldassare, The Book of the Courtier, 29
catharsis, 14, 17–18, 36, 185, 249
Cervantes, Miguel de, Don Quixote, 149
Chapelain, Jean, 41
character versus action, 14, 47
characteristic, the (Romantic concept of), 71, 81, 249
charity, principle of, 25
Charles II, 41
Chase, Richard, 194–5
Chaucer, William, 22, 30, 46–7
  The Canterbury Tales, 22, 30
Chekhov, Anton, 97, 114–15
Chernyshevsky, Nikolai, 85–6, 88
'Chevy Chase, The Ballad of', 48
Chicago Critics, 194, 196
Chomskyan linguistics, 16
chosisme, 102, 273 f.21
Cicero, 4, 5, 25
circulating libraries, 49
Classical (period), 1–21, 23, 24, 28–30, 32–3, 48, 53, 61, 89, 98, 117, 126, 164, 235, 249, 259, 261
Classics, the, 31–3, 36, 167, 249
code, 52, 74–5, 131, 232–4
cogito, 202–3, 249–50
Coleridge, Samuel Taylor, 59–60, 61, 66–7, 70–1, 75, 76, 79–80, 170, 185, 253
  'Frost at Midnight', 59
commentary (as mode of criticism), 18, 26–7, 200
commodity fetishism, 137, 143, 144
concretisation, 205–7, 230
condensation (Freudian), 131, 250

connote, connotation, 132, 183, 235, 251
Constance School, 204, 210
contiguity, 105, 154, 224–5, 229, 256
convention, 48, 103, 151, 153, 156, 161, 198, 207, 226, 231, 235–6, 259
copyright laws, 49
Corneille, Pierre, 45
correspondences, *correspondances*, 104–6, 109, 113, 114, 122, 174, 250
Courbet, Gustave, 98
Crabbe, George, 96
Crane, R. S., 194
critical relativism, 3–4, 63, 86, 110, 151, 156–7, 164, 209, 255
critique, 3, 115, 142–3, 217, 239
Culler, Jonathan, 233–4
Cultural Materialists (British), 165

Daniel, Samuel, 'Defence of Rhyme', 32
Dante Alighieri, 27–8, 31–2, 33, 63, 90, 121
  Convivio, 27
  'Epistle to Cangrande', 27, 265n.7
  De Vulgari Eloquentia, 31
  The Divine Comedy, 33, 90
Dark Ages, the, 29
Darwin, Charles, 10, 101, 130
  The Origin of Species, 101
De Man, Paul, 204
De Quincy, Thomas, *Confessions of an English Opium Eater*, 196
De Sanctis, Francesco, 91
deconstruction, deconstructionism, 78, 133, 204, 243
decorum, 16–17, 45, 47, 250
deep structures, 220, 223, 224–5, 228–9
defamiliarisation, 150–1, 153–4, 155, 207, 251
Degas, Edgar, 107
Deleuze, Gilès, 239
Demetrius, 5, 235
Dennis, John, 53
denote, denotation, 183, 235, 251
Derrida, Jacques, 7, 133, 239, 243
Descartes, René, 65, 249–50
Desportes, Philippe, 40
detective novel, 232–3, 236

dialectic, 64–5, 145, 230, 259
dialogical novel, 159–61, 251
dialogism, 57, 158–61, 251
Dickens, Charles, 81, 181, 281n.56
  Little Dorrit, 181
diction, 3, 58, 74–5, 194, 250
Diderot, Dennis, 56–7
  'Letter on the Blind', 56
  'Letter on the Deaf and Dumb', 56
  'The Paradox of Acting', 56
diegesis, 6–7, 251–60
Dionysius of Halicarnassus, 5
Dionysus, 126
disappearance of the poet, 108
displacement (Freudian), 131–2, 252
dissociation of sensibility, 123
distinctive features, 222–3, 228
Dobrolyubov, Nikolai, 85–7, 88, 139
dominant, the, 151–2
Dos Passos, John, 161
Dostoevsky, Fyodor, 159–60, 162
  Notes from Underground, 159
  The Brothers Karamazov, 160
  The Devils, 160
Dryden, John, 40, 46–7, 60, 123
  'An Essay of Dramatic Poesy', 46–7
Du Bellay, Joachim, 32, 40
  Defence and Illustration of the French Language, 32

Eagleton, Terry, xi, 209
écriture feminine, 215–16, 218, 252
Eikhenbaum, Boris, 146–7, 149–52, 163
  The Young Tolstoy, 152
Einfühlung, 72, 75, 252
Eisenstein, Sergei, 141
ekstasis, 19
Eliot, George, 81, 82
  Middlemarch, 82
Eliot, T.S., 116, 117, 120–4, 168, 171, 178, 182, 190, 193, 234, 249, 257, 262, 275n.98
  'Tradition and the Individual Talent', 122
  The Waste Land, 122, 168, 171
  Four Quartets, 257
Emerson, Ralph Waldo, 79–80, 202
empiricism, 8, 48, 70, 92, 199, 220, 223, 231

Empson, William, 173–6, 180, 182, 188, 189, 194, 240, 280n.24
Seven Types of Ambiguity, 173–5, 280n.24
entelechy, 10
epic, 1, 2, 5, 6–8, 12–13, 26, 30, 33, 34, 36, 43, 94, 160–1, 215, 225
epic theatre, 142–3
epiphany, 114
Euripides, 2
Existentialism, 201–2, 208, 213, 216, 218–19, 254
explication de texte, 200
Expressionism, 115
extension (as word-meaning), 183

fabula (Russian), 148, 154, 252–3
fabula, fabulae (Medieval), 24, 26
fancy, 70, 253
fantastic, the, 232
Faulkner, William, 182
Fergusson, Francis, 194
Fiedler, Leslie, 194–5
Fielding, Henry, 161, 206
Joseph Andrews, 206
figmentum, figmenta, 24
figure (of speech), 4–5, 19, 23, 27, 56, 261
Flaubert, Gustave, 81, 98, 100, 102, 180, 235
Madame Bovary, 100
'A Simple Heart', 235
folk-poetry, 62–3, 84
Formalism (Russian), xii, 124, 146–52, 153, 155, 156–8, 163, 172, 235
general, 177, 221
Foucault, Michel, 4, 243
fragment form, 62
Frank, Joseph 'Spatial Form in Modern Literature', 283,n.11
Frankfurt School, 143–5
Freud, Sigmund, 73, 79, 95, 130–5, 136, 175, 241, 250, 252
Frye, Northrop, 195–9, 219, 231, 232, 253
Anatomy of Criticism, 195, 198
Fugitive program, 182
Fulgentius, 26–7, 187
Exposition of the Content of Virgil, 26

function (Proppian, narratological), 153–4, 228, 230, 253
furor poeticus, 33, 36
fusion of horizons, 209, 212
Futurism, 115, 124, 146–7, 153

Gadamer, Hans-Georg, 208–10, 212, 242, 254
Gaskell, Elizabeth, 179
Gautier, Théophile, 103–4, 109
Genette, Gérard, 113, 220, 226
Geneva Critics, 201–4, 250
genius (of the poet), 17, 42, 46, 50, 51–2, 55, 60, 68, 73, 78, 129, 141, 152, 214, 218
genre, 1, 12–13, 16, 19, 33, 43, 48, 70, 84, 91, 151, 153, 160, 161, 162–4, 194, 195, 196, 197, 199, 203, 227, 231–4, 250, 253–4
historical *vs* theoretical, 231–2, 254
Geoffrey of Vinsauf, 23
Gestalt psychology, 200, 206
ghost stories, 232
Giraldi ('Cinthio'), Giovambattista, 33
Goethe, Johann Wolfgang von, 59, 61, 68, 71, 94
Gogol, Nikolai, 81, 84, 163
Goncourt Brothers, 96, 99, 100
Germinie Lacerteux, 96, 100
Gongorism, 39
Gorgias, 3
Gosson, Stephen, 34
Gothic, 53, 59, 152, 253
Gottsched, Johann Christoph, 58
Gracian, Balthazar, 39
Gray, Thomas, 193
Greimas, A.-J., 219, 226, 227–31, 247, 259
Structural Semantics, 227
Grün, Karl, 94–5

hamartia, 14
Hamlet, 134
Harland, Richard, *Beyond Superstructuralism*, xii, 105, 137, 169, 223
Hartmann, Geoffrey, 195
Hawthorne, Nathaniel, 202
Hazlitt, William, 74
Hegel, G. W. F., Hegelianism, 61, 64–5, 90–1, 93, 95, 259

Heidegger, Martin, 201, 208
Heine, Heinrich, 149
Heinsius, Daniel, 46
Henry, O., 150–1
Herder, Johann Gottfried, 62–3, 65, 72–3, 90–1
hermeneutics, 73–4, 208–10
heroic couplet, 40
higher-order signifying, 193, 233, 235, 241
histoire, 148, 252
historical novel, 82
Hobbes, Thomas, 49, 65
Hogg, James, *Confessions of a Justified Sinner*, 196
Hölderlin, J. C. F., 61
Hollywood, 141, 143
Horace, 15–18, 33, 36, 41, 43, 45, 68
Ars Poetica, 15, 36
horizon, 201, 205, 209–12, 254
Horkheimer, Max, 143
Hulme, T. E., 116–20, 150, 183, 249, 275n.85
Humanism, 28, 29, 182
Hume, David, 44, 48–9
Hurd, Richard, 53, 63
Husserl, Edmund, 200–2, 204–6

Ibsen, Henrik, 97, 114
Idealism (German philosophical), 61, 79
ideology, 9, 88, 93–5, 160, 163, 186, 236, 242, 249, 251, 258
image (poetic), 9, 45–6, 54–5, 65, 71–3, 87, 119–21, 162–3, 183, 188–90, 193, 194, 200, 221, 223, 260
imagination, 34, 38, 52, 54–6, 58, 66, 70, 72, 76, 82, 94, 102, 105, 111–12, 143, 205, 253–4
Coleridge's distinction of Primary *vs* Secondary, 66–7, 70–1
Imagism, 115, 117
impersonality, doctrine of authorial, 104, 112–13, 120
Impressionist Criticism, 110–11, 166
Industrial Revolution, 60, 137, 143, 178, 182
intension, 183
Intentional Fallacy, 175, 191–3, 254
interinanimation, 170

intertextuality, 122, 241, 254
irony, 33, 116, 151, 161, 190, 191, 195, 255, 261
Iser, Wolfgang, 204, 206–8, 210

Jakobson, Roman, 146–7, 153, 155, 221–6, 228, 229
James, Henry, 111–13, 148, 178
Jauss, Hans-Robert, 204, 208, 210–12, 254
'Literary History as a Challenge to Literary Theory', 210
je ne sais quoi, 45
Jensen, Wilhelm, *Gradiva*, 134
Jiménez, Juan Ramón, 116
John of Garland, 23
Johnson, Samuel, 41, 47–8, 50–1, 176–7
Rasselas, 41
Jones, Ernest, 134
Jonson, Ben, 46
journalist-critics, 83
Joyce, James, 161, 164, 178, 199
Jung, Carl, 194–6, 197

Kafka, Franz, 144
kanon, 18, 248–9; *see also* canon
Kant, Immanuel, 61, 65–67, 69, 73, 126, 127, 170
Critique of Judgement, 65
Critique of Pure Reason, 65
katharsis, 14, 249; *see also* catharsis
Keats, John, 59, 74–5, 193
'Ode to a Nightingale', 59
Knight, G. Wilson, 195
Knights, L. C., 'How Many Children had Lady Macbeth?', 176
Konstanz School, 204

La Rochefoucauld, *Maximes*, 40
Lamb, Charles, 74
langue, 135–6, 137, 158, 162, 222, 232, 234, 240, 255
Lawrence, D. H., 177
Women in Love, 177
Leavis, F. R., 176–81, 281n.56
New Bearings, 177–8
The Great Tradition, 179
Leavis, Q. D., 176, 281n.56
Leavisite, 176–81, 182, 199, 248

Lessing, Gotthold, *Laocoön*, 58–9
Lévi-Strauss, Claude, 219, 220, 221, 223,
  224, 229, 230
linguistic turn, 109, 240
literariness (Russian Formalist
  concept), 147–8, 151, 156, 255
little magazine, 116, 166
Locke, John, 49, 65
Logical Atomism, 169
Logical Positivism, 169
Longinus, 18–21, 53, 54
  Peri Hupsous (On the Sublime), 19
Lubbock, Percy, *The Craft of Fiction*,
  113
Lukács, Georg, 137–40, 142, 144, 157,
  209
lyric, 2, 5, 6, 8, 16, 60, 74, 97, 194, 205,
  253, 256

Macbeth, 173–4, 176, 282n.80
Macrobius, *Dream of Scipio*, 24
Malherbe, François de, 40
Mallarmé, Stéphane, 96, 104–5, 106–8,
  114, 117, 120
manly virtues, 46
Marinism, 39
Marvell, Andrew, 124
marvellous, the, 11, 33, 34, 36, 232
Marx, Karl, 93–5, 137, 142, 209, 241
  Das Capital, 137
Marxism, 93–5, 137–9, 143, 158, 209
materialism, 87, 88, 93, 94, 95, 165, 241
Maturin, Charles, *Melmoth the
  Wanderer*, 196
Maupassant, Guy de, 230
Mayakovsky, Vladimir, 116
Mazzoni, Jacopo, 33
Medvedev, Pavel, 157–8, 164–5
  Formalism and Marxism, 164
Menander, 2
Menippean satire, 163–4
Meredith, George, 179
meta-language, 237, 255
metaphor, 4, 19, 39, 56, 118, 128–9, 131,
  132, 147, 150, 183, 190, 223, 224–5,
  233, 256, 261
Metaphysical poets, 39, 46, 123–4, 152,
  193, 195, 262
metonymy, 4–5, 128, 131, 223–5, 256,
  260, 261

Miller, J. Hillis, 203, 204
Milton, John, 21, 48, 50, 52, 53, 75, 90,
  123, 180, 193, 195
  Paradise Lost, 48
mimesis, mimetic, 6–8, 9, 10, 11, 14, 15,
  17, 18, 23, 33, 36, 129, 196, 200, 251,
  256–7
Minturno, Antonio, 36, 38–9
Modern Language Association (MLA), 182
Modernism, 74–5, 78, 80, 81, 96–9, 104,
  108, 109, 113–17, 120, 122–5, 131,
  132, 135, 139–40, 143–4, 147. 149,
  152–3, 163, 168, 171, 175–8, 182,
  183–4, 188, 193, 194–5, 198, 200,
  205, 212, 213–16, 219, 221, 225,
  238–9, 241, 248, 253, 255–7, 260,
  262
  avant-garde Modernists *vs*
    Symbolist-Modernists, 116
monological novel, 160, 251
Montaigne, Michel de, 40
moods of the verb, 227
Moscow Linguistic Circle, 227
Mukarovsky, Jan, 155–7
Myth Criticism, 194–9, 219, 253–4
mythological thinking, 56, 72, 223
mythos, 196

naive (*vs* sentimental), 63–4
narrative grammar, 226–7, 229–30
narratology, 225–31, 234, 252, 253
Nashe, Thomas, *The Unfortunate
  Traveller*, 30
Naturalism, 9, 57–8, 81, 95, 96–103, 104,
  108, 111–12, 114, 115, 117, 119,
  138–9, 142, 214
Nature (concepts of), 10, 11, 43, 44–5,
  46–8, 55, 58, 60, 63, 71, 79, 103, 109,
  214, 217
Nazi Germany, 143
negative dialectic, 145
Neo-Aristotelian Chicago school, 194, 196
Neoclassicism, xii, 18, 29, 56, 58–9, 61–3,
  70–1, 74, 81, 85, 96, 98, 103, 210,
  214, 248, 250, 253, 256, 258, 260–2
Neo-Platonism, 9–10, 24, 25
New Critics, New Criticism, xi, 125, 155,
  174–6, 180, 182–6, 187–94, 195, 196,
  199, 220, 221, 223, 225–6, 231, 234,
  240, 242, 247, 248–9, 254

New Historicists, 165
New Humanism, 182
Newton, Sir Isaac, *Principia Mathematica*, 40
Nietzsche, Friedrich, 125–30
    The Birth of Tragedy, 126
nouveau roman, 236

objective correlative, 121, 257
objectivity, 2, 8–9, 42, 43, 66–7, 73, 86, 102, 108, 110, 121, 127, 130, 139, 157, 158, 172, 173, 184, 201, 204, 209, 212, 220, 239, 257
obscurity, 54, 106
Odyssey, The, 24
oeuvre, 203
Ogden, C. K., *The Meaning of Meaning* (with I. A. Richards), 169
Olsen, Elder, 194
OPOJAZ, 146
oratory, 2–5, 18, 19, 23
organic unity, organic form, 69–70, 163, 170, 190–1
Origen, 25, 25
originality, 7, 9, 11, 17, 27, 51–2, 56, 61, 73, 77–8, 110, 120, 134, 143, 203, 209, 210, 211, 242
Ortega y Gasset, 116
ostranenie, 150–1, 155, 251, 257
Over-soul, 79
overdetermination, 132, 250, 257

Pallavicino, Sforza, 39
paradigmatic relations, 221–5, 257
paradox, 57, 110, 126, 149, 189, 191
paraphrase, 52, 171, 191
    heresy of, 191
parapraxis, 133
parole, 135, 158, 232, 240, 255, 257
Parzifal, 22
Pater, Walter, 109–10
Patrizi, Francesco, 33
patronage, 29–30, 49, 60, 257–8
perspicuity, 41, 54, 258
Petrarch (Francesco Petrarca), 29, 31
Phenomenology, 200–1, 203–5, 209, 254
Philosophical Aesthetics, 48–9, 53–4, 73
Pisarev, Dmitri, 85–6
    'The Destruction of Aesthetics', 86
Piso, 15

Plato, 2, 6–10, 11, 13, 14, 23, 24, 33, 48, 251–2
    Republic, 6, 9
    Ion, 33
    Phaedrus, 33
Platonism (Renaissance), 33, 35–6, 37, 38
Pléiade poets, 32
plot, 13, 14, 24, 39, 47, 68, 148, 151, 196, 225, 253, 261
Plotinus, 9, 48–9
Poe, Edgar Allan, 79, 80
    'The Philosophy of Composition', 80
poetic justice, 36, 164, 199, 231, 232, 234
poetics, 36, 164, 199, 231, 232, 234
poiesis, poesis, 2, 3, 6, 8, 9, 10, 15, 17–8, 36, 49
point of view, 43, 112–13, 139, 160, 217, 251, 258
polyglossia, 162, 258
polyphonic novel, 160, 251, 259
Pope, Alexander, 40, 42–5, 46, 52, 175, 190, 193
    Essay on Man, 40
    Essay on Criticism, 42, 175
    The Rape of the Lock, 190
popular entertainment, 30, 38, 83, 97, 115–16, 143, 144, 152, 165, 168, 183, 198, 199, 206, 212, 232, 247, 249
Porphyry of Tyre, 24
Postcolonial theory, 32, 218, 243
Postmodernism, 45, 57, 78, 81, 87, 109, 111, 122, 132, 143, 165, 176, 185, 207, 219, 232, 238–43, 259, 261
Poststructuralism, 27, 32, 103, 110, 185, 186, 234, 236, 237, 239–43, 248, 254
Poulet, Georges, 201–3
Pound, Ezra, 116, 117, 118, 119–20, 188, 249
Prague Linguistic Circle, 155
praise of beauties, *see* beauties, praise of
Proclus, 10, 24–5
Propp, Vladimir, 153–5, 226, 228, 229, 230, 253
    Morphology of the Folktale, 153, 226
Protagoras, 3
provinciality, 88, 272n.20
pseudo-statement, 171
Pudovkin, Vsevolod, 141

Pushkin, Alexander, 85

quantitative metre, 32
Quiller-Couch, Sir Arthur, 166
Quintilian, 4, 5

Rabelais, Francois, *Gargantua and Pantagruel*, 164–5
Racine, Jean, 40, 234
Raleigh, Walter, 166
Rambler, The, 48
Ransom, John Crowe, 182–4, 190
Rapin, René, 41, 45
Raymond, Marcel, 201
reader-response theory, 207, 243
reading public, 48, 49, 100
realism, 9, 11, 14, 17, 37, 48, 77–102, 138, 146, 148–9, 151, 152, 153, 157, 195, 196, 197, 199, 225, 235–6, 247, 253, 256, 259, 261, 262
reality effect, 235, 259, 262
Reception Aesthetics, 204, 212
récit, 148, 253
reification, 128, 137, 139
Relevance, Doctrine of, 183
Restoration (English), 41, 46, 82, 123, 262
rhetoric, 2, 3–6, 9, 15, 19, 20, 21, 23, 40, 55, 77, 128, 161, 186, 191, 259, 261
Richards, I. A, 168–73, 174, 182, 190
Practical Criticism, 168
The Meaning of Meaning (with C. K. Ogden), 169
Richardsonian novel (Samuel Richardson), 50
Rilke, Rainer Maria, 116
Rimbaud, Arthur, 96
Robbe-Grillet, Alain, 103 273n.21
Romance of the Rose, The, 22
romance, 33, 34, 43, 52, 82, 112, 195, 196–7
Romanticism, 21, 44, 51, 54–6, 59, 60–80, 81–2, 84, 85, 91, 96, 98–9, 103–4, 108, 109, 111, 116–17, 120, 123, 129–30, 149, 152, 157, 169–70, 180, 182, 193, 195–6, 203, 213–14, 225, 238, 248–9, 252–3, 256, 276n.21

Sainte-Beuve, Charles-Augustin, 77–9, 91

Saintsbury, George, 166
Sartre, Jean-Paul, 209, 216, 219
satire, 16, 40, 49, 163–4, 253
Saussure, Ferdinand de, 135–8, 162, 219, 220, 221–2, 228, 236, 257, 259
Scaliger, Julius Caesar, 36, 38, 39, 41
Schiller, Friedrich, 61, 63–4, 68, 149
'On Naive and Sentimental Poetry', 63
Wallenstein, 149
Schlegel, August Wilhelm, 61, 64, 66, 69, 70, 270n.31
Schlegel, Friedrich, 64, 66, 70, 72–4
Schleiermacher, Friedrich, 73–4, 77, 208
Scholasticism, 28
Schopenhauer, Arthur, 61, 68, 69, 125–6, 127, 129
Schorer, Mark, 193–4
Scott, Sir Walter, 82, 138
semantics, 227
semiology, semiologist, 137, 236, 259
semiotics, 229, 259
semiotic square, 229–30, 259
Sensibility (Age of), 49–55, 57, 58, 61, 67, 68, 74
sentimental (*vs* naive), 63–4
Shaftesbury, Lord, *Characteristics*, 48
Shelley, Percy Bysshe, 61, 74, 76–7, 78, 89, 111, 195
'A Defence of Poetry', 76
Shklovsky, Viktor, 148, 149–50, 152, 153, 156, 157, 163, 251
Sidney, Sir Philip, 34–5, 36
'An Apology for Poetry' ('Defence of Poesy'), 34, 36
Arcadia, 34
skaz, 163
Socialist Realism, 157
Sophism, 3–4
Sophocles, 2, 12, 20
Oedipus Tyrannus, 12
Southern Renaissance, 182
Spectator, The, 48
Spenser, Edmund, 33, 50, 52, 53
The Faerie Queene, 33
Speroni, Sperone, 37
spy novels, 232
St Augustine, 25, 26
St Isidore of Seville, 26
St Paul, *Galatians*. 25

St Thomas Aquinas, 26
de Staël, Germaine de (Madame de
    Staël) 213–14
  'Literature Considered in its Relation
    to Social Institutions', 213
Stalin, Stalinism, 146, 157–8
Stendhal, 198
Sterne, Lawrence, 161, 180
  Tristram Shandy, 150–1, 197
story, 113, 148, 151, 191, 226, 227, 228,
    252–3
Structural Anthropology, 219–20, 221,
    223
Structural Linguistics, 135, 137, 158,
    219–20, 221, 257
Structuralism
  French, xii, 32, 42, 103, 110, 155, 199,
    219–37, 238–9, 240, 241, 248, 253,
    257
  Czech, 155–7, 172
Sturm und Drang, 59, 61–2
sublime, the, 19, 20, 52, 53–4, 55, 61,
    259–60; *vs* the beautiful, 53–4,
    259–60
subversion, 145, 240–2
Swinburne, Charles Algernon, 109
symbol, 25–6, 71–2, 79–80, 121, 131,
    132, 169, 174, 185, 186, 188–9, 193,
    236, 241, 248, 257, 260
Symbolism, 57–8, 72, 75, 80, 96–8, 99,
    103–9, 113, 114, 115, 116, 117, 122,
    125, 131, 140, 146, 147, 163, 171,
    174, 185, 188, 193, 225, 238, 250,
    260
symptom, 77, 97, 135, 241
synechdoche, 4, 131, 225, 260
syntagmatic relations, 222, 224, 226,
    229, 257
syntax, 18, 20, 21, 105, 222, 224, 226
synthesis, 66, 73, 156, 170, 190, 259
syuzhet, 148, 252–3

Taine, Hippolyte, 91–2, 93, 95, 99
Tasso, Torquato, 34
taste, 5, 30, 43–4, 48, 49, 50, 52, 53, 88,
    138, 119, 212, 260
Tate, Allen, 182–4
Tatler, The, 48
Tel Quel, 236
Tennyson, Lord Alfred, 193

tenor (in metaphor), 256
tension (in poetry), 183
Tesauro, Emmanuele, 39
Theagenes of Rhegium, 24
theme, 174, 188–9, 191, 195, 250
Theophrastus, 2
thriller novels, 232
thusness, 81, 249
Todorov, 219, 226–8, 231–3, 253–4
  Grammaire du Decameron, 226, 231
  The Fantastic, 232
Tolstoy, 81–2, 150, 152, 160–2, 197
  War and Peace, 82
  Resurrection, 197
Tomashevsky, Boris, 146–8, 151, 261
touchstone, 90, 261
trace (Poststructuralist conception of),
    241
Transcendentalism (American), 79
Traversi, Derek, 176
Trollope, Anthony, 112, 179
trope, 4, 5, 56, 261
Turgenev, Ivan, 85, 112, 149
Tynyanov, Yuri, 146, 148, 149, 151, 153,
    155, 156, 157, 163
typology, 79

uncanny, the, 133, 232
unconscious, the, 74, 95, 128, 130–4,
    138, 175, 252
unheimlich, 133
unities, the, 13, 39, 41, 50, 53, 63, 163,
    170–1, 190–1, 199, 261
  unity of time, 39, 50, 261
  unity of place, 39, 50, 261
  unity of action, 39, 261
  unity of design, 53, 261
  rejected by Johnson, 50–1
utile dulci, 18, 34

Valéry, Paul, 104–8, 116, 117, 120, 122,
    273n.36
  La Jeune Parque, 122
vehicle (in metaphor), 256
verisimilitude, 36–8, 47, 48, 67, 262
vernacular, vernacular literature, 22, 27,
    31–2, 163, 262
Veselovsky, Alexander, 262
Vico, Giambattista, 55, 56, 62, 72
  Scienza Nuova, 56

Virgil, 26, 35, 43, 52
  Aeneid, 26
  Eclogues, 26
volksgeist, 90, 94, 262
Voloshinov, V. N., 157–8, 162, 251
  *Marxism and the Philosophy of
    Language*, 158
Vorticism, 115

Walton, Isaac, *The Compleat Angler*,
  196
Warren, Robert Penn, 187, 190
  Understanding Poetry (with Cleanth
    Brooks), 187
Warton, Joseph, 52
  'Essay on the Genius and Writings of
    Pope', 52
Warton, Thomas, 52–3
Wellek, René, 187
Wheelwright, Philip, 194
Whitman, Walt, 202
Wilde, Oscar, 109–11
  'The Critic as Artist', 110–11
Will to Power, 126–7, 129

Will to Truth, 127
Wimsatt, W. K., 184, 190, 192–3, 247,
  254, 282n.71
  'The Intentional Fallacy' (with
    Monroe Beardsley), 192–3, 254
Winckelmann, J. J., 61
Winters, Yvor, 184
wit, 49, 52, 124, 190, 253, 262
Wordsworth, William, 67, 74–5, 76–7,
  89, 111, 168, 177, 193, 250
  'Preface to Lyrical Ballads', 74
  'Essay upon Epitaphs', 75–6
writer-critics, 116, 120, 124, 166, 219,
  220

Young, Edward, 51–2
  'Conjectures on Original
    Composition', 51

zeitgeist, 90–1, 94, 252, 262
Zola, Emile, 96, 99–101, 102, 197
  'The Experimental Novel', 101
  Germinal, 96, 197
  Therese Raquin, 96, 100, 102